THE OLD FARMER'S ALMANAC

CALCULATED ON A NEW AND IMPROVED PLAN FOR THE YEAR OF OUR LORD

Being Leap Year and (until July 4) 244th year of American Independence

FITTED FOR BOSTON AND THE NEW ENGLAND STATES, WITH SPECIAL CORRECTIONS AND CALCULATIONS TO ANSWER FOR ALL THE UNITED STATES.

Containing, besides the large number of Astronomical Calculations and the Farmer's Calendar for every month in the year, a variety of

NEW, USEFUL, & ENTERTAINING MATTER.

ESTABLISHED IN 1792
BY ROBERT B. THOMAS (1766–1846)

The best thing about the future is that it comes one day at a time.
–Abraham Lincoln, 16th U.S. president (1809–65)

Cover design registered U.S. Trademark Office

Copyright © 2019 by Yankee Publishing Incorporated
ISSN 0078-4516

Library of Congress Card No. 56-29681

Cover illustration by Steven Noble • Original wood engraving (above) by Randy Miller

THE OLD FARMER'S ALMANAC • DUBLIN, NH 03444 • 603-563-8111 • ALMANAC.COM

CONTENTS

8

18

2020 TRENDS
Forecasts, Facts, and Fascinating Ideas 6

156

58

"TO BE CONTINUED"

Welcome, patrons! Join us as we celebrate another year as North America's oldest continuously published—and most beloved—annual. This 228th edition aims once again to fulfill your expectations by being the same (the facts, the fun, the forecasts) but different (news, novelties, and a little nonsense) from page to page—a compendium of curiosities to carry you through the year.

Yes, another year. Already.

Here, from our barn-red headquarters in Dublin, New Hampshire (see our live webcam at Almanac.com or Almanac.ca), as we ponder and proof each page, we watch the seasons roll past, the months march forward, and the days yield one to next and we think of *you!* Not by name or face, of course but by your interests—matters of concern to you as well as to folks across North America and beyond.

One of these concerns, as you may know, is the environment and how we relate to it. A recent report suggests that a shift is under way from digital dependence to personal transcendence: People want more "face time" with Mother Nature, more engagement with "she" and less with "me." More green time, less screen time. Fewer algorithms, more of nature's rhythms. Less keying in, more being in–volved with the environment. Outdoors is the new indoors, and bringing the outdoors in—with daylight, fresh air, and plants—is a new "Like" for people of all generations. We have new awareness of the high-speed connections between the Sun and a seed, between bees and flower buds, and to the Moon's effect on such seemingly (but not so!) mundane occurrences as catching fish, cutting hair, and cultivating a garden. Today, "going wild" is less about misbehaving and more about saving the planet, with native plants, natural products, and traditional practices.

Sound familiar?

These interests define the values and intentions of this Almanac! Thanks to centuries of encouragement and support from folks like you, we have always celebrated nature's precision, rhythm, and glory from sunrise to sunrise and in every moment in between—and we will continue to do so!

–J. S., JUNE 2019

However, it is by our works and not our words that we would be judged. These, we hope, will sustain us in the humble though proud station we have so long held in the name of

Your obedient servant,

4

2020 TRENDS

IN THE KITCHEN

We will see more restaurants promoting zero-waste cooking on their menus and through the media.

–Jeremy Abbey, director of culinary programs, American Culinary Federation

TOP ORGANIC FOODS BY SALES VALUE, IN 2018:

1. Cow's milk
2. Prepackaged salads
3. Chicken eggs
4. Health and nutrition bars
5. Fresh chicken

–Nielsen

PEOPLE ARE TALKING ABOUT . . .

- drinking fermented apple cider pressed from foraged fruit

- ordering steak from menus that specify the source animal's feeding regimen and age at "harvest"

- catching fish orders from in-restaurant tanks (fishing poles and bait are provided)

BY THE NUMBERS: U.S.

43%: amount of air in an average bag of chips

44% of workers have a snack drawer

8: pounds of fresh strawberries consumed, on average, per person, per year

9% of Americans have tried a meal kit

40% of Millennial parents eat their kids' leftovers to avoid waste

39% of U.S. adults say that at least some of their food is organic

31% of Americans participate in meat-free days once per week

NEW FOODS

- ginger and fennel juice *digestifs*

- algae protein bars and shakes

FOLLOW US:

- candy sweetened with pear juice or tapioca syrup and colored with turmeric or beet juice

- fruit with the taste and texture of meat: grilled watermelon "ham," cantaloupe "burgers," toasted coconut "bacon," and pumpkin "ribs"

BUZZWORD
Hyperlocal = food grown at a restaurant or grocery

BY THE NUMBERS: CANADA

9.4% are vegan or vegetarian

54% dine out at least once a week

57% change a menu order after reading nutrition information, at least sometimes

$411: average increase in family groceries spending from 2018 to 2019

COMING SOON . . .
- devices for "pressing" your own fun-shape chicken nuggets

- self-driving grocery store fleets from which people can choose groceries.

IN THE GARDEN

Balcony gardening, small space gardening, and any gardening that can be done in a community plot will increase, due to more people living in smaller spaces as cities around the world continue to densify.

–*Cynthia Sayre, curator of collections, VanDusen Botanical Garden, Vancouver, B.C.*

(continued)

Photos, from top: ArtCookStudio/Shutterstock; courtesy of Robomart; tapui/Getty Images

OUT-OF-POCKET
- U.S. gardeners annually spend, on average:
$84 on vegetables
$76 on flowers
$58 on container gardening
$52 on herbs
$43 on houseplants
–2018 National Gardening Survey

DEFINING SPACES
Gardeners are designating spaces for quiet meditation and reflection.
–Dave Forehand, vice president of gardens, Dallas Arboretum

- Parents of teenagers are creating areas with fireplaces and plants to provide privacy and absorb noise.

- Gardeners are using logs to edge gardens

and as habitats for beneficial insects.

IN DEMAND OUTDOORS
- turf alternatives: Pennsylvania sedge for shade; perennial grasses for low- or no-traffic lawns

- mosses and succulents between pathway stones

PHENOLOGY RISING
Nature is becoming a more and more reliable source to tell us when to plant seeds, apply insect and weed controls, and begin other seasonal gardening projects.
–Kerry Ann Mendez, The Budget-Wise Gardener *(St. Lynn's Press, 2018)*
Learn some of these signs on page 233.

SMALL IS ALL
Homeowners want plants that are smaller, more compact, and

easy to grow. The need for instant gratification, limited time, smaller budgets, and smaller overall growing space is driving this trend.
–Thomas Soulsby, senior horticulturist, Chicago Botanic Garden

For example . . .
- dwarf versions of evergreen trees

- small-scale perennials (bee balm, hydrangeas, blueberry)

- mini meadows

COLOR COMMENTS . . .
- The trend is toward more color, both tropical and perennial, with variegated foliage on trees and shrubs and more bodacious blooms.
–Julie Hess, senior horticulturist, Missouri Botanical Garden

- Uncommon hues like coral, apricot,

FOLLOW US:

brown, and even gray will rise in popularity. These colors read well in the dramatically backlit age of Instagram.

–Adam Dooling, curator of outdoor gardens, The New York Botanical Garden

BEE FRIENDS

Diverse plantings that support a wide variety of pollinators—flies, moths, and bats—will be just as important as bee habitats.

–Soulsby

Such as . . .

- milkweed *(Asclepias syriaca)*
- showy milkweed *(Asclepias speciosa)*
- Arizona series hummingbird mint
- 'Big Blue' salvia

–Ginger Long, spokesperson, Park Seed

SHOWY MILKWEED

EARTH-FRIENDLY ENDEAVORS

- cultivating grains (wheat, barley, oats, rice, sorghum, corn)

SORGHUM

from seed to cover open spaces and to feed the birds

- setting bed edges with garlic, onion, bitter 'Micrette' basil, and arugula to deter browsing mammals

–Brie Arthur, The Foodscape Revolution (St. Lynn's Press, 2017)

GROW FOR THE GLOW

"People are designing gardens for entertaining under the Moon."

With . . .

- light-color plants to reflect the Moon's glow
- night-blooming plants
- plants with fragrance to enjoy day and night

–Katie Dubow, creative director, Garden Media Group

GREENING AND SCREENING

"Indoor houseplants have struck a chord with younger shoppers. Now they're taking this trend outdoors and onto patios and balconies."

With . . .

- glossy foliage ('Cannova' canna)
- enveloping trellises ('Solar Tower' ipomoea)
- wall-climbing plants (mandevilla and dipladenia)

–Katie Rotella, Ball Horticultural Company

DIPLADENIA

BY THE NUMBERS: U.S.

5: days after harvest when tomatoes taste best, says recent research

$503: amount the average household spends on a garden

77% of households garden

(continued)

FOLLOW US:

FIGHT BACK...
Against Mosquitoes & Ticks

MOSQUITO DUNKS ®

Kills mosquitoes *before* they're old enough to bite! ®

- *Kills mosquito larvae and nothing else.*
- Use for *long term control*—30 days or more.
- Use in bird baths, rain barrels, ponds— or any standing water.

CHEMICAL FREE!
Biological *BTI Control*
100% NATURAL
100% EFFECTIVE

FOR ORGANIC PRODUCTION

Kills Mosquitoes *that Transmit Viruses —*
ZIKA & WEST NILE

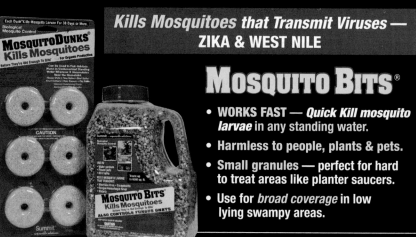

MOSQUITO BITS ®

- **WORKS FAST — *Quick Kill mosquito larvae*** in any standing water.
- **Harmless to people, plants & pets.**
- **Small granules — perfect for hard to treat areas like planter saucers.**
- Use for *broad coverage* in low lying swampy areas.

Summit®
Tick & Flea Spray

- *Quickly kills Ticks & Fleas —* including Deer Ticks (which carry Lyme Disease).

- Spray tick and flea habitats such as the yard perimeter, and weedy, bushy areas.

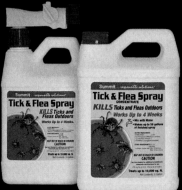

WE LOVE OUR PETS

High-tech pet products are adding health features, including trackers for exercise and food and water consumption.

–Phillip Cooper, president, Pet Industry Expert

ONLY THE BEST

Manufacturers are targeting pets by age, weight, breed characteristics, or specific health issues.
–Jacinthe Moreau, World Pet Association

With . . .

- shampoos for hairless breeds
- vets in retail stores
- raised feeding systems for pets with achy joints

GOTTA-HAVES

- subscription meal plans
- facial recognition food and water bowls
- microchips allowing pets to enter and exit homes at certain times

CURE-ALLS

- Pet products will mirror human health care trends.
–Tierra Bonaldi, pet lifestyle expert

With . . .

- food to improve gut health
- DNA testing to learn lineage

BY THE NUMBERS: CANADA

8.2 million: household dogs (2018)

8.3 million: household cats (2018)

–Canadian Animal Health Institute

BY THE NUMBERS: U.S.

26% of pets have had massages, physical therapy, chiropractic, or acupuncture

52% of pet owners say that they feed their pets better than themselves

56% of pet owners own pet-specific technology

–Michelson Found Animals Foundation

OH. *THAT.*

- *Coming for cats:* litter boxes that monitor cats' weight and frequency of litter box use
- *In development for dogs:* indoor toilets that package waste
(continued)

FOLLOW US:

BUZZWORD
Pre-tirees = people who leave the traditional workforce but work at home

MONEY MATTERS

People are taking a back-to-basics approach to financial health: putting down the devices, eating right, getting enough sleep, and realizing that the little choices matter.

–*Jonathan DeYoe*, Mindful Money *(New World Library, 2017)*

THE FUTURE OF WORK

- Intergenerational collaboration.

–*Paul Irving, chairman, Milken Institute Center for the Future of Aging*

- People will retire from the office but not from work.

–*Sharon Emek, founder and CEO, Work At Home Vintage Experts*

REAL ESTATE REALITIES

- People are swapping homes (for quick sales and to bypass fees).

- Sellers are letting potential buyers spend a night in the property that they're considering.

- Agents are specializing in energy-efficient, eco-friendly homes.

GOING AWAY . . .

- Dollars spent for travel annually:
Boomers: $6,600
Gen Xers: $5,400
Millennials: $4,400

–*AARP Research*

BY THE NUMBERS: U.S.

$732: estimate of beekeeper earnings, per hive, per season

12: times the average American switches jobs by age 50

4.2: median years workers have been at their current employer

48% of Americans do not know their tax bracket

BY THE NUMBERS: CANADA

156: number of shopping trips made by Canadians annually, on average

–*Nielsen Homescan*

(continued)

FOLLOW US:

Train at home to

Work at Home

Be a Medical Coding & Billing Specialist

WORK AT HOME!

✓ Be home for your family
✓ Be your own boss
✓ Choose your own hours

SAVE MONEY!

✓ No day care, commute, or office wardrobe/lunches
✓ Possible tax breaks
✓ Tuition discount for eligible military and their spouses
✓ Military education benefits & MyCAA approved

Train at home in as little as 4 months to earn up to $38,000 a year!*

Now you can train in the comfort of your own home to work in a medical office, or from home as your experience and skills increase.

Make great money...up to $38,000 a year with experience! It's no secret, healthcare providers need Medical Coding & Billing Specialists. **In fact, the U.S. Department of Labor projects 13.9% growth, 2016 to 2026, for specialists doing coding and billing.

| 10 Years | **13.9%** |
| 5 Years | **Increase In Demand!**** |

No previous medical experience required. Compare the money you can make!

Coders earn great money because they make a lot of money for the people they work for. Entering the correct codes on medical claims can mean the difference in thousands of dollars in profits for doctors, hospitals and clinics. Since each and every medical procedure must be coded and billed, there's plenty of work available for well-trained Medical Coding & Billing Specialists.

Get FREE Facts. Contact Us Today!

SENT FREE!

U.S. Career Institute®
2001 Lowe St., Dept. FMAB2A99
Fort Collins, CO 80525

1-800-388-8765
Dept. FMAB2A99
www.uscieducation.com/FMA99

YES! Rush me my free Medical Coding & Billing information package.

Name _____ Age _____

Address _____ Apt _____

City, State, Zip _____

E-mail _____ Phone _____

Accredited • Affordable • Approved
Celebrating over 35 years of education excellence!

CB010

✷DEAC
DISTANCE EDUCATION ACCREDITING COMMISSION

BBB ACCREDITED BUSINESS
A+ Rating

*With experience, https://www.bls.gov/oes/current/oes292071.htm, http://www.bls.gov/oes/current/oes433021.htm, 5/15/18
**https://www.bls.gov/ooh/office-and-administrative-support/financial-clerks.htm#tab-6, https://www.bls.gov/ooh/healthcare/medical-records-and-health-information-technicians.htm#tab-6, 5/15/18

and *Transformers* figures

TAKE MY STUFF, PLEASE
- Parents are enlisting appraisers to educate their family on their antiques' history and significance, in hope that the children will become caretakers.
–Kelly Juhasz, principal, Fine Art Appraisal and Services, Canada

DID YOU KNOW?
- A 1976 Apple-1 computer sold for **$375,000.**

COLLECTIBLES & STUFF

Collectibles are shifting from being nostalgia-based to being a transactional, speculation-based market.
–James Gallo, owner/operator of Toy and Comic Heaven

BUYERS SEEK
- vintage sports pennants for bikes
- World's Fair trinkets
- Sears Wish Books from the '50s and '60s
- limited-release sneakers and jackets

TECH IS TREASURE
- Collectors are paying hundreds for early, brick-size cell phones and thousands for unused first-generation iPhones.
–Karen Knapstein, editor, Antique Trader

HOT TOYS
- from the 1960s: "Mod" Barbie dolls
- '70s: toys from fast-food meals
- '80s: *Masters of the Universe* (He-Man)

OLD IS NEW
- Buyers are snapping up items for function, not as collectibles.
–Gayle Skluzacek, president, Abigail Hartmann Associates

Such as . . .
- '50s-era enameled cast-iron cookware
- '60s-era stereos
- '70s-era gaming consoles
- '80s-era cassette players or boom boxes

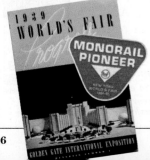

FOLLOW US:

AROUND THE HOUSE

We'll continue to see advancements with creative textiles and building materials that use recycled or sustainable raw materials.

–Hadley Keller, news editor, Architectural Digest's AD PRO

BRAINY BATHROOMS
- showerheads adjust water usage based on the bather's distance from it
- colors signal the gallons of water used
- colors indicate weight on a scale

RE-INVENTIONEERING
- making tables and glasses from old smartphone screens
- café chairs from discarded coffee cups and lids

PEOPLE ARE TALKING ABOUT . . .
- dry-flush and (coming soon) toilets that turn liquid waste into clean water
- homes made of noncombustibles (concrete, glass, steel), with exterior sprinklers in case of wildfires
- homes moored to posts, in case of flood
- cone-shape roofs on homes with rounded corners to dissipate hurricane winds

DESIGNS IN DEMAND:
- glass doors and walls
- navy or forest green walls
- counter-to-ceiling backsplashes
- oddly shaped rugs

(continued)

BY THE NUMBERS: U.S.

15%: decrease of average single-family home lot size

10%: increase in average single-family home size

53% of homeowners tackle home improvement projects to outdo the neighbors

ON THE FARM

We're getting young people back to the farm by introducing the variety of ag careers available to them.

–Zippy Duvall, president, American Farm Bureau Federation

BY THE NUMBERS: CANADA

77,830 Canadian farmers are female

1,051 is the average acreage rented/leased by females (818 for males)

10,629 Canadians are beekeepers

2.3 million: number of agricultural jobs in Canada

16% of young farmers live in cities

–Statistics Canada

HOW NOW, COW?
● Wearable devices powered by bovine body heat can track a cow's health and use facial recognition to check its food and drink consumption.

FOOD NEWS
Plant breeders and chefs are creating
● 'Badger Flame' mild, sweet beets
● 'Primero Red' mild-heat habaneros
● blue fenugreek: tastes buttery, smells like maple syrup

A CLASS THAT'S A BLAST
● Soon, high schools will teach kids how to operate ag drones.

WHY BUY LOCAL?
● Apps will connect local grocery buyers with local food producers to order fresh products

● Edible bar codes on produce can identify its source farm and row from which picked.

O, CANADA
● Expensive, large-scale, indoor, hydroponic vertical growing systems are generating loads of money and excitement from investors.

–Mike Levenston, executive director, City Farmer, Vancouver, B.C.

(continued)

FOLLOW US:

When it's built by *hand,*

It's connected to the *Heart.*

For three generations, the builders, blacksmiths and craftsmen at Country Carpenters have put their hands and their hearts into designing and building the finest New England Style buildings available. Hand-selected materials, hand-forged hardware, all hand-built and hand-finished by real people. You can feel the difference in your heart.

NEW ENGLAND STYLE
Country Carpenters INC.
POST & BEAM BUILDINGS

COUNTRY BARNS, CARRIAGE HOUSES, POOL & GARDEN SHEDS, CABINS

Visit our models on display!

326 Gilead Street, Hebron, CT 06248 • 860.228.2276 • countrycarpenters.com

BUZZWORD
trashercise
= to clean up garbage while running or walking

TO OUR HEALTH

Mental hygiene is becoming as important as, if not more important than, physical hygiene.

–Richard Davidson, PhD, founder, The Center for Healthy Minds, University of Wisconsin–Madison

DOCTORS' RX

● Mindfulness . . . to recognize the importance of social and emotional intelligence.
–Allan Donsky, MD, clinical associate professor, University of Calgary

● "Garden bathing"— immersion in natural scenery—as a healing and stress-reduction opportunity.
–Brian White, PhD, professor, Royal Roads University, Victoria, B.C.

DOCS' TO-DO

● We're reconsidering hygiene practices due to research showing that a more diverse microbiome aids our health.
–Kathleen Wolf, PhD, researcher, University of Washington

● Physicians . . . will be required to learn to meditate.
–Darshan Mehta, MD, MPH, medical director, Benson-Henry Institute for Mind Body Medicine

PEOPLE ARE TALKING ABOUT . . .

● diets based on gut bacteria

● blood tests to determine best diet

BY THE NUMBERS: U.S.

288: calories burned per hour picking up litter while jogging (vs. 235 just jogging)

32%: increase in physical activity for workers in open office settings, compared to private offices or cubicles

● heart-rate monitors that indicate workout intensity levels

● slow mornings: rising early to enjoy A.M. solitude and quiet

(continued)

FOLLOW US:

WE ARE WHAT WE WEAR

Look out for more in-store experiences
and collaborations with social media influencers.

–Suzanne Cotton, chair of fashion design, Columbus College of Art & Design

PEOPLE ARE TALKING ABOUT . . .

- younger women dyeing their hair silvery shades and older women keeping their gray locks
- flat shoes in vending machines in airports
- tours to learn how shoes, jewelry, and clothing are made
- discounts on new items in exchange for old clothing

FORGET FORM-FITTING

- We'll see lots of slouchy, oversize, tailored, menswear-inspired pieces to wear in layers.

–Cotton

MENSWEAR

- corduroy pants with bungee closures at the ankle
- coats with a sleeve of a color different from the rest of the coat
- khakis rolled up to reveal bright-color socks
- shirts with large blocks of camouflage colors
- puffy jackets in plaid patterns

BY THE NUMBERS: U.S.

25% of women put on makeup for gym workouts

600: pieces of clothing thrown away in the average American's lifetime

43% of people do not read care instructions before doing laundry

FASHIONISTA FLAIR

- unmatched sandals
- plastic lunch pails resembling handbags
- heavily feathered shoes and handbags

(continued)

FOLLOW US:

OUR CULTURE

To find joy, consumers are ceasing constant multitasking, to do one thing at a time during spare time.

–Lorenza Della-Santa, consultant, Euromonitor International

PEOPLE ARE TALKING ABOUT . . .

- falling asleep to videos of people whispering, tapping, or crinkling newspaper

- listening to music on sunglasses with tiny speakers in the temple pieces

- engine-driven boards for "surfing" over waveless waters

WE LOVE PODS

- public soundproof rooms for karaoke practice

- glass-enclosed office booths for private talks

- rentable napping pods in city buildings

FAVE PASTIMES

- running marathons backward

BY THE NUMBERS: U.S.

2.1: hours spent on housework daily by fathers of young kids

2.6: hours spent on housework daily by mothers of young kids

–U.S. Bureau of Labor Statistics American Time Use Survey

- visiting cafés with free-roaming wild animals (raccoons, wallabies, chinchillas, meerkats)

OUR HOTEL PERKS

- shower hammocks

- in-room or phone consultations with pet psychics

SIGNS OF THE TIMES

Employers are . . .

- providing meditation training

- teaching workers how to make eye contact and shake hands

- inviting employees' parents to observe their children at work

COMING SOON . . .

- driverless flying taxis

- waterproof tents for undersea camping

- recycled plastic roads placed down like Lego blocks ■

FOLLOW US:

Choose Life
Grow Young with HGH

From the landmark book Grow Young with HGH comes the most powerful, over-the-counter health supplement in the history of man. Human growth hormone was first discovered in 1920 and has long been thought by the medical community to be necessary only to stimulate the body to full adult size and therefore unnecessary past the age of 20. Recent studies, however, have overturned this notion completely, discovering instead that the natural decline of Human Growth Hormone (HGH), from ages 21 to 61 (the average age at which there is only a trace left in the body) and is the main reason why the body ages and fails to regenerate itself to its 25 year-old biological age.

Like a picked flower cut from the source, we gradually wilt physically and mentally and become vulnerable to a host of degenerative diseases, that we simply weren't susceptible to in our early adult years.

Modern medical science now regards aging as a disease that is treatable and preventable and that "aging", the disease, is actually a compilation of various diseases and pathologies, from everything, like a rise in blood glucose and pressure to diabetes, skin wrinkling and so on. All of these aging symptoms can be stopped and rolled back by maintaining Growth Hormone levels in the blood at the same levels HGH existed in the blood when we were 25 years old.

There is a receptor site in almost every

cell in the human body for HGH, so its regenerative and healing effects are very comprehensive.

Growth Hormone, first synthesized in 1985 under the Reagan Orphan drug act, to treat dwarfism, was quickly recognized to stop aging in its tracks and reverse it to a remarkable degree. Since then, only the lucky and the rich have had access to it at the cost of $10,000 US per year.

The next big breakthrough was to come in 1997 when a group of doctors and scientists, developed an all-natural source product which would cause your own natural HGH to be released again and do all the remarkable things it did for you in your 20's. Now available to every adult for about the price of a coffee and donut a day.

GHR now available in America, just in time for the aging Baby Boomers and everyone else from age 30 to 90 who doesn't want to age rapidly but would rather stay young, beautiful and healthy all of the time.

The new HGH releasers are winning converts from the synthetic HGH users as well, since GHR is just as effective, is oral instead of self-injectable and is very affordable.

GHR is a natural releaser, has no known side effects, unlike the synthetic version and has no known drug interactions. Progressive doctors admit that this is the direction medicine is seeking to go, to get the body to heal itself instead of employing drugs. GHR is truly a revolutionary paradigm shift in medicine and, like any modern leap frog advance, many others will be left in the dust holding their limited, or useless drugs and remedies.

It is now thought that HGH is so comprehensive in its healing and regenerative powers that it is today, where the computer industry was twenty years ago, that it will displace so many prescription and non-prescription drugs and health remedies that it is staggering to think of.

The president of BIE Health Products stated in a recent interview, I've been waiting for these products since the 70's. We knew they would come, if only we could stay healthy and live long enough to see them! If you want to stay on top of your game, physically and mentally as you age, this product is a boon, especially for the highly skilled professionals who have made large investments in their education, and experience. Also with the failure of Congress to honor our seniors with pharmaceutical coverage policy, it's more important than ever to take pro-active steps to safeguard your health. Continued use of GHR will make a radical difference in your health, HGH is particularly helpful to the elderly who, given a choice, would rather stay independent in their own home, strong, healthy and alert enough to manage their own affairs, exercise and stay involved in their communities. Frank, age 85, walks two miles a day, plays golf, belongs to a dance club for seniors, had a girl friend again and doesn't need Viagra, passed his drivers test and is hardly ever home when we call - GHR delivers.

HGH is known to relieve symptoms of Asthma, Angina, Chronic Fatigue, Constipation, Lower back pain and Sciatica, Cataracts and Macular Degeneration, Menopause, Fibromyalgia, Regular and Diabetic Neuropathy, Hepatitis, helps Kidney Dialysis and Heart and Stroke recovery.

For more information or to order call
877-849-4777
www.biehealth.us

These statements have not been evaluated by the FDA. Copyright © 2000. Code OFA.

THE
FLOWER
WITH A
FACE

PANSIES ARE NO SHRINKING VIOLETS!

BY MARE-ANNE JARVELA

Pansy, spring's vibrant and ubiquitous bloom, has a colorful place in history and commanding presence in today's gardens.

PANSY'S PAST

Pansies are descendants of the wild violet *(Viola tricolor)* and the sweet violet *(V. odorata)*. Violets were grown in Europe as early as the 4th century B.C.

In medieval times, the blossoms were mixed into potpourri, added to both sweet and savory dishes, and used both to flavor alcoholic drinks and to perfume linens.

It is said that Napoleon gave Josephine violets on their wedding anniversary. "Violet" was a password during the Emperor's exile, and his loyalists made it their symbol of hope for his return.

In Britain, Adm. James Gambier (1756–1833) and his gardener, William Thompson, began crossing various wild species of the *Viola* family in the early 1800s. Lady

THE ROSE IS RED, THE VIOLET'S BLUE, THE HONEY'S SWEET, AND SO ARE YOU.

—Gammer Gurton's Garland
(a collection of English nursery rhymes), 1784

PANSY LOVE

According to ancient Greek mythology, the pansy got its colors from Cupid's arrow, which turned purple after piercing the heart of a white flower, causing it to bleed purple. It was said that just one drop of the flower's juice would cause lovesickness, and this belief inspired yet another name for the flower: love-in-idleness.

THE PENSIVE PANSY

The name "pansy" comes from the French word *pensée,* meaning "thought." It was so named because the flower's dark center resembles a human face, and, as each bloom matures, it nods forward, looking as though it were deep in thought. In the language of flowers, the pansy means "I'm thinking of you." Other names for violets and pansies include . . .

- call-me-to-you
- faces-under-the-hood
- godfathers and godmothers
- heartsease
- Jack-jump-up-and-kiss-me
- Johnny-jump-up
- kiss-her-in-the-pantry
- monkey's face
- peeping Tom
- three faces in a hood
- tickle-my-fancy

In German and Scottish folklore, pansies were called stepmothers: The large lower petal was the mother, the two petals to either side were daughters, and the two small upper petals were stepdaughters.

Mary Elizabeth Bennet (1785–1861) and her gardener, William Richardson, crossbred violets during the same period and showcased their new pansies to gardeners in 1813.

Further hybridization of *V. tricolor, V. lutea,* and *V. altaica* led to more unusual colors, different color combinations, and larger flowers.

By 1850, the pansy had been introduced to North America; by the late 1800s, it had become the continent's most popular flower grown from seed.

Today, the pansy is considered one of the world's most beloved flowers, with just about every color you can imagine represented in the more than 250 cultivars of *V.* x *wittrockiana.* *(continued)*

IF YOU DREAM OF PANSIES, YOU CAN EXPECT
TROUBLES WITH A GOOD FRIEND.
–folklore

> TO PLANT PANSIES IN
> THE SHAPE OF A HEART
> IS A SURE SIGN THAT
> THEY WILL FLOURISH.
> –folklore

PANSY POTIONS

- To gargle with pansy tea was believed to cure a toothache.
- Pliny the Elder recommended that a garland of violets be worn on the head to ward off headaches and dizzy spells.
- The wild violet flower was used to treat epilepsy in ancient times.
- The Celts made the dried leaves into a tea and used it both as a love potion and to cure a broken heart.

PANSY PLANTING

Pansies are classified as cool-season annuals because they can withstand cool temperatures. They typically bloom profusely from spring through early summer but wane in the heat of midsummer. In southern states, pansies tend to thrive in fall and winter.

You can start pansy seeds indoors 6 to 8 weeks before you plan to transplant them in the spring. In Zones 6 and warmer, seeds can also be started in late summer for fall and winter bloom. The seeds germinate best in darkness and at temperatures around 70°F.

Pansies thrive in rich, well-drained soil that receives morning sun and afternoon shade. Set five to seven plants in groups—such as in containers or as a border or ground cover—spacing them about 8 inches apart for strong visual impact and to prevent crowding. Many varieties reach 8 to 10 inches in height, with a similar spread.

Water regularly and deadhead (remove spent blossoms) as needed. For continuous bloom, apply a balanced fertilizer a couple of times during the growing season. Prune spring-blooming pansies back to about 2 inches in July for possible repeated bloom in early fall. Pansies may also reseed if left in the ground.

(continued)

Photos, from left: fermate/Getty Images; Pixabay

Anytime 'Iris' Pansiola

PARTICULAR PANSIES

As 'Yesterday, Today, & Tomorrow' matures, its blooms change color from creamy white to medium blue to, finally, deep lavender.

Trailing pansies from the Cool Wave and WonderFall series can spread to over 2 feet long, making them ideal candidates for hanging baskets. They are available in many colors.

The Anytime series is heat-tolerant and will bloom throughout the summer. It has a semi-trailing habit, perfect for containers. The series includes blooms of purple, shimmering pale blue and white, pure white, purple and yellow, and bright yellow.

Chianti Mix pansies have semi-ruffled flowers with streaked faces in soft shades of terra-cotta, salmon, creamy caramel, bronzed chocolate, rose, and wine red.

PANSIES AT A PARTY

High in vitamins A and C, pansy and violet petals and leaves are edible, and their presence in the kitchen inspires gaiety.

Pick mildly mint-tasting pansy flowers and the stronger-tasting leaves in the morning, when their water content is at its highest. (Don't let folklore's warning of rain on page 36 deter you.)

Put fresh blooms into a bowl of cold water for 5 minutes, then place them on a paper towel and roll the towel gently around the flowers. You can put the rolled flowers in the refrigerator until needed, but it is best to use the flowers as soon as possible. Here are a few ideas:

• Add colorful fresh blossoms to green salads, soups, and desserts.

• Freeze violet or pansy flowers into ice cubes or an ice ring to float in punch. *(continued)*

Photos, from left: Proven Winners; ThitareeSarmkasat/Getty Images

I LIKE TO SEE THE
FLOWERS GROW,
TO SEE THE PANSIES
IN A ROW;
I THINK A WELL-KEPT
GARDEN'S FINE,
AND WISH THAT SUCH
A ONE WERE MINE . . .

–Edgar Albert Guest,
English-born
American poet
(1881–1959)

IF YOU PICK A PANSY,
RAIN WILL FALL.
–folklore

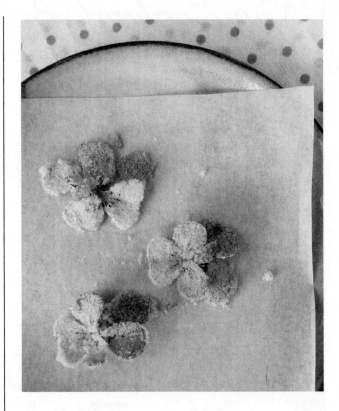

• Mix the smaller violet petals into cookie dough or decorate a cake with pansies.

• Candy the flowers to use as decorations on cakes or place them on top of a fruit salad: Mix powdered egg whites or meringue powder with water, according to the package directions, and beat until frothy. Using a small brush, paint each flower with the mixture. Sprinkle with superfine sugar and place on waxed paper to dry for at least 12 hours.

When gathering edible flowers, don't choose those growing near a road, as they have been exposed to dirt and exhaust. Also, don't use flowers from florists or garden centers because they may have been treated with pesticides. ■

Mare-Anne Jarvela enjoys both pansies and wild violets in her hillside New Hampshire garden. She uses the edible flowers in salads and as colorful accents on cakes.

Dwarf Tomatoes

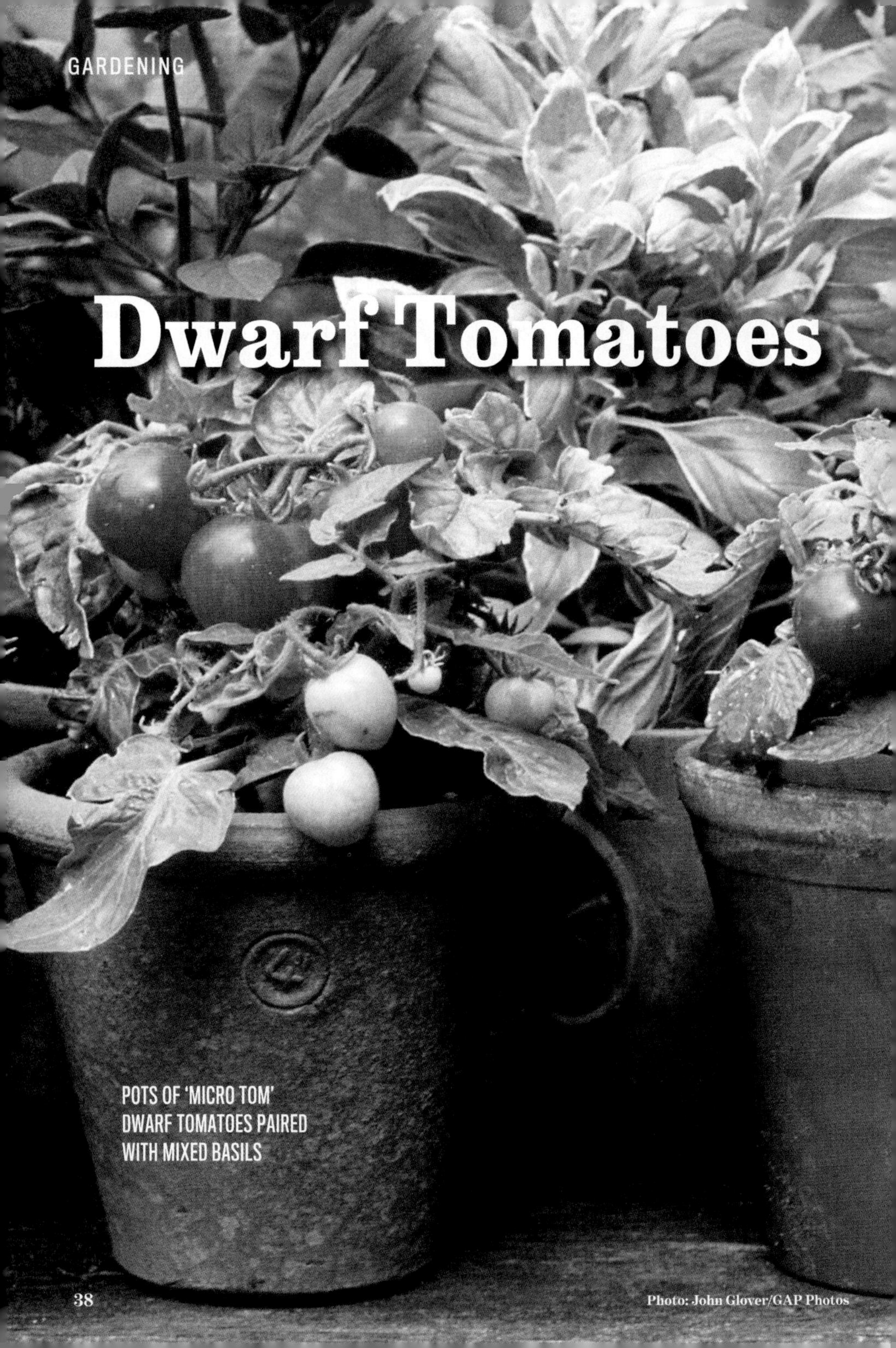

POTS OF 'MICRO TOM' DWARF TOMATOES PAIRED WITH MIXED BASILS

Photo: John Glover/GAP Photos

STAND TALL

Mini tomato plants have colossal appeal.

BY GAYLA TRAIL

(continued on page 41)

Got Neuropathy Pain?

Learn how Dr. Tammi Chapman, DPM helps her patients.

"I can't sleep at night – the shooting, prickling pain keeps me awake."

"Can I get pain relief without the drowsy side effects?"

"I need a pain relief product that won't interfere with my medications."

"I don't need to run marathons again – I just want to take a pain-free walk."

Have you said these same words? If so, you'll want to keep reading. Dr. Tammi Chapman, DPM in Robinson, Illinois explains why she recommends Frankincense & Myrrh Neuropathy to her neuropathy patients. "I believe in it. It has helped a good 75% of my patients find temporary relief."

> *"It has helped a good 75% of my patients find temporary neuropathy relief."*
> *-Dr. Tammi Chapman*

F&M: How would you describe Frankincense & Myrrh Neuropathy?

Dr. Chapman: Frankincense & Myrrh Neuropathy is a safe, non-drowsy, topical rubbing oil that won't interfere with other medications. It has helped many of my patients get a better night's sleep and move better during the day. While it doesn't help all my patients, a good 75% find temporary relief. For those it doesn't help, Frankincense & Myrrh comes with a satisfaction guarantee which offers a full product refund. I tell all my neuropathy patients, "Give it a try. You have nothing to lose and a lot to gain."

F&M: Why do you recommend Frankincense & Myrrh Neuropathy?

Dr. Chapman: I believe in this product!

It's a great, non-prescription option, and we are seeing good results with our patients who use it. I have not found many effective topical pain relief products on the market. This one works.

Many of my patients are on a plethora of medications. I can recommend Frankincense & Myrrh Neuropathy to help take the edge off their pain without negative interactions with their other medications.

F&M: How do you encourage patients to try Frankincense & Myrrh Neuropathy?

Dr. Chapman: It seems neuropathy pain is more acute at night. I encourage my neuropathy patients to rub a few drops on their feet at bedtime. I say, "It will help you sleep better and it can't hurt anything. At least try it."

Find Frankincense & Myrrh Neuropathy in the diabetic care aisle at **Walgreens, CVS, Walmart, Meijer, Sprouts** and online at **Amazon.com.** Visit frankincensemyrrh.com to download a $3.00 off product coupon and learn more or clip coupon on facing page.

Dr. Tammi Chapman, DPM has been in private practice 22 years. Her practice, TLC Foot Doc, Ltd, is located at 1000 N. Allen Street, Robinson, IL. Reach her at tlcfootdoc@gmail.com.

DWARF TOMATOES (CONTINUED)

When most of us think about tomatoes, we imagine big, sprawling vines bejeweled in cascading clusters of fruit. These monstrous indeterminate (vining) plants, especially if they are colorful heirloom varieties, do tend to be the most delicious. Unfortunately, we don't all have an in-ground garden in which to grow them, or our plot may be plagued by poorly draining soil, a lack of sun, or blight.

Fortunately, there are excellent diminutive options bred specifically for growing in pots. Allow me to introduce you to the dwarf tomato.

HOW DWARFS ARE DIFFERENT

Tomatoes tend toward two main forms (with a few rogue growth habits that fall in between): We have the tall, vining indeterminates that keep growing vertically, producing fruit until exhaustion, a hard frost, or disease cuts them down. Then there are the shorter determinates that leaf out into a bush, produce most of their fruit all at once, and then expire.

Dwarfs can be both and are neither; they reside in their own special category. In general, dwarf tomatoes are stocky, compact plants that mature at no more than 5 feet tall. Their leaves are often puckered or pleated (called "rugose"),

(continued on page 186)

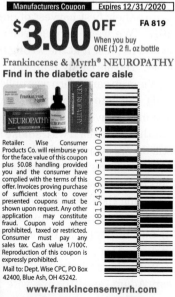

GROWING FARMERS

Stories, inspirations, and advice from folks who grow our food.

BY STACEY KUSTERBECK AND KAREN DAVIDSON

Farmers in the U.S. and Canada are diversifying. Their reasons for this range from generating additional income to helping the community to just plain survival. All have one thing in common: They truly love working the land.

BALDWIN FARMS
MCPHERSON, KANSAS

Will it pop? That question gave the owners of Baldwin Farms sleepless nights just before their first harvest of popcorn in 2017. "We were very nervous that we would harvest it at the wrong moisture level," recalls Cindy Baldwin.

When an ear of corn was pulled off the stalk, put into a paper bag, and placed in a microwave oven, nothing popped— but the house filled with smoke from the still damp, overheated cob.

The waiting game began as the kernels dried a few more days in the field.

During the next test, cobs popped in the microwave, in a stovetop pot, and in an air popper. "We all did a high five—and then we ate it," smiles Cindy.

With that, Cindy, husband Dwight, son Adam, and Adam's wife Kim became the niche marketers of Papa Baldy's Popcorn. For four decades, wheat, field corn, and soybeans have been the Baldwins' only crops, as the farm increased to several thousand acres. Then crop prices began to fall. "When commodity prices go down, if you have more acres, you have a tendency to lose more money," Dwight notes.

After a meeting with popcorn breeders, the family decided to try 'Jumbo Mushroom' popcorn and devoted a 5-acre field to it.

Dwight took on sales, offering free samples at countless sales venues. Today, the Baldwins have a diverse mix of retail customers. Yields aren't nearly as high as they are for field corn, but popcorn's selling price is much higher.

The farm allocated an additional 3 acres to popcorn in 2018, and the family is experimenting with poppable sorghum. "We had a good first year, and we are hoping for a good second year," says Dwight. "We're just going to see where this goes." *(continued)*

DWIGHT BALDWIN

BEECH HILL FARM

HOPKINTON, NEW HAMPSHIRE

In the 1800s, Beech Hill Farm delivered to customers raw bottled milk, produced by purebred Ayrshire cattle, in horse-drawn wagons. Today, folks travel to the farm, many for its famous make-your-own-sundae bar.

About 20 years ago, owners Holly Kimball and her father had to make some tough decisions. "Dairy farming became too difficult for many reasons," she remembers. They, with her oldest son Nate, decided to reinvent the 150-acre farm as an agritourism destination.

"The biggest challenge that we faced was figuring out how to bring people off the beaten path to our farm in rural New Hampshire," she reports. The first attractions were a walk-up ice cream stand and a cut-your-own-bouquet flower patch. She promoted the new features to local businesses and on the farm's Web site. Word of mouth spread.

A milking barn became an ice cream and gift shop. A former cow barn now hosts fund-raisers, concerts, parties, and Scout activities. Another building became a museum, with items and apparatus dating from the 1800s on display.

Outdoors, visitors enjoy the animals (cows, sheep, lambs, goats, a pony, donkeys, chickens, a bunny, piglets, peacocks, and an alpaca), nature trails, and corn maze. "We use every opportunity that we get to educate the public about agriculture," says Holly.

Nate completed the University of New Hampshire agricultural diversification and business management program with three future farm goals in mind: convert to solar energy, start a maple sugaring operation, and raise all-natural beef and pork. "Over the past 5 years, all of these initiatives have become a reality," notes Holly.

The diverse offerings bring relief and promise to all three generations, but one thing has not changed: "Weather affects us just as much or more than it did when we were only farming." *(continued)*

BREAKING NEWS...

CoQ10's Failure Leaves Millions Wanting

Use this pill to supercharge your brain and think better than ever.

NASA-discovered nutrient is stunning the medical world by activating more youthful energy, vitality and health than CoQ10.

BREAKING NEWS: Millions of Americans take the supplement CoQ10. It's the "jet fuel" that supercharges your cells' power generators, known as mitochondria.

As you age, your mitochondria begin to die. In fact, by age 67, you lose 80% of the mitochondria you had at age 25. But if you're taking CoQ10, there's something important you should know.

As powerful as CoQ10 is, there is a critical thing it just can't do — create new mitochondria in your cells.

Taking CoQ10 is not enough

"There's a little-known NASA nutrient that multiplies the number of new power generators in your cells by up to 55%," says Dr. Al Sears, owner of the Sears Institute for Anti-Aging Medicine in Royal Palm Beach, Florida. "Now you can make your heart, brain and body young again.

"I tell my patients the most important thing I can do is increase their 'health span.' This is the length of time you can live free of disease and with all your youthful abilities and faculties intact."

Medical first: Multiply the "power generators" in your cells

Al Sears, M.D., recently released an energy-boosting supplement based on this NASA nutrient that has become so popular, he's having trouble keeping it in stock.

Dr. Sears is the author of over 500 scientific papers on anti-aging and recently spoke at the WPBF 25 Health & Wellness Festival featuring Dr. Oz and special guest Suzanne Somers.

Thousands of people listened to Dr. Sears speak on his anti-aging breakthroughs and attended his book signing at the event.

Now, Dr. Sears has come up with what his peers consider his greatest contribution to anti-aging medicine yet — a newly discovered nutrient that multiplies the number of tiny, energy-producing "engines" located inside the body's cells, shattering the limitations of CoQ10 supplements.

Why mitochondria matter

A single cell in your body can contain between 200 to 2,000 mitochondria. But because of changes in cells, stress and poor diet, most people's power generators begin to malfunction and die off as they age.

Health problems such as heart issues, blood sugar concerns and vision and hearing difficulties can all be connected to a decrease in mitochondria.

Dr. Sears and his researchers combined the most powerful form of CoQ10 available — ubiquinol — with a newly discovered natural compound called PQQ (Pyrroloquinoline quinone) that has the remarkable ability to stimulate new mitochondria. Together, the two powerhouses are now available in a supplement called Ultra Accel II.

Science stands behind the power of PQQ

Biochemical Pharmacology reports that PQQ is up to 5,000 times more efficient in sustaining energy production than common antioxidants.

"PQQ has been a game changer for my patients," says Dr. Sears.

"With the PQQ in Ultra Accel II, I have energy I never thought possible," says Colleen R., one of Dr. Sears' patients. "I am in my 70s but feel 40 again."

Increase your 'health span' today

The demand for this supplement is so high, Dr. Sears is having trouble keeping it in stock. Right now the only way to get this potent combination of PQQ and super-powered CoQ10 is with Dr. Sears' breakthrough Ultra Accel II formula.

To secure bottles of this hot, new supplement, buyers should contact the Sears Health Hotline at 1-877-353-0632 within the next 48 hours. "The Hotline allows us to ship the product directly to the customer," says Dr. Sears.

Dr. Sears feels so strongly about this product, he offers a 100%, money-back guarantee on every order. "Just send me back the bottle and any unused product within 90 days of purchase, and I'll send you your money back," says Dr. Sears.

Call 1-877-353-0632 to secure your limited supply of Ultra Accel II. You don't need a prescription, and those who call in the first 24 hours qualify for a significant discount. To take advantage of this great offer use Promo Code FARM2019UA when you call in.

CHINOOK HONEY COMPANY & CHINOOK ARCH MEADERY
OKOTOKS, ALBERTA

Art and Cherie Andrews never imagined that when they grounded their aviation careers, they would embark on a flight with honeybees. Their hobby apiary is now an agritourism destination in the foothills of Alberta's Rocky Mountains.

"We grew from two hives in 1995 to more than 300 in 2008," reports Cherie, "but since then, our numbers have declined to 150 hives." Disease and harsh winters have taken a toll. The August drought and early September snows of 2018 dashed hopes of continuing "to pull honey" (extract it from frames), a process that usually lasts into October. "In the early days, it was common to lose about 10 percent of the hives over winter, but now those losses are closer to 30 percent. Weak queens are also an emerging issue."

In the meantime, Art, a beer maker, had been experimenting with making mead, an alcoholic beverage derived from fermented honey. "At the time, there were no masters of mead-making in western Canada," says Cherie.

Several years and 50 batches later, Art found himself with a perfect recipe—and plans to sell the liquid gold. He consulted sparkling wine experts in British Columbia's Okanagan Valley and imported equipment from Italy. Harder to procure was a provincial license; the government had no category for mead. However, after input from Cherie and some of Alberta's beekeepers and fruit growers, in 2007 the provincial government was persuaded to create the Estate Winery License, which facilitated the sale of Art's beverage in provincial liquor outlets.

Today, Art annually produces almost 5,000 gallons of mead in 12 flavors, including black currant and cherry (fruit-infused mead is called "melomel"). The farm is abuzz with customers for raw honey; honey-infused jams, jellies, and sauces; and, of course, mead. *(continued)*

Photos: courtesy of Chinook Honey Company & Chinook Arch Meadery

FRESH FUTURE FARM
NORTH CHARLESTON, SOUTH CAROLINA

When Germaine Jenkins and her children lived in an apartment building, she promised them that they'd have a garden someday. When she moved to the Low Country to attend culinary school and became a homeowner, she kept her word. The first step was digging up and giving away the azaleas in the front yard. In their place, she planted blueberries, orange trees, and sweet potatoes, and she kept chickens in the back for egg production and manure. Curious kids riding by on bikes would ask, "Is this a farm?"

The question was prescient. Jenkins soon convinced North Charleston city officials to lease her a .81-acre vacant lot. She marked its boundaries with fruit trees and, over time, it became Fresh Future Farm. "Slowly, we built up the farm," she recalls.

Today, the farm is the source of an astounding variety of the freshest, most nutritious produce that some locals have ever had. Fresh eggs come from the farm's chickens; compost, from garden waste; mulch, from cardboard boxes donated by a local business; the store building, from the owner of a rental car company who no longer needed it.

The five employees who manage the store and field are paid through donations and store revenue. Volunteers, ages 15 to 73, prepare the fields, plant, and harvest. "Everyone who works here either volunteered, interned, or shopped here for months before they got the job," reports Jenkins.

Families, school kids, and tourists visit the farm and learn about its sustainable ways, like capturing rainwater and keeping bees for pollination. Jenkins plans an online class on "agricultural entrepreneurship": "It will show the basics, so that the next person who does this skips all of the mistakes that I made. We don't just want to grow food. We want to grow gardeners."

(continued)

HERRLE'S COUNTRY FARM MARKET
ST. AGATHA, ONTARIO

I n 1964, Howard and Elsie Herrle (HER-lee) were growing a few acres of sweet corn and selling it from their garage near St. Agatha, Ontario. The harvest lasted for just a few weeks, but the quality of their produce and their friendly service earned them the loyalty of the local community. Before long, they were offering tender peas, spinach, and beans. Come August, shelves groaned with baskets of squash varieties and pumpkins. By 1988, the Herrles had built a farm market and bakery. Customers were coming from increasingly greater distances!

As the Herrles' reputation grew, so did their vision. In 1995, local Mennonite craftsmen built them a hand-notched and -pegged post-and-beam addition. By 2005, the market was offering salads, dairy products, and frozen (heritage) meats. The Herrles sought the freshest produce from local farmers—Niagara's famous peaches, for example. Over the years, they added ready-to-eat items. "If consumers don't want to make a meal from scratch," says Howard, "they can buy our homemade corn chowder."

The family has long supported the community. From July through October, the Food Bank of Waterloo Region and House of Friendship social service agency are grateful recipients of 40,000 pounds of fresh produce—all grown specifically for donation. Every fall, a total of about 2,500 schoolchildren come for a tour to see how their food is grown. Occasionally local chefs arrange to film cooking videos on-site.

Today, Howard and Elsie's son James, a fifth-generation descendant of Peter Herrle, who purchased the land in 1858, says that diversification has allowed six family members to remain fully employed and provided jobs for about 60 others. The staff—more like a family—greets an estimated 100,000 customers annually.

(continued)

Photos: courtesy of Herrle's Country Farm Market

CAROLYN BISHOP

NOGGINS CORNER FARM MARKET
GREENWICH, NOVA SCOTIA

The Noggins Corner Farm Market can be traced back to the cradle of agriculture in Nova Scotia. The Bishop family was granted 500 acres on the Cornwallis River in 1755 as part of an offer to entice New England settlers with free land. Within a few years, they had established apple and pear orchards and a dairy. By the late 1800s, commerce was flourishing on a wagon track and weary travelers were buying noggins (quarter pints) of rum from an old farmhouse in Greenwich.

Skip forward to 1992. Descendant Andrew Bishop incorporated the farm, anticipating more growth. Today, he produces more than 50 varieties of apples and pears, and his vision is to diversify into tender fruit such as apricots and nectarines. Some of the pears and apples are made into fruit ciders. New apple products include purées and leathers (made by pouring puréed apples onto a flat surface for drying). Several family members are involved in growing, marketing, and trucking, while Andrew's brother Stirling operates a dairy farm as a separate venture.

Andrew's daughter, Patricia, and her husband, Josh, own and run Taproot Farms. The organic farm's prodigious vegetable harvest serves 350 families each year through community-shared agriculture boxes and is also marketed or sold at Noggins Corner Farm Market as well as four other markets in the province.

Andrew's other daughter, Carolyn, manages this diverse enterprise. Still, at the heart of it all is apples and apple products. "We're always looking for more ideas on how to sell one more apple," Carolyn says. *(continued)*

Photo: Karen Davidson

SANTA CRUZ FARM
SANTA CRUZ, NEW MEXICO

At Santa Cruz Farm, 72 varieties of organic produce grow on just 3½ acres. "It's a beautiful, small, diverse farm. I farm the same land that my ancestors farmed 400 years ago, basically using the same techniques," says owner Don Bustos.

As a child, Bustos could often be found behind a mule, plowing for his grandfather on the family's farm. Over time, the property became overgrown. Then, in 1983, he began farming it again—this time, to grow organic produce.

The tiny farm is a four-man operation: Bustos and two employees work the land, and his nephew handles sales at six local farmers' markets, all within 25 miles. "We have a little bit of wholesale here and there, but direct sales seem to be more profitable for us," reports Bustos. Customers know that Santa Cruz Farm is the only place to find locally grown blackberries and strawberries—and cucumbers off-season.

Success stems from tried-and-true practices paired with cautious, low-cost innovations. "Being a small farm, we are very risk-averse," notes Bustos. "But small investments add up to big profits, if done correctly." High tunnels were added to extend the growing season. Switching to a root-zone heating system saved money; the heating bill for the small greenhouse, once $750 a month, is now just pennies a day. "This is what allows us to grow greens in the middle of the winter," says Bustos.

He is passionate about training beginning farmers: "My philosophy is not to grow the farm, but to grow more people to farm. It's not about just one person. It's about the whole community flourishing."

His advice: Go all in. "If you approach farming as a full-time job, you will be successful. But if you try to farm and do something else on the side, then you marginalize your chances." *(continued)*

VALE FARMS GRASSROOTS LTD.

LUMBY, BRITISH COLUMBIA

When Michael and Charlotte Ruechel immigrated from Germany in 1975, looking for an idyllic ranch setting, they found it in a valley close to the Monashee Mountains. The area had ample hay and pasture acreage supported by a good water supply. There they founded Vale Farm beef ranch. Today, the beef herd numbers about 60 cattle, many of which are Canadian Speckle Parks. Developed in the Prairie provinces, the breed derives from Teeswater Shorthorn, Aberdeen Angus, and English cattle. "This breed does very well on grass," observes Charlotte. "They're not spoiled with grain." The resulting meat is well marbled and flavorful.

The Ruechels' beef ranch has slowly evolved into Vale Farms Grassroots Limited, a source of organic meats. Charlotte converted to organic practices in 1999, almost a decade after a horse-riding accident left Michael with life-altering injuries. While caring for him, she realized that "my only tool was nutrition"—and renewed her interest in bone broth, which she had enjoyed as a regular part of German cuisine.

Charlotte attended health conferences and came to believe that nutrient-dense foods helped to build strong bones. With a plentiful supply of beef bones, she started to experiment with a recipe, adding root vegetables and herbs. In 2014, she became certified organic and began to sell the broth commercially.

Today, daughter Emily and her husband, Don Hladich, are responsible for the beef herd and an organic dairy with 60 milking cows. Daughter Lorna, with her husband, Chris Church, purchased an adjacent acreage in 2008. They called it Grassy Gnome Acres and raise turkeys, pigs, and lambs there. "We like raising animals the old-fashioned way—on pasture," adds Charlotte. ■

The profiles of the U.S. farmers were written by **Stacey Kusterbeck,** a regular contributor to the Almanac. **Karen Davidson,** editor of *The Grower,* a leading Canadian horticultural magazine, and frequent contributor to the Almanac, wrote the profiles of the Canadian farmers.

Photos: courtesy of Vale Farms Grassroots Ltd.

A SOUND HISTORY OF NOISE

BY TIM CLARK
ILLUSTRATIONS BY TIM ROBINSON

There is a common condition of modern life that disturbs our sleep, disrupts our emotions, impairs our thinking, and literally drives us crazy. This threat exists at almost every place on the planet; those where it does not exist are disappearing every day. It has been present throughout human history, and it is getting worse all the time.

It is noise.

Not all sound is noise. Defined as unwanted sound, "noise" shares its linguistic DNA with words like "annoying" and "noisome." But one person's noise may be another's music. In 1845, Henry David Thoreau wrote, "The commonest and cheapest sounds, as the barking of a dog, produce the same effect on fresh and healthy ears as the rarest music does. It depends on your appetite for sound."

On that note, let the cacophony begin!

For nearly as long as we have been making noise, we have been trying to control it. One of its earliest uses was for protection. Some 50,000 years ago, dogs were domesticated and began to serve as living security systems, barking at other animals that approached. Ever since, one of the most common sources of unwanted sound has been barking dogs.

Burglar alarms employing bells and trip wires date from the 18th century. But when the first electric alarm—a "burglar annunciator"—was registered in Boston in 1853, as essayist Nelson Smith noted in 1997, it began a "raucous encroachment of private distress on the public

domain." Residents of Windsor, Ontario, and some surrounding communities have experienced such an intrusion. Since 2011, they have endured an unexplainable low-frequency hum that they claim causes mood disorders, heart and sleeping problems, nausea, and more.

oise has long been a potent weapon. According to the Old Testament Book of Joshua, in 1400 B.C., the invading Israelites toppled the walls of the Canaanite city of Jericho at God's command by blowing ram's-horn trumpets and giving a great shout. Later, Aztec warriors blew on a "death whistle" that sounded like human screams, and in World War II, German Stuka dive-bombers were equipped with a "Jericho horn" that emitted a piercing shriek that terrified soldiers and civilians targeted by the Luftwaffe. In 1989,

U.S. troops struck a different chord: They drove Panamanian dictator Manuel Noriega out of hiding by playing rock music at extreme volumes.

Even in the realm of sport, noise plays an aggressive role. The student body of Mississippi State University was so famous for ringing cowbells (to disrupt the composure and communications of visiting football teams) that the practice was banned by the Southeastern Conference in 1975. Undeterred, the team's fans came up with alternatives such as shaking bells from which the clangers had been removed while roaring "Ding, Dong, Damnit!" Eventually, after threats of a lawsuit, the SEC gave in and let the Bulldogs ring their bells. *(continued)*

By the Numbers

Noise is measured in decibels. A decibel (1 dB) is one-tenth of a bel, a unit named for Alexander Graham Bell. Here's a sampling of common sounds, with their volume in decibels:

Softest sound that a person with normal hearing can hear	0 dB
Normal breathing	10
A quiet library	40
Heavy traffic	85
Car horn	110
Chainsaw	120
Shotgun firing	170
Volcanic eruption	180
Blue whale song	190

The composition of Earth's atmosphere is such that no sound can be louder than 194 dB. Beyond that level, the event creates a shock wave that pushes the air forward instead of creating sound waves that move through it.

s long as we have sought to employ noise, we have striven to lower the volume. In the 6th century B.C., the first known noise ordinance banned roosters inside the walls of a Greek city. The Greek physician Hippocrates identified the condition now known as "tinnitus" ("ringing in the ears") and suggested that it might be caused by exposure to loud noises. Julius Caesar regulated the legal hours of wagon driving in Rome. And in 1595, the City of London forbade men to beat their wives at night—not to spare the wives, but to let the neighbors sleep. Nearly three centuries later, the city authorities were still trying to quell the din: In 1864, "The Act for Better Regulation of Street Music in the Metropolis" was passed in London.

Yet for each successful attempt to mute the racket, some new technology made things worse. In 1770, Scotland's James Watt invented the steam engine, a powerful new source of noise. In 1819, the French baron Charles Cagniard de la Tour demonstrated a noisemaking machine that worked underwater. He called it the siren, after beautiful

women who lure sailors to their death in Greek myths. And in 1860, Belgian Jean Joseph Etienne Lenoir built the first practical gas-powered internal combustion engine. No longer would the clip-clop of horses' hooves be the most common sound on city streets.

But the louder the noise, the more alarming the effects on human and animal health. When the first steam-powered foghorn was installed at the lighthouse on Sandy Hook, New Jersey, in 1867, it was blamed for curdling milk, killing chicks in their eggs, and making people lose weight.

Over time, the resistance grew louder, too. In 1906, Julia Barnett Rice founded the Society for the Suppression of Unnecessary Noise in New York City, where her house overlooked the Hudson River. Her lobbying resulted in 1907's Bennett Act, which banned the

excessive blowing of steam whistles on boats in New York Harbor. Having stilled the boats, she then went after automobiles. Ironically, the first man to own a car in Manhattan was her husband, who enjoyed roaring through Central Park in it, tooting its Klaxon horn (ah-OO-gah!), invented in 1908 by Miller Reese Hutchison (who, a few years earlier, had developed the first portable electric hearing aid).

Invention begat rejection: In 1913, an unknown prisoner from Denver invented the first mechanical car alarm. In 1950, Aldo Vandermolen invented a gasoline-powered leaf blower whose noise level can exceed 80 decibels. In 1957, Chicago passed the nation's first zoning ordinance that sets maximum allowable noise levels in certain densely populated areas. By 1975, communities like Beverly Hills, California, were banning leaf blowers. In 1994, the New York City Police Department reported

that car alarms could be making the crime problem worse, citing a case in 1992 where a thief deliberately rocked a car, setting off its alarm, to mask the sound of him breaking into a building.

While some fought against the industrial noise complex, others tried to thwart it with technology. In 1962, the Marpac Sleep Mate, a

mechanical producer of random or "white" noise to help people sleep, went on the market. In 1969, an agency of the United Nations proposed a "right to silence" to combat the intrusion of recorded or broadcast music in quiet places. In 1989, Dr. Amar Bose, a pioneer in improved sound recording who had wearied of the noise on a commercial airliner, scribbled some notes on a napkin. Fifteen years and $50 million in research and development later, he debuted the first noise-canceling headphones.

Perhaps the patron saint of the anti-noise revolution should be primary school teacher Annalisa Flanagan, from Northern Ireland. In 1994, she was credited with the world's loudest shout (as loud as a jet engine) by the *Guinness Book of World Records.* The word she shouted? "Quiet!"

However, the 21st century brought troubling news: We may be evolving to prefer the screech, the whine, the rumble, and the roar. In 2014, a University of Virginia study put hundreds of volunteers in an empty, quiet room alone for 15 minutes. One-quarter of the women and two-thirds of the men later testified that they would prefer painful electric shocks to silence. ∎

Tim Clark lives in Dublin, New Hampshire, with his wife and two very noisy dogs.

GOT A Craving

Coconuts can be found throughout the tropics, but they are not all the same. There are over 1,300 types of coconut, all of which can be traced back to two genetic strains from either the Pacific or the Indian Ocean. The coconut is the fruit of the coconut palm tree, and, technically, it is a drupe, not a nut. A drupe is a fruit that has an outer layer covering a fibrous, fleshy part that in turn surrounds a shell that contains a seed. Coconuts found in grocery stores have had this hairy outer part removed.

Why is it called a "nut"? *Coco* comes from the Portuguese word for "grinning face," because 16th-century Portuguese sailors thought that the three indentations on the shell resembled a grinning monkey. *Nut* was added later by English-speakers, presumably because they thought that it resembled a large nut.

Coconuts have many uses, but their most familiar place is in the kitchen. Whether you cook with coconut oil, milk, or flour or coconut's white meat (called "copra" when dried), it's good to know that coconuts are full of vitamins and minerals and add a taste of the tropics to any dish.

(continued)

CRACK THE COCONUT

Kids are fascinated by whole, fresh coconuts. Buy one to show them where coconut meat comes from! To choose a good one, shake it and listen for the liquid inside. At home, with a screwdriver and hammer, make two holes at one end of the coconut. Pour out the liquid and reserve it to drink later. Hit the coconut repeatedly around its equator until it cracks open. Continue striking the pieces, making them smaller. Separate the meat from the shell using a knife as a wedge. Peel away any brown skin. Cut the coconut meat into 1-inch pieces and shred it, using a box grater or food processor. Freeze any coconut that you do not use.

FOR Coconut?

Try a taste of the tropics to warm up chilly nights!

BY SARAH PERREAULT
RECIPE PHOTOS: SAMANTHA JONES • STYLING: KENZA SALEM
QUINN BREIN COMMUNICATIONS

HOW TO TOAST COCONUT

Use toasted coconut to jazz up dishes that call for it shredded and sprinkle some on oatmeal, salad, and yogurt.

Toast shredded coconut in a nonstick skillet over medium-high heat for 4 to 6 minutes, or until golden brown. Stir constantly. (The more you stir, the more evenly the coconut will toast.) Immediately transfer to a plate. When cool, store in an airtight container for up to 1 month.

COCONUT CURRY PORK AND CRANBERRIES

1½ cups basmati or jasmine rice

zest of 1 lime

1 teaspoon kosher or sea salt, divided

¾ cup light coconut milk

1 tablespoon Thai red curry paste

1 tablespoon fish sauce

1 tablespoon soy sauce

1 tablespoon brown sugar

1 tablespoon fresh lime juice

3 tablespoons vegetable oil

1 pound pork tenderloin, cut into strips about ½ inch wide and 2 inches long

2 cups sliced button mushrooms

4 cloves garlic, minced

2 tablespoons minced fresh ginger

4 cups thinly sliced Napa cabbage

½ cup dried sweetened cranberries

½ cup chopped fresh scallions, for topping

½ cup chopped fresh cilantro, for topping

⅓ cup chopped salted peanuts, for topping

In a pot, combine rice and 2½ cups of water. Let sit for 15 minutes, then stir in lime zest and ½ teaspoon salt. Cover pot and bring to a boil. Reduce heat to low and cook for 15 minutes, or until rice absorbs the water. Set aside.

In a bowl, whisk together coconut milk, curry paste, fish sauce, soy sauce, brown sugar, and lime juice. Set aside.

In a frying pan or wok over high heat, warm oil until it shimmers. Add pork and remaining ½ teaspoon salt. Cook, stirring often, for 2 minutes or until no longer pink. Add mushrooms and cook, stirring, for 2 minutes. Add garlic, ginger, cabbage, and cranberries, stirring for 1 minute. Add coconut milk mixture and simmer for 3 minutes.

Divide rice among six bowls and top with pork mixture. Pass scallions, cilantro, and peanuts at the table for topping.

Makes 6 servings.   *(continued)*

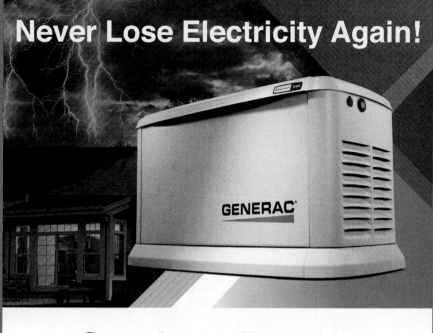

COCONUT CREAM PIE

FILLING:
½ cup sugar
3½ tablespoons cornstarch
pinch of salt
2 cups milk
3 egg yolks
2 tablespoons (¼ stick)
  unsalted butter, cut into
  pieces
1 teaspoon vanilla extract
½ teaspoon coconut extract
1 cup sweetened flaked
  coconut
your favorite prepared
  piecrust

CREAM:
¾ cup cold heavy cream
3 tablespoons sifted
  confectioners' sugar
½ teaspoon vanilla extract

½ cup toasted coconut flakes

For filling: In a nonstick saucepan, whisk together sugar, cornstarch, and salt. Whisk in milk and yolks. Place over medium heat and cook for 5 to 7 minutes, whisking until mixture thickens and starts to boil. Remove from heat and whisk in butter, one piece at a time. Whisk in vanilla, coconut extract, and coconut.

Pour filling into pie shell and smooth top with a spoon. Cover with plastic wrap and smooth to remove any air gaps. Transfer pie to a rack and cool completely. Refrigerate overnight.

For cream: Chill a bowl and electric mixer's beaters in the freezer for 5 minutes. Beat cream until it holds soft peaks, then beat in confectioners' sugar. Add vanilla and beat until cream is stiff but not grainy. Spread over pie and sprinkle with toasted coconut. Refrigerate until ready to serve.

Makes 8 servings. *(continued)*

70

LEMON COCONUT COOKIES

1 cup (2 sticks)
  unsalted butter,
  softened
½ cup sugar
1½ tablespoons
  grated lemon
  zest
1 teaspoon vanilla
  extract
½ teaspoon lemon
  extract
2 cups all-purpose
  flour
¼ teaspoon
  kosher or sea
  salt
1 cup toasted
  coconut flakes
confectioners'
  sugar

Using an electric hand or stand mixer, cream butter and sugar until light and fluffy. Beat in lemon zest and vanilla and lemon extracts. Add flour and salt and beat well. Stir in coconut.

Cut dough in half and place each half on a sheet of wax paper. Form each half into an 8-inch log. Wrap each log in wax paper and refrigerate for at least 4 hours (or overnight).

Preheat oven to 300°F. Grease baking sheets or line with parchment paper.

With a sharp knife, cut logs into ¼-inch-thick slices and arrange 2 inches apart on prepared baking sheets. Bake for 25 to 30 minutes, or until lightly golden. Transfer cookies to cooling racks and sift generously with confectioners' sugar. Let cool and dust lightly with more confectioners' sugar.

Makes about 4 dozen cookies. ■

Sarah Perreault is the food editor of *The Old Farmer's Almanac.*

2019 PASTA
RECIPE CONTEST WINNERS

Many thanks to the hundreds of you who submitted recipes!

PHOTOGRAPHY: SAMANTHA JONES · STYLING: KENZA SALEM
QUINN BREIN COMMUNICATIONS

FIRST PRIZE: $300
SPINACH ARTICHOKE DIP STUFFED PASTA SHELLS

36 jumbo pasta shells
1 container (16 ounces) cottage
   cheese or ricotta
1 can (14 ounces) artichoke
   hearts, drained and coarsely
   chopped
1 box (10 ounces) chopped
   spinach, thawed and
   squeezed dry
4 ounces cream cheese, softened
½ cup freshly grated Parmesan
   cheese
⅓ cup sour cream
⅓ cup mayonnaise
½ teaspoon garlic powder
½ teaspoon onion powder
½ teaspoon salt
¼ teaspoon freshly ground
   black pepper
⅛ teaspoon ground nutmeg,
   or to taste
1½ cups french-fried onions
1 jar (24 ounces) red pepper
   pasta sauce or favorite pasta
   sauce
1½ cups shredded mozzarella
   cheese
chopped fresh parsley,
   for garnish

Preheat oven to 350°F. Grease a 13x9-inch baking dish.

Cook pasta shells for 2 minutes less than package directions, then drain and rinse in cold water.

In a bowl, combine cottage cheese, artichoke hearts, spinach, cream cheese, Parmesan, sour cream, mayonnaise, garlic powder, onion powder, salt, pepper, and nutmeg. Fold in french-fried onions.

Cover bottom of prepared baking dish with a layer of pasta sauce. Stuff shells with artichoke mixture and place in baking dish. Spoon remaining sauce over shells and top with mozzarella cheese. Cover with foil and bake for 30 minutes. Remove foil and bake for another 15 minutes, or until sauce is bubbly and cheese is melted. Garnish with parsley.

Makes 8 to 10 servings.

–Kellie Braddell, West Point, California
(continued)

SECOND PRIZE: $200

QUICK SOUTHWEST PASTA

1 pound small shell pasta
1 pound chorizo pork sausage, sliced
¼ onion, diced
4 cloves garlic, minced
1 can (15.5 ounces) black beans, drained and rinsed
1 can (15 ounces) tomato sauce
1 can (4 ounces) diced green chiles
1 cup frozen corn
1 teaspoon salt
½ teaspoon dark chili powder
½ teaspoon dried oregano
¼ teaspoon cumin
¼ teaspoon freshly ground black pepper
¼ cup Cotija cheese, for topping
15 sprigs cilantro, chopped, for topping

Prepare pasta according to package directions. Drain and set aside.

In a skillet over medium heat, cook chorizo until browned. Add onions and cook for 5 minutes, or until translucent. Add garlic and cook for 2 minutes. Add black beans, tomato sauce, green chiles, corn, salt, chili powder, oregano, cumin, pepper, and 1 cup of water to skillet. Cook for 15 minutes. Add pasta and cook for 3 minutes.

Serve individual portions topped with Cotija and cilantro.

Makes 6 servings.

–*Chelsea Madren, Fullerton, California*
(continued)

ENTER THE 2020 RECIPE CONTEST: APPETIZERS
Got a great recipe for an appetizer that's loved by family and friends? It could win! See contest rules on page 251.

THIRD PRIZE: $100
BACON HORSERADISH PENNE PASTA SALAD

SALAD:
½ pound penne pasta
6 slices bacon, diced and cooked crisp
1 cup chopped broccoli, steamed
¾ cup halved cherry tomatoes
½ cup sliced kalamata olives
¼ cup chopped red onion

DRESSING:
½ cup mayonnaise
⅓ cup sour cream
1½ teaspoons horseradish sauce
½ teaspoon brown mustard
salt and freshly ground black pepper, to taste

For salad: Cook pasta according to package directions for al dente. Drain and rinse in cold water.

In a bowl, combine pasta, bacon, broccoli, tomatoes, olives, and onions.

For dressing: In a bowl, thoroughly combine mayonnaise, sour cream, horseradish sauce, mustard, and salt and pepper.

Add dressing to salad and stir to combine. Refrigerate salad for at least 1 hour before serving.

Makes 6 servings.

–Mona Grandbois, Biddeford, Maine

HONORABLE MENTION
RAISIN, PINE NUT, SWISS CHARD, APPLE, AND SAUSAGE PASTA

6 tablespoons raisins
¾ cup lukewarm water
3 tablespoons extra virgin olive oil
2 cloves garlic, minced
1 pound sweet Italian sausage, casings removed
4 sprigs rosemary
2 red apples, peeled, cored, and diced
1 cup dry white wine or chicken broth
1 teaspoon salt
½ teaspoon freshly ground black pepper
1 pound Swiss chard, stalks removed, julienned
1 pound spaghetti or other thin ribbon pasta
½ cup pine nuts
¾ cup grated Parmesan cheese

Soak raisins in lukewarm water.

In a skillet over medium heat, warm oil. Add garlic and cook, stirring, until just golden, about 1 minute. Add sausage and rosemary. Increase heat to medium high and cook for 3 minutes, breaking up sausage as it cooks. Reduce heat to low, add apples, stir for 1 minute, then add wine. Cook until wine reduces by half, another 4 to 5 minutes. Season with salt and pepper and remove rosemary stems.

Bring a pot of salted water to a boil. Add Swiss chard and return to a boil. Add pasta and cook according to package instructions for al dente. Drain, reserving ½ cup of pasta cooking water.

Add pasta and Swiss chard to skillet. Toss gently, adding reserved pasta cooking water if needed.

Transfer to a serving bowl. Drain raisins and add to pasta along with pine nuts. Toss to combine. Sprinkle Parmesan over pasta. Serve immediately.

Makes 4 to 6 servings.

–Donna Pochoday-Stelmach, Morristown, New Jersey ■

WHERE **GLACIERS** STOPPED

. . . AND TRAFFIC HALTS FOR REPTILES

BY MICHAEL JEFFORDS AND SUSAN POST

Driving across Illinois has been compared to "zipping through eye-level corduroy"—an homage to the endless flat landscape of corn and soybeans. All of Illinois, however, is not so agriculturally dominated.

Heading south out of Mt. Vernon, the topography begins to get rougher and wilder. Amid rugged hills known as the Shawnee Escarpment stand massive outcroppings of ancient sandstone, limestone, and shale bedrock, weathered and exposed. This area, extending across the southern part of the state from near the mouth of the Wabash River in the east to the Mississippi River in the west (approximately 80 miles), is known as the Shawnee Hills and contains the 289,000-acre Shawnee National Forest.

Cloaked in deep forests interspersed with cool ravines, these mammoth rocks mark the southernmost extent of the great North American continental glaciers of the Pleistocene epoch (said to have begun some 2.6 million years ago and ended 11,700 years ago). This

ONCE FARMED, NOW FORESTED

By the early 20th century, this land had mostly become ruined, gullied farmland due to attempts by settlers to farm the rugged topography. In 1939, it was declared a national forest by President Franklin D. Roosevelt and named for the Native American tribe that called the area home. Today, the land is a mix of many hardwood tree species dotted with islands of planted pines, courtesy of the Civilian Conservation Corps in the 1930s and '40s.

THREE WARRIORS ROCK FORMATION

Photos, from top: FSTOPLIGHT/Getty Images; baluzek/Getty Images

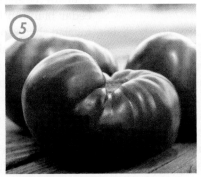

CAMEL ROCK, THE LANDMARK OF
THE GARDEN OF THE GODS

area avoided burial by glacial soil and rock deposits that filled in much of the landscape to the north.

As a result, geological diversity is on full display.

The signature site here is Garden of the Gods Recreation Area, with its landmark Camel Rock—an outcrop resembling a humped desert ungulate. Other prominent features of Garden of the Gods can be observed along a half-mile trail. Rock ledges are clothed with lichens and mosses. Clifftop vegetation here is intimately attuned to the violent fluctuations in moisture. Consequently, most rock ledge plants grow and flower in spring,

when rainfall is plentiful: bluets, false garlic, and yellow star grass appear in shallow depressions in the ledges and at borders, where the sandstone slips beneath the soil of the scraggly oak and cedar bluff-top forests that leaf out in myriad shades of green. The landscape is also predictably spectacular in the fall, the colors courtesy of huge, old-growth oak, maple, and tulip trees.

The ancient sandstone harbors odd formations: giant's kettles (weathered holes in rock) and Liesegang Rings (vibrantly colored concentric circles of rock). The Rings, composed of iron-rich minerals, appear on cliff faces as raised, dark red patterns. Chemical changes solidified the iron oxides *(continued on page 190)*

Burro Into This

... and don't make a donkey out of yourself in the process.

by Karen L. Kirsch

They've been around for thousands of years and today they're a rapidly growing segment of the equine industry, yet donkeys remain subjects of undue ridicule and ignorance. Contrary to misperceptions, a donkey is not a horse with big ears. A donkey is a burro (that name is Spanish) and a donkey is an ass *(Equus africanus asinus,* to be precise), but donkey aficionados simply call them longears.

Donkeys are unique physically, intellectually, and emotionally. They come in many colors and in sizes ranging from mini to mammoth. Like horses, donkeys are measured in "hands" calculated from the ground to their "withers," the highest point on their back (a hand is 4 inches). Miniature donkeys can not exceed 9 hands (36 inches), but mammoth donkeys measure 14 hands and more—and can live for more than 50 years.

Their memory is extraordinary, and they can remember people, places, and other donkeys from 25 years past. Donkeys are the smallest members of the Equidae family, but pound for pound, they're stronger than horses. As social creatures, lone donkeys are not happy. Like people, they need friends and build lasting bonds.   *(continued)*

By Many Other Names

A female is a jenny or jennet. An intact male is a jack, and a castrated male is a john. Donkeys have 62 chromosomes, making them genetically incompatible with horses, which have 64, so crossbreeding produces almost-always sterile offspring with 63. But without jackasses (male donkeys), there would be no mules (for which donkeys are often mistaken). Mules are the long-eared progeny of a donkey jack and a horse mare. Crossing a jenny with a horse stallion produces a hinny, which more closely resembles a pony. A cross with a zebra creates a sterile, hybrid zedonk (*below;* also called a zonkey, zebroid, or zebrass). Gestation time averages 12 months, with the jenny having a single foal, usually every other year.

Photos, from top: tepic/Getty Images; Top Photo Corporation/Getty Images

Donkeys, by Design

Some say that they look like they were made with leftover parts, but form follows function, which has allowed them to survive essentially unchanged for millennia. Those big ears enhance their hearing. They have a sharp sense of smell and can detect water a mile away. Their upright hooves can dig water holes in arid environments or strike out in defense.

Donkeys have no forelock, and their mane and tail hair is stiff and scruffy. Skinny tails terminate with a "brush" that looks as if it were stolen from a cow. And that bizarre voice! Their larynx, nostrils, and nasal passages differ anatomically from horses', resulting in a loud bray (rather than a horse's neigh) that's necessary for communication and warding off predators. *(continued on page 192)*

(continued on page 192)

Photo: YiorgosGR/Getty Images

A KING AND A BRAYER

• According to the Bible, strongman Samson slew 1,000 Philistines with the jawbone of a donkey.

• George Washington believed donkeys to be superior to horses and other draft animals and desired to breed them at Mount Vernon. At the time, the world's best donkeys were from Spain, and permission of the king of Spain was required to procure one. Eventually, the king gave Washington two Spanish donkeys. "Royal Gift" arrived in 1785; the other was lost at sea en route.

• Beginning in the 1880s, teams of 20 mules were used to pull the wagons that hauled borax, a naturally occurring mineral that was mined in Death Valley, California. For years borax was considered a useful cleaning agent. (It was the sponsor of the popular radio and later TV show *Death Valley Days*.) Today, borax is believed to have harmful side effects.

• The most expensive cheese in the world is made from the milk of Balkan donkeys in the town of Zasavica, Serbia. *Pule* (a Serbian word for "foal") is priced at about $600 per pound. Donkeys there are milked three times daily and produce about a third- to a half-gallon of milk per day.

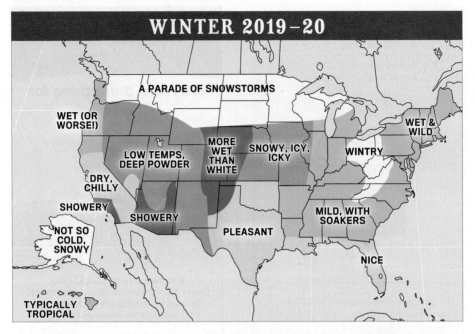

WINTER 2019–20

- A PARADE OF SNOWSTORMS
- WET (OR WORSE!)
- WET & WILD
- LOW TEMPS, DEEP POWDER
- MORE WET THAN WHITE
- SNOWY, ICY, ICKY
- WINTRY
- DRY, CHILLY
- SHOWERY
- SHOWERY
- MILD, WITH SOAKERS
- NOT SO COLD, SNOWY
- PLEASANT
- NICE
- TYPICALLY TROPICAL

These weather maps correspond to the winter and summer predictions in the General Weather Forecast (opposite) and on the regional forecast pages, 206–223. To learn more about how we make our forecasts, turn to page 202.

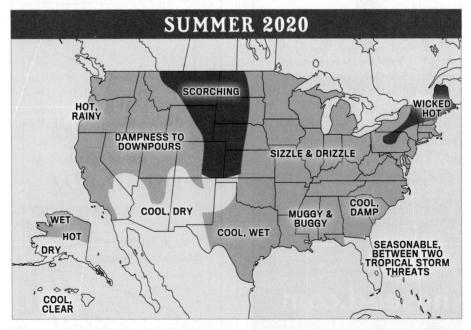

SUMMER 2020

- SCORCHING
- HOT, RAINY
- WICKED HOT
- DAMPNESS TO DOWNPOURS
- SIZZLE & DRIZZLE
- COOL, DRY
- COOL, DAMP
- WET
- MUGGY & BUGGY
- HOT
- DRY
- COOL, WET
- SEASONABLE, BETWEEN TWO TROPICAL STORM THREATS
- COOL, CLEAR

Maps: AccuWeather, Inc.

THE GENERAL WEATHER REPORT AND FORECAST

FOR REGIONAL FORECASTS, SEE PAGES 206-223.

W hat's shaping the weather? Solar Cycle 24, possibly the smallest since the early 1800s' Dalton Minimum, is close to its end. Nascent Cycle 25 is also expected to bring low solar activity. Although such minimal activity has historically meant cooler average temperatures across Earth, we believe that recent warming trends will dominate in the eastern and northern parts of the nation this winter, with below-normal average temperatures limited to the Southwest.

WINTER temperatures will be below normal from the Heartland westward to the Pacific and in the Desert Southwest, Pacific Southwest, and Hawaii but above normal elsewhere. Precipitation will be below normal in Florida and the Gulf Coast area, Texas, Oklahoma, the Upper Midwest, the western Desert Southwest, central California, and western Hawaii and above normal elsewhere.

Snowfall will be above normal from the southern Appalachians northward through western Pennsylvania and most of Ohio, in the Heartland, from northern Michigan westward to Puget Sound, and in the Intermountain region, eastern Desert Southwest, and Alaska and below normal in most other areas.

SPRING will be warmer than normal in Alaska and the eastern two-thirds of the Lower 48, near normal in the Pacific Northwest, and cooler than normal elsewhere from the High Plains westward and in Hawaii. Precipitation will be below normal in the Northeast, southern Florida, eastern Great Lakes, Heartland, Pacific Northwest, and Hawaii and near or above normal elsewhere.

SUMMER temperatures will be below normal from Florida northward through

the Southeast, from Texas and Oklahoma westward through southern and central California, and in the Intermountain region and Hawaii and above normal elsewhere. Rainfall will be above normal from most of Texas northward to Canada and eastward to the Atlantic (except for in Florida, where it will be below normal), in the Intermountain and Pacific regions, and in northern Alaska and below normal elsewhere.

Watch for a major **HURRICANE** in mid-September along the Florida–North Carolina coast. **TROPICAL STORM** threats are foreseen for the same area in mid- to late June, in Florida in mid- to late July and mid- to late October, and from the Deep South and Southeast northeastward to New England in early to mid-October.

AUTUMN temperatures will be cooler than normal in most of Texas, Oklahoma, and New Mexico and in the Pacific Southwest, Alaska, and Hawaii and near or above normal elsewhere. Precipitation will be above normal from the Deep South and Southeast northeastward to New England, from central California northward through the Pacific Northwest, and in southern Alaska; near normal in the Desert Southwest; and below normal elsewhere.

TO GET A SUMMARY OF THE RESULTS OF OUR FORECAST FOR LAST WINTER, TURN TO PAGE 204.

THE OLD
FARMER'S ALMANAC

Established in 1792 and published every year thereafter

ROBERT B. THOMAS, *founder* (1766–1846)

YANKEE PUBLISHING INC.

EDITORIAL AND PUBLISHING OFFICES

P.O. Box 520, 1121 Main Street, Dublin, NH 03444

Phone: 603-563-8111 • Fax: 603-563-8252

EDITOR *(13th since 1792):* Janice Stillman
ART DIRECTOR: Colleen Quinnell
MANAGING EDITOR: Jack Burnett
SENIOR EDITORS: Sarah Perreault, Heidi Stonehill
EDITORIAL ASSISTANTS: Tim Clark,
Benjamin Kilbride
WEATHER GRAPHICS AND CONSULTATION:
AccuWeather, Inc.

V.P., NEW MEDIA AND PRODUCTION:
Paul Belliveau
PRODUCTION DIRECTORS:
Susan Gross, David Ziarnowski
SENIOR PRODUCTION ARTISTS:
Jennifer Freeman, Janet Selle, Susan Shute

WEB SITE: ALMANAC.COM

DIGITAL EDITOR: Catherine Boeckmann
DIGITAL ASSISTANT EDITOR: Christopher Burnett
NEW MEDIA DESIGNERS: Lucio Eastman, Amy O'Brien
E-COMMERCE DIRECTOR: Alan Henning
PROGRAMMING: Peter Rukavina

CONTACT US

We welcome your questions and comments about articles in and topics for this Almanac. Mail all editorial correspondence to Editor, The Old Farmer's Almanac, P.O. Box 520, Dublin, NH 03444-0520; fax us at 603-563-8252; or contact us through Almanac.com/Feedback. *The Old Farmer's Almanac* can not accept responsibility for unsolicited manuscripts and will not acknowledge any hard-copy queries or manuscripts that do not include a stamped and addressed return envelope.

Thank you for buying this Almanac! We hope that you find it "useful, with a pleasant degree of humor." Thanks, too, to everyone who had a hand in it, including advertisers, distributors, printers, and sales and delivery people.

OUR CONTRIBUTORS

Bob Berman, our astronomy editor, is the director of Overlook Observatory in Woodstock and Storm King Observatory in Cornwall, both in New York. With Jim Metzner, he is a co-host of the "Astounding Universe" podcast, a freewheeling exploration of the world of science. Listen for free at Almanac.com/podcast.

Julia Shipley, a journalist and poet, wrote the Farmer's Calendar essays that appear in this edition. She raises animals and vegetables on a small farm in northern Vermont. Her recordings of the essays are available free at Almanac.com/Podcast.

Tim Clark, a retired English teacher from New Hampshire, has composed the weather doggerel on the Calendar Pages since 1980.

Bethany E. Cobb, our astronomer, is an Associate Professor of Honors and Physics at George Washington University. She conducts research on gamma-ray bursts and specializes in teaching astronomy and physics to non–science majoring students. When she is not scanning the sky, she enjoys rock climbing, figure skating, and reading science fiction.

Celeste Longacre, our astrologer, often refers to astrology as "a study of timing, and timing is everything." A New Hampshire native, she has been a practicing astrologer for more than 25 years. Her book, *Celeste's Garden Delights* (2015), is available for sale on her Web site, www.celestelongacre.com.

Michael Steinberg, our meteorologist, has been forecasting weather for the Almanac since 1996. In addition to college degrees in atmospheric science and meteorology, he brings a lifetime of experience to the task: He began predicting weather when he attended the only high school in the world with weather Teletypes and radar.

THE OLD
FARMER'S ALMANAC

Established in 1792 and published every year thereafter

ROBERT B. THOMAS, *founder* (1766–1846)

YANKEE PUBLISHING INC.
P.O. Box 520, 1121 Main Street, Dublin, NH 03444
Phone: 603-563-8111 • Fax: 603-563-8252

PUBLISHER *(23rd since 1792):* Sherin Pierce
EDITOR IN CHIEF: Judson D. Hale Sr.

FOR DISPLAY ADVERTISING RATES
Go to Almanac.com/AdvertisingInfo or
call 800-895-9265, ext. 109

Stephanie Bernbach-Crowe • 914-827-0015
Steve Hall • 800-736-1100, ext. 320

FOR CLASSIFIED ADVERTISING
Cindy Levine, RJ Media • 212-986-0016

AD PRODUCTION COORDINATOR:
Janet Selle • 800-895-9265, ext. 168

PUBLIC RELATIONS
Quinn Brein • 206-842-8922
Ginger Vaughan • ginger@quinnbrein.com

CONSUMER MAIL ORDERS
Call 800-ALMANAC (800-256-2622)
or go to Almanac.com/Shop

RETAIL SALES
Stacey Korpi • 800-895-9265, ext. 160
Janice Edson, ext. 126

DISTRIBUTORS
NATIONAL: Curtis Circulation Company
New Milford, NJ
BOOKSTORE: Houghton Mifflin Harcourt
Boston, MA

Old Farmer's Almanac publications are available for sales promotions or premiums. Contact Beacon Promotions, info@beaconpromotions.com.

YANKEE PUBLISHING INCORPORATED
Jamie Trowbridge, *President;* Judson D. Hale Sr., *Senior Vice President;* Paul Belliveau, Jody Bugbee, Judson D. Hale Jr., Brook Holmberg, Sandra Lepple, Sherin Pierce, *Vice Presidents.*

The Old Farmer's Almanac/Yankee Publishing Inc. assumes no responsibility for claims made by advertisers or failure by its advertisers to deliver any goods or services advertised herein. Publication of any advertisement by The Old Farmer's Almanac/Yankee Publishing Inc. is not an endorsement of the product or service advertised therein.

PRINTED IN U.S.A.

Leading Acid Reflux Pill Becomes an Anti-Aging Phenomenon

Clinical studies show breakthrough acid reflux treatment also helps maintain vital health and helps protect users from the serious conditions that accompany aging such as fatigue and poor cardiovascular health

"ACCIDENTAL" ANTI-AGING BREAKTHROUGH: Originally developed for digestive issues, AloeCure not only ends digestion nightmares... it revitalizes the entire body. Some are calling it the greatest accidental discovery in decades.

Stewart Blum
Health Correspondence

Seattle, WA – A clinical study on a leading acid reflux pill shows that its key ingredient relieves digestive symptoms while suppressing the inflammation that contributes to premature aging in men and women.

And, if consumer sales are any indication of a product's effectiveness, this 'acid reflux pill turned anti-aging phenomenon' is nothing short of a miracle.

Sold under the brand name AloeCure, it was already backed by clinical data documenting its ability to provide all day and night relief from heartburn, acid reflux, constipation, irritable bowel, gas, bloating, and more.

But soon doctors started reporting some incredible results...

"With AloeCure, my patients started reporting less joint pain, more energy, better sleep, and even less stress and better skin, hair, and nails" explains Dr. Liza Leal; a leading integrative health specialist and company spokesperson.

AloeCure contains an active ingredient that helps improve digestion by acting as a natural acid-buffer that improves the pH balance of your stomach.

Scientists now believe that this acid imbalance is what contributes to painful inflammation throughout the rest of the body.

The daily allowance of AloeCure has shown to calm this inflammation which is why AloeCure is so effective.

Relieving other stressful symptoms related to GI health like pain, bloating, fatigue, cramping, constipation, diarrhea, heartburn, and nausea.

Now, backed with new clinical studies, AloeCure is being recommended by doctors everywhere to help improve digestion, calm painful inflammation, soothe joint pain, and even reduce the appearance of wrinkles – helping patients to look and feel decades younger.

FIX YOUR GUT & FIGHT INFLAMMATION

Since hitting the market, sales for AloeCure have taken off and there are some very good reasons why.

To start, the clinical studies have been impressive. Participants taking the active ingredient in AloeCure saw a stunning 100% improvement in digestive symptoms, which includes fast and lasting relief from reflux.

Users also experienced higher energy levels and endurance, relief from chronic discomfort and better sleep. Some even reported healthier looking skin, hair, and nails.

Doctors are calling AloeCure the greatest accidental health discovery in decades!

EXCITING RESULTS FROM PATIENTS

To date over 5 million bottles of AloeCure have been sold, and the community seeking non-pharma therapy for their GI health continues to grow.

According to Dr. Leal, her patients are absolutely thrilled with their results and are often shocked by how fast it works.

"For the first time in years, they are free from concerns about their digestion and almost every other aspect of their health," says Dr. Leal, "and I recommend it to everyone who wants to improve GI health

without resorting to drugs, surgery, or OTC medications."

With so much positive feedback, it's easy to see why the community of believers is growing and sales for the new pill are soaring.

THE SCIENCE BEHIND ALOECURE

AloeCure is a pill that's taken just once daily. The pill is small. Easy to swallow. There are no harmful side effects and it does not require a prescription.

The active ingredient is a rare Aloe Vera component known as acemannan.

Made from of 100% organic Aloe Vera, AloeCure uses a proprietary process that results in the highest quality, most bio-available levels of acemannan known to exist.

According to Dr. Leal and several of her colleagues, improving the pH balance of your stomach and restoring gut health is the key to revitalizing your entire body.

When your digestive system isn't healthy, it causes unwanted stress on your immune system, which results in inflammation in the rest of the body.

The recommended daily allowance of acemannan in AloeCure has been proven to support digestive health, and calm painful inflammation without side effects or drugs.

This would explain why so many users are experiencing impressive results so quickly.

HOW TO GET ALOECURE

In order to get the word out about AloeCure, the company is offering special introductory discounts to all who call. Discounts will automatically be applied to all callers, but don't wait. This offer may not last forever. Call toll-free: 1-800-547-0173

ECLIPSES

There will be six eclipses in 2020, two of the Sun and four of the Moon. Solar eclipses are visible only in certain areas and require eye protection to be viewed safely. Lunar eclipses are technically visible from the entire night side of Earth, but during a penumbral eclipse, the dimming of the Moon's illumination is slight. See the **Astronomical Glossary, page 110,** for explanations of the different types of eclipses.

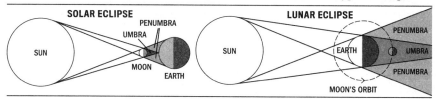

JANUARY 10: PENUMBRAL ECLIPSE OF THE MOON. This eclipse is visible from North America only in far northwestern and northeastern regions. The Moon will enter the penumbra at 12:06 P.M. EST (8:06 P.M. AKST) and leave the penumbra at 4:14 P.M. EST (12:14 P.M. AKST).

JUNE 5: PENUMBRAL ECLIPSE OF THE MOON. This eclipse is not visible from North America. (The eclipse is visible only from the western Pacific Ocean and parts of Australasia, Asia, Antarctica, Europe, Africa, and South America.)

JUNE 21: ANNULAR ECLIPSE OF THE SUN. This eclipse is not visible from North America. (The annular solar eclipse is visible from parts of Africa, Europe, the Middle East, Asia, Indonesia, and Micronesia.)

JULY 4-5: PENUMBRAL ECLIPSE OF THE MOON. This eclipse is visible from North America, except in northernmost regions. The Moon will enter the penumbra at 11:04 P.M. EDT (8:04 P.M. PDT) on July 4 and leave the penumbra at 1:56 A.M. EDT on July 5 (10:56 P.M. PDT on July 4). *Only a small portion of the Moon will fall within the penumbra during this eclipse.*

NOVEMBER 29-30: PENUMBRAL ECLIPSE OF THE MOON. This eclipse is visible from North America. The Moon will enter the penumbra at 2:30 A.M. EST on November 30 (11:30 P.M. PST on November 29) and leave the penumbra at 6:56 A.M. EST (3:56 A.M. PST) on November 30.

DECEMBER 14: TOTAL ECLIPSE OF THE SUN. This eclipse is not visible from North America. (The eclipse is visible only from the southern Pacific Ocean, the Galápagos Islands, and parts of South America, Antarctica, and Africa.)

TRANSIT OF MERCURY. Mercury's proximity to the Sun makes the planet difficult to observe. In 2020, Mercury is best viewed from the Northern Hemisphere during early February (after sunset), late May to early June, and mid-November (before sunrise). Look for a conjunction between Mercury and Venus after sunset on May 22.

THE MOON'S PATH

The Moon's path across the sky changes with the seasons. Full Moons are very high in the sky (at midnight) between November and February and very low in the sky between May and July.

FULL-MOON DATES (ET)				
	2020	2021	2022	2023	2024
JAN.	10	28	17	6	25
FEB.	9	27	17	5	24
MAR.	9	28	18	7	25
APR.	7	26	16	6	23
MAY	7	26	16	5	23
JUNE	5	24	14	3	21
JULY	5	23	13	3	21
AUG.	3	22	11	1 & 30	19
SEPT.	2	20	10	29	17
OCT.	1 & 31	20	9	28	17
NOV.	30	19	8	27	15
DEC.	29	18	7	27	15

2020   The Old Farmer's Almanac   103

BRIGHT STARS

TRANSIT TIMES

This table shows the time (ET) and altitude of a star as it transits the meridian (i.e., reaches its highest elevation while passing over the horizon's south point) at Boston on the dates shown. The transit time on any other date differs from that of the nearest date listed by approximately 4 minutes per day. To find the time of a star's transit for your location, convert its time at Boston using Key Letter C (see **Time Corrections, page 238**).

STAR	CONSTELLATION	MAGNITUDE	TIME OF TRANSIT (ET) BOLD = P.M. LIGHT = A.M.						ALTITUDE (DEGREES)
			JAN. 1	MAR. 1	MAY 1	JULY 1	SEPT. 1	NOV. 1	
Altair	Aquila	0.8	**12:53**	8:57	5:57	1:57	**9:49**	**4:49**	56.3
Deneb	Cygnus	1.3	**1:43**	9:47	6:47	2:47	**10:40**	**5:40**	92.8
Fomalhaut	Psc. Aus.	1.2	**3:59**	**12:03**	9:03	5:03	1:00	**7:56**	17.8
Algol	Perseus	2.2	**8:09**	**4:13**	**1:13**	9:13	5:10	1:10	88.5
Aldebaran	Taurus	0.9	**9:36**	**5:41**	**2:41**	10:41	6:37	1:37	64.1
Rigel	Orion	0.1	**10:15**	**6:19**	**3:19**	11:19	7:15	2:16	39.4
Capella	Auriga	0.1	**10:17**	**6:22**	**3:22**	11:22	7:18	2:18	93.6
Bellatrix	Orion	1.6	**10:25**	**6:30**	**3:30**	11:30	7:26	2:26	54.0
Betelgeuse	Orion	var. 0.4	**10:55**	**6:59**	**4:00**	**12:00**	7:56	2:56	55.0
Sirius	Can. Maj.	−1.4	**11:45**	**7:49**	**4:49**	**12:49**	8:46	3:46	31.0
Procyon	Can. Min.	0.4	12:43	**8:43**	**5:43**	**1:44**	9:40	4:40	52.9
Pollux	Gemini	1.2	12:49	**8:50**	**5:50**	**1:50**	9:46	4:46	75.7
Regulus	Leo	1.4	3:12	**11:12**	**8:12**	**4:12**	**12:09**	7:09	59.7
Spica	Virgo	var. 1.0	6:28	2:32	**11:28**	**7:29**	**3:25**	10:25	36.6
Arcturus	Boötes	−0.1	7:18	3:22	12:23	**8:19**	**4:15**	11:15	66.9
Antares	Scorpius	var. 0.9	9:32	5:36	2:36	**10:32**	**6:29**	**1:29**	21.3
Vega	Lyra	0	11:39	7:43	4:43	12:43	**8:35**	**3:35**	86.4

RISE AND SET TIMES

To find the time of a star's rising at Boston on any date, subtract the interval shown at right from the star's transit time on that date; add the interval to find the star's setting time. To find the rising and setting times for your city, convert the Boston transit times above using the Key Letter shown at right before applying the interval (see **Time Corrections, page 238**). Deneb, Algol, Capella, and Vega are circumpolar stars—they never set but appear to circle the celestial north pole.

STAR	INTERVAL (H. M.)	RISING KEY	DIR.*	SETTING KEY	DIR.*
Altair	6 36	B	EbN	E	WbN
Fomalhaut	3 59	E	SE	D	SW
Aldebaran	7 06	B	ENE	D	WNW
Rigel	5 33	D	EbS	B	WbS
Bellatrix	6 27	B	EbN	D	WbN
Betelgeuse	6 31	B	EbN	D	WbN
Sirius	5 00	D	ESE	B	WSW
Procyon	6 23	B	EbN	D	WbN
Pollux	8 01	A	NE	E	NW
Regulus	6 49	B	EbN	D	WbN
Spica	5 23	D	EbS	B	WbS
Arcturus	7 19	A	ENE	E	WNW
Antares	4 17	E	SEbE	A	SWbW

*b = "by"

THE TWILIGHT ZONE/METEOR SHOWERS

Twilight is the time when the sky is partially illuminated preceding sunrise and again following sunset. The ranges of twilight are defined according to the Sun's position below the horizon. **Civil twilight** occurs when the Sun's center is between the horizon and 6 degrees below the horizon (visually, the horizon is clearly defined). **Nautical twilight** occurs when the center is between 6 and 12 degrees below the horizon (the horizon is distinct). **Astronomical twilight** occurs when the center is between 12 and 18 degrees below the horizon (sky illumination is imperceptible). When the center is at 18 degrees (**dawn** or **dark**) or below, there is no illumination.

LENGTH OF ASTRONOMICAL TWILIGHT (HOURS AND MINUTES)

LATITUDE	JAN. 1-APR. 10	APR. 11-MAY 2	MAY 3-MAY 14	MAY 15-MAY 25	MAY 26-JULY 22	JULY 23-AUG. 3	AUG. 4-AUG. 14	AUG. 15-SEPT. 5	SEPT. 6-DEC. 31
25°N to 30°N	1 20	1 23	1 26	1 29	1 32	1 29	1 26	1 23	1 20
31°N to 36°N	1 26	1 28	1 34	1 38	1 43	1 38	1 34	1 28	1 26
37°N to 42°N	1 33	1 39	1 47	1 52	1 59	1 52	1 47	1 39	1 33
43°N to 47°N	1 42	1 51	2 02	2 13	2 27	2 13	2 02	1 51	1 42
48°N to 49°N	1 50	2 04	2 22	2 42	–	2 42	2 22	2 04	1 50

TO DETERMINE THE LENGTH OF TWILIGHT: The length of twilight changes with latitude and the time of year. See the **Time Corrections, page 238,** to find the latitude of your city or the city nearest you. Use that figure in the chart above with the appropriate date to calculate the length of twilight in your area.

TO DETERMINE ARRIVAL OF DAWN OR DARK: Calculate the sunrise/sunset times for your locality using the instructions in **How to Use This Almanac, page 116.**

Subtract the length of twilight from the time of sunrise to determine when dawn breaks. Add the length of twilight to the time of sunset to determine when dark descends.

EXAMPLE:
BOSTON, MASS. (LATITUDE 42°22')

Sunrise, August 1	5:37 A.M. ET
Length of twilight	- 1 52
Dawn breaks	3:45 A.M.
Sunset, August 1	8:03 P.M. ET
Length of twilight	+1 52
Dark descends	9:55 P.M.

PRINCIPAL METEOR SHOWERS

SHOWER	BEST VIEWING	POINT OF ORIGIN	DATE OF MAXIMUM*	NO. PER HOUR**	ASSOCIATED COMET
Quadrantid	Predawn	N	Jan. 4	25	–
Lyrid	Predawn	S	Apr. 22	10	Thatcher
Eta Aquarid	Predawn	SE	May 4	10	Halley
Delta Aquarid	Predawn	S	July 30	10	–
Perseid	**Predawn**	**NE**	**Aug. 11-13**	**50**	**Swift-Tuttle**
Draconid	Late evening	NW	Oct. 9	6	Giacobini-Zinner
Orionid	Predawn	S	Oct. 21-22	15	Halley
Taurid	Late evening	S	Nov. 9	3	Encke
Leonid	Predawn	S	Nov. 17-18	10	Tempel-Tuttle
Andromedid	Late evening	S	Nov. 25-27	5	Biela
Geminid	**All night**	**NE**	**Dec. 13-14**	**75**	–
Ursid	Predawn	N	Dec. 22	5	Tuttle

*May vary by 1 or 2 days   **In a moonless, rural sky   **Bold** = most prominent

New Arthritis Painkiller Works on Contact and Numbs the Pain in Minutes

New cream works faster and is more targeted than oral medications. Key ingredients penetrate the skin within minutes to relieve joint arthritis pain. Users report significant immediate relief.

Apeaz™: Quick Acting Pain and Arthritis Cream is Now Available Without a Prescription

By Robert Ward
Associated Health Press

BOSTON – Innovus Pharmaceuticals has introduced a new arthritis pain relief treatment that works in minutes.

Sold under the brand name Apeaz™, the new pain relief cream numbs the nerves right below the skin.

When applied to an arthritic joint, or a painful area on the body, it delivers immediate relief that lasts for hours and hours.

The powerful painkilling effect is created by the creams active ingredients, three special medical compounds.

Anesthetics are used in hospitals during surgery. They block nerve signals from the brain so that patients don't feel pain and they work fast.

The anesthetic found in Apeaz™ is the strongest available without a prescription.

The cream form allows users to directly target their area of pain. It works where it is applied. The company says this is why the product is so effective and fast acting.

"Users can expect to start feeling relief immediately after applying," explains Dr. Bassam Damaj, President of Innovus Pharmaceuticals.

"There will be a pleasant warming sensation that is followed by a cool, soothing one. This is how you know that the active ingredients have reached the affected joint and tissue."

Works In Minutes

For arthritis suffers, Apeaz™ offers impressive advantages over traditional medications. The most obvious is how quickly it relieves pain discomfort.

The cream contains the maximum approved OTC dose of a top anesthetic, which penetrates the skin in a matter of minutes to numb the area that's in pain. This relief lasts for several hours.

Published pre-clinical animal studies have shown that the ingredients in Apeaz™ can also prevent further bone and cartilage destruction.

There are also no negative side effects like from oral medication. Apeaz™ delivers its ingredients through the skin. Oral medications are absorbed in the digestive tract. Overtime, the chemicals in pills can tear the delicate lining of the stomach, causing ulcers and bleeding.

When compared to other arthritis medications, Apeaz™ is a fraction of the cost. At less than $2 a day, the cream quickly is becoming a household name.

Those with terrible arthritis in their hands and fingers, love how easy Apeaz™ is to open. The jar fits in the palm of the hand, which makes it much easier to use.

Instant Pain Relief Without a Prescription

Many Apeaz™ users report significant improvements in daily aches and pain. Many more report increased flexibility and less stiffness. They are moving with less pain for the first time in years, like Henry Esber, an early user of Apeaz™.

"I've tried more pills than I can count. I've also had a handful of cortisone shots. Nothing is as effective as this product. With Apeaz™, I get relief right away. I rub a little on my hands. It keeps the pain away. It also prevents the pain from getting really bad. It's completely changed my life."

How It Works

Apeaz™ contains the highest, non-prescription OTC dose of a medical compound that fights pain on contact. When applied to the skin it goes to work within minutes by penetrating right to the source of your pain, numbing the nerve endings.

"This is why Apeaz™ is so effective for people with arthritis pain. It reduces pain while adding an additional potential layer of joint support," explains Damaj.

How to Get Apeaz™

In order to get the word out about Apeaz™, the company is offering special introductory discounts to all who call. Discounts will automatically be applied to all callers, but don't wait. This offer may not last forever. Call toll-free: 1-800-411-8480.

THE VISIBLE PLANETS

Listed here for Boston are viewing suggestions for and the rise and set times (ET) of Venus, Mars, Jupiter, and Saturn on specific days each month, as well as when it is best to view Mercury. Approximate rise and set times for other days can be found by interpolation. Use the Key Letters at the right of each listing to convert the times for other localities **(see pages 116 and 238).**

FOR ALL PLANET RISE AND SET TIMES BY ZIP CODE, VISIT ALMANAC.COM/ASTRONOMY.

VENUS

Venus has an eye-catching year, opening with the brightest planet a conspicuous evening star after sunset. This fine apparition shifts rightward into the northwestern sky as winter turns to spring, reaches its peak elevation and brilliance in April, and remains excellent through May. For the rest of the year, Venus is a fine morning star. May 21 brings a wonderful close conjunction between Venus and Mercury, 10 degrees above the western horizon in evening twilight.

Jan. 1	set	7:09	B	Apr. 1	set	11:19	E	July 1	rise	3:15	B	Oct. 1	rise	3:15	B
Jan. 11	set	7:34	B	Apr. 11	set	11:28	E	July 11	rise	2:51	B	Oct. 11	rise	3:35	B
Jan. 21	set	7:59	B	Apr. 21	set	11:27	E	July 21	rise	2:33	B	Oct. 21	rise	3:56	C
Feb. 1	set	8:24	C	May 1	set	11:14	E	Aug. 1	rise	2:21	B	Nov. 1	rise	3:21	C
Feb. 11	set	8:46	C	May 11	set	10:43	E	Aug. 11	rise	2:17	B	Nov. 11	rise	3:43	D
Feb. 21	set	9:07	D	May 21	set	9:51	E	Aug. 21	rise	2:19	B	Nov. 21	rise	4:07	D
Mar. 1	set	9:26	D	June 1	set	8:30	E	Sept. 1	rise	2:27	B	Dec. 1	rise	4:32	D
Mar. 11	set	10:45	E	June 11	rise	4:31	A	Sept. 11	rise	2:40	B	Dec. 11	rise	4:56	E
Mar. 21	set	11:03	E	June 21	rise	3:48	B	Sept. 21	rise	2:56	B	Dec. 21	rise	5:21	E
												Dec. 31	rise	5:43	E

MARS

2020 is a superb year for Mars, which achieves an unusually big (21 arcseconds) and bright (magnitude –2.6) appearance unequaled until the year 2033. Plus, the Red Planet is nicely high up in Pisces during its October opposition. As this year opens, the red-orange orb is an unimpressive dim second-magnitude morning star in Libra. But chugging eastward and brightening, it breaks the 0-magnitude threshold on June 1, in Aquarius. Summer finds Mars brightening explosively. When it rises at 11:00 P.M. in August, in Pisces, it equals the brilliance of Jupiter in September. Out all night at its October 13 opposition, it remains brightly visible through year's end. Mars is close to Saturn in early April and—in a worthy conjunction—very close to the Moon on October 2.

Jan. 1	rise	4:00	E	Apr. 1	rise	3:36	E	July 1	rise	12:22	D	Oct. 1	rise	7:11	C
Jan. 11	rise	3:55	E	Apr. 11	rise	3:19	E	July 11	rise	11:54	C	Oct. 11	rise	6:22	C
Jan. 21	rise	3:50	E	Apr. 21	rise	3:01	E	July 21	rise	11:28	C	Oct. 21	set	6:18	D
Feb. 1	rise	3:43	E	May 1	rise	2:41	D	Aug. 1	rise	10:58	C	Nov. 1	set	4:23	D
Feb. 11	rise	3:35	E	May 11	rise	2:20	D	Aug. 11	rise	10:28	C	Nov. 11	set	3:40	D
Feb. 21	rise	3:27	E	May 21	rise	1:59	D	Aug. 21	rise	9:57	C	Nov. 21	set	3:03	D
Mar. 1	rise	3:17	E	June 1	rise	1:34	D	Sept. 1	rise	9:19	C	Dec. 1	set	2:33	D
Mar. 11	rise	4:06	E	June 11	rise	1:11	D	Sept. 11	rise	8:40	C	Dec. 11	set	2:07	D
Mar. 21	rise	3:52	E	June 21	rise	12:47	D	Sept. 21	rise	7:58	C	Dec. 21	set	1:46	D
												Dec. 31	set	1:28	D

BOLD = P.M. LIGHT = A.M.

Find more heavenly details at Almanac.com/Astronomy.

JUPITER

The solar system's largest planet opens 2020 as a predawn morning star in Sagittarius and is visible the entire year to the right of Saturn. During March, Jupiter bunches together with Mars and Saturn; the Moon joins the trio on the 18th. Opposition occurs on July 14, in Sagittarius, when Jupiter rises at sunset and is visible all night; it is highest at 1:00 A.M. By autumn, Jupiter is seen only during the night's first half. It crosses into Capricornus on December 15, meets the Moon on the next night, and passes extremely close to Saturn from December 20 to 22—being closest on December 21, the solstice. This will be the finest planetary "great" conjunction of our lives—the premier astronomical event of the year.

Jan. 1	rise	7:00	E	Apr. 1	rise	3:09	E	July 1	**rise**	**9:07**	E	Oct. 1	**set**	**11:51**	A
Jan. 11	rise	6:30	E	Apr. 11	rise	2:34	E	July 11	**rise**	**8:23**	E	Oct. 11	**set**	**11:16**	A
Jan. 21	rise	5:59	E	Apr. 21	rise	1:57	E	July 21	set	4:56	A	Oct. 21	**set**	**10:41**	A
Feb. 1	rise	5:26	E	May 1	rise	1:20	E	Aug. 1	set	4:06	A	Nov. 1	**set**	**9:05**	A
Feb. 11	rise	4:54	E	May 11	rise	12:42	E	Aug. 11	set	3:21	A	Nov. 11	**set**	**8:33**	A
Feb. 21	rise	4:23	E	May 21	**rise**	**11:58**	E	Aug. 21	set	2:38	A	Nov. 21	**set**	**8:03**	A
Mar. 1	rise	3:54	E	June 1	**rise**	**11:14**	E	Sept. 1	set	1:51	A	Dec. 1	**set**	**7:33**	A
Mar. 11	rise	4:21	E	June 11	**rise**	**10:32**	E	Sept. 11	set	1:11	A	Dec. 11	**set**	**7:04**	A
Mar. 21	rise	3:47	E	June 21	**rise**	**9:50**	E	Sept. 21	set	12:32	A	Dec. 21	**set**	**6:35**	A
												Dec. 31	**set**	**6:07**	A

SATURN

Expect to first glimpse the Ringed Planet in February in Sagittarius as a low predawn star. It spends the year to the left of Jupiter. Saturn's rings are angled fairly open and are gorgeous through any telescope using more than 30x. By June, Saturn rises at midnight; during its opposition on July 20, it's up at nightfall and out all night. Sinking lower in the autumn, it becomes visible only before midnight until December 21, when it stands 14 degrees high in the evening and meets Jupiter in the must-see event of 2020.

Jan. 1	**set**	**5:12**	A	Apr. 1	rise	3:30	E	July 1	**rise**	**9:26**	E	Oct. 1	set	12:32	A
Jan. 11	**set**	**4:38**	A	Apr. 11	rise	2:52	E	July 11	**rise**	**8:45**	E	Oct. 11	**set**	**11:49**	A
Jan. 21	rise	6:46	E	Apr. 21	rise	2:14	E	July 21	**rise**	**8:03**	E	Oct. 21	**set**	**11:12**	A
Feb. 1	rise	6:07	E	May 1	rise	1:36	E	Aug. 1	set	4:45	A	Nov. 1	**set**	**9:31**	A
Feb. 11	rise	5:31	E	May 11	rise	1:01	E	Aug. 11	set	4:02	A	Nov. 11	**set**	**8:55**	A
Feb. 21	rise	4:56	E	May 21	rise	12:17	E	Aug. 21	set	3:19	A	Nov. 21	**set**	**8:19**	A
Mar. 1	rise	4:23	E	June 1	**rise**	**11:29**	E	Sept. 1	set	2:33	A	Dec. 1	**set**	**7:44**	A
Mar. 11	rise	4:47	E	June 11	**rise**	**10:49**	E	Sept. 11	set	1:52	A	Dec. 11	**set**	**7:10**	A
Mar. 21	rise	4:10	E	June 21	**rise**	**10:08**	E	Sept. 21	set	1:12	A	Dec. 21	**set**	**6:36**	A
												Dec. 31	**set**	**6:02**	A

MERCURY

The innermost planet whirls so closely around the Sun that we see it only in twilight. Mercury is marginally visible in the last half of February and October but well seen throughout June. It can be glimpsed during the first halves of January and April but is best seen in August, except at the end of that month, and from mid-November to mid-December. Mercury hovers below the Moon and Mars on November 24 and between them the next evening.

DO NOT CONFUSE: *Mars with Saturn in the southeast before dawn from March 29 to April 3: Mars is orange and brighter. • Venus with Mercury, May 20 to 24, very low in the west after sunset: Venus is brighter. • Jupiter with Saturn all year: Jupiter is much brighter. • The Geminid meteor shower from December 13 to 14 with stray meteors: The Geminids come from the northeast overhead around midnight, while stray shooting stars fly in random directions.*

ASTRONOMICAL GLOSSARY

APHELION (APH.): The point in a planet's orbit that is farthest from the Sun.

APOGEE (APO.): The point in the Moon's orbit that is farthest from Earth.

CELESTIAL EQUATOR (EQ.): The imaginary circle around the celestial sphere that can be thought of as the plane of Earth's equator projected out onto the sphere.

CELESTIAL SPHERE: An imaginary sphere projected into space that represents the entire sky, with an observer on Earth at its center. All celestial bodies other than Earth are imagined as being on its inside surface.

CIRCUMPOLAR: Always visible above the horizon, such as a circumpolar star.

CONJUNCTION: The time at which two or more celestial bodies appear closest in the sky. **Inferior (Inf.):** Mercury or Venus is between the Sun and Earth. **Superior (Sup.):** The Sun is between a planet and Earth. Actual dates for conjunctions are given on the **Right-Hand Calendar Pages, 121–147;** the best times for viewing the closely aligned bodies are given in **Sky Watch** on the **Left-Hand Calendar Pages, 120–146.**

DECLINATION: The celestial latitude of an object in the sky, measured in degrees north or south of the celestial equator; comparable to latitude on Earth. This Almanac gives the Sun's declination at noon.

ECLIPSE, LUNAR: The full Moon enters the shadow of Earth, which cuts off all or part of the sunlight reflected off the Moon. **Total:** The Moon passes completely through the umbra (central dark part) of Earth's shadow. **Partial:** Only part of the Moon passes through the umbra. **Penumbral:** The Moon passes through only the penumbra (area of partial darkness surrounding the umbra). **See page 102** for more information about eclipses.

ECLIPSE, SOLAR: Earth enters the shadow of the new Moon, which cuts off all or part of the Sun's light. **Total:** Earth passes through the umbra (central dark part) of the Moon's shadow, resulting in totality for observers within a narrow band on Earth. **Annular:** The Moon appears silhouetted against the Sun, with a ring of sunlight showing around it. **Partial:** The Moon blocks only part of the Sun.

ECLIPTIC: The apparent annual path of the Sun around the celestial sphere. The plane of the ecliptic is tipped 23½° from the celestial equator.

ELONGATION: The difference in degrees between the celestial longitudes of a planet and the Sun. **Greatest Elongation (Gr. Elong.):** The greatest apparent distance of a planet from the Sun, as seen from Earth.

EPACT: A number from 1 to 30 that indicates the Moon's age on January 1 at Greenwich, England; used in determining the date of Easter.

EQUINOX: When the Sun crosses the celestial equator. This event occurs two times each year: **Vernal** is around March 20 and **Autumnal** is around September 22.

EVENING STAR: A planet that is above the western horizon at sunset and less than 180° east of the Sun in right ascension.

GOLDEN NUMBER: A number in the 19-year Metonic cycle of the Moon, used in determining the date of Easter. See **page 149** for this year's Golden Number.

MAGNITUDE: A measure of a celestial object's brightness. **Apparent magnitude** measures the brightness of an object as seen from Earth. Objects with an apparent magnitude of 6 or less are observable to the naked eye. The lower the magnitude, the greater the brightness; an object with a magnitude of –1, e.g., is brighter than one with a magnitude of +1.

(continued)

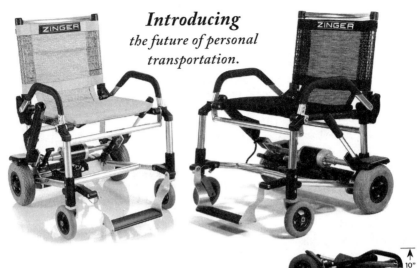

Introducing
the future of personal transportation.

The Zinger folds to a mere 10 inches.

It's not a Wheelchair...
It's not a Power Chair...
It's a Zinger Chair!

Years of work by innovative engineers have resulted in a mobility device that's truly unique. They created a battery that provides powerful energy at a fraction of the weight of most batteries. The *Zinger* features two steering levers, one on either side of the seat. The user pushes both levers down to go forward, pulls them both up to brake, and pushes one while pulling the other to turn to either side. This enables great mobility, the ability to turn on a dime and to pull right up to tables or desks. The controls are right on the steering lever so it's simple to operate and its exclusive footrest swings out of the way when you stand up or sit down. With its rugged yet lightweight aluminum frame, the *Zinger* is sturdy and durable yet convenient and comfortable! What's more, it easily folds up for storage in a car seat or trunk– you can even gate-check it at the airport like a stroller. Think about it, you can take your *Zinger* almost anywhere, so you don't have to let mobility issues rule your life. It folds in seconds without tools and is safe and reliable. It holds up to 275 pounds, and it goes up to 6 mph and operates for up to 8 hours on a single charge.

Why spend another day letting mobility issues hamper your independence and quality of life?

Zinger Chair
Call now and receive a utility basket absolutely FREE with your order.

1-888-610-1701
Mention code 111581 when ordering.

Zinger is not a wheelchair or medical device and is not covered by Medicare or Medicaid.

83952

© 2019 *first*STREET for Boomers and Beyond, Inc.

ASTRONOMICAL GLOSSARY

MIDNIGHT: Astronomically, the time when the Sun is opposite its highest point in the sky. Both 12 hours before and after noon (so, technically, both A.M. and P.M.), midnight in civil time is usually treated as the beginning of the day. It is displayed as 12:00 A.M. on 12-hour digital clocks. On a 24-hour cycle, 00:00, not 24:00, usually indicates midnight.

MOON ON EQUATOR: The Moon is on the celestial equator.

MOON RIDES HIGH/RUNS LOW: The Moon is highest above or farthest below the celestial equator.

MOONRISE/MOONSET: When the Moon rises above or sets below the horizon.

MOON'S PHASES: The changing appearance of the Moon, caused by the different angles at which it is illuminated by the Sun. **First Quarter:** Right half of the Moon is illuminated. **Full:** The Sun and the Moon are in opposition; the entire disk of the Moon is illuminated. **Last Quarter:** Left half of the Moon is illuminated. **New:** The Sun and the Moon are in conjunction; the Moon is darkened because it lines up between Earth and the Sun.

MOON'S PLACE, Astronomical: The position of the Moon within the constellations on the celestial sphere at midnight. **Astrological:** The position of the Moon within the tropical zodiac, whose twelve 30° segments (signs) along the ecliptic were named more than 2,000 years ago after constellations within each area. Because of precession and other factors, the zodiac signs no longer match actual constellation positions.

MORNING STAR: A planet that is above the eastern horizon at sunrise and less than 180° west of the Sun in right ascension.

NODE: Either of the two points where a celestial body's orbit intersects the ecliptic. **Ascending:** When the body is moving from south to north of the ecliptic. **Descending:** When the body is moving from north to south of the ecliptic.

OCCULTATION (OCCN.): When the Moon or a planet eclipses a star or planet.

OPPOSITION: The Moon or a planet appears on the opposite side of the sky from the Sun (elongation 180°).

PERIGEE (PERIG.): The point in the Moon's orbit that is closest to Earth.

PERIHELION (PERIH.): The point in a planet's orbit that is closest to the Sun.

PRECESSION: The slowly changing position of the stars and equinoxes in the sky caused by a slight wobble as Earth rotates around its axis.

RIGHT ASCENSION (R.A.): The celestial longitude of an object in the sky, measured eastward along the celestial equator in hours of time from the vernal equinox; comparable to longitude on Earth.

SOLSTICE, Summer: When the Sun reaches its greatest declination (23½°) north of the celestial equator, around June 21. **Winter:** When the Sun reaches its greatest declination (23½°) south of the celestial equator, around December 21.

STATIONARY (STAT.): The brief period of apparent halted movement of a planet against the background of the stars shortly before it appears to move backward/westward (retrograde motion) or forward/eastward (direct motion).

SUN FAST/SLOW: When a sundial is ahead of (fast) or behind (slow) clock time.

SUNRISE/SUNSET: The visible rising/setting of the upper edge of the Sun's disk across the unobstructed horizon of an observer whose eyes are 15 feet above ground level.

TWILIGHT: See page 106. ∎

2019

JANUARY
S	M	T	W	T	F	S
		1	2	3	4	5
6	7	8	9	10	11	12
13	14	15	16	17	18	19
20	21	22	23	24	25	26
27	28	29	30	31		

FEBRUARY
S	M	T	W	T	F	S
					1	2
3	4	5	6	7	8	9
10	11	12	13	14	15	16
17	18	19	20	21	22	23
24	25	26	27	28		

MARCH
S	M	T	W	T	F	S
					1	2
3	4	5	6	7	8	9
10	11	12	13	14	15	16
17	18	19	20	21	22	23
24	25	26	27	28	29	30
31						

APRIL
S	M	T	W	T	F	S
	1	2	3	4	5	6
7	8	9	10	11	12	13
14	15	16	17	18	19	20
21	22	23	24	25	26	27
28	29	30				

MAY
S	M	T	W	T	F	S
			1	2	3	4
5	6	7	8	9	10	11
12	13	14	15	16	17	18
19	20	21	22	23	24	25
26	27	28	29	30	31	

JUNE
S	M	T	W	T	F	S
						1
2	3	4	5	6	7	8
9	10	11	12	13	14	15
16	17	18	19	20	21	22
23	24	25	26	27	28	29
30						

JULY
S	M	T	W	T	F	S
	1	2	3	4	5	6
7	8	9	10	11	12	13
14	15	16	17	18	19	20
21	22	23	24	25	26	27
28	29	30	31			

AUGUST
S	M	T	W	T	F	S
				1	2	3
4	5	6	7	8	9	10
11	12	13	14	15	16	17
18	19	20	21	22	23	24
25	26	27	28	29	30	31

SEPTEMBER
S	M	T	W	T	F	S
1	2	3	4	5	6	7
8	9	10	11	12	13	14
15	16	17	18	19	20	21
22	23	24	25	26	27	28
29	30					

OCTOBER
S	M	T	W	T	F	S
		1	2	3	4	5
6	7	8	9	10	11	12
13	14	15	16	17	18	19
20	21	22	23	24	25	26
27	28	29	30	31		

NOVEMBER
S	M	T	W	T	F	S
					1	2
3	4	5	6	7	8	9
10	11	12	13	14	15	16
17	18	19	20	21	22	23
24	25	26	27	28	29	30

DECEMBER
S	M	T	W	T	F	S
1	2	3	4	5	6	7
8	9	10	11	12	13	14
15	16	17	18	19	20	21
22	23	24	25	26	27	28
29	30	31				

2020

JANUARY
S	M	T	W	T	F	S
			1	2	3	4
5	6	7	8	9	10	11
12	13	14	15	16	17	18
19	20	21	22	23	24	25
26	27	28	29	30	31	

FEBRUARY
S	M	T	W	T	F	S
						1
2	3	4	5	6	7	8
9	10	11	12	13	14	15
16	17	18	19	20	21	22
23	24	25	26	27	28	29

MARCH
S	M	T	W	T	F	S
1	2	3	4	5	6	7
8	9	10	11	12	13	14
15	16	17	18	19	20	21
22	23	24	25	26	27	28
29	30	31				

APRIL
S	M	T	W	T	F	S
			1	2	3	4
5	6	7	8	9	10	11
12	13	14	15	16	17	18
19	20	21	22	23	24	25
26	27	28	29	30		

MAY
S	M	T	W	T	F	S
					1	2
3	4	5	6	7	8	9
10	11	12	13	14	15	16
17	18	19	20	21	22	23
24	25	26	27	28	29	30
31						

JUNE
S	M	T	W	T	F	S
	1	2	3	4	5	6
7	8	9	10	11	12	13
14	15	16	17	18	19	20
21	22	23	24	25	26	27
28	29	30				

JULY
S	M	T	W	T	F	S
			1	2	3	4
5	6	7	8	9	10	11
12	13	14	15	16	17	18
19	20	21	22	23	24	25
26	27	28	29	30	31	

AUGUST
S	M	T	W	T	F	S
						1
2	3	4	5	6	7	8
9	10	11	12	13	14	15
16	17	18	19	20	21	22
23	24	25	26	27	28	29
30	31					

SEPTEMBER
S	M	T	W	T	F	S
		1	2	3	4	5
6	7	8	9	10	11	12
13	14	15	16	17	18	19
20	21	22	23	24	25	26
27	28	29	30			

OCTOBER
S	M	T	W	T	F	S
				1	2	3
4	5	6	7	8	9	10
11	12	13	14	15	16	17
18	19	20	21	22	23	24
25	26	27	28	29	30	31

NOVEMBER
S	M	T	W	T	F	S
1	2	3	4	5	6	7
8	9	10	11	12	13	14
15	16	17	18	19	20	21
22	23	24	25	26	27	28
29	30					

DECEMBER
S	M	T	W	T	F	S
		1	2	3	4	5
6	7	8	9	10	11	12
13	14	15	16	17	18	19
20	21	22	23	24	25	26
27	28	29	30	31		

2021

JANUARY
S	M	T	W	T	F	S
					1	2
3	4	5	6	7	8	9
10	11	12	13	14	15	16
17	18	19	20	21	22	23
24	25	26	27	28	29	30
31						

FEBRUARY
S	M	T	W	T	F	S
	1	2	3	4	5	6
7	8	9	10	11	12	13
14	15	16	17	18	19	20
21	22	23	24	25	26	27
28						

MARCH
S	M	T	W	T	F	S
	1	2	3	4	5	6
7	8	9	10	11	12	13
14	15	16	17	18	19	20
21	22	23	24	25	26	27
28	29	30	31			

APRIL
S	M	T	W	T	F	S
				1	2	3
4	5	6	7	8	9	10
11	12	13	14	15	16	17
18	19	20	21	22	23	24
25	26	27	28	29	30	

MAY
S	M	T	W	T	F	S
						1
2	3	4	5	6	7	8
9	10	11	12	13	14	15
16	17	18	19	20	21	22
23	24	25	26	27	28	29
30	31					

JUNE
S	M	T	W	T	F	S
		1	2	3	4	5
6	7	8	9	10	11	12
13	14	15	16	17	18	19
20	21	22	23	24	25	26
27	28	29	30			

JULY
S	M	T	W	T	F	S
				1	2	3
4	5	6	7	8	9	10
11	12	13	14	15	16	17
18	19	20	21	22	23	24
25	26	27	28	29	30	31

AUGUST
S	M	T	W	T	F	S
1	2	3	4	5	6	7
8	9	10	11	12	13	14
15	16	17	18	19	20	21
22	23	24	25	26	27	28
29	30	31				

SEPTEMBER
S	M	T	W	T	F	S
			1	2	3	4
5	6	7	8	9	10	11
12	13	14	15	16	17	18
19	20	21	22	23	24	25
26	27	28	29	30		

OCTOBER
S	M	T	W	T	F	S
					1	2
3	4	5	6	7	8	9
10	11	12	13	14	15	16
17	18	19	20	21	22	23
24	25	26	27	28	29	30
31						

NOVEMBER
S	M	T	W	T	F	S
	1	2	3	4	5	6
7	8	9	10	11	12	13
14	15	16	17	18	19	20
21	22	23	24	25	26	27
28	29	30				

DECEMBER
S	M	T	W	T	F	S
			1	2	3	4
5	6	7	8	9	10	11
12	13	14	15	16	17	18
19	20	21	22	23	24	25
26	27	28	29	30	31	

A CALENDAR OF THE HEAVENS FOR 2020

–Beth Krommes

The Calendar Pages (120–147) are the heart of *The Old Farmer's Almanac.* They present sky sightings and astronomical data for the entire year and are what make this book a true almanac, a "calendar of the heavens." In essence, these pages are unchanged since 1792, when Robert B. Thomas published his first edition. The long columns of numbers and symbols reveal all of nature's precision, rhythm, and glory, providing an astronomical look at the year 2020.

HOW TO USE THE CALENDAR PAGES

The astronomical data on the **Calendar Pages (120–147)** are calculated for Boston (where Robert B. Thomas learned to calculate the data for his first Almanac). Guidance for calculating the times of these events for your locale appears on **pages 116–117.** Note that the results will be *approximate.* For the *exact* time of any astronomical event at your locale, go to **Almanac.com/Astronomy** and enter your zip code. While you're there, print the month's "Sky Map," useful for viewing with "Sky Watch" in the Calendar Pages.

For a list of 2020 holidays and observances, see **pages 148–149.** Also check out the **Glossary of Almanac Oddities** on **pages 152 and 154,** which describes some of the more obscure entries traditionally found on the **Right-Hand Calendar Pages (121–147).**

ABOUT THE TIMES: All times are given in ET (Eastern Time), except where otherwise noted as AT (Atlantic Time, +1 hour), CT (Central Time, –1), MT (Mountain Time, –2), PT (Pacific Time, –3), AKT (Alaska Time, –4), or HAT (Hawaii-Aleutian Time, –5). Between 2:00 A.M., March 8, and 2:00 A.M., November 1, Daylight Saving Time is assumed in those locales where it is observed.

ABOUT THE TIDES: Tide times for Boston appear on **pages 120–146;** for Boston tide heights, see **pages 121–147.** Tide Corrections for East Coast locations appear on **pages 236–237.** Tide heights and times for locations across the United States and Canada are available at **Almanac.com/Tides.**

The Left-Hand Calendar Pages, 120 to 146

On these pages are the year's astronomical predictions for Boston (42°22' N, 71°3' W). Learn how to calculate the times of these events for your locale here or go to **Almanac.com/Rise** and enter your zip code.

A SAMPLE MONTH

SKY WATCH: The paragraph at the top of each Left-Hand Calendar Page describes the best times to view conjunctions, meteor showers, planets, and more. (Also see **How to Use the Right-Hand Calendar Pages, p. 118.**)

			1		2		3	4	5		6				7	8
DAY OF YEAR	DAY OF MONTH	DAY OF WEEK	☼ RISES H. M.	RISE KEY	☼ SETS H. M.	SET KEY	LENGTH OF DAY H. M.	SUN FAST M.	SUN DECLINATION ° '	HIGH TIDE TIMES BOSTON	☾ RISES H. M.	RISE KEY	☾ SETS H. M.	SET KEY	☾ ASTRON. PLACE	☾ AGE
60	1	Fr.	6:20	D	5:34	C	11 14	4	7 s. 30	7¼ 8	3:30	E	12:58	B	SAG	25
61	2	Sa.	6:18	D	5:35	C	11 17	4	7 s. 07	8¼ 9	4:16	E	1:51	B	SAG	26
62	3	**F**	6:17	D	5:36	C	11 19	4	6 s. 44	9¼ 9¾	4:56	E	2:47	B	CAP	27
63	4	M.	6:15	D	5:37	C	11 22	4	6 s. 21	10 10½	5:31	E	3:45	C	CAP	28

1. To calculate the sunrise time in your locale: Choose a day. Note its Sun Rise Key Letter. Find your (nearest) city on **page 238**. Add or subtract the minutes that correspond to the Sun Rise Key Letter to/from the sunrise time for Boston.

EXAMPLE:

To calculate the sunrise time in Denver, Colorado, on day 1:

Sunrise, Boston,
with Key Letter D (above)   6:20 A.M. ET

Value of Key Letter D
for Denver (p. 238)   + 11 minutes

Sunrise, Denver   6:31 A.M. MT

To calculate your sunset time, repeat, using Boston's sunset time and its Sun Set Key Letter value.

2. To calculate the length of day: Choose a day. Note the Sun Rise and Sun Set Key Letters. Find your (nearest) city on **page 238**. Add or subtract the minutes that correspond to the Sun Set Key Letter to/from Boston's length of day. *Reverse* the sign (e.g., minus to plus) of the

Sun Rise Key Letter minutes. Add or subtract it to/from the first result.

EXAMPLE:

To calculate the length of day in Richmond, Virginia, on day 1:

Length of day, Boston (above)   11h.14m.
Sunset Key Letter C
for Richmond (p. 242)   + 25m.
                                     11h.39m.
Reverse sunrise Key Letter D
for Richmond (p. 242, +17 to -17)   - 17m.
Length of day, Richmond   11h.22m.

3. Use Sun Fast to change sundial time to clock time. A sundial reads natural (Sun) time, which is neither Standard nor Daylight time. To calculate clock time on a sundial in Boston, subtract the minutes given in this column; add the minutes when preceded by an asterisk [*].

−Beth Krommes

To convert the time to your (nearest) city, use Key Letter C on **page 238.**

EXAMPLE:

To change sundial to clock time in Boston or Salem, Oregon, on day 1:

Sundial reading (Boston or Salem)	12:00 noon
Subtract Sun Fast (p. 116)	- 4 minutes
Clock time, Boston	11:56 A.M. ET
Use Key Letter C for Salem (p. 241)	+ 27 minutes
Clock time, Salem	12:23 P.M. PT

4. This column gives the degrees and minutes of the Sun from the celestial equator at noon ET.

5. This column gives the approximate times of high tide in Boston. For example, the first high tide occurs at 7:15 A.M. and the second occurs at 8:00 P.M. the same day. (A dash indicates that high tide occurs on or after midnight and is recorded on the next day.) Figures for calculating approximate high tide times for localities other than Boston are given in the **Tide Corrections** table on page **236.**

6. To calculate the moonrise time in your locale: Choose a day. Note the Moon Rise Key Letter. Find your (nearest) city on **page 238.** Add or subtract the minutes that correspond to the Moon Rise Key Letter to/from the moonrise time given for Boston. (A dash indicates that the moonrise occurs on/after midnight and is recorded on the next day.) Find the longitude of your (nearest) city on **page**

LONGITUDE OF CITY	CORRECTION MINUTES	LONGITUDE OF CITY	CORRECTION MINUTES
58°–76°	0	116°–127°	+4
77°–89°	+1	128°–141°	+5
90°–102°	+2	142°–155°	+6
103°–115°	+3		

238. Add a correction in minutes for your city's longitude (see table, bottom left). Use the same procedure with Boston's moonset time and the Moon Set Key Letter value to calculate the time of moonset in your locale.

EXAMPLE:

To calculate the time of moonset in Lansing, Michigan, on day 1:

Moonset, Boston, with Key Letter B (p. 116)	12:58 P.M. ET
Value of Key Letter B for Lansing (p. 240)	+ 53 minutes
Correction for Lansing longitude, 84°33'	+ 1 minute
Moonset, Lansing	1:52 P.M. ET

7. This column gives the Moon's *astronomical* position among the constellations (not zodiac) at midnight. For *astrological* data, see **pages 224–227.**

Constellations have irregular borders; on successive nights, the midnight Moon may enter one, cross into another, and then move to a new area of the previous. It visits the 12 zodiacal constellations, as well as Auriga **(AUR),** a northern constellation between Perseus and Gemini; Cetus **(CET),** which lies south of the zodiac, just south of Pisces and Aries; Ophiuchus **(OPH),** primarily north of the zodiac but with a small corner between Scorpius and Sagittarius; Orion **(ORI),** whose northern limit first reaches the zodiac between Taurus and Gemini; and Sextans **(SEX),** which lies south of the zodiac except for a corner that just touches it near Leo.

8. This column gives the Moon's age: the number of days since the previous new Moon. (The average length of the lunar month is 29.53 days.) *(continued)*

The Right-Hand Calendar Pages, 121 to 147

The Right-Hand Calendar Pages contain celestial events; religious observances; proverbs and poems; civil holidays; historical events; folklore; tide heights; weather prediction rhymes; Farmer's Calendar essays; and more.

A SAMPLE MONTH

1	2	3	4	5	6	7	8	9	10
1	Fr.	ALL FOOLS' •	*If you want to make a fool of yourself, you'll find a lot of people ready to help you.*				*Flakes*	an inch long, who
2	Sa.	Tap dancer Charles "Honi" Coles born, 1911 •			Tides { 9.5 / 9.0		*alive!*	in fresh water, pro pond across the
3	**B**	2nd ⚏. of Easter •	Writer F. Scott Fitzgerald married Zelda Sayre, 1920			*Spring's*	emerged a month
4	M.	Annunciation T • ♂♆☾ •	*Ben Hur* won 11 Academy Awards, 1960			*arrived!*	to spend the next 3
5	Tu.	☾ AT ☍ •	Blizzard left 27.2" snow, St. John's, Nfld., 1999 •	Tides { 10.8 / 10.8		*Or is this*	on land before ret their wet world.
6	W.	☾ ON EQ. • ♂♀☾ •	Twin mongoose lemurs born, Busch Gardens, Tampa, Fla., 2012			*warmth*	You can't mis

1. The bold letter is the Dominical Letter (from A to G), a traditional ecclesiastical designation for Sunday determined by the date on which the year's first Sunday falls. For 2020, the Dominical Letter is **E** through February. It then reverts to **D** for the rest of the year.

2. Civil holidays and astronomical events.

3. Religious feasts: A T indicates a major feast that the church has this year temporarily transferred to a date other than its usual one.

4. Sundays and special holy days.

5. Symbols for notable celestial events. For example, ♂♆☾ on the 4th day means that a conjunction (♂) of Neptune (♆) and the Moon (☾) occurs.

6. Proverbs, poems, and adages.

7. Noteworthy historical events, folklore, and legends.

8. High tide heights, in feet, at Boston, Massachusetts.

9. Weather prediction rhyme.

10. Farmer's Calendar essay.

Celestial Symbols

☉ Sun	⊕ Earth	♅ Uranus	♂ Conjunction	☋ Descending node
○●☾ Moon	♂ Mars	♆ Neptune	(on the same	☌ Opposition
☿ Mercury	♃ Jupiter	♇ Pluto	celestial longitude)	(180 degrees
♀ Venus	♄ Saturn		☊ Ascending node	from Sun)

PREDICTING EARTHQUAKES

Note the dates in the Right-Hand Calendar Pages when the Moon rides high or runs low. The date of the high begins the most likely 5-day period of earthquakes in the Northern Hemisphere; the date of the low indicates a similar 5-day period in the Southern Hemisphere. Also noted are the 2 days each month when the Moon is on the celestial equator, indicating the most likely time for earthquakes in either hemisphere.

EARTH AT PERIHELION AND APHELION

Perihelion: January 5, 2020 (EST). Earth will be 91,398,199 miles from the Sun. **Aphelion:** July 4, 2020 (EDT). Earth will be 94,507,635 miles from the Sun.

Why We Have Seasons

The seasons occur because as Earth revolves around the Sun, its axis remains tilted at 23.5 degrees from the perpendicular. This tilt causes different latitudes on Earth to receive varying amounts of sunlight throughout the year.

In the Northern Hemisphere, the summer solstice marks the beginning of summer and occurs when the North Pole is tilted toward the Sun. The winter solstice marks the beginning of winter and occurs when the North Pole is tilted away from the Sun.

The equinoxes occur when the hemispheres equally face the Sun. At this time, the Sun rises due east and sets due west. The vernal equinox marks the beginning of spring; the autumnal equinox marks the beginning of autumn.

In the Southern Hemisphere, the seasons are the reverse of those in the Northern Hemisphere.

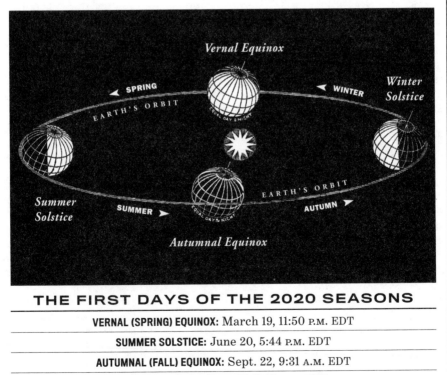

THE FIRST DAYS OF THE 2020 SEASONS

VERNAL (SPRING) EQUINOX: March 19, 11:50 P.M. EDT

SUMMER SOLSTICE: June 20, 5:44 P.M. EDT

AUTUMNAL (FALL) EQUINOX: Sept. 22, 9:31 A.M. EDT

WINTER SOLSTICE: Dec. 21, 5:02 A.M. EST

NOVEMBER

SKY WATCH: Mercury transits the Sun's face on the 11th, starting at 7:37 A.M. and continuing for over 5 hours. All of the United States (except Alaska) and Canada can see at least part of it (a "solar telescope" is required). From the 1st to the 14th, low in the predawn east, returning orange Mars meets Virgo's blue star, Spica. During the month's second half, bright Mercury appears below Mars. On the 24th, the crescent Moon hovers to the left of Mars, with Mercury below. On the 25th, a predawn lineup has blue Spica highest, above orange Mars, then orange Mercury, and finally the Moon, lowest. In the west after sunset, Venus and Jupiter hover side-by-side on the 23rd and 24th but quite low in twilight. The Moon floats just above brilliant Venus on the 28th.

◐ **FIRST QUARTER** 4th day 5:23 A.M.   ◑ **LAST QUARTER** 19th day 4:11 P.M.

○ **FULL MOON** 12th day 8:34 A.M.   ● **NEW MOON** 26th day 10:06 A.M.

After 2:00 A.M. on November 3, Eastern Standard Time is given.

GET THESE PAGES WITH TIMES SET TO YOUR ZIP CODE AT ALMANAC.COM/ACCESS.

DAY OF YEAR	DAY OF MONTH	DAY OF WEEK	☼ RISES H. M.	RISE KEY	☼ SETS H. M.	SET KEY	LENGTH OF DAY H. M.	SUN FAST M.	SUN DECLINATION ° ′	HIGH TIDE TIMES BOSTON		☾ RISES H. M.	RISE KEY	☾ SETS H. M.	SET KEY	☾ ASTRON. PLACE	☾ AGE
305	1	Fr.	7:17	D	5:38	B	10 21	32	14 s. 29	2¾	3	12:05	E	9:21	B	SAG	5
306	2	Sa.	7:18	D	5:37	B	10 19	32	14 s. 48	3¾	4	12:57	E	10:17	B	SAG	6
307	3	**F**	6:20	D	4:35	B	10 15	32	15 s. 07	3¾	3¾	12:42	E	10:16	B	SAG	7
308	4	M.	6:21	D	4:34	B	10 13	32	15 s. 25	4½	4¾	1:19	E	11:16	B	CAP	8
309	5	Tu.	6:22	E	4:33	B	10 11	32	15 s. 43	5½	5¾	1:51	E	—	-	CAP	9
310	6	W.	6:23	E	4:32	B	10 09	32	16 s. 01	6½	6¾	2:19	E	12:16	C	AQU	10
311	7	Th.	6:25	E	4:31	B	10 06	32	16 s. 19	7½	7¾	2:44	D	1:15	C	AQU	11
312	8	Fr.	6:26	E	4:29	B	10 03	32	16 s. 37	8¼	8½	3:08	D	2:15	D	PSC	12
313	9	Sa.	6:27	E	4:28	B	10 01	32	16 s. 54	9	9¼	3:31	C	3:14	D	CET	13
314	10	**F**	6:28	E	4:27	B	9 59	32	17 s. 11	9½	10	3:56	C	4:14	D	PSC	14
315	11	M.	6:30	E	4:26	B	9 56	32	17 s. 28	10¼	10½	4:22	C	5:16	E	CET	15
316	12	Tu.	6:31	E	4:25	B	9 54	32	17 s. 44	10¾	11¼	4:51	B	6:19	E	ARI	16
317	13	W.	6:32	E	4:24	B	9 52	32	18 s. 00	11½	—	5:25	B	7:23	E	TAU	17
318	14	Th.	6:33	E	4:23	B	9 50	31	18 s. 16	12	12	6:05	B	8:28	E	TAU	18
319	15	Fr.	6:35	E	4:22	B	9 47	31	18 s. 31	12½	12¾	6:53	B	9:31	E	TAU	19
320	16	Sa.	6:36	E	4:22	B	9 46	31	18 s. 46	1¼	1½	7:49	B	10:30	E	GEM	20
321	17	**F**	6:37	E	4:21	B	9 44	31	19 s. 01	2¼	2¼	8:53	B	11:22	E	GEM	21
322	18	M.	6:38	E	4:20	B	9 42	31	19 s. 15	3	3¼	10:02	B	12:08	E	CAN	22
323	19	Tu.	6:40	E	4:19	B	9 39	30	19 s. 29	4	4¼	11:13	C	12:48	E	LEO	23
324	20	W.	6:41	E	4:18	B	9 37	30	19 s. 43	5	5¼	—	-	1:23	E	LEO	24
325	21	Th.	6:42	E	4:18	B	9 36	30	19 s. 56	6	6¼	12:26	C	1:54	D	LEO	25
326	22	Fr.	6:43	E	4:17	B	9 34	30	20 s. 09	7	7¼	1:39	D	2:23	D	VIR	26
327	23	Sa.	6:44	E	4:16	B	9 32	29	20 s. 22	7¾	8¼	2:53	D	2:52	C	VIR	27
328	24	**F**	6:46	E	4:16	A	9 30	29	20 s. 34	8¾	9¼	4:07	E	3:23	C	VIR	28
329	25	M.	6:47	E	4:15	A	9 28	29	20 s. 46	9½	10¼	5:20	E	3:56	B	LIB	29
330	26	Tu.	6:48	E	4:15	A	9 27	28	20 s. 58	10½	11	6:34	E	4:34	B	LIB	0
331	27	W.	6:49	E	4:14	A	9 25	28	21 s. 09	11¼	11¾	7:44	E	5:18	B	OPH	1
332	28	Th.	6:50	E	4:14	A	9 24	28	21 s. 19	12	—	8:49	E	6:07	B	SAG	2
333	29	Fr.	6:51	E	4:13	A	9 22	27	21 s. 30	12¾	12¾	9:47	D	7:02	B	SAG	3
334	30	Sa.	6:52	E	4:13	A	9 21	27	21 s. 40	1½	1½	10:36	D	8:01	B	SAG	4

NOVEMBER

Chill winds sweep down the mountain way,
The skies are leaden-like and gray.
–**James Berry Bensel**

DAY OF MONTH	DAY OF WEEK	DATES, FEASTS, FASTS, ASPECTS, TIDE HEIGHTS, AND WEATHER	
1	Fr.	All Saints' • ☾ RUNS LOW • ☾ AT ☋ • U.S. First Lady Mamie Eisenhower died, 1979	*An*
2	Sa.	All Souls' • Sadie Hawkins Day • ☌♄☾ • ☌♇☾ • Tides {9.5 / 10.2}	*echo*
3	**F**	**21st S. af. P.** • **Daylight Saving Time ends, 2:00 a.m.** • Tides {9.0 / 9.7}	*of*
4	M.	Manufacturer Benjamin F. Goodrich born, 1841 • {8.7 / 9.3}	*summer,*
5	Tu.	**Election Day** • GPS system patented, 1996 • {8.6 / 9.0}	*before*
6	W.	☌♆☾ • Posthumous Victoria Cross recipient James Robertson died, 1917 • {8.6 / 9.0}	*rain's*
7	Th.	☾ AT APO. • U.S. president FDR re-elected for 4th term, 1944 • {8.9 / 9.1}	*drummer*
8	Fr.	Mont. statehood (Dakotas, Nov. 2; Wash., Nov. 11), 1889 • Tides {9.2 / 9.2}	*sends*
9	Sa.	☾ ON EQ. • 1st documented Canadian gridiron football game played, Univ. of Toronto, Ont., 1861	*the*
10	**F**	**22nd S. af. P.** • ☌♅☾ • TV's *Sesame Street* debuted, 1969	*last*
11	M.	St. Martin of Tours • **Veterans Day** • ☿ IN INF. ☌ • ☿ TRANSIT OVER ☉ • {10.1 / 9.5}	*leaves*
12	Tu.	Indian Summer • **FULL BEAVER** ○ • Voters OK'd creation of Nunavut territory, 1992 • {10.3 / 9.5}	*fleeing.*
13	W.	*Set trees poor, and they will grow rich; set them rich, and they will grow poor.* • Tides {10.5 / 9.5}	*Rain*
14	Th.	Just after launch, *Apollo 12* struck twice by lightning, 1969 • Tides {10.6 / —}	*turns*
15	Fr.	Judge Joseph Wapner born, 1919 • Tides {9.4 / 10.6}	*to*
16	Sa.	☾ RIDES HIGH • ☾ AT ☊ • Meteor fireball turned night into day, Finland, 2017 • {9.3 / 10.5}	*snow*
17	**F**	**23rd S. af. P.** • 1800s champagne sampled from Baltic Sea shipwreck, 2010 • {9.2 / 10.4}	*and*
18	M.	St. Hilda of Whitby • *November take flail, Let ships no more sail.* • {9.1 / 10.3}	*thoughts*
19	Tu.	David L. Pickens granted patent for "registered pedigree stuffed animals," 2002 • {9.2 / 10.1}	*turn*
20	W.	☿ STAT. • Tucson Municipal Flying Field, Ariz., 1st municipal airport in U.S., 1919 • {9.3 / 10.0}	*to*
21	Th.	N.C. statehood, 1789 • Dusting of snow, central Fla., 2006 • Tides {9.7 / 10.1}	*skiing.*
22	Fr.	☾ ON EQ. • Humane Society of the United States founded, 1954 • Writer George Eliot born, 1819	*Turkey's*
23	Sa.	St. Clement • ☾ AT PERIG. • Thespis 1st actor on record in Greek drama, 534 B.C. • {10.7 / 10.4}	*been*
24	**F**	**24th S. af. P.** • ☌☿☾ • ☌♀♃ • ☌♂☾ • Tides {11.2 / 10.5}	*fixed;*
25	M.	U.S. chess champion John Donaldson wed Soviet champion Elena Akhmilovskaya, 1988	*precipitation's*
26	Tu.	**NEW** ● • 1.5" rain fell in 1 minute, setting world record, Barot, Guadeloupe, 1970 • {11.7 / 10.5}	*mixed.*
27	W.	♆ STAT. • *Better some of a pudding than none of a pie.* • Tides {11.7 / 10.3}	*So*
28	Th.	**Thanksgiving Day** • ☾ AT ☋ • ☌♀☾ • ☌♃☾ • ☿ GR. ELONG. (20° WEST)	*are*
29	Fr.	☾ RUNS LOW • ☌♄☾ • ☌♇☾ • 1st governor-general of Canada, Sir Charles Stanley, died, 1894	*our*
30	Sa.	St. Andrew • Discovery of 215 fossilized pterosaur eggs in Gobi Desert, China, announced, 2017	*feelings.*

Farmer's Calendar

The rungs had rattled my mind for months, as I wondered what I might see from the silo's cusp. One night shy of the full Moon, I climbed up. During the growing season, a homesteader is devoted to the ground: trundling hoses, sinking fence posts, dumping manure, stooping to tend everything. And then, suddenly, there is nothing left to weed or harvest and her focus can drift upward. Twice I'd queried the neighbors for permission to scale their tower of corn silage and twice they'd declined. So, what happened next might just be a lie. At dusk, I crept to the silo with a friend who boosted me to the ladder's bottom rung. From there, I scrambled up to where the view was generous, expansive. At height, the three nearby farmhouses appeared as diminutive as butter pats. The neighbors' dairy barn seemed no bigger than a mailbox amid the shorn cornfield with its plaid of tractor ruts. As the neighbors' lights snapped out, my friend waited gamely by the ladder's start. Maybe I was the highest living thing in our valley? Just then a Canada goose squawked, correcting me, as it soared over the silo toward the Milky Way.

DECEMBER

SKY WATCH: The year ends with a planetary whimper. All of the superior planets are on the far side of the Sun, near their dimmest magnitudes and further diminished by solar glare. Several farewell conjunctions provide compensation. On the 1st, low in the west at evening twilight, float Jupiter (highest), Venus, Saturn, and the crescent Moon. Venus meets Saturn on the 10th and 11th. Meanwhile, Mars rises a bit higher as a predawn morning star, but it's still low and shines at a mere magnitude 2. The Geminid meteors on the 13th are spoiled by a nearly full Moon parked in Gemini that very night. Winter begins with the solstice on the 21st at 11:19 P.M.

◑ **FIRST QUARTER** 4th day 1:58 A.M.　　◐ **LAST QUARTER** 18th day 11:57 P.M.
○ **FULL MOON** 12th day 12:12 A.M.　　● **NEW MOON** 26th day 12:13 A.M.

All times are given in Eastern Standard Time.

GET THESE PAGES WITH TIMES SET TO YOUR ZIP CODE AT ALMANAC.COM/ACCESS.

DAY OF YEAR	DAY OF MONTH	DAY OF WEEK	☼ RISES H. M.	RISE KEY	☼ SETS H. M.	SET KEY	LENGTH OF DAY H. M.	SUN FAST M.	SUN DECLINATION ° ′	HIGH TIDE TIMES BOSTON		☽ RISES H. M.	RISE KEY	☽ SETS H. M.	SET KEY	☽ ASTRON. PLACE	☽ AGE
335	1	F	6:53	E	4:13	A	9 20	27	21 s. 49	2¼	2½	11:17	E	9:02	B	CAP	5
336	2	M.	6:54	E	4:12	A	9 18	26	21 s. 58	3	3¼	11:52	E	10:03	C	CAP	6
337	3	Tu.	6:55	E	4:12	A	9 17	26	22 s. 07	4	4¼	12:21	E	11:03	C	AQU	7
338	4	W.	6:57	E	4:12	A	9 15	26	22 s. 15	4¾	5	12:47	D	—	-	AQU	8
339	5	Th.	6:58	E	4:12	A	9 14	25	22 s. 23	5¾	6	1:11	D	12:03	C	AQU	9
340	6	Fr.	6:58	E	4:12	A	9 14	25	22 s. 30	6½	7	1:35	C	1:02	D	CET	10
341	7	Sa.	6:59	E	4:12	A	9 13	24	22 s. 37	7½	7¾	1:58	C	2:01	D	CET	11
342	8	F	7:00	E	4:11	A	9 11	24	22 s. 43	8¼	8½	2:23	C	3:02	E	PSC	12
343	9	M.	7:01	E	4:11	A	9 10	23	22 s. 49	8¾	9¼	2:51	B	4:04	E	ARI	13
344	10	Tu.	7:02	E	4:12	A	9 10	23	22 s. 55	9½	10	3:23	B	5:09	E	TAU	14
345	11	W.	7:03	E	4:12	A	9 09	23	23 s. 00	10¼	10¾	4:01	B	6:14	E	TAU	15
346	12	Th.	7:04	E	4:12	A	9 08	22	23 s. 05	11	11½	4:47	B	7:19	E	TAU	16
347	13	Fr.	7:05	E	4:12	A	9 07	22	23 s. 09	11½	—	5:41	B	8:22	E	GEM	17
348	14	Sa.	7:05	E	4:12	A	9 07	21	23 s. 13	12¼	12¼	6:44	B	9:18	E	GEM	18
349	15	F	7:06	E	4:12	A	9 06	21	23 s. 16	1	1¼	7:52	B	10:08	E	CAN	19
350	16	M.	7:07	E	4:13	A	9 06	20	23 s. 19	1¾	2	9:04	C	10:50	E	CAN	20
351	17	Tu.	7:07	E	4:13	A	9 06	20	23 s. 21	2¾	3	10:17	C	11:26	E	LEO	21
352	18	W.	7:08	E	4:13	A	9 05	19	23 s. 23	3½	4	11:29	D	11:58	D	LEO	22
353	19	Th.	7:09	E	4:14	A	9 05	19	23 s. 24	4½	5	—	-	12:27	D	VIR	23
354	20	Fr.	7:09	E	4:14	A	9 05	18	23 s. 25	5½	6	12:41	D	12:55	C	VIR	24
355	21	Sa.	7:10	E	4:15	A	9 05	18	23 s. 26	6½	7	1:52	E	1:24	C	VIR	25
356	22	F	7:10	E	4:15	A	9 05	17	23 s. 26	7½	8	3:04	E	1:55	B	LIB	26
357	23	M.	7:11	E	4:16	A	9 05	17	23 s. 25	8½	9	4:15	E	2:30	B	LIB	27
358	24	Tu.	7:11	E	4:16	A	9 05	16	23 s. 24	9¼	10	5:26	E	3:10	B	SCO	28
359	25	W.	7:12	E	4:17	A	9 05	16	23 s. 23	10¼	10¾	6:32	E	3:56	B	OPH	29
360	26	Th.	7:12	E	4:17	A	9 05	15	23 s. 21	11	11½	7:33	E	4:48	B	SAG	0
361	27	Fr.	7:12	E	4:18	A	9 06	15	23 s. 18	11¾	—	8:27	E	5:46	B	SAG	1
362	28	Sa.	7:13	E	4:19	A	9 06	14	23 s. 16	12¼	12½	9:12	E	6:47	B	CAP	2
363	29	F	7:13	E	4:20	A	9 07	14	23 s. 12	1	1¼	9:50	E	7:48	C	CAP	3
364	30	M.	7:13	E	4:20	A	9 07	13	23 s. 09	1¾	2	10:22	E	8:50	C	CAP	4
365	31	Tu.	7:13	E	4:21	A	9 08	13	23 s. 04	2½	2¾	10:49	E	9:50	C	AQU	5

Send the ruddy firelight higher;
Draw your easy chair up nigher.
–Ina Donna Coolbrith

DAY OF MONTH	DAY OF WEEK	DATES, FEASTS, FASTS, ASPECTS, TIDE HEIGHTS, AND WEATHER	
1	**F**	**1st S. of Advent** • Winnie (bear Pooh named after) donated to London Zoo, 1919	*Deck*
2	M.	St. Viviana • 1st T. Eaton Co. Santa Claus parade, Toronto, Ont., 1905 • Tides {8.9 / 9.6	*the*
3	Tu.	*Pioneer 11* Jupiter flyby, 1974 • 68°F, Portland, Maine, 2009 • Tides {8.7 / 9.2	*halls;*
4	W.	☾ at apo. • ☌♆☾ • French statesman Armand-Jean du Plessis (Cardinal de Richelieu) died, 1642	*hit*
5	Th.	Pusuke, a Shiba Inu mix and world's oldest dog at time (26 yrs., 8 mos.), died, 2011 • Tides {8.6 / 8.7	*the*
6	Fr.	St. Nicholas • ☾ on eq. • Kitty O'Neil reached 512.71 mph land speed, 1976	*malls;*
7	Sa.	St. Ambrose • **Nat'l Pearl Harbor Remembrance Day** • Tides {9.1 / 8.7	*scan*
8	**F**	**2nd S. of Advent** • ☌♅☾ • Astronaut John Glenn died, 2016 • {9.4 / 8.8	*the*
9	M.	Quebec adopted new coat of arms, 1939 • Tides {9.8 / 9.0	*Web*
10	Tu.	St. Eulalia • ☌♀♄ • *All doors open to courtesy.* –Thomas Fuller • {10.1 / 9.2	*with*
11	W.	United Nations International Children's Emergency Fund (UNICEF) established, 1946 • {10.4 / 9.3	*passion!*
12	Th.	**Our Lady of Guadalupe** • **Full Cold** ○ • Paul Martin became Canada's 21st prime minister, 2003	*These*
13	Fr.	St. Lucia • ☾ rides high • ☾ at ☊ • ☌♀♇ • Tides {10.9 / —	*mild*
14	Sa.	Halcyon Days begin. • Ala. statehood, 1819 • Millau Viaduct opened, France, 2004	*days*
15	**F**	**3rd S. of Advent** • *Dec. 14–15:* Windstorm caused flooding/power outages, Wash./Oreg., 2006	*are*
16	M.	9,000th episode of *All My Children* aired, 2004 • Tides {9.6 / 10.8	*flashin' by—*
17	Tu.	Project Blue Book (UFO investigations) terminated, 1969 • {9.6 / 10.6	*Snowstorm's*
18	W.	Ember Day • ☾ at perig. • Freezing rain caused 170 auto accidents, Memphis, Tenn., 1989	*crashin'*
19	Th.	Beware the Pogonip. • *A snow year, a rich year.* • {9.8 / 10.0	*Santa's*
20	Fr.	Ember Day • ☾ on eq. • Calif. angler caught 230-lb. Nile perch, Lake Nasser, Egypt, 2000 • {10.0 / 9.8	*party!*
21	Sa.	St. Thomas • Ember Day • **Winter Solstice** • Tides {10.3 / 9.7	*May*
22	**F**	**4th S. of Advent** • Chanukah begins at sundown • ☌♂☾ • {10.6 / 9.7	*your*
23	M.	Entrepreneur Madam C. J. Walker born, 1867 • –50°F, Williston, N.Dak., 1983 • Tides {10.9 / 9.7	*Yule*
24	Tu.	Clement Moore's "A Visit From St. Nicholas" likely written, 1822 • Tides {11.1 / 9.8	*be filled*
25	W.	**Christmas** • ☌☿☾ • *Be merry and wise.* • Tides {11.2 / 9.8	*with*
26	Th.	**Boxing Day (Canada)** • **1st day of Kwanzaa** • **New** ● • **Eclipse** ☉ • ☾ runs low • ☾ at ☋ • ☌♃☾	
27	Fr.	St. John • ☌♃☉ • ☌♄☾ • ☌♇☾ • ALH 84001 Mars meteorite found, Antarctica, 1984	*plenty*
28	Sa.	Holy Innocents • ☌♀☾ • 2nd U.S. chewing gum patent went to William Semple, 1869 • {9.6 / 10.7	*and*
29	**F**	**1st S. af. Ch.** • American Meteorological Society founded, 1919 • {9.4 / 10.4	*likewise*
30	M.	Social reformer Amelia Bloomer died, 1894 • Tides {9.2 / 10.0	*your*
31	Tu.	St. Sylvester • ☌♆☾ • *Plan your life at New Year's eve, your day at dawn.* • {9.0 / 9.6	*2020!*

Farmer's Calendar

"Can you tell the difference between a balsam and a Fraser?" Steve Moffatt grills his tree hauler, Seth Johnson, a young farmer. "Yep," replies Seth, who grows beans and wheat, raises beef and horses, and moonlights as a trucker when his growing season stalls. Together they load the culmination of Steve's decade of labor—planting, fertilizing, weeding, grooming, harvesting, and baling. Now Seth climbs onto his trailer and begins driving in the bed stakes that will gird this precious cargo. Then Steve hands over the first of 500 eight-foot balsams and Fraser firs. Seth lays them in like shingles, butts and tips sheltering each other, protecting each tree's topmost branch. In the cold, it can snap like glass, and a tree without a tip, as both driver and grower know, is useless. The cold air fills with a balsam perfume as the Christmas tree layers accrue. Finally, Seth stretches his cables and cinches the load. He climbs into his cab, equipped with his CB radio, Thermos, and Santa hat. As Seth's truck eases onto Wild Branch Road, Steve watches the results of his labor—the forest he began 10 years ago—glide off in a diesel sleigh.

JANUARY

SKY WATCH: This extraordinary year for planets—the best year of our lives—begins rather quietly. In January, only Venus dominates, but for 5 months this brilliant evening star will be a beacon in the west. Earth is closest to the Sun on the 5th. Mars begins 2020 in Libra, visible before dawn at magnitude 2, its dimmest of the year, and quickly moves into Scorpius, passing above the star named after it, the famously orange Antares. They form a triangle with the crescent Moon on the 20th. By month's end, also before dawn, Jupiter first appears low in the east. In evening twilight, the crescent Moon dangles below Venus on the 27th in Aquarius and stands to its left on the 28th.

◑ **FIRST QUARTER** 2nd day 11:45 P.M.　　◐ **LAST QUARTER** 17th day 7:58 A.M.
○ **FULL MOON** 10th day 2:21 P.M.　　● **NEW MOON** 24th day 4:42 P.M.

All times are given in Eastern Standard Time.

GET THESE PAGES WITH TIMES SET TO YOUR ZIP CODE AT ALMANAC.COM/ACCESS.

DAY OF YEAR	DAY OF MONTH	DAY OF WEEK	☼ RISES H. M.	RISE KEY	☼ SETS H. M.	SET KEY	LENGTH OF DAY H. M.	SUN FAST M.	SUN DECLINATION ° '	HIGH TIDE TIMES BOSTON		☾ RISES H. M.	RISE KEY	☾ SETS H. M.	SET KEY	☾ ASTRON. PLACE	☾ AGE
1	1	W.	7:13	E	4:22	A	9 09	12	23 s. 00	3¼	3½	11:14	D	10:49	D	AQU	6
2	2	Th.	7:13	E	4:23	A	9 10	12	22 s. 55	4	4¼	11:37	D	11:48	D	PSC	7
3	3	Fr.	7:13	E	4:24	A	9 11	11	22 s. 49	5	5¼	12:00	C	—	-	CET	8
4	4	Sa.	7:13	E	4:25	A	9 12	11	22 s. 43	5¾	6¼	12:24	C	12:47	E	PSC	9
5	5	**E**	7:13	E	4:26	A	9 13	11	22 s. 36	6½	7	12:50	C	1:48	E	CET	10
6	6	M.	7:13	E	4:27	A	9 14	10	22 s. 29	7½	8	1:20	B	2:51	E	ARI	11
7	7	Tu.	7:13	E	4:28	A	9 15	10	22 s. 22	8¼	8¾	1:54	B	3:55	E	TAU	12
8	8	W.	7:13	E	4:29	A	9 16	9	22 s. 14	9	9¾	2:36	B	5:01	E	TAU	13
9	9	Th.	7:13	E	4:30	A	9 17	9	22 s. 06	9¾	10½	3:27	B	6:05	E	ORI	14
10	10	Fr.	7:13	E	4:31	A	9 18	8	21 s. 57	10½	11¼	4:27	B	7:06	E	GEM	15
11	11	Sa.	7:12	E	4:32	A	9 20	8	21 s. 48	11¼	—	5:36	B	8:00	E	GEM	16
12	12	**E**	7:12	E	4:33	A	9 21	8	21 s. 38	12	12	6:49	C	8:47	E	CAN	17
13	13	M.	7:12	E	4:34	A	9 22	7	21 s. 28	12¾	1	8:04	C	9:26	E	LEO	18
14	14	Tu.	7:11	E	4:35	A	9 24	7	21 s. 18	1½	1¾	9:18	D	10:00	E	LEO	19
15	15	W.	7:11	E	4:36	A	9 25	7	21 s. 07	2½	2¾	10:32	D	10:31	D	VIR	20
16	16	Th.	7:10	E	4:38	A	9 28	6	20 s. 56	3¼	3½	11:44	E	10:59	D	VIR	21
17	17	Fr.	7:10	E	4:39	A	9 29	6	20 s. 44	4¼	4½	—	-	11:28	C	VIR	22
18	18	Sa.	7:09	E	4:40	A	9 31	6	20 s. 32	5¼	5¾	12:55	E	11:58	B	LIB	23
19	19	**E**	7:09	E	4:41	B	9 32	5	20 s. 20	6¼	6¾	2:05	E	12:30	B	LIB	24
20	20	M.	7:08	E	4:42	B	9 34	5	20 s. 07	7¼	7¾	3:15	E	1:08	B	SCO	25
21	21	Tu.	7:08	E	4:44	B	9 36	5	19 s. 54	8¼	8¾	4:21	E	1:50	B	OPH	26
22	22	W.	7:07	E	4:45	B	9 38	4	19 s. 41	9	9¾	5:23	E	2:40	B	SAG	27
23	23	Th.	7:06	E	4:46	B	9 40	4	19 s. 27	10	10½	6:19	E	3:35	B	SAG	28
24	24	Fr.	7:05	E	4:47	B	9 42	4	19 s. 12	10¾	11¼	7:06	E	4:34	B	SAG	0
25	25	Sa.	7:05	E	4:49	B	9 44	4	18 s. 58	11½	—	7:47	E	5:35	B	CAP	1
26	26	**E**	7:04	E	4:50	B	9 46	3	18 s. 43	12	12	8:21	E	6:37	C	CAP	2
27	27	M.	7:03	E	4:51	B	9 48	3	18 s. 28	12¾	12¾	8:50	E	7:38	C	AQU	3
28	28	Tu.	7:02	E	4:53	B	9 51	3	18 s. 12	1¼	1½	9:16	D	8:38	C	AQU	4
29	29	W.	7:01	E	4:54	B	9 53	3	17 s. 56	2	2¼	9:40	D	9:37	D	PSC	5
30	30	Th.	7:00	E	4:55	B	9 55	3	17 s. 40	2½	2¾	10:03	C	10:35	D	CET	6
31	31	F.	6:59	E	4:56	B	9 57	3	17 s. 23	3¼	3¾	10:26	C	11:35	E	PSC	7

JANUARY

Arise, New Year! Receive our earnest greeting,
Our promises to do the best we may.
–Georgiana Bennet

DAY OF MONTH	DAY OF WEEK	DATES, FEASTS, FASTS, ASPECTS, TIDE HEIGHTS, AND WEATHER	
1	W.	Holy Name • **New Year's Day** • ☾ at apo. • Tides {8.7 / 9.0}	*Flakes*
2	Th.	☾ on Eq. • ☌☿♃ • *Luna 1* 1st spacecraft to leave Earth's gravity (and later, to orbit Sun), 1959	*floating;*
3	Fr.	*A little wind kindles, too much puts out the fire.* • {8.6 / 8.4}	*better*
4	Sa.	St. Elizabeth Ann Seton • ☌♅☾ • Blizzard, New England/ eastern Canada, 2018 • {8.7 / 8.2}	*for*
5	**E**	**2nd S. af. Ch.** • Twelfth Night • ⊕ at perihelion • {8.9 / 8.2}	*boating!*
6	M.	**Epiphany** • James Plimpton rec'd patent for improved roller skates, 1863 • {9.2 / 8.3}	*Stop-*
7	Tu.	Distaff Day • U.S. military plane *Question Mark* completed 150-hr., 40-min. nonstop flight, 1929	*and-*
8	W.	Entertainer Elvis Presley born, 1935 • Tides {10.0 / 8.8}	*go*
9	Th.	☾ at ☊ • 6.5 earthquake off shore of Eureka, Calif., 2010 • Tides {10.5 / 9.1}	*snow,*
10	Fr.	**Full Wolf** ○ • **Eclipse** ☾ • ☾ rides high • ☿ in sup. ☌ • {10.9 / 9.4}	*ten*
11	Sa.	☌☿♄ • ♅ stat. • Canadian prime minister Sir John A. Macdonald born, 1815	*above*
12	**E**	**1st S. af. Ep.** • ☌☿♇ • Civil rights activist James Leonard Farmer Jr. born, 1920	*to*
13	M.	St. Hilary • Plough Monday • ☾ at perig. • ☌♄☉ • ☌♄♇ • ☌♇☉	*ten*
14	Tu.	*A summerish January, a winterish spring.* • {10.1 / 11.2}	*below.*
15	W.	Online encyclopedia Wikipedia launched, 2001 • Tides {10.2 / 10.9}	*Northern*
16	Th.	☾ on Eq. • Prohibition went into effect in U.S., 1920 • Tides {10.3 / 10.4}	*snowy,*
17	Fr.	U.S. statesman Benjamin Franklin born, 1706 • Tides {10.3 / 9.8}	*southern*
18	Sa.	Ice trapped Antarctic explorer E. Shackleton's ship *Endurance* until sank Nov. 21, Weddell Sea, 1915	*soupy,*
19	**E**	**2nd. S. af. Ep.** • Astronaut Roberta Bondar 1st Canadian woman selected for space mission, 1990	*mild*
20	M.	**Martin Luther King Jr.'s Birthday, observed** • ☌♂☾ • {10.3 / 9.0}	*and*
21	Tu.	Kiwanis International founded, 1915 • –19°F, Caesars Head, S.C., 1985 • {10.4 / 9.0}	*gloopy.*
22	W.	St. Vincent • ☾ runs low • ☾ at ☋ • ☌♃☾ • {10.5 / 9.1}	*Cold*
23	Th.	☌♄☾ • ☌♇☾ • January thaw traditionally begins about now. • {10.6 / 9.2}	*enough*
24	Fr.	**New** ● • *Knowledge is a treasure, but practice is the key to it.* • Tides {10.6 / 9.2}	*to make*
25	Sa.	Conversion of Paul • **Chinese New Year (Rat)** • ☌☿☾ • {10.5 / —}	*us*
26	**E**	**3rd. S. af. Ep.** • Agricultural scientist Richard Keith Downey born, 1927	*flinch—*
27	M.	☌♀♆ • Writer J. D. Salinger died, 2010 • Tides {9.2 / 10.1}	*snow*
28	Tu.	St. Thomas Aquinas • ☌♀☾ • ☌♆☾ • Tides {9.2 / 9.9}	*accumulating*
29	W.	☾ at apo. • "Great Olympic Blowdown" windstorm struck Wash. coast, toppling timber, 1921	*inch*
30	Th.	☾ on Eq. • Funds approved to purchase T. Jefferson's library to rebuild Library of Congress, 1815	*by*
31	Fr.	☌♅☾ • Raccoons mate now. • 0°F, San Antonio, Tex., 1949 • {8.9 / 8.7}	*inch!*

Farmer's Calendar

The woodstove purrs and spurts, burning through logs from a tree that may have sprouted from an acorn during Lincoln's presidency. This oak that grew through two centuries of summers warms the house tonight. I knew moving to this 1850s farmhouse meant taking care of a leaky roof and a buckled retaining wall, as well as a pair of trees looming broad and tall beside the driveway. But recently I failed in that stewardship. Sometimes when it rains a lot, Matt Forrester, the aptly named tree surgeon, explained, a tree will absorb so much water that its weight becomes unsustainable and it drops a limb or collapses. And, regretfully, that's what happened to one of the long-standing oaks: One spring, after torrential rains, the giant closest to the road shed its most gargantuan limb. It raked down power lines, crushed our truck, and blocked the road. Over the following days, a crew extricated the truck and brought down the remaining trunk. We rented a chipper and spent a weekend feeding it branches. Later, over the din of a wood-splitter, we discussed the red oak's silver lining: Its demise supplied a bonanza of firewood. As I type by its cozy fire, some of the tree's story keeps growing.

SKY WATCH: Early this month, Saturn materializes as a low morning star before dawn, joining higher-up Jupiter and Mars, all in Sagittarius. These three superior planets bunch closer together as the month progresses. The waning crescent Moon offers a strikingly close conjunction with Mars before dawn on the 18th. The Moon then passes to the right of Jupiter on the 19th to be just below Saturn on the 20th, providing easy identification of these two gas giants that will astonish the world in December. Meanwhile, in the western evening sky, during this month's first 12 days, Mercury has its best showing of 2020 at a very bright magnitude 0, far below the more dazzling Venus, which stands 10 degrees high 40 minutes after local sunset.

| ◖ FIRST QUARTER | 1st day | 8:42 P.M. | ◗ LAST QUARTER | 15th day | 5:17 P.M. |
| ○ FULL MOON | 9th day | 2:33 A.M. | ● NEW MOON | 23rd day | 10:32 A.M. |

All times are given in Eastern Standard Time.

GET THESE PAGES WITH TIMES SET TO YOUR ZIP CODE AT ALMANAC.COM/ACCESS.

DAY OF YEAR	DAY OF MONTH	DAY OF WEEK	☼ RISES H. M.	RISE KEY	☼ SETS H. M.	SET KEY	LENGTH OF DAY H. M.	SUN FAST M.	SUN DECLINATION ° '	HIGH TIDE TIMES BOSTON		☽ RISES H. M.	RISE KEY	☽ SETS H. M.	SET KEY	☽ ASTRON. PLACE	☽ AGE
32	1	Sa.	6:58	E	4:58	B	10 00	2	17 s. 06	4	4½	10:50	C	—	-	CET	8
33	2	**E**	6:57	E	4:59	B	10 02	2	16 s. 49	5	5½	11:17	B	12:36	E	ARI	9
34	3	M.	6:56	E	5:00	B	10 04	2	16 s. 31	5¾	6¼	11:49	B	1:38	E	TAU	10
35	4	Tu.	6:55	E	5:02	B	10 07	2	16 s. 14	6¾	7¼	**12:26**	B	2:42	E	TAU	11
36	5	W.	6:54	D	5:03	B	10 09	2	15 s. 56	7½	8¼	**1:12**	B	3:46	E	TAU	12
37	6	Th.	6:53	D	5:04	B	10 11	2	15 s. 37	8½	9	**2:07**	B	4:48	E	GEM	13
38	7	Fr.	6:52	D	5:06	B	10 14	2	15 s. 19	9¼	10	**3:12**	B	5:45	E	GEM	14
39	8	Sa.	6:50	D	5:07	B	10 17	2	15 s. 00	10¼	10¾	**4:24**	B	6:36	E	CAN	15
40	9	**E**	6:49	D	5:08	B	10 19	2	14 s. 41	11	11½	**5:41**	C	7:19	E	LEO	16
41	10	M.	6:48	D	5:09	B	10 21	2	14 s. 21	11¾	—	**6:58**	D	7:57	E	LEO	17
42	11	Tu.	6:47	D	5:11	B	10 24	2	14 s. 02	12¼	12½	**8:15**	D	8:30	D	LEO	18
43	12	W.	6:45	D	5:12	B	10 27	2	13 s. 42	1¼	1½	**9:30**	E	9:00	D	VIR	19
44	13	Th.	6:44	D	5:13	B	10 29	2	13 s. 22	2	2¼	**10:44**	E	9:30	C	VIR	20
45	14	Fr.	6:43	D	5:15	B	10 32	2	13 s. 01	2¾	3¼	**11:57**	E	10:00	C	VIR	21
46	15	Sa.	6:41	D	5:16	B	10 35	2	12 s. 41	3¾	4¼	—	-	10:32	B	LIB	22
47	16	**E**	6:40	D	5:17	B	10 37	2	12 s. 20	4¾	5¼	1:07	E	11:08	B	LIB	23
48	17	M.	6:38	D	5:19	B	10 41	2	11 s. 59	5¾	6½	2:15	E	11:49	B	OPH	24
49	18	Tu.	6:37	D	5:20	B	10 43	2	11 s. 38	6¾	7½	3:18	E	**12:36**	B	SAG	25
50	19	W.	6:36	D	5:21	B	10 45	2	11 s. 17	7¾	8¾	4:15	E	**1:28**	B	SAG	26
51	20	Th.	6:34	D	5:22	B	10 48	2	10 s. 56	8¾	9½	5:04	E	**2:26**	B	SAG	27
52	21	Fr.	6:33	D	5:24	B	10 51	2	10 s. 34	9¾	10¼	5:46	E	**3:26**	B	CAP	28
53	22	Sa.	6:31	D	5:25	B	10 54	2	10 s. 12	10½	11	6:22	E	**4:27**	C	CAP	29
54	23	**E**	6:30	D	5:26	B	10 56	3	9 s. 50	11¼	11½	6:52	E	**5:28**	C	AQU	0
55	24	M.	6:28	D	5:27	B	10 59	3	9 s. 28	11¾	—	7:19	D	**6:29**	C	AQU	1
56	25	Tu.	6:27	D	5:29	B	11 02	3	9 s. 06	12¼	12½	7:43	D	**7:28**	D	AQU	2
57	26	W.	6:25	D	5:30	B	11 05	3	8 s. 43	12¾	1	8:06	D	**8:27**	D	CET	3
58	27	Th.	6:23	D	5:31	C	11 08	3	8 s. 21	1½	1¾	8:29	C	**9:26**	E	CET	4
59	28	Fr.	6:22	D	5:32	C	11 10	3	7 s. 58	2	2¼	8:52	C	**10:25**	E	PSC	5
60	29	Sa.	6:20	D	5:34	C	11 14	4	7 s. 36	2¾	3	9:18	B	**11:26**	E	ARI	6

FEBRUARY

The little birds twitter and cheep
To their loves on the leafless larch.
–**John Addington Symonds**

DAY OF MONTH	DAY OF WEEK	DATES, FEASTS, FASTS, ASPECTS, TIDE HEIGHTS, AND WEATHER	
1	Sa.	St. Brigid • Sailor Alexander Selkirk (stranded on isle for 4+ years) found, 1709	*Temperatures*
2	E	Candlemas • Groundhog Day • Philosopher Bertrand Russell died, 1970	*tumble,*
3	M.	62-yr.-old Laysan albatross hatched chick, Midway Atoll National Wildlife Refuge, 2013	*groundhogs*
4	Tu.	*If you will not hear Reason, she will surely rap your knuckles.* • Tides 9.1 / 8.1	*grumble,*
5	W.	St. Agatha • William Stephenson invested as Companion of Order of Canada, 1980	*burrows*
6	Th.	☾ RIDES HIGH • ☾ AT ☊ • SpaceX launched E. Musk's Starman mannequin in Tesla roadster, 2018	*buried*
7	Fr.	Writer Sinclair Lewis born, 1885 • Tides 10.6 / 9.3	*under*
8	Sa.	Ellen MacArthur set record for solo, nonstop sail around globe (71 days, 14 hrs., 18 mins., 33 secs.), 2005	*snow.*
9	E	**Septuagesima** • FULL SNOW ○ • Ice storm began in parts of U.S. South, 1994	*Rain*
10	M.	☾ AT PERIG. • ☿ GR. ELONG. (18° EAST) • Olympic swimmer Mark Spitz born, 1950	*impending*
11	Tu.	John Buchan, 15th governor-general of Canada, died, 1940 • Tides 10.7 / 11.8	*as*
12	W.	☾ ON EQ. • U.S. president Abraham Lincoln born, 1809 • Tides 10.9 / 11.5	*it's*
13	Th.	Last original *Peanuts* comic strip ran in newspapers, 2000 • Tides 11.0 / 11.0	*trending*
14	Fr.	Sts. Cyril & Methodius • VALENTINE'S DAY • YouTube founded, 2005 • 10.9 / 10.4	*warmer.*
15	Sa.	NATIONAL FLAG OF CANADA DAY • Social reformer Susan B. Anthony born, 1820 • 10.6 / 9.7	*Skiers*
16	E	**Sexagesima** • ☿ STAT. • 1st U.S. patent for fruit tree (peach) issued, 1932	*muddle*
17	M.	PRESIDENTS' DAY • Winter's back breaks. • Tides 10.1 / 8.7	*through*
18	Tu.	☾ AT ☋ • OCCN. ♂☾ • Elm Farm Ollie 1st cow to fly in plane, 1930 • 9.9 / 8.6	*each*
19	W.	☾ RUNS LOW • ☌♃☾ • 25" snow in 24 hrs., Dover, Del., 1979 • Tides 9.9 / 8.7	*puddle.*
20	Th.	☌♄☾ • ☌♇☾ • Tchaikovsky's ballet *Swan Lake* premiered, 1877 • 10.0 / 8.8	*Could*
21	Fr.	*Love can neither be bought nor sold; its only price is love.* • Tides 10.1 / 9.0	*this*
22	Sa.	U.S. president George Washington born, 1732 • Tides 10.2 / 9.2	*be a*
23	E	**Quinquagesima** • NEW ● • ☌☿☾ • 10.2 / 9.3	*thaw?*
24	M.	St. Matthias • ☌♆☾ • Pilots of 2 planes reported UFO over Ariz., 2018	*Naw!*
25	Tu.	Shrove Tuesday • ☿ IN INF. ☌ • 1st U.S. presidential Cabinet meeting held, 1793 • 9.4 / 10.0	*Pile*
26	W.	**Ash Wednesday** • ☾ ON EQ. • ☾ AT APO. • Tides 9.5 / 9.8	*wood*
27	Th.	☌♀☾ • 16-yr.-old Tiger Woods, youngest PGA golfer in 35 years, teed off in L.A. Open, 1992	*higher*
28	Fr.	St. Romanus • ☌⛢☾ • Skunks mate now. • Tides 9.4 / 9.2	*on the*
29	Sa.	LEAP DAY • *Look ere you leap.* • Tides 9.3 / 8.8	*fire!*

What is worse than raining cats and dogs? Hailing taxicabs.

Farmer's Calendar

One day while zigzagging around the garden, working alone, thinning carrots, hoeing onions, and sowing more beans, I noticed a collection of bees, hundreds of them, forming a beard-shape swarm along the fence line. For months I'd seen them zip around as individuals, making solo forays to the apple blossoms and the foxglove's speckled bells and then to the blue bachelor's buttons and the orange calendula. But now they acted as one organism as they clung to our barbed wire fence until the apiarist arrived in his white attire and snipped the fence so that they poured into his hive. Living in a sparsely populated area, I often wonder what it feels like to belong to a throng, to behave in simultaneity, like a swarm of bees. Then one colorless midwinter day I attended a farmers' meeting. Twenty of us sat in a circle, until a late attendee stepped in from the ongoing snow bearing a huge sack whose contents he spilled at our feet: The floor filled with hundreds of seed packets, each featuring vivid pictures of flowers—the cerulean cuff of morning glory, spires of purple lupine, deep hues of yellow zinnia and red-orange tithonia—and without thinking, in a simultaneous motion, we all zoomed to our knees.

MARCH

SKY WATCH: Set your sights on the eastern sky just before dawn. Superior planets Mars, Jupiter, and Saturn bunch together in a line starting on the 17th. The waning crescent Moon joins this party on the 18th, just below the planets, with dim orange Mars on the right, brilliant Jupiter in the middle, and medium-bright Saturn farther left. This is a don't-miss conjunction, with the four celestial bodies standing 17 degrees high 40 minutes before local sunrise, easily seen with the naked eye. The three planets, minus the Moon, again form a nice grouping from the 28th to the 31st, with Jupiter on the right and Saturn on the left. The vernal equinox—the earliest in 124 years!—falls on the 19th at 11:50 P.M. EDT.

◑ FIRST QUARTER	2nd day	2:57 P.M.	◐ LAST QUARTER	16th day	5:34 A.M.
○ FULL MOON	9th day	1:48 P.M.	● NEW MOON	24th day	5:28 A.M.

After 2:00 A.M. on March 8, Eastern Daylight Time is given.

GET THESE PAGES WITH TIMES SET TO YOUR ZIP CODE AT ALMANAC.COM/ACCESS.

DAY OF YEAR	DAY OF MONTH	DAY OF WEEK	☼ RISES H. M.	RISE KEY	☼ SETS H. M.	SET KEY	LENGTH OF DAY H. M.	SUN FAST M.	SUN DECLINATION ° '	HIGH TIDE TIMES BOSTON	☾ RISES H. M.	RISE KEY	☾ SETS H. M.	SET KEY	☾ ASTRON. PLACE	☾ AGE
61	1	D	6:19	D	5:35	C	11 16	4	7 s. 13	3¼ 3¾	9:47	B	—	-	TAU	7
62	2	M.	6:17	D	5:36	C	11 19	4	6 s. 50	4¼ 4¾	10:21	B	12:28	E	TAU	8
63	3	Tu.	6:15	D	5:37	C	11 22	4	6 s. 27	5 5¾	11:01	B	1:31	E	TAU	9
64	4	W.	6:14	D	5:38	C	11 24	4	6 s. 04	6 6¾	11:50	B	2:32	E	GEM	10
65	5	Th.	6:12	D	5:40	C	11 28	5	5 s. 40	7 7¾	12:49	B	3:30	E	GEM	11
66	6	Fr.	6:10	C	5:41	C	11 31	5	5 s. 17	8 8½	1:56	B	4:23	E	CAN	12
67	7	Sa.	6:09	C	5:42	C	11 33	5	4 s. 54	8¾ 9½	3:11	C	5:09	E	CAN	13
68	8	D	7:07	C	6:43	C	11 36	5	4 s. 30	10¾ 11¼	5:28	C	6:49	E	LEO	14
69	9	M.	7:05	C	6:44	C	11 39	6	4 s. 07	11¾ —	6:47	D	7:24	E	LEO	15
70	10	Tu.	7:04	C	6:45	C	11 41	6	3 s. 43	12¼ 12½	8:06	D	7:56	D	VIR	16
71	11	W.	7:02	C	6:47	C	11 45	6	3 s. 20	1 1¼	9:23	E	8:27	C	VIR	17
72	12	Th.	7:00	C	6:48	C	11 48	6	2 s. 56	1¾ 2¼	10:39	E	8:57	C	VIR	18
73	13	Fr.	6:59	C	6:49	C	11 50	7	2 s. 32	2½ 3	11:54	E	9:30	B	LIB	19
74	14	Sa.	6:57	C	6:50	C	11 53	7	2 s. 09	3½ 4	—	-	10:05	B	LIB	20
75	15	D	6:55	C	6:51	C	11 56	7	1 s. 45	4¼ 5	1:05	E	10:46	B	OPH	21
76	16	M.	6:53	C	6:52	C	11 59	7	1 s. 21	5¼ 6	2:12	E	11:32	B	OPH	22
77	17	Tu.	6:52	C	6:54	C	12 02	8	0 s. 58	6¼ 7¼	3:12	E	12:23	B	SAG	23
78	18	W.	6:50	C	6:55	C	12 05	8	0 s. 34	7½ 8¼	4:04	E	1:20	B	SAG	24
79	19	Th.	6:48	C	6:56	C	12 08	8	0 s. 10	8½ 9¼	4:48	E	2:19	B	CAP	25
80	20	Fr.	6:47	C	6:57	C	12 10	9	0 N. 13	9½ 10¼	5:25	E	3:20	B	CAP	26
81	21	Sa.	6:45	C	6:58	C	12 13	9	0 N. 36	10½ 11	5:56	E	4:21	C	AQU	27
82	22	D	6:43	C	6:59	C	12 16	9	1 N.00	11 11½	6:23	E	5:21	C	AQU	28
83	23	M.	6:41	C	7:01	C	12 20	10	1 N. 24	11¾ —	6:48	D	6:21	D	AQU	29
84	24	Tu.	6:40	C	7:02	C	12 22	10	1 N. 47	12¼ 12½	7:11	D	7:20	D	PSC	0
85	25	W.	6:38	C	7:03	C	12 25	10	2 N. 11	12¾ 1	7:33	C	8:19	D	CET	1
86	26	Th.	6:36	C	7:04	C	12 28	10	2 N. 34	1¼ 1½	7:56	C	9:19	E	PSC	2
87	27	Fr.	6:34	C	7:05	C	12 31	11	2 N. 58	1¾ 2¼	8:21	B	10:19	E	CET	3
88	28	Sa.	6:33	C	7:06	D	12 33	11	3 N. 21	2½ 3	8:48	B	11:21	E	ARI	4
89	29	D	6:31	C	7:07	D	12 36	11	3 N. 45	3 3½	9:20	B	—	-	TAU	5
90	30	M.	6:29	C	7:08	D	12 39	12	4 N. 08	3¾ 4¼	9:57	B	12:22	E	TAU	6
91	31	Tu.	6:27	C	7:10	D	12 43	12	4 N. 31	4½ 5¼	10:41	B	1:23	E	TAU	7

RUSH!
Priority Order!

NO POSTAGE
NECESSARY
IF MAILED
IN THE
UNITED STATES

BUSINESS REPLY MAIL
FIRST-CLASS MAIL PERMIT NO. 51 PALM COAST FL

POSTAGE WILL BE PAID BY ADDRESSEE

The Old Farmer's Almanac
Subscriptions
PO BOX 420001
PALM COAST FL 32142-9900

RUSH!
Priority Order!

NO POSTAGE
NECESSARY
IF MAILED
IN THE
UNITED STATES

BUSINESS REPLY MAIL
FIRST-CLASS MAIL PERMIT NO. 51 PALM COAST FL

POSTAGE WILL BE PAID BY ADDRESSEE

The Old Farmer's Almanac
Subscriptions
PO BOX 420001
PALM COAST FL 32142-9900

THE THIRD MONTH • 2020

MARCH

MARCH HATH 31 DAYS

Spring, with her golden suns and silver rain,
Is with us once again.
–**Henry Timrod**

DAY OF MONTH	DAY OF WEEK	DATES, FEASTS, FASTS, ASPECTS, TIDE HEIGHTS, AND WEATHER	
1	**D**	**1st. S. in Lent** • 13.7" snow, Norfolk, Va., 1980 • {9.2 / 8.4	*March*
2	M.	Clean Monday • St. Chad • Space probe *Pioneer 10* launched, 1972 • {9.1 / 8.1	*plods*
3	Tu.	Astronomer James Ludlow Elliot died, 2011 • Tides {9.1 / 8.0	*in*
4	W.	Ember Day • ☾ RIDES HIGH • ☾ AT ☊ • Deadly avalanche, Rogers Pass, B.C., 1910	*with*
5	Th.	St. Piran • Boston Massacre, 1770 • Tides {9.6 / 8.5	*snowy*
6	Fr.	Ember Day • *March, many weathers.* • Tides {10.1 / 9.0	*feet,*
7	Sa.	St. Perpetua • Ember Day • 1st coin-operated locker patented, 1911 • {10.7 / 9.7	*trailing*
8	**D**	**2nd. S. in Lent** • **DAYLIGHT SAVING TIME BEGINS, 2:00 A.M.** • ☌♆☉	*rain*
9	M.	**FULL WORM** ○ • ☌♀⛢ • ☿ STAT. • Hummingbirds migrate north now.	*and*
10	Tu.	☾ AT PERIG. • 5.12" rain, Wilmington, N.C., 1936 • Tides {11.0 / 11.9	*mud*
11	W.	☾ ON EQ. • Great white shark circled fisherman's kayak for over 1 hr., Maui, Hawaii, 2017	*and*
12	Th.	Canadian WWI ace Billy Barker died, 1930 • Tides {11.6 / 11.5	*sleet,*
13	Fr.	Opera singer Luciano Pavarotti rec'd 15-min. standing ovation, 2004 • Tides {11.6 / 11.0	*keeping*
14	Sa.	Marc Garneau chosen as 1st Canadian astronaut to go into space, 1984 • Tides {11.3 / 10.3	*up*
15	**D**	**3rd. S. in Lent** • Beware the ides of March. • Maine statehood, 1820	*the*
16	M.	☾ AT ☋ • N.Y. Stock Exchange's slowest day: 31 shares traded, 1830 • {10.3 / 9.0	*heaping*
17	Tu.	**ST. PATRICK'S DAY** • ☾ RUNS LOW • *A stout heart crushes ill luck.* • {9.9 / 8.6	*up*
18	W.	☌♂☾ • ☌♃☾ • ☌♄☾ • ☌♇☾ • Tides {9.6 / 8.5	*and*
19	Th.	St. Joseph • **VERNAL EQUINOX** • 5.38"-wide, 9.8-oz. hail fell, Walter, Ala., 2018	*sweeping*
20	Fr.	☌♂♃ • Skier Lauren Woolstencroft won her 5th gold medal of Winter Paralympic Games, 2010	*up*
21	Sa.	☌☿☾ • Rajveer Meena recited 70,000 decimal places of pi, 2015 • {9.7 / 9.1	*the*
22	**D**	4th. S. in Lent • ☌♆☾ • 9th day of March record highs (78°–87°F), Chicago, Ill., 2012	*street!*
23	M.	☌♂♇ • ☿ GR. ELONG. (28° WEST) • Botanist John Bartram born, 1699 • {9.9 / —	*It's*
24	Tu.	NEW ● • ☾ ON EQ. • ☾ AT APO. • ♀ GR. ELONG. (46° EAST) • {9.6 / 9.9	*dark*
25	W.	**Annunciation** • *Mar. 22–25:* Blizzard hit Okla./Tex. panhandles, 1957 • {9.7 / 9.8	*as*
26	Th.	☌⛢☾ • Chipmunks emerge from hibernation now. • Tides {9.8 / 9.7	*a*
27	Fr.	50-lb. carp caught, MacArthur Park Lake, Los Angeles, Calif., 2017 • Tides {9.8 / 9.4	*dungeon,*
28	Sa.	☌♀☾ • Peggy Fortnum, 1st illustrator of Paddington Bear children's book series, died, 2016	*and*
29	**D**	**5th. S. in Lent** • 1st wedding at White House, D.C., 1812 • {9.7 / 8.8	*the*
30	M.	*A good recorder / Sets all in order.* • Tides {9.5 / 8.6	*temperature's*
31	Tu.	☾ AT ☊ • ☌♂♄ • Longview Bridge (Lewis and Clark Bridge) opened, Wash./Ore., 1930	*plungin'.*

Farmer's Calendar

Backyard sugaring—if you are factoring in time and energy—is not a rational endeavor. And yet, on a certain day each winter, the backyard sugar-er grabs her cordless drill and stomps into her snowy woods, ambling from maple to maple, standing within kissing distance as she bores a 3/8-inch hole. Then she inserts a metal spout, or spile. Last, she hangs a bucket. Sun warms her shoulder as she trudges between the trees and hears the season's beginning: plunk, plunk, plunk—like a quickening heartbeat—the first drops of sap plummeting into her newly hung buckets. By late afternoon, the woods sport 100 taps and 100 buckets and she is "tapped out," an expression that describes the first phase of making maple syrup but is also slang for how she'll feel in 6 weeks when she's running on the dregs of her energy, having gathered perhaps a thousand gallons and boiled it late into the night. It takes 40 gallons of sap to distill 1 gallon of sweet stuff. Why bother? While animals shed their winter coats and migratory birds swerve north, perhaps she's compelled—the urge flowing in her as surely as sap's drawn up through the trees.

APRIL

SKY WATCH: The year's closest Moon is on the 7th. It's in the full phase, so the media will call it a "supermoon," even if the super size is not apparent to observers. Saturn and Mars, very close together on the 1st, have crossed into Capricornus, with brilliant Jupiter lingering to their right in Sagittarius. Mars then speeds away to the left, leaving the three planets in a line during most of the month. The Moon hovers below them on the 15th: This striking conjunction rises by 4:00 A.M. and is well seen in the southeast as dawn begins. In the evening sky, Venus, in Taurus, reaches her brightest and highest at a shadow-casting magnitude –4.7; she stands above the Moon on the 25th and to its right on the 26th.

◑ **FIRST QUARTER** 1st day 6:21 A.M.   ● **NEW MOON** 22nd day 10:26 P.M.
○ **FULL MOON** 7th day 10:35 P.M.   ◐ **FIRST QUARTER** 30th day 4:38 P.M.
◑ **LAST QUARTER** 14th day 6:56 P.M.

All times are given in Eastern Daylight Time.

GET THESE PAGES WITH TIMES SET TO YOUR ZIP CODE AT ALMANAC.COM/ACCESS.

DAY OF YEAR	DAY OF MONTH	DAY OF WEEK	☼ RISES H. M.	RISE KEY	☼ SETS H. M.	SET KEY	LENGTH OF DAY H. M.	SUN FAST M.	SUN DECLINATION ° '	HIGH TIDE TIMES BOSTON	☾ RISES H. M.	RISE KEY	☾ SETS H. M.	SET KEY	☾ ASTRON. PLACE	☾ AGE
92	1	W.	6:26	C	7:11	D	12 45	12	4 N. 54	5½ 6¼	11:35	B	2:21	E	GEM	8
93	2	Th.	6:24	C	7:12	D	12 48	12	5 N. 17	6½ 7¼	12:36	B	3:14	E	GEM	9
94	3	Fr.	6:22	C	7:13	D	12 51	13	5 N. 40	7½ 8¼	1:46	B	4:01	E	CAN	10
95	4	Sa.	6:21	C	7:14	D	12 53	13	6 N. 03	8½ 9¼	3:00	C	4:43	E	LEO	11
96	5	D	6:19	C	7:15	D	12 56	13	6 N. 26	9½ 10	4:17	C	5:19	E	LEO	12
97	6	M.	6:17	B	7:16	D	12 59	14	6 N. 48	10½ 11	5:35	D	5:51	D	LEO	13
98	7	Tu.	6:16	B	7:17	D	13 01	14	7 N. 11	11¼ 11¾	6:53	E	6:22	D	VIR	14
99	8	W.	6:14	B	7:19	D	13 05	14	7 N. 33	12¼ —	8:12	E	6:52	C	VIR	15
100	9	Th.	6:12	B	7:20	D	13 08	14	7 N. 55	12½ 1	9:30	E	7:24	C	VIR	16
101	10	Fr.	6:11	B	7:21	D	13 10	15	8 N. 17	1¼ 2	10:46	E	7:59	B	LIB	17
102	11	Sa.	6:09	B	7:22	D	13 13	15	8 N. 39	2¼ 2¾	11:58	E	8:38	B	SCO	18
103	12	D	6:07	B	7:23	D	13 16	15	9 N. 01	3 3¾	—	-	9:23	B	OPH	19
104	13	M.	6:06	B	7:24	D	13 18	15	9 N. 23	4 4¾	1:03	E	10:14	B	SAG	20
105	14	Tu.	6:04	B	7:25	D	13 21	16	9 N. 45	4¾ 5¾	2:00	E	11:11	B	SAG	21
106	15	W.	6:02	B	7:26	D	13 24	16	10 N. 06	6 6¾	2:47	E	12:11	B	CAP	22
107	16	Th.	6:01	B	7:28	D	13 27	16	10 N. 27	7 7¾	3:27	E	1:12	B	CAP	23
108	17	Fr.	5:59	B	7:29	D	13 30	16	10 N. 48	8 8¾	4:00	E	2:14	C	CAP	24
109	18	Sa.	5:58	B	7:30	D	13 32	17	11 N. 09	9 9½	4:28	E	3:14	C	AQU	25
110	19	D	5:56	B	7:31	D	13 35	17	11 N. 30	10 10¼	4:53	D	4:14	C	AQU	26
111	20	M.	5:55	B	7:32	D	13 37	17	11 N. 50	10½ 11	5:16	D	5:13	D	PSC	27
112	21	Tu.	5:53	B	7:33	D	13 40	17	12 N. 10	11¼ 11½	5:39	C	6:12	D	CET	28
113	22	W.	5:52	B	7:34	D	13 42	17	12 N. 31	12 —	6:01	C	7:12	E	PSC	0
114	23	Th.	5:50	B	7:36	D	13 46	18	12 N. 50	12¼ 12½	6:25	C	8:13	E	CET	1
115	24	Fr.	5:49	B	7:37	D	13 48	18	13 N. 10	12¾ 1¼	6:51	B	9:14	E	ARI	2
116	25	Sa.	5:47	B	7:38	D	13 51	18	13 N. 30	1¼ 1¾	7:21	B	10:17	E	TAU	3
117	26	D	5:46	B	7:39	D	13 53	18	13 N. 49	2 2½	7:56	B	11:18	E	TAU	4
118	27	M.	5:44	B	7:40	D	13 56	18	14 N. 08	2½ 3¼	8:38	B	—	-	TAU	5
119	28	Tu.	5:43	B	7:41	E	13 58	18	14 N. 27	3¼ 4	9:28	B	12:17	E	GEM	6
120	29	W.	5:41	B	7:42	E	14 01	18	14 N. 45	4 4¾	10:26	B	1:11	E	GEM	7
121	30	Th.	5:40	B	7:43	E	14 03	19	15 N. 03	5 5¾	11:31	B	1:59	E	CAN	8

To use this page, see p. 116; for Key Letters, see p. 238. LIGHT = A.M. BOLD = P.M.   2020

CALENDAR

APRIL

The work is done; no more to man is given;
The grateful Farmer trusts the rest to Heaven.
–Robert Bloomfield, of planting

DAY OF MONTH	DAY OF WEEK	DATES, FEASTS, FASTS, ASPECTS, TIDE HEIGHTS, AND WEATHER	
1	W.	**All Fools'** • ☽ rides high • Misao Okawa died at age 117, 2015 • {9.4 / 8.3	*Wetter*
2	Th.	Writer Hans Christian Andersen born, 1805 • Pope John Paul II died, 2005 • {9.5 / 8.5	*days*
3	Fr.	St. Richard of Chichester • ☌☿♆ • Pony Express began postal service, 1860 • {9.8 / 8.9	*lead*
4	Sa.	U.S. Army SFC Paul Ray Smith rec'd Medal of Honor posthumously, 2005 • Tides {10.2 / 9.6	*to*
5	**D**	**Palm Sunday** • Bobby Orr 1st NHL defenseman to win scoring title, 1970	*better*
6	M.	☌♃♇ • *Intelsat-1,* 1st commercial geosynchronous communications satellite, launched, 1965	*days,*
7	Tu.	**Full Pink** ○ • ☽ on eq. • ☽ at perig. • Tides {11.6 / 11.6	*sunny*
8	W.	Passover begins at sundown • Sunspot enlarged to 330+ times Earth's area, 1947 • {11.7 / —	*and*
9	Th.	Maundy Thursday • Photographer Eadweard Muybridge born, 1830 • {12.0 / 11.6	*warmish.*
10	Fr.	**Good Friday** • *Rain on Good Friday foreshows a fruitful year.* • {12.1 / 11.2	*Now*
11	Sa.	Astronomer Samuel Heinrich Schwabe died, 1875 • Tides {11.9 / 10.7	*it's*
12	**D**	**Easter** • ☽ at ☋ • Salk polio vaccine declared safe and effective, 1955	*stormish,*
13	M.	Easter Monday • ☽ runs low • U.S. president Thomas Jefferson born, 1743	*and*
14	Tu.	☌♃☽ • ☌♇☽ • "Black Sunday" dust storm hit southern Plains, 1935 • {10.2 / 9.0	*the*
15	W.	☌♄☽ • U.S. president Abraham Lincoln died, 1865 • 1st Can. small penny coin released, 1920	*wind's*
16	Th.	☌♂☽ • Scientist Isaac Newton knighted, 1705 • Tides {9.4 / 8.6	*biting.*
17	Fr.	*He that has but four and spends five has no need of a purse.* • Tides {9.2 / 8.7	*Precipitating*
18	Sa.	104°F, Del Rio, Tex., 2006 • Tides {9.3 / 9.0	*without*
19	**D**	**2nd S. of Easter** • **Orthodox Easter** • ☌♆☽	*abating.*
20	M.	☽ at apo. • Deadly F3 tornado hit Utica, Ill., 2004 • Tides {9.5 / 9.6	*Inviting,*
21	Tu.	☽ on eq. • ☌☿☽ • Writer Mark Twain died, 1910 • {9.6 / 9.8	*but*
22	W.	**Earth Day** • **new** ● • 1st Earth Day celebrated in U.S., 1970 • {9.6 / —	*still*
23	Th.	St. George • Ramadan begins at sundown • ☌⛢☽ • {10.0 / 9.6	*cool.*
24	Fr.	*The Old Farmer's Almanac* founder Robert B. Thomas born, 1766 • Tides {10.1 / 9.5	*Drip,*
25	Sa.	St. Mark • 1st guide dog, Buddy, presented to Morris Frank, 1928 • {10.1 / 9.3	*drip,*
26	**D**	**3rd S. of Easter** • ☌♀☽ • ☌⛢☉ • ♇ stat.	*more*
27	M.	☽ at ☊ • ♀ gr. illum. ext. • 27" 24-hour snowfall, Minot, N.Dak., 1984	*precip;*
28	Tu.	☽ rides high • Six endangered red wolf pups born, Museum of Life and Science, Durham, N.C., 2017	*milder*
29	W.	Poplars leaf out about now. • Tides {9.8 / 8.7	*as a*
30	Th.	☌☿⛢ • *Every bird likes its own nest.* • Tides {9.8 / 8.8	*rule.*

Farmer's Calendar

Growing a potato could make anyone feel like a magician—that is, after the ground thaws. Throughout the winter, a few bushels of our Corollas—the bald, soap-shape staples of our winter diet—lurk in the underground part of the house, the cellar. Each week, I descend and retrieve a shirt-hem's worth for dinner. About the time I tire of ever tasting them again is when they're starting to wrinkle anyway and launch spooky white shoots from their "eyes." To ensure another cellar full of winter fare—*pomme de terre,* the soil's fruit—we plant chunks of the sprouting spuds in early spring. From that buried nub a shoot will rear and spread its leaves. Then we'll mound the soil around them. Even as they bloom, we'll push more soil against their shoulders, as if trying to rebury them alive. By the time the Canada geese are angling in the sky, all these potato plants will have withered and died, until all that remains is a clutch of slumping stalks. "After you loosen the soil, plunge your hands in," I once told my dirt-averse mother. She obliged, and replied, "There's nothing here." Then, like a girl who'd just won a prize, "Oh, look!" she exclaimed, as she exhumed an enormous tuber.

Listen to the Farmer's Calendar at Almanac.com/Podcast.

MAY

SKY WATCH: Venus is a dazzlingly gorgeous evening star in the northwest on the 1st, but each night she steadily sinks lower into the dusk until she is gone by month's end. Mercury, standing 12 degrees high in fading twilight 40 minutes after sunset in the second half of the month, offers a fine evening apparition. Look for Venus and Mercury to form a fine, close conjunction on the 21st, only 10 degrees high in fading twilight, a very worthy target. These inferior planets create a striking dinnertime triangle with the thin crescent Moon on the 23rd. After 4:00 A.M., look for the Moon below Jupiter and Saturn on the 12th and below steadily brightening Mars on the 15th.

○ FULL MOON	7th day	6:45 A.M.	● NEW MOON	22nd day	1:39 P.M.
◑ LAST QUARTER	14th day	10:03 A.M.	◐ FIRST QUARTER	29th day	11:30 P.M.

All times are given in Eastern Daylight Time.

GET THESE PAGES WITH TIMES SET TO YOUR ZIP CODE AT ALMANAC.COM/ACCESS.

DAY OF YEAR	DAY OF MONTH	DAY OF WEEK	☼ RISES H. M.	RISE KEY	☼ SETS H. M.	SET KEY	LENGTH OF DAY H. M.	SUN FAST M.	SUN DECLINATION ° '	HIGH TIDE TIMES BOSTON		☾ RISES H. M.	RISE KEY	☾ SETS H. M.	SET KEY	☾ ASTRON. PLACE	☾ AGE
122	1	Fr.	5:39	B	7:44	E	14 05	19	15 N. 21	6	6¾	12:41	C	2:41	E	CAN	9
123	2	Sa.	5:37	B	7:46	E	14 09	19	15 N. 39	7	7¾	1:54	C	3:17	E	LEO	10
124	3	D	5:36	B	7:47	E	14 11	19	15 N. 57	8	8¾	3:09	D	3:50	D	LEO	11
125	4	M.	5:35	B	7:48	E	14 13	19	16 N. 14	9	9½	4:26	D	4:20	D	VIR	12
126	5	Tu.	5:33	B	7:49	E	14 16	19	16 N. 31	10	10½	5:43	E	4:49	C	VIR	13
127	6	W.	5:32	B	7:50	E	14 18	19	16 N. 48	11	11¼	7:01	E	5:19	C	VIR	14
128	7	Th.	5:31	B	7:51	E	14 20	19	17 N. 04	11¾	—	8:19	E	5:51	B	LIB	15
129	8	Fr.	5:30	B	7:52	E	14 22	19	17 N. 20	12	12¾	9:35	E	6:28	B	LIB	16
130	9	Sa.	5:29	B	7:53	E	14 24	19	17 N. 36	1	1½	10:46	E	7:11	B	OPH	17
131	10	D	5:28	B	7:54	E	14 26	19	17 N. 52	1¾	2½	11:49	E	8:00	B	SAG	18
132	11	M.	5:26	B	7:55	E	14 29	19	18 N. 07	2¾	3¼	—	-	8:56	B	SAG	19
133	12	Tu.	5:25	B	7:56	E	14 31	19	18 N. 22	3½	4¼	12:42	E	9:57	B	SAG	20
134	13	W.	5:24	B	7:57	E	14 33	19	18 N. 36	4½	5¼	1:26	E	11:00	B	CAP	21
135	14	Th.	5:23	B	7:59	E	14 36	19	18 N. 51	5½	6¼	2:02	E	12:03	C	CAP	22
136	15	Fr.	5:22	B	8:00	E	14 38	19	19 N. 05	6½	7¼	2:32	E	1:05	C	AQU	23
137	16	Sa.	5:21	B	8:01	E	14 40	19	19 N. 19	7½	8	2:58	D	2:05	C	AQU	24
138	17	D	5:20	B	8:02	E	14 42	19	19 N. 32	8¼	9	3:22	D	3:05	D	AQU	25
139	18	M.	5:19	B	8:03	E	14 44	19	19 N. 45	9¼	9½	3:44	D	4:04	D	CET	26
140	19	Tu.	5:18	A	8:04	E	14 46	19	19 N. 58	10	10¼	4:06	C	5:03	E	PSC	27
141	20	W.	5:18	A	8:05	E	14 47	19	20 N. 10	10¾	11	4:29	C	6:04	E	PSC	28
142	21	Th.	5:17	A	8:05	E	14 48	19	20 N. 22	11½	11½	4:54	B	7:06	E	ARI	29
143	22	Fr.	5:16	A	8:06	E	14 50	19	20 N. 34	12	—	5:23	B	8:09	E	TAU	0
144	23	Sa.	5:15	A	8:07	E	14 52	19	20 N. 45	12¼	12¾	5:56	B	9:12	E	TAU	1
145	24	D	5:14	A	8:08	E	14 54	19	20 N. 56	12¾	1½	6:36	B	10:12	E	TAU	2
146	25	M.	5:14	A	8:09	E	14 55	19	21 N. 07	1½	2¼	7:24	B	11:09	E	GEM	3
147	26	Tu.	5:13	A	8:10	E	14 57	19	21 N. 17	2¼	3	8:20	B	11:59	E	GEM	4
148	27	W.	5:12	A	8:11	E	14 59	18	21 N. 27	3	3¾	9:23	B	—	-	CAN	5
149	28	Th.	5:12	A	8:12	E	15 00	18	21 N. 36	3¾	4½	10:31	B	12:42	E	CAN	6
150	29	Fr.	5:11	A	8:13	E	15 02	18	21 N. 45	4¾	5½	11:42	C	1:19	E	LEO	7
151	30	Sa.	5:11	A	8:13	E	15 02	18	21 N. 54	5¾	6¼	12:54	C	1:52	E	LEO	8
152	31	D	5:10	A	8:14	E	15 04	18	22 N. 02	6¾	7¼	2:08	D	2:22	D	VIR	9

To use this page, see p. 116; for Key Letters, see p. 238. LIGHT = A.M. **BOLD = P.M.**   **2020**

What can better please, / When your mind is well at ease,
Than a walk among the green fields in May?
–**William Allingham**

DAY OF MONTH	DAY OF WEEK	DATES, FEASTS, FASTS, ASPECTS, TIDE HEIGHTS, AND WEATHER	
1	Fr.	Sts. Philip & James • MAY DAY • Scofield Mine disaster, Utah, 1900	*Springlike!*
2	Sa.	St. Athanasius • *Good Housekeeping* magazine debuted, 1885 • {10.0 / 9.5	*We'll*
3	**D**	**4th S. of Easter** • John McCrae wrote "In Flanders Fields," 1915 • {10.3 / 10.2	*sing*
4	M.	☾ ON EQ. • ☿ IN SUP. ☌ • American Academy of Arts and Sciences incorporated, Boston, Mass., 1780	*like*
5	Tu.	☾ AT PERIG. • *Sow beans in the mud, And they'll grow like a wood.* • {10.9 / 11.5	*thrushes!*
6	W.	Lt.-Col. Maryse Carmichael became 1st female commander of Canadian Snowbirds, 2010	*Meltwater*
7	Th.	Vesak • FULL FLOWER ○ • Tornado hit Natchez, Miss., 317 lives lost, 1840	*rushes*
8	Fr.	St. Julian of Norwich • V-E Day, WWII, 1945 • Tides {12.1 / 11.0	*through*
9	Sa.	St. Gregory of Nazianzus • 40-lb. 4-oz. brown trout caught, Little Red River, Ark., 1992	*meadow*
10	**D**	**5th. S. of. Easter** • MOTHER'S DAY • ☾ AT ☋ • {11.8 / 10.3	*and*
11	M.	☾ RUNS LOW • ♄ STAT. • Three • Tides {11.3 / 9.9	*rill,*
12	Tu.	☌♃☾ • ☌♄☾ • ☌♇☾ • Chilly • Tides {10.7 / 9.4	*giving*
13	W.	♀ STAT. • 136-mph wind gust, Grissom AFB, Peru, Ind., 1995 • Saints	*the*
14	Th.	☌♂☾ • ♃ STAT. • Cranberries in bud now. • Tides {9.6 / 8.8	*winter-*
15	Fr.	Tennis player Andy Murray born, 1987 • {9.2 / 8.8	*weary*
16	Sa.	☌♆☾ • Joan of Arc canonized, 1920 • Tides {9.0 / 8.9	*a*
17	**D**	**Rogation Sunday** • Peter Phillips, son of British Princess Anne, wed Canadian Autumn Kelly, 2008	*thrill.*
18	M.	VICTORIA DAY (CANADA) • ☾ ON EQ. • ☾ AT APO. • {9.0 / 9.4	*Daffodil-icious!*
19	Tu.	St. Dunstan • Dark Day (dark sky due to fires in west, clouds, smoke), New England, 1780	*Gardeners*
20	W.	☌♅☾ • *To him who watches, everything reveals itself.* • Tides {9.2 / 9.9	*brandishing*
21	Th.	**Ascension** • Social worker Jane Addams died, 1935 • Tides {9.2 / 10.1	*hoes*
22	Fr.	NEW ● • ☌☿♀ • Cat Tiffany Two died at age 27 yrs., 2 mos., 9 days, 2015	*and*
23	Sa.	☌♀☾ • New York Public Library established, N.Y.C., 1895 • Tides {10.3 / 9.2	*squishing*
24	**D**	**1st S. af. Asc.** • ☾ AT ☊ • ☌☿☾ • {10.4 / 9.2	*their*
25	M.	St. Bede • MEMORIAL DAY, OBSERVED • ☾ RIDES HIGH • {10.4 / 9.2	*bare*
26	Tu.	For a few days, Galveston, Tex., shores had abnormally blue water due to change in ocean current, 2018	*toes*
27	W.	*Deeds are fruits, words are leaves.* • Tides {10.3 / 9.1	*in the*
28	Th.	**Orthodox Ascension** • Shavuot begins at sundown • Astronomer Frank Drake born, 1930	*dirt:*
29	Fr.	R.I. statehood, 1790 • *Discovery* 1st space shuttle to dock with ISS, 1999 • {10.2 / 9.4	*Loam,*
30	Sa.	Pierre-Joseph-Olivier Chauveau, 1st premier of Quebec after Confederation, born, 1820 • {10.1 / 9.7	*sweet*
31	**D**	**Whit S.** • **Pentecost** • Stratolaunch plane debuted, 2017 • {10.1 / 10.1	*loam!*

Farmer's Calendar

Months since the crickets quit, followed by a hundred nights with no terrestrial ruckus, we lie awake at night listening for that very first peep. Finally, on an evening slightly more balmy than chilly, it begins. Like the dying battery on a smoke alarm, a single chirp. Did we really hear it? Yes! A soprano note peeps again, serious and ponderous. Then it repeats its query, possibly expressing, Am I alone? For one night: It's alone. Then: a zany mayhem, as the evening hours fill with the high-pitch cheeping of peepers. Several years ago, when our land held only a damp gulch, nothing croaked or creaked or peeped. Then an excavator clawed us a small pond, and almost overnight a boisterous amphibian orchestra commenced as dozens of frogs—wood frogs, tree frogs, northern leopard frogs, and spring peepers—announced their new residence. Is there no middle ground with these creatures? All or nothing, silence or cacophony? Case in point: Yesterday's pond was clear; today, it's clouded by thousands of frogs' eggs floating in the shallows. Were we sleeping when the pond's inhabitants released their progeny? This evidence suggests one thing: We'll hear gulpers, croakers, and another bout of temporary soloists come next year's unsilent spring.

JUNE

SKY WATCH: Change prevails, as Venus crosses over to be a morning star in Taurus. Binoculars may help to spot a very low but spectacularly close Moon–Venus conjunction in bright twilight on the 19th. In the first half of June, Mercury is the evening star in Gemini; now in the dimmer half of its orbit, it was easier to see last month. Mars hits an eye-catching 0 magnitude in Aquarius and rises by 2:00 A.M. at midmonth. Saturn, with brilliant Jupiter to its right, rises at midnight and is one-third of the way up the southern sky before dawn. The same calendar vagaries that gave us our extraordinarily early spring now bring an early summer, with the solstice on the 20th at 5:44 P.M. EDT.

○ **FULL MOON** 5th day 3:12 P.M. ● **NEW MOON** 21st day 2:41 A.M.
◐ **LAST QUARTER** 13th day 2:24 A.M. ◑ **FIRST QUARTER** 28th day 4:16 A.M.

All times are given in Eastern Daylight Time.

GET THESE PAGES WITH TIMES SET TO YOUR ZIP CODE AT ALMANAC.COM/ACCESS.

DAY OF YEAR	DAY OF MONTH	DAY OF WEEK	☼ RISES H. M.	RISE KEY	☼ SETS H. M.	SET KEY	LENGTH OF DAY H. M.	SUN FAST M.	SUN DECLINATION ° '	HIGH TIDE TIMES BOSTON		☽ RISES H. M.	RISE KEY	☽ SETS H. M.	SET KEY	☽ ASTRON. PLACE	☽ AGE
153	1	M.	5:10	A	8:15	E	15 05	18	22 N.10	7¾	8¼	3:22	D	2:50	D	VIR	10
154	2	Tu.	5:09	A	8:16	E	15 07	18	22 N.18	8¾	9¼	4:37	E	3:18	C	VIR	11
155	3	W.	5:09	A	8:16	E	15 07	17	22 N.25	9¾	10	5:53	E	3:48	C	LIB	12
156	4	Th.	5:08	A	8:17	E	15 09	17	22 N.32	10¾	11	7:09	E	4:22	B	LIB	13
157	5	Fr.	5:08	A	8:18	E	15 10	17	22 N.38	11½	11¾	8:23	E	5:01	B	SCO	14
158	6	Sa.	5:08	A	8:18	E	15 10	17	22 N.44	12½	—	9:31	E	5:47	B	OPH	15
159	7	D	5:08	A	8:19	E	15 11	17	22 N.50	12½	1¼	10:30	E	6:40	B	SAG	16
160	8	M.	5:07	A	8:20	E	15 13	16	22 N.55	1½	2¼	11:19	E	7:40	B	SAG	17
161	9	Tu.	5:07	A	8:20	E	15 13	16	23 N.00	2¼	3	12:00	E	8:43	B	CAP	18
162	10	W.	5:07	A	8:21	E	15 14	16	23 N.04	3	3¾	—	-	9:48	B	CAP	19
163	11	Th.	5:07	A	8:21	E	15 14	16	23 N.08	4	4¾	12:33	E	10:52	C	AQU	20
164	12	Fr.	5:07	A	8:22	E	15 15	16	23 N.12	4¾	5½	1:01	E	11:54	C	AQU	21
165	13	Sa.	5:07	A	8:22	E	15 15	15	23 N.15	5¾	6½	1:26	D	12:54	D	AQU	22
166	14	D	5:07	A	8:23	E	15 16	15	23 N.18	6¾	7¼	1:48	D	1:53	D	PSC	23
167	15	M.	5:07	A	8:23	E	15 16	15	23 N.20	7½	8	2:10	C	2:53	D	CET	24
168	16	Tu.	5:07	A	8:23	E	15 16	15	23 N.22	8½	8¾	2:33	C	3:53	E	PSC	25
169	17	W.	5:07	A	8:24	E	15 17	15	23 N.24	9¼	9½	2:57	C	4:54	E	ARI	26
170	18	Th.	5:07	A	8:24	E	15 17	14	23 N.25	10¼	10¼	3:24	B	5:57	E	ARI	27
171	19	Fr.	5:07	A	8:24	E	15 17	14	23 N.25	11	11	3:55	B	7:00	E	TAU	28
172	20	Sa.	5:07	A	8:25	E	15 18	14	23 N.26	11¾	11¾	4:33	B	8:03	E	TAU	29
173	21	D	5:08	A	8:25	E	15 17	14	23 N.26	12¼	—	5:18	B	9:02	E	TAU	0
174	22	M.	5:08	A	8:25	E	15 17	14	23 N.25	12½	1	6:12	B	9:56	E	GEM	1
175	23	Tu.	5:08	A	8:25	E	15 17	13	23 N.24	1	1¾	7:14	B	10:42	E	GEM	2
176	24	W.	5:08	A	8:25	E	15 17	13	23 N.23	1¾	2½	8:22	B	11:22	E	CAN	3
177	25	Th.	5:09	A	8:25	E	15 16	13	23 N.21	2¾	3¼	9:33	C	11:56	E	LEO	4
178	26	Fr.	5:09	A	8:25	E	15 16	13	23 N.19	3½	4¼	10:45	C	—	-	LEO	5
179	27	Sa.	5:09	A	8:25	E	15 16	12	23 N.16	4½	5	11:58	D	12:26	D	VIR	6
180	28	D	5:10	A	8:25	E	15 15	12	23 N.13	5¼	6	1:10	D	12:54	D	VIR	7
181	29	M.	5:10	A	8:25	E	15 15	12	23 N.10	6¼	7	2:23	E	1:21	C	VIR	8
182	30	Tu.	5:11	A	8:25	E	15 14	12	23 N.06	7½	7¾	3:37	E	1:49	C	VIR	9

THE SIXTH MONTH · 2020 **JUNE** JUNE HATH 30 DAYS

I love my garden—dearly love
That little spot of ground.
–**Caroline Bowles Southey**

DAY OF MONTH	DAY OF WEEK	DATES, FEASTS, FASTS, ASPECTS, TIDE HEIGHTS, AND WEATHER	
1	M.	Visit. of Mary[T] • ☾ON EQ. • Twin auto inventors Francis and Freelan Stanley born, 1849	*Showers*
2	Tu.	☾AT PERIG. • 65 tornadoes hit parts of Midwest, 1990 • Tides {10.2 11.2	*are*
3	W.	Ember Day • ♀IN INF. ☌ • John Adams 1st U.S. president to live in D.C., 1800	*sprinkling,*
4	Th.	☿GR. ELONG. (24° EAST) • Hockey player Gordie Howe retired at age 52, 1980 • {10.4 11.8	*then*
5	Fr.	St. Boniface • Ember Day • **FULL STRAWBERRY** ○ • **ECLIPSE** ☾	*in*
6	Sa.	Ember Day • D-Day, 1944 • ☾AT ☋ • Tides {10.4 —	*a*
7	**D**	**Trinity** • Orthodox Pentecost • ☾RUNS LOW • Tides {11.8 10.2	*twinkling,*
8	M.	☌♃☾ • ☌♄☾ • ☌♇☾ • Tides {11.5 9.9	*it's*
9	Tu.	1st degree earned via radio given to Clifford Lideen by State University of Iowa, 1925 • {11.1 9.6	*turning*
10	W.	*The whispering grove tells of a storm to come.* • {10.6 9.3	*steamy!*
11	Th.	St. Barnabas • Ben Franklin invented Franklin stove, 1742 • Tides {10.0 9.1	*Prom*
12	Fr.	Ember Day • ☌♂☾ • ☌♆☾ • ☌♂♆ • {9.6 9.0	*is*
13	Sa.	Raccoon completed climb of 20+-story skyscraper, St. Paul, Minn., 2018 • {9.2 8.9	*dreamy,*
14	**D**	**Corpus Christi** • Orthodox All Saints' • **FLAG DAY** • ☾ON EQ. • ☾AT APO.	*perfect*
15	M.	Great Smoky Mountains Nat'l Park (Tenn./N.C.) established, 1934 • Tides {8.7 9.2	*for*
16	Tu.	☌♅☾ • 14" rain, Palmer Lake and Larkspur, Colo., 1965 • Tides {8.6 9.4	*teen*
17	W.	☿STAT. • Battle of Bunker Hill, Charlestown, (Mass.), Am. Revolution, 1775	*romance.*
18	Th.	*At a great bargain, make a pause.* • Tides {8.8 9.9	*Let*
19	Fr.	☌♀☾ • 1st U.S. observance of Father's Day, Spokane, Wash., 1910 • {8.9 10.2	*thunder*
20	Sa.	**SUMMER SOLSTICE** • Lightning strikes sparked hundreds of fires in northern Calif., 2008	*salute*
21	**D**	**FATHER'S DAY** • **NEW** ● • **ECLIPSE** ☉ • ☾RIDES HIGH • ☾AT ☊	*the*
22	M.	St. Alban • ☌☿☾ • Killdeer nest held up prep for RBC Bluesfest, Ottawa, Ont., 2018	*grads'*
23	Tu.	♆STAT. • Sprinter Wilma Rudolph born, 1940 • Tides {10.7 9.4	*big toot*
24	W.	Nativ. John the Baptist • **MIDSUMMER DAY** • ♀STAT. • {10.8 9.5	*while*
25	Th.	*June 25–26:* Snow fell in N.L., 2018 • Tides {10.8 9.6	*the*
26	Fr.	*Follow love, and it will flee; Flee love, and it will follow thee.* • Tides {10.7 9.8	*band*
27	Sa.	Liberty Bell returned from Allentown to Philadelphia, Pa., 1778 • {10.5 10.0	*plays*
28	**D**	**4th S. af. P.** • ☾ON EQ. • ☌♃♇ • {10.2 10.3	*"Pomp and*
29	M.	Sts. Peter & Paul • ☾AT PERIG. • Tides {10.0 10.6	*Circumstance"!*
30	Tu.	☿IN INF. ☌ • Original desert tortoise spring prognosticator Mojave Max died, Nev., 2008	

Farmer's Calendar

How pleasing to see the grass thicken and rise until we realize that—yikes!—it's got to be cut, a task that asks for either loud machines or diligent livestock. I'm partial to a third option: the scythe. This Old World tool looks like a musical notation that leapt out of the score, expanded in size, and, when not in service, abides in our shed beside the retired weed-whacker. I loathed that contraption with its dervish-ing string driven by the sniveling engine. Not to mention the backache that it created, along with its habit of spattering grass across my jeans. Another mowing plan involves allowing the cows and sheep out to feed on our lawn. But as they meander and munch, their work is predictably uneven. Plus they leave behind untouched patches, along with excretions. That's when I reach for my sharpened scythe to dispatch the tall grass. In the morning when everything's still wet with dew, I wield my scythe like a kooky broom, swinging its curved blade from side to side, as if sweeping. The undercut stems become instant fringe. So quiet: I can hear anything sing. For as long as the growing season lasts—wherever grass rises, I'll scythe it.

JULY

SKY WATCH: The two inferior planets occupy the predawn sky, with Venus brightening to a riveting magnitude –4.7 and climbing higher each successive morning. On the 13th, she is close to Aldebaran in Taurus. The Moon joins them on the 17th and hovers to the left of Mercury on the 19th. Mercury is observable in the second half of the month but stays quite low. Jupiter comes into opposition on the 14th, when it rises at sunset and is out all night. Saturn's opposition is on the 20th. The two giant planets, now at their brightest of the year, increase their separation as Jupiter's rightward retrograde motion carries it farther westward in Sagittarius. The Moon hangs beneath them to form a triangle on the 6th.

○ **FULL MOON**	5th day	12:44 A.M.
☽ **LAST QUARTER**	12th day	7:29 P.M.
● **NEW MOON**	20th day	1:33 P.M.
☾ **FIRST QUARTER**	27th day	8:33 A.M.

All times are given in Eastern Daylight Time.

GET THESE PAGES WITH TIMES SET TO YOUR ZIP CODE AT ALMANAC.COM/ACCESS.

DAY OF YEAR	DAY OF MONTH	DAY OF WEEK	☼ RISES H. M.	RISE KEY	☼ SETS H. M.	SET KEY	LENGTH OF DAY H. M.	SUN FAST M.	SUN DECLINATION ° ′	HIGH TIDE TIMES BOSTON		☾ RISES H. M.	RISE KEY	☾ SETS H. M.	SET KEY	☾ ASTRON. PLACE	☾ AGE
183	1	W.	5:11	A	8:25	E	15 14	12	23 N. 02	8½	8¾	4:51	E	2:20	B	LIB	10
184	2	Th.	5:12	A	8:25	E	15 13	12	22 N. 57	9½	9¾	6:04	E	2:56	B	SCO	11
185	3	Fr.	5:12	A	8:24	E	15 12	11	22 N. 52	10½	10½	7:13	E	3:38	B	OPH	12
186	4	Sa.	5:13	A	8:24	E	15 11	11	22 N. 47	11¼	11½	8:16	E	4:27	B	SAG	13
187	5	**D**	5:14	A	8:24	E	15 10	11	22 N. 41	12¼	—	9:10	E	5:24	B	SAG	14
188	6	M.	5:14	A	8:23	E	15 09	11	22 N. 35	12¼	1	9:54	E	6:26	B	SAG	15
189	7	Tu.	5:15	A	8:23	E	15 08	11	22 N. 28	1	1¾	10:31	E	7:31	B	CAP	16
190	8	W.	5:16	A	8:23	E	15 07	11	22 N. 21	2	2½	11:01	E	8:36	C	CAP	17
191	9	Th.	5:16	A	8:22	E	15 06	10	22 N. 14	2¾	3¼	11:28	D	9:40	C	AQU	18
192	10	Fr.	5:17	A	8:22	E	15 05	10	22 N. 06	3½	4	11:51	D	10:41	C	AQU	19
193	11	Sa.	5:18	A	8:21	E	15 03	10	21 N. 58	4¼	4¾	—	-	11:42	D	PSC	20
194	12	**D**	5:19	A	8:21	E	15 02	10	21 N. 49	5	5½	12:13	C	12:41	D	CET	21
195	13	M.	5:19	A	8:20	E	15 01	10	21 N. 40	6	6½	12:36	C	1:40	E	PSC	22
196	14	Tu.	5:20	A	8:20	E	15 00	10	21 N. 31	6¾	7¼	12:59	C	2:41	E	CET	23
197	15	W.	5:21	A	8:19	E	14 58	10	21 N. 21	7¾	8	1:24	B	3:43	E	ARI	24
198	16	Th.	5:22	A	8:18	E	14 56	10	21 N. 11	8¾	8¾	1:53	B	4:46	E	TAU	25
199	17	Fr.	5:23	A	8:17	E	14 54	10	21 N. 01	9½	9¾	2:28	B	5:49	E	TAU	26
200	18	Sa.	5:24	A	8:17	E	14 53	9	20 N. 50	10¼	10½	3:10	B	6:50	E	TAU	27
201	19	**D**	5:25	A	8:16	E	14 51	9	20 N. 39	11	11¼	4:01	B	7:47	E	GEM	28
202	20	M.	5:26	A	8:15	E	14 49	9	20 N. 28	12	—	5:00	B	8:37	E	GEM	0
203	21	Tu.	5:26	A	8:14	E	14 48	9	20 N. 16	12	12¾	6:08	B	9:20	E	CAN	1
204	22	W.	5:27	B	8:13	E	14 46	9	20 N. 04	12¾	1½	7:20	C	9:56	E	LEO	2
205	23	Th.	5:28	B	8:13	E	14 45	9	19 N. 52	1½	2¼	8:34	C	10:28	E	LEO	3
206	24	Fr.	5:29	B	8:12	E	14 43	9	19 N. 39	2¼	3	9:48	D	10:57	D	LEO	4
207	25	Sa.	5:30	B	8:11	E	14 41	9	19 N. 26	3¼	3¾	11:01	D	11:25	C	VIR	5
208	26	**D**	5:31	B	8:10	E	14 39	9	19 N. 12	4¼	4¾	12:14	E	11:53	C	VIR	6
209	27	M.	5:32	B	8:09	E	14 37	9	18 N. 59	5	5½	1:27	E	—	-	VIR	7
210	28	Tu.	5:33	B	8:08	E	14 35	9	18 N. 45	6	6½	2:40	E	12:23	B	LIB	8
211	29	W.	5:34	B	8:07	E	14 33	9	18 N. 30	7¼	7½	3:52	E	12:56	B	LIB	9
212	30	Th.	5:35	B	8:05	E	14 30	9	18 N. 16	8¼	8½	5:02	E	1:35	B	OPH	10
213	31	Fr.	5:36	B	8:04	E	14 28	9	18 N. 01	9¼	9½	6:06	E	2:20	B	SAG	11

To use this page, see p. 116; for Key Letters, see p. 238. LIGHT = A.M. **BOLD = P.M.**   **2020**

THE SEVENTH MONTH • 2020 **JULY** JULY HATH 31 DAYS

The brightest day that ever shown on earth,
The day that Liberty received her birth.
–William Emmons

DAY OF MONTH	DAY OF WEEK	DATES, FEASTS, FASTS, ASPECTS, TIDE HEIGHTS, AND WEATHER	
1	W.	**CANADA DAY** • "O Canada" officially became Canada's national anthem, 1980 • {9.7 11.1	*The*
2	Th.	F3 tornado, Kawacatoose First Nation, Raymore, Sask., 2010 • Tides {9.7 11.3	*Fourth*
3	Fr.	Dog Days begin. • ☾ AT ☋ • Idaho statehood, 1890 • {9.8 11.4	*will feature*
4	Sa.	**INDEPENDENCE DAY** • ☾ RUNS LOW • ⊕ AT APHELION • {9.8 11.4	*some*
5	**D**	**5th. S. af. P.** • FULL BUCK ○ • ECLIPSE ☾ • ☌♃☾ • ☌♇☾	
6	M.	☌♄☾ • 1st human treated with Louis Pasteur's rabies vaccine, 1885 • {11.3 9.7	*fireworks*
7	Tu.	Armadillos mate now. • Tides {11.1 9.6	*from*
8	W.	*No tempest, good July, Lest corn come off blue by* [mildew]. • Tides {10.7 9.5	*Nature.*
9	Th.	After boating accident, 7-yr.-old Roger Woodward survived plunge over Horseshoe (Niagara) Falls, Ont., 1960	
10	Fr.	☌♆☾ • ♀ GR. ILLUM. EXT. • Wyo. statehood, 1890 • {9.9 9.2	*Sunstroke*
11	Sa.	☌♂☾ • Cornscateous air is everywhere. • {9.5 9.1	*is no*
12	**D**	**6th. S. af. P.** • ☾ ON EQ. • ☾ AT APO. • ☿ STAT. • {9.1 9.1	*joke:*
13	M.	Roman statesman Julius Caesar born about now, 100 B.C. • 106°F, Chicago, Ill., 1995	*Protect*
14	Tu.	Bastille Day • ☌⛢☾ • ♃ AT ☍ • Tides {8.5 9.2	*your*
15	W.	St. Swithin • ♇ AT ☍ • St. Frances Xavier Cabrini, 1st U.S. saint, born, 1850	*pate*
16	Th.	Dr. Emily Howard Stowe, 1st woman to practice medicine in Canada, received medical license, 1880	*before*
17	Fr.	☌♀☾ • *The better day, the better deed.* • Tides {8.5 9.9	*it's*
18	Sa.	☾ AT ☊ • ☌☿☾ • Astronomer Eugene Shoemaker died, 1997 • {8.7 10.2	*too*
19	**D**	**7th. S. af. P.** • ☾ RIDES HIGH • 26th Summer Olympics began, Atlanta, Ga., 1996	*late!*
20	M.	NEW ● • ♄ AT ☍ • 18.18" rain, Edgerton, Mo., 1965 • {9.2 10.9	*Thunder*
21	Tu.	Pathologist George Frederick Dick born, 1881 • Tides {9.5 —	*mutters*
22	W.	St. Mary Magdalene • ☿ GR. ELONG. (20° WEST) • Tides {11.1 9.8	*while*
23	Th.	Black-eyed Susans in bloom now. • Tides {11.2 10.1	*rain*
24	Fr.	*July:* Hottest avg. monthly temp. in world, 108.1°F, Death Valley, Calif., 2018 • {11.2 10.3	*rattles*
25	Sa.	St. James • ☾ ON EQ. • ☾ AT PERIG. • Tides {11.0 10.5	*gutters.*
26	**D**	**8th. S. af. P.** • Benjamin Franklin became 1st U.S. postmaster general, 1775	*Blazing!*
27	M.	Adult gypsy moths emerge. • Marathon runner Gérard Côté born, 1913 • {10.2 10.7	*Jupiter*
28	Tu.	Ornithologist Roger Tory Peterson died, 1996 • Tides {9.8 10.7	*is*
29	W.	St. Martha • 184-pound wahoo caught, Cabo San Lucas, Mex., 2005 • {9.5 10.7	*up—*
30	Th.	Astronomer Galileo Galilei 1st to observe what we now know are Saturn's rings, 1610 • {9.3 10.8	*and*
31	Fr.	St. Ignatius of Loyola • ☾ AT ☋ • *Toasted cheese hath no master.* • {9.3 10.8	*amazing!*

Farmer's Calendar

A nearby farmer swears she hears field corn growing on muggy nights—says it sounds like a drawn-out squeak. In the decade I've lived beside 80 acres of it, I've never heard its rising stalks sing. Nor, during all those years, did I grow my own corn, for fear of wind-borne cross-pollination. Recently, the big field changed hands. Now it grows other plants. So we sowed our own kernels in hope of reaping a choir's worth. While working on other farms, I'd harvested the ripe corn in the morning. Shuffling into its narrow forest, I towed a flimsy sack that fattened as I snapped off ears with the thickest girths. The dewy leaves scratched like a cat's tongue, and by the time I emerged on the field's far side dragging a bulging bag, I was scoured and damp and bearing enough corn for an orchestra. But this year I emerged from our stalks with hardly enough for our two-part harmony. I'd underguessed its ripeness until I spotted one shucked cob dropped on the lawn. Every kernel was gouged. Inspecting the rest of the patch, I noticed that the plants were nearly earless. Robbed, all I could do was feast my eyes and imagine a moonlit raccoon's chomping.

AUGUST

SKY WATCH: Jupiter and Saturn are optimally visible all night long, standing one-third of the way up the southern sky at midnight. The Moon dangles just below Jupiter on the 1st, with Saturn to the left. Mars, now very bright in Pisces, rises at 11:00 P.M. On the 11th, the Perseid meteors are best seen before midnight (exceptionally early)—before the Moon rises to create unwanted brightness. Meanwhile, just before dawn, Venus in Gemini remains extremely bright and not too low, with Mercury much lower but at a very bright and easy magnitude –1 in the month's first week. Below Venus on the 15th, the Moon stands close to Jupiter on the 28th—a worthy conjunction—before hanging below Saturn on the 29th.

○ **FULL MOON**	3rd day	11:59 A.M.
☽ **LAST QUARTER**	11th day	12:45 P.M.
● **NEW MOON**	18th day	10:42 P.M.
☽ **FIRST QUARTER**	25th day	1:58 P.M.

All times are given in Eastern Daylight Time.

GET THESE PAGES WITH TIMES SET TO YOUR ZIP CODE AT ALMANAC.COM/ACCESS.

DAY OF YEAR	DAY OF MONTH	DAY OF WEEK	☼ RISES H. M.	RISE KEY	☼ SETS H. M.	SET KEY	LENGTH OF DAY H. M.	SUN FAST M.	SUN DECLINATION ° '	HIGH TIDE TIMES BOSTON		☾ RISES H. M.	RISE KEY	☾ SETS H. M.	SET KEY	☾ ASTRON. PLACE	☾ AGE
214	1	Sa.	5:37	B	8:03	E	14 26	10	17 N. 46	10¼	10½	7:02	E	3:13	B	SAG	12
215	2	**D**	5:38	B	8:02	E	14 24	10	17 N. 30	11¼	11¼	7:49	E	4:12	B	SAG	13
216	3	M.	5:39	B	8:01	E	14 22	10	17 N. 14	12	—	8:28	E	5:16	B	CAP	14
217	4	Tu.	5:40	B	7:59	E	14 19	10	16 N. 58	12	12¾	9:01	E	6:21	B	CAP	15
218	5	W.	5:41	B	7:58	E	14 17	10	16 N. 42	12¾	1½	9:29	D	7:26	C	AQU	16
219	6	Th.	5:42	B	7:57	E	14 15	10	16 N. 25	1½	2	9:53	D	8:29	C	AQU	17
220	7	Fr.	5:43	B	7:56	E	14 13	10	16 N. 08	2¼	2¾	10:16	D	9:30	D	AQU	18
221	8	Sa.	5:44	B	7:54	E	14 10	10	15 N. 51	3	3½	10:38	C	10:30	D	CET	19
222	9	**D**	5:45	B	7:53	E	14 08	10	15 N. 34	3¾	4	11:01	C	11:29	E	PSC	20
223	10	M.	5:47	B	7:52	E	14 05	11	15 N. 16	4½	4¾	11:25	B	12:29	E	CET	21
224	11	Tu.	5:48	B	7:50	E	14 02	11	14 N. 58	5¼	5½	11:52	B	1:29	E	ARI	22
225	12	W.	5:49	B	7:49	D	14 00	11	14 N. 40	6¼	6½	—	–	2:31	E	TAU	23
226	13	Th.	5:50	B	7:47	D	13 57	11	14 N. 22	7	7¼	12:24	B	3:34	E	TAU	24
227	14	Fr.	5:51	B	7:46	D	13 55	11	14 N. 03	8	8¼	1:02	B	4:35	E	TAU	25
228	15	Sa.	5:52	B	7:44	D	13 52	11	13 N. 44	9	9	1:48	B	5:33	E	GEM	26
229	16	**D**	5:53	B	7:43	D	13 50	12	13 N. 25	9¾	10	2:43	B	6:26	E	GEM	27
230	17	M.	5:54	B	7:42	D	13 48	12	13 N. 06	10½	10¾	3:48	B	7:13	E	CAN	28
231	18	Tu.	5:55	B	7:40	D	13 45	12	12 N. 47	11½	11½	4:59	B	7:53	E	CAN	0
232	19	W.	5:56	B	7:38	D	13 42	12	12 N. 27	12¼	—	6:14	C	8:27	E	LEO	1
233	20	Th.	5:57	B	7:37	D	13 40	13	12 N. 07	12½	1	7:30	C	8:58	D	LEO	2
234	21	Fr.	5:58	B	7:35	D	13 37	13	11 N. 47	1¼	1¾	8:46	D	9:27	C	VIR	3
235	22	Sa.	5:59	B	7:34	D	13 35	13	11 N. 27	2	2½	10:01	D	9:55	C	VIR	4
236	23	**D**	6:00	B	7:32	D	13 32	13	11 N. 06	3	3½	11:16	E	10:24	C	VIR	5
237	24	M.	6:01	B	7:31	D	13 30	14	10 N. 46	3¾	4¼	12:31	E	10:57	B	LIB	6
238	25	Tu.	6:02	B	7:29	D	13 27	14	10 N. 25	4¾	5¼	1:44	E	11:34	B	LIB	7
239	26	W.	6:04	B	7:27	D	13 23	14	10 N. 04	5¾	6¼	2:55	E	—	–	OPH	8
240	27	Th.	6:05	B	7:26	D	13 21	15	9 N. 43	7	7¼	4:00	E	12:17	B	OPH	9
241	28	Fr.	6:06	B	7:24	D	13 18	15	9 N. 22	8	8¼	4:58	E	1:07	B	SAG	10
242	29	Sa.	6:07	B	7:22	D	13 15	15	9 N. 00	9	9¼	5:47	E	2:04	B	SAG	11
243	30	**D**	6:08	B	7:21	D	13 13	15	8 N. 39	10	10¼	6:28	B	3:06	B	CAP	12
244	31	M.	6:09	B	7:19	D	13 10	16	8 N. 17	11	11	7:02	E	4:10	B	CAP	13

AUGUST

Hence, let me haste into the mid wood shade,
Where scarce a sunbeam wanders through the gloom.
–James Thompson

DAY OF MONTH	DAY OF WEEK	DATES, FEASTS, FASTS, ASPECTS, TIDE HEIGHTS, AND WEATHER	
1	Sa.	Lammas Day • ☾ runs low • ☌♃☾ • Tides {9.3 / 10.9	*Warm*
2	D	9th. S. af. P. • ☌♄☾ • ☌♇☾ • Tides {9.4 / 10.9	*and*
3	M.	Civic Holiday (Canada) • Full Sturgeon ○ • {9.5 / —	*motherly,*
4	Tu.	*Every couple is not a pair.* • Tides {10.8 / 9.6	*lightning*
5	W.	Royal Canadian Navy (through B.C. premier) acquired 1st subs, 1914 • Tides {10.7 / 9.6	*southerly.*
6	Th.	Transfiguration • ☌♆☾ • Damaging hailstorm, Colorado Springs, Col., 2018	*Hot*
7	Fr.	Gray squirrels have second litters now. • {10.2 / 9.5	*stuff!*
8	Sa.	St. Dominic • ☾ on Eq. • Florence Chadwick swam English Channel, 13 hrs. 20 mins., 1950	*Moon's*
9	D	10th. S. af. P. • ☾ at apo. • ☌♂☾ • Tides {9.4 / 9.3	*too*
10	M.	St. Lawrence • ☌♅☾ • Canadian Bill of Rights enacted, 1960 • {9.0 / 9.2	*bright*
11	Tu.	St. Clare • Dog Days end. • Conservationist Gifford Pinchot born, 1865 • {8.6 / 9.1	*for*
12	W.	♀ Gr. Elong. (46° West) • Fossil hunter Susan Hendrickson found T-rex bones near Faith, S.Dak., 1990	*a*
13	Th.	*The day has eyes; the night has ears.* • Tides {8.2 / 9.2	*Perseids*
14	Fr.	☾ at ☊ • Ragweed in bloom. • Tides {8.2 / 9.5	*sight.*
15	Sa.	Assumption • ☾ rides high • ☌♀☾ • ♅ stat. • {8.4 / 9.8	*Cool*
16	D	11th. S. af. P. • *August:* Furry "sea monster" remains discovered, Kamchatka Peninsula, 2018	*and*
17	M.	Cat Nights commence. • ☿ in sup. ☌ • {9.1 / 10.8	*mist-kissed.*
18	Tu.	New ● • ☌☿☾ • 19th Amendment ratified, 1920 • Tides {9.6 / 11.2	*Nights*
19	W.	First of Muharram begins at sundown • Scientist Axel Cronstedt died, 1765 • {10.1 / —	*full*
20	Th.	*When woodpeckers are much heard, rain will follow.* • Tides {11.5 / 10.6	*of*
21	Fr.	☾ on Eq. • ☾ at perig. • Deadly tornado struck Goderich, Ont., 2011 • {11.6 / 10.9	*boomers,*
22	Sa.	Writer Ray Bradbury born, 1920 • Tides {11.5 / 11.1	*an*
23	D	12th. S. af. P. • Storm formed that later became Hurricane Katrina, 2005	*occasional*
24	M.	St. Bartholomew • GPS off by up to 3' for 3 hrs. due to rocket-made ionospheric hole, 2017	*squall—*
25	Tu.	*Voyager-2*'s closest approach to Neptune, 1989 • Tides {10.1 / 10.8	*trees*
26	W.	Saint (Mother) Teresa of Calcutta born, 1910 • {9.6 / 10.6	*whisper*
27	Th.	☾ at ☋ • Hummingbirds migrate south. • {9.2 / 10.4	*rumors*
28	Fr.	St. Augustine of Hippo • ☾ runs low • ☌♃☾ • {9.0 / 10.3	*of*
29	Sa.	St. John the Baptist • ☌♄☾ • ☌♇☾ • {9.0 / 10.3	*frosts*
30	D	13th. S. af. P. • Tennis player Greg Rusedski served ball at 141 mph, U.S. Open, N.Y.C., 1997	*and*
31	M.	Nat'l Agricultural Center and Hall of Fame chartered, Bonner Springs, Kans., 1960 • {9.3 / 10.4	*fall.*

Farmer's Calendar

Most of what we grew, the summer I first worked as part of a crew of farming apprentices, was annuals: carrots, lettuce, peas, watermelons—plants whose entire life span transpires within a single season. We sowed and reaped the "one-time offer" as opposed to a "lifetime guarantee." But eventually we began to harvest something that we had not planted—garlic, whose cloves are all clones of the mother bulb. The previous year's apprentices had left us this gift; they'd pressed those individual cloves into the soil, cloves that endured through winter, sprouted in spring, and developed into whole new garlic heads. We grabbed onto each stalk and yanked up this crop, as if taking up a baton left by the previous crew, a baton that was now ours to carry into the barn to let cure throughout the waning summer days. Before we left the farm to begin our winter jobs, we tucked hundreds of garlic cloves in the ground—something for yet another set of hands to recover. It's been 20 growing seasons since I pawed that farm's soil. Yet each summer I draw on the one-time memory while harvesting my garlic. For days afterward, my hands remain un-scrubbably pungent.

SEPTEMBER

SKY WATCH: Wonders abound: Jupiter finishes retrograding and resumes direct motion toward Saturn; the pair hover due south at 8:30 P.M. and are joined by the Moon on the 24th and 25th. Keep your eye on this duo as their gap narrows in preparation for their amazing and historic "Great Conjunction" in 3 months. Mars brightens spectacularly to magnitude –2, equaling Jupiter; in Pisces, the Red Planet rises at 9:00 P.M. on September 1 and near 7:00 P.M. by month's end. It is closely joined by the Moon on the 5th. In the predawn eastern sky, Venus still looks wonderfully striking, especially when she meets the crescent Moon on the 14th. Mercury becomes an evening star but remains very low. Autumn arrives with the equinox on the 22nd at 9:31 A.M. EDT.

○ **FULL MOON**	2nd day 1:22 A.M.	● **NEW MOON**	17th day 7:00 A.M.
◑ **LAST QUARTER**	10th day 5:26 A.M.	◐ **FIRST QUARTER**	23rd day 9:55 P.M.

All times are given in Eastern Daylight Time.

GET THESE PAGES WITH TIMES SET TO YOUR ZIP CODE AT ALMANAC.COM/ACCESS.

DAY OF YEAR	DAY OF MONTH	DAY OF WEEK	☀ RISES H. M.	RISE KEY	☀ SETS H. M.	SET KEY	LENGTH OF DAY H. M.	SUN FAST M.	SUN DECLINATION ° '	HIGH TIDE TIMES BOSTON		☾ RISES H. M.	RISE KEY	☾ SETS H. M.	SET KEY	☾ ASTRON. PLACE	☾ AGE
245	1	Tu.	6:10	B	7:17	D	13 07	16	7 N. 55	11½	11¾	7:31	E	5:14	C	AQU	14
246	2	W.	6:11	B	7:16	D	13 05	16	7 N. 33	12¼	—	7:56	D	6:18	C	AQU	15
247	3	Th.	6:12	C	7:14	D	13 02	17	7 N. 11	12½	1	8:19	D	7:19	D	AQU	16
248	4	Fr.	6:13	C	7:12	D	12 59	17	6 N. 49	1¼	1½	8:41	C	8:20	D	CET	17
249	5	Sa.	6:14	C	7:10	D	12 56	17	6 N. 27	1¾	2	9:03	C	9:19	D	CET	18
250	6	D	6:15	C	7:09	D	12 54	18	6 N. 04	2½	2¾	9:27	B	10:19	E	PSC	19
251	7	M.	6:16	C	7:07	D	12 51	18	5 N. 42	3¼	3½	9:52	B	11:19	E	ARI	20
252	8	Tu.	6:17	C	7:05	D	12 48	18	5 N. 19	3¾	4	10:21	B	12:20	E	ARI	21
253	9	W.	6:18	C	7:04	D	12 46	19	4 N. 57	4¾	5	10:56	B	1:21	E	TAU	22
254	10	Th.	6:19	C	7:02	D	12 43	19	4 N. 34	5½	5¾	11:37	B	2:22	E	TAU	23
255	11	Fr.	6:20	C	7:00	D	12 40	19	4 N. 11	6½	6¾	—	-	3:21	E	TAU	24
256	12	Sa.	6:21	C	6:58	D	12 37	20	3 N. 48	7¼	7½	12:28	B	4:15	E	GEM	25
257	13	D	6:22	C	6:56	D	12 34	20	3 N. 25	8¼	8½	1:27	B	5:04	E	GEM	26
258	14	M.	6:24	C	6:55	C	12 31	20	3 N. 02	9¼	9½	2:34	B	5:46	E	CAN	27
259	15	Tu.	6:25	C	6:53	C	12 28	21	2 N. 39	10	10¼	3:47	C	6:22	E	LEO	28
260	16	W.	6:26	C	6:51	C	12 25	21	2 N. 16	11	11¼	5:04	C	6:55	D	LEO	29
261	17	Th.	6:27	C	6:49	C	12 22	22	1 N. 53	11¾	—	6:21	D	7:25	D	VIR	0
262	18	Fr.	6:28	C	6:48	C	12 20	22	1 N. 29	12	12½	7:39	D	7:54	C	VIR	1
263	19	Sa.	6:29	C	6:46	C	12 17	22	1 N. 06	12¾	1¼	8:57	E	8:23	C	VIR	2
264	20	D	6:30	C	6:44	C	12 14	23	0 N. 43	1¾	2	10:15	E	8:55	B	LIB	3
265	21	M.	6:31	C	6:42	C	12 11	23	0 N. 19	2½	3	11:31	E	9:32	B	LIB	4
266	22	Tu.	6:32	C	6:41	C	12 09	23	0 S. 03	3½	3¾	12:45	E	10:14	B	SCO	5
267	23	W.	6:33	C	6:39	C	12 06	24	0 S. 26	4½	4¾	1:54	E	11:03	B	OPH	6
268	24	Th.	6:34	C	6:37	C	12 03	24	0 S. 50	5½	5¾	2:55	E	11:58	B	SAG	7
269	25	Fr.	6:35	C	6:35	C	12 00	24	1 S. 13	6¾	7	3:47	E	—	-	SAG	8
270	26	Sa.	6:36	C	6:34	C	11 58	25	1 S. 36	7¾	8	4:30	E	12:59	B	CAP	9
271	27	D	6:37	C	6:32	C	11 55	25	2 S. 00	8¾	9	5:05	E	2:02	B	CAP	10
272	28	M.	6:38	C	6:30	C	11 52	25	2 S. 23	9¾	10	5:35	E	3:06	C	CAP	11
273	29	Tu.	6:40	C	6:28	C	11 48	26	2 S. 46	10½	10¾	6:01	D	4:09	C	AQU	12
274	30	W.	6:41	C	6:27	C	11 46	26	3 S. 10	11¼	11½	6:24	D	5:11	C	AQU	13

To use this page, see p. 116; for Key Letters, see p. 238. LIGHT = A.M. BOLD = P.M.   2020

But sweet and joyful sound the rural talk,
And merry laugh, amidst the happy crowd.
–Thomas Francis, of harvest day

DAY OF MONTH	DAY OF WEEK	DATES, FEASTS, FASTS, ASPECTS, TIDE HEIGHTS, AND WEATHER	
1	Tu.	Alta. and Sask. became Canadian provinces, 1905 • {9.5 10.4	*At*
2	W.	FULL CORN ○ • ☌♆☾ • 1st ATM in U.S. debuted, Rockville Centre, N.Y., 1969 • {9.6 —	*the*
3	Th.	1.67-lb. hailstone measuring 17.5" in circumference found, Coffeyville, Kans., 1970 • {10.3 9.7	*bus*
4	Fr.	☾ ON EQ. • 50-years-overdue library book returned to Lexington, Ky., public library, 2018 • {10.2 9.7	*stop,*
5	Sa.	*A round-topped cloud, with flattened base, Carries rainfall in its face.* • Tides {9.9 9.7	*kids*
6	**D**	**14th. S. af. P.** • ☾ AT APO. • ☌♂☾ • ☌♅☾ • {9.6 9.6	*hop*
7	M.	LABOR DAY • Painter Grandma Moses born, 1860 • Tides {9.3 9.5	*to*
8	Tu.	Deadliest U.S. hurricane, w/15' storm surge, killed est. 8,000, Galveston, Tex., 1900 • {8.9 9.3	*stay*
9	W.	♂ STAT. • Calif. statehood, 1850 • Businessman Harland Sanders born, 1890	*warm.*
10	Th.	☾ AT ☊ • Cranberry bog harvest begins, Cape Cod, Mass. • Tides {8.3 9.2	*It's*
11	Fr.	PATRIOT DAY • ♆ AT ☍ • ICE spacecraft met its 1st comet (Giacobini-Zinner), 1985	*wet*
12	Sa.	☾ RIDES HIGH • ♃ STAT. • Basketball player Yao Ming born, 1980 • Tides {8.2 9.5	*out*
13	**D**	**15th. S. af. P.** • "Little Bear" children's writer Else H. Minarik born, 1920 • {8.5 9.9	*as*
14	M.	Holy Cross • ☌♀☾ • Crayola announced crayon name "Bluetiful," 2017 • {9.0 10.4	*all*
15	Tu.	Landscape architect André Le Nôtre died, 1700 • Writer Agatha Christie born, 1890	*get-out!*
16	W.	Ember Day • *Good words cost nothing, but are worth much.* • Tides {10.2 11.4	*Up*
17	Th.	NEW ● • Bottle message from April Caribbean cruise found in Sunset Beach, N.C., 2018	*north,*
18	Fr.	Ember Day • Rosh Hashanah begins at sundown • ☾ ON EQ. • ☾ AT PERIG. • ☌☿☾	*there's*
19	Sa.	Ember Day • 7.1 earthquake, Ayutla, Puebla, Mex., 2017 • Tides {11.7 11.7	*glory*
20	**D**	**16th. S. af. P.** • Adirondack tornado traveled 275 miles across N.Y., 1845	*in the*
21	M.	St. Matthew • Hurricane Igor struck N.L., 2010 • Tides {11.1 11.6	*notches;*
22	Tu.	Harvest Home • AUTUMNAL EQUINOX • Baseball player Yogi Berra died, 2015	*everyone*
23	W.	☾ AT ☋ • Capt. John Paul Jones: "I have not yet begun to fight!," Am. Rev., 1779	*watches*
24	Th.	☾ RUNS LOW • USS *Enterprise*, 1st U.S. nuclear aircraft carrier, launched, Newport News, Va., 1960	*the*
25	Fr.	☌♃☾ • ☌♄☾ • ☌♇☾ • Tides {9.1 10.1	*leaf*
26	Sa.	Frontiersman Daniel Boone died, 1820 • Sir Louis-Olivier Taillon, 8th premier of Quebec, born, 1840	*revue,*
27	**D**	**17th. S. af. P.** • Yom Kippur begins at sundown • Tides {9.0 9.9	*ever*
28	M.	♄ STAT. • 15th prime minister of Canada Pierre Trudeau died, 2000 • {9.2 10.0	*familiar,*
29	Tu.	St. Michael • ☌♆☾ • *One hour today is worth two tomorrow.* • {9.4 10.0	*ever*
30	W.	St. Gregory the Illuminator • Woodchucks hibernate now. • Tides {9.6 10.0	*new.*

Farmer's Calendar

A reclusive neighbor sometimes asks me to tend his pair of elderly cashmere goats. Then twice a day I'll bike his class 4 road, a single dirt track that runs through hayfields and birch groves, past boulders and ferns, and terminates in front of his remote goat barn. Far more private and wild than our roadside pastures and garden, these fields are where I'll sometimes startle a doe that goes bounding into the bushes or hear a hermit thrush utter its haunting trill. Once, hurrying along before a thunderstorm, I passed a paw print in the mud of a low spot in the road. As I stopped and knelt beside it, I noted four toe pads. Not a coyote print, nor fox. Not in the dog family at all. No claw marks like a bear would leave, but it was big: I held my left hand out beside it, fingers spread wide—yes, as big. The Department of Fish and Wildlife insists that our state's catamounts are extinct. Still, locals swear by their sightings, "I'm telling ya, that weren't no bobcat." Regardless, doubt prevails. So the next day I dragged my husband right over to the print to prove it, but the creature's secret remains—by then, the big cat's evidence lay under a pool of rain.

OCTOBER

SKY WATCH: Mars reaches opposition on the 13th, following an unusually close approach on the 6th. (It won't come closer to Earth until 2035!) This brings Mars to an atypically brilliant magnitude –2.6, outshining even Jupiter this month; look for the Red Planet to closely meet the full Moon on the 2nd. Meanwhile, Jupiter and Saturn, pulling nearer together, are due south at nightfall in Sagittarius. Before dawn on the 13th and 14th, Venus meets the crescent Moon in Leo. Uranus comes into opposition on Halloween, an easy green binocular target in eastern Pisces, far to the left of Mars. At magnitude 5.7, it can be faintly glimpsed with the naked eye in rural locations.

○ **FULL MOON** 1st day 5:05 P.M. ☽ **FIRST QUARTER** 23rd day 9:23 A.M.
☾ **LAST QUARTER** 9th day 8:40 P.M. ○ **FULL MOON** 31st day 10:49 A.M.
● **NEW MOON** 16th day 3:31 P.M.

All times are given in Eastern Daylight Time.

GET THESE PAGES WITH TIMES SET TO YOUR ZIP CODE AT ALMANAC.COM/ACCESS.

DAY OF YEAR	DAY OF MONTH	DAY OF WEEK	☀ RISES H. M.	RISE KEY	☀ SETS H. M.	SET KEY	LENGTH OF DAY H. M.	SUN FAST M.	SUN DECLINATION ° ′	HIGH TIDE TIMES BOSTON		☾ RISES H. M.	RISE KEY	☾ SETS H. M.	SET KEY	☾ ASTRON. PLACE	☾ AGE
275	1	Th.	6:42	C	6:25	C	11 43	26	3 s. 33	11¾	—	6:46	D	6:12	D	PSC	14
276	2	Fr.	6:43	C	6:23	C	11 40	27	3 s. 56	12	12½	7:08	C	7:11	D	CET	15
277	3	Sa.	6:44	C	6:21	C	11 37	27	4 s. 19	12¾	1	7:30	C	8:11	E	PSC	16
278	4	**D**	6:45	D	6:20	C	11 35	27	4 s. 42	1¼	1½	7:55	B	9:11	E	CET	17
279	5	M.	6:46	D	6:18	C	11 32	28	5 s. 05	2	2¼	8:22	B	10:12	E	ARI	18
280	6	Tu.	6:47	D	6:16	C	11 29	28	5 s. 28	2¾	2¾	8:54	B	11:13	E	TAU	19
281	7	W.	6:48	D	6:15	C	11 27	28	5 s. 51	3¼	3½	9:32	B	12:14	E	TAU	20
282	8	Th.	6:50	D	6:13	C	11 23	28	6 s. 14	4	4¼	10:18	B	1:12	E	TAU	21
283	9	Fr.	6:51	D	6:11	C	11 20	29	6 s. 37	5	5	11:12	B	2:07	E	GEM	22
284	10	Sa.	6:52	D	6:10	C	11 18	29	7 s. 00	5¾	6	—	-	2:57	E	GEM	23
285	11	**D**	6:53	D	6:08	C	11 15	29	7 s. 22	6¾	7	12:14	B	3:40	E	CAN	24
286	12	M.	6:54	D	6:06	C	11 12	29	7 s. 45	7¾	8	1:23	B	4:18	E	CAN	25
287	13	Tu.	6:55	D	6:05	B	11 10	30	8 s. 07	8¾	9	2:36	C	4:51	E	LEO	26
288	14	W.	6:56	D	6:03	B	11 07	30	8 s. 29	9½	10	3:52	C	5:21	D	LEO	27
289	15	Th.	6:58	D	6:01	B	11 03	30	8 s. 51	10½	10¾	5:09	D	5:50	D	VIR	28
290	16	Fr.	6:59	D	6:00	B	11 01	30	9 s. 13	11¼	11¾	6:28	E	6:19	C	VIR	0
291	17	Sa.	7:00	D	5:58	B	10 58	31	9 s. 35	12	—	7:47	E	6:50	C	VIR	1
292	18	**D**	7:01	D	5:57	B	10 56	31	9 s. 57	12½	12¾	9:07	E	7:25	B	LIB	2
293	19	M.	7:02	D	5:55	B	10 53	31	10 s. 19	1½	1¾	10:26	E	8:06	B	LIB	3
294	20	Tu.	7:03	D	5:54	B	10 51	31	10 s. 40	2¼	2½	11:40	E	8:53	B	OPH	4
295	21	W.	7:05	D	5:52	B	10 47	31	11 s. 01	3¼	3½	12:47	E	9:48	B	SAG	5
296	22	Th.	7:06	D	5:51	B	10 45	31	11 s. 23	4¼	4½	1:44	E	10:49	B	SAG	6
297	23	Fr.	7:07	D	5:49	B	10 42	32	11 s. 43	5¼	5½	2:30	E	11:53	B	SAG	7
298	24	Sa.	7:08	D	5:48	B	10 40	32	12 s. 04	6¼	6½	3:08	E	—	-	CAP	8
299	25	**D**	7:09	D	5:46	B	10 37	32	12 s. 25	7½	7¾	3:40	E	12:58	B	CAP	9
300	26	M.	7:11	D	5:45	B	10 34	32	12 s. 45	8½	8¾	4:06	E	2:02	C	AQU	10
301	27	Tu.	7:12	D	5:43	B	10 31	32	13 s. 05	9¼	9½	4:30	D	3:04	C	AQU	11
302	28	W.	7:13	D	5:42	B	10 29	32	13 s. 25	10	10¼	4:52	D	4:05	D	PSC	12
303	29	Th.	7:14	D	5:41	B	10 27	32	13 s. 45	10¾	11	5:13	C	5:04	D	CET	13
304	30	Fr.	7:16	D	5:39	B	10 23	32	14 s. 05	11¼	11¾	5:35	C	6:04	E	PSC	14
305	31	Sa.	7:17	D	5:38	B	10 21	32	14 s. 24	11¾	—	5:59	B	7:04	E	CET	15

OCTOBER

OCTOBER HATH 31 DAYS

Ruffling the colors of the forest leaves,
The winds make music as they come and go.
–John Critchley Prince

DAY OF MONTH	DAY OF WEEK	DATES, FEASTS, FASTS, ASPECTS, TIDE HEIGHTS, AND WEATHER	
1	Th.	FULL HARVEST ○ • ☾ ON EQ. • ☿ GR. ELONG. (26° EAST) • {9.8 / —	*Cool*
2	Fr.	Sukkoth begins at sundown • ☌♂☾ • Thurgood Marshall sworn in as U.S. Supreme Court justice, 1967	*as*
3	Sa.	☾ AT APO. • Watch for banded woolly bear caterpillars now. • Tides {9.9 / 10.0	*a cuke—*
4	**D**	18th. S. af. P. • ☌♅☾ • ♇ STAT. • Tides {9.7 / 9.9	*that*
5	M.	Laurie Skreslet 1st Canadian to summit Mt. Everest, 1982 • *A red Sun has water in its eye.* • {9.4 / 9.8	*shower's*
6	Tu.	♂ AT CLOSEST APPROACH • Opera singer Jenny Lind born, 1820 • {9.1 / 9.7	*no*
7	W.	☾ AT ☊ • Lynette Woodard 1st woman to play with Harlem Globetrotters, 1985 • {8.8 / 9.5	*fluke:*
8	Th.	Writer Frank P. Herbert born, 1920 • Tides {8.5 / 9.4	*We're*
9	Fr.	☾ RIDES HIGH • Deadly fire leveled Baudette and Spooner, Minn., 1910 • Tides {8.3 / 9.3	*in*
10	Sa.	U.S. Naval Academy founded, Annapolis, Md., 1845 • {8.3 / 9.3	*for*
11	**D**	19th. S. af. P. • Little brown bats hibernate now. • Tides {8.4 / 9.6	*some*
12	M.	COLUMBUS DAY, OBSERVED • INDIGENOUS PEOPLES' DAY • THANKSGIVING DAY (CANADA)	*weather!*
13	Tu.	☌♀☾ • ♂ AT ☍ • Manufacturer Milton Hershey died, 1945 • {9.4 / 10.4	*Sunshine*
14	W.	☿ STAT. • Video tweet posted of miniature horse seen in back seat of neighboring car, Iowa, 2017	*flickers*
15	Th.	☾ ON EQ. • *Set not your loaf in till the oven's hot.* • Tides {10.9 / 11.3	*through*
16	Fr.	NEW ● • ☾ AT PERIG. • Engineer Wallace Rupert Turnbull born, 1870	*orchard*
17	Sa.	St. Ignatius of Antioch • ☌☿☾ • Canadian heroine (War of 1812) Laura Secord died, 1868	*rows*
18	**D**	20th. S. af. P. • 47" snow, Gouverneur, N.Y., 1930 • {11.5 / 12.2	*while*
19	M.	St. Luke[T] • St. Luke's little summer. • Writer Jonathan Swift died, 1745 • {11.3 / 12.1	*busy*
20	Tu.	☾ AT ☋ • Architect Sir Christopher Wren born, 1632 • Tides {10.8 / 11.8	*pickers*
21	W.	☾ RUNS LOW • Native American Kateri Tekakwitha canonized, 2012 • {10.3 / 11.3	*don*
22	Th.	☌♃☾ • ☌♄☾ • ☌♇☾ • Cellist Pablo Casals died, 1973 • {9.7 / 10.7	*their*
23	Fr.	St. James of Jerusalem • 25,000 women marched for suffrage, N.Y.C., 1915 • {9.3 / 10.1	*slickers*
24	Sa.	Painter Franklin Carmichael died, 1945 • Tides {9.0 / 9.7	*and*
25	**D**	21st. S. af. P. • ☿ IN INF. ☌ • Tides {8.9 / 9.5	*fill*
26	M.	Timber rattlesnakes move to winter dens. • {9.0 / 9.5	*their*
27	Tu.	☌♆☾ • Harvard expedition observed solar eclipse in British-occupied Penobscot Bay, Maine, 1780	*buckets*
28	W.	Sts. Simon & Jude • 3rd most powerful solar flare ever recorded, 2003 • Tides {9.5 / 9.6	*with*
29	Th.	☾ ON EQ. • ☌♂☾ • Man paddled 1,364-lb. pumpkin down River Ouse, Yorkshire, England, 2018	*bounty*
30	Fr.	☾ AT APO. • *If you wish to live and thrive, Let a spider run alive.* • {9.9 / 9.6	*that glows.*
31	Sa.	All Hallows' Eve • Reformation Day • FULL HUNTER'S ○ • ☌♅☾ • ♅ AT ☍	

Farmer's Calendar

"The Pumpking" is what his parents called this enterprising guy, their son, because he arrives on their lawn at dawn and dismounts his ATV to inspect his 6,000 loyal subjects: pumpkins, arranged in tidy rows, like a royal court, a crowd of orange faces. Consider that Ben, in his mid-30s, can say that he's been sovereign, the reigning monarch of squash in his quadrant of northeastern Vermont, for more than a quarter-century, growing his business since the ripe old age of 6. Now he lives adjacent to his parents and grows 20 pumpkinds, ranging from the diminutive fists of 'Jack Be Little' to the chunky orbs of 'Howden' to a hassock-size cucurbit called 'Dill's Atlantic Giant'. There must be enough raw jack-o'-lantern material here to gratify every kid in a 30-mile vicinity. I am a mere kindergartener when it comes to this business, selling just a few dozen of one variety—'New England Pie'—from my 5-year-old roadside shanty. Yet Ben and I have at least one thing in common, which is that we refuse to outgrow our love for the round, orange vegetables of Halloween. Nor do we fear leftover inventory—it'll just mean a preponderance of pumpkin pie for the great banquet at Thanksgiving.

SKY WATCH: Except for Mercury in the predawn east, all of the planets fade a bit. Venus sinks lower each morning but is still conspicuous before dawn. Look for the thin crescent Moon between Mercury and Venus on the 13th and below them on the 14th. Venus hovering above Mercury is an easy observation from the 8th to the 18th, 40 minutes before sunrise, for those with an unobstructed eastern horizon. When evening dusk fades, Jupiter continues its steady march toward Saturn, with the pair now visible only in the first few hours of each night. The Moon floats near the two planets on the 18th and 19th.

CALENDAR

| ☽ LAST QUARTER | 8th day | 8:46 A.M. | ☾ FIRST QUARTER | 21st day | 11:45 P.M. |
| ● NEW MOON | 15th day | 12:07 A.M. | ○ FULL MOON | 30th day | 4:30 A.M. |

After 2:00 A.M. on November 1, Eastern Standard Time is given.

GET THESE PAGES WITH TIMES SET TO YOUR ZIP CODE AT ALMANAC.COM/ACCESS.

DAY OF YEAR	DAY OF MONTH	DAY OF WEEK	☼ RISES H. M.	RISE KEY	☼ SETS H. M.	SET KEY	LENGTH OF DAY H. M.	SUN FAST M.	SUN DECLINATION ° ′	HIGH TIDE TIMES BOSTON		☽ RISES H. M.	RISE KEY	☽ SETS H. M.	SET KEY	☽ ASTRON. PLACE	☽ AGE
306	1	D	6:18	D	4:37	B	10 19	32	14 s. 43	12¼	11½	5:25	B	7:05	E	ARI	16
307	2	M.	6:19	D	4:36	B	10 17	32	15 s. 02	12	12	5:55	B	8:06	E	TAU	17
308	3	Tu.	6:21	D	4:34	B	10 13	32	15 s. 21	12½	12½	6:31	B	9:08	E	TAU	18
309	4	W.	6:22	D	4:33	B	10 11	32	15 s. 39	1¼	1¼	7:14	B	10:07	E	TAU	19
310	5	Th.	6:23	E	4:32	B	10 09	32	15 s. 57	2	2	8:04	B	11:03	E	GEM	20
311	6	Fr.	6:24	E	4:31	B	10 07	32	16 s. 15	2¾	2¾	9:03	B	11:54	E	GEM	21
312	7	Sa.	6:26	E	4:30	B	10 04	32	16 s. 33	3½	3½	10:08	B	12:38	E	CAN	22
313	8	D	6:27	E	4:29	B	10 02	32	16 s. 50	4½	4½	11:17	C	1:17	E	CAN	23
314	9	M.	6:28	E	4:28	B	10 00	32	17 s. 07	5¼	5½	—	-	1:50	E	LEO	24
315	10	Tu.	6:29	E	4:26	B	9 57	32	17 s. 24	6¼	6½	12:29	C	2:20	D	LEO	25
316	11	W.	6:31	E	4:25	B	9 54	32	17 s. 40	7¼	7½	1:43	D	2:48	D	VIR	26
317	12	Th.	6:32	E	4:25	B	9 53	32	17 s. 56	8	8½	2:58	D	3:16	C	VIR	27
318	13	Fr.	6:33	E	4:24	B	9 51	31	18 s. 12	9	9½	4:16	D	3:45	C	VIR	28
319	14	Sa.	6:34	E	4:23	B	9 49	31	18 s. 27	9¾	10¼	5:35	E	4:17	B	LIB	29
320	15	D	6:36	E	4:22	B	9 46	31	18 s. 43	10¾	11¼	6:56	E	4:55	B	LIB	0
321	16	M.	6:37	E	4:21	B	9 44	31	18 s. 57	11½	—	8:15	E	5:40	B	OPH	1
322	17	Tu.	6:38	E	4:20	B	9 42	31	19 s. 12	12	12¼	9:28	E	6:33	B	OPH	2
323	18	W.	6:39	E	4:19	B	9 40	30	19 s. 26	1	1¼	10:32	E	7:33	B	SAG	3
324	19	Th.	6:40	E	4:19	B	9 39	30	19 s. 40	2	2	11:25	E	8:39	B	SAG	4
325	20	Fr.	6:42	E	4:18	B	9 36	30	19 s. 53	2¾	3	12:08	E	9:45	B	CAP	5
326	21	Sa.	6:43	E	4:17	B	9 34	30	20 s. 06	3¾	4	12:42	E	10:51	C	CAP	6
327	22	D	6:44	E	4:17	B	9 33	29	20 s. 19	4¾	5	1:11	E	11:55	C	AQU	7
328	23	M.	6:45	E	4:16	A	9 31	29	20 s. 32	5¾	6	1:35	D	—	-	AQU	8
329	24	Tu.	6:46	E	4:15	A	9 29	29	20 s. 43	6¾	7	1:58	D	12:56	D	AQU	9
330	25	W.	6:48	E	4:15	A	9 27	29	20 s. 55	7½	8	2:19	C	1:57	D	CET	10
331	26	Th.	6:49	E	4:14	A	9 25	28	21 s. 06	8¼	8¾	2:40	C	2:56	D	PSC	11
332	27	Fr.	6:50	E	4:14	A	9 24	28	21 s. 17	9	9½	3:03	C	3:56	E	PSC	12
333	28	Sa.	6:51	E	4:13	A	9 22	28	21 s. 27	9¾	10¼	3:28	B	4:56	E	ARI	13
334	29	D	6:52	E	4:13	A	9 21	27	21 s. 37	10¼	11	3:57	B	5:58	E	TAU	14
335	30	M.	6:53	E	4:13	A	9 20	27	21 s. 47	11	11½	4:31	B	7:00	E	TAU	15

THE ELEVENTH MONTH · 2020 **NOVEMBER** NOVEMBER HATH 30 DAYS

The genuine food / Of every plant is earth: hence their increase, Their strength and substance.
–**Robert Dodsley**

DAY OF MONTH	DAY OF WEEK	DATES, FEASTS, FASTS, ASPECTS, TIDE HEIGHTS, AND WEATHER	
1	D	All Saints' • Daylight Saving Time ends, 2:00 A.M. • Tides {9.5 9.4	*Mild,*
2	M.	All Souls' • For 1st time since 1908, Chicago Cubs won World Series, 2016 • {10.1 —	*murky;*
3	Tu.	Election Day • ☾ at ☊ • ☿ stat. • Tides {9.2 10.0	*order*
4	W.	*A high wind prevents frost.* • *EPOXI* spacecraft flew by comet Hartley 2, 2010 • Tides {9.0 9.9	*the*
5	Th.	☾ rides high • 2" snow, Salisbury, Mo., 1995 • Tides {8.7 9.7	*turkey!*
6	Fr.	Deadly tornado struck near Evansville, Ind., 2005 • {8.6 9.6	*White-*
7	Sa.	Sadie Hawkins Day • Last spike of transcontinental Can. Pacific Rwy. driven, Craigellachie, B.C., 1885	*out,*
8	D	23rd. S. af. P. • 1st storm warning (for Great Lakes) by U.S. Signal Corps weather service, 1870	*then*
9	M.	Astronomer Carl Sagan born, 1934 • Tides {8.8 9.6	*bright*
10	Tu.	☿ gr. elong. (19° west) • 71°F, East Milford, N.H., 2009 • {9.3 9.9	*out.*
11	W.	St. Martin of Tours • Veterans Day • G. Bowering 1st Parliamentary Poet Laureate (Can.), 2002	*Great*
12	Th.	Indian Summer • ☾ on eq. • ☌♀☾ • Tides {10.6 10.6	*for*
13	Fr.	☌☿☾ • ☌♃♇ • Writer Robert Louis Stevenson born, 1850 • {11.3 10.9	*animal*
14	Sa.	☾ at perig. • *Do good, if you expect to receive it.* • Tides {11.9 11.0	*tracks*
15	D	24th. S. af. P. • new ● • ♂ stat. • {12.2 11.0	*exposed:*
16	M.	☾ at ☋ • Inaugural concert of Philadelphia Orchestra, 1900 • {12.3 —	*First*
17	Tu.	St. Hugh of Lincoln • Douglas C. Engelbart received patent for computer mouse, 1970 • {10.8 12.1	*it*
18	W.	St. Hilda of Whitby • ☾ runs low • Tides {10.5 11.7	*rains,*
19	Th.	☌♃☾ • ☌♄☾ • ☌♇☾ • Tides {10.0 11.1	*then it*
20	Fr.	U.S. attorney general Robert F. Kennedy born, 1925 • Tides {9.6 10.5	*snows.*
21	Sa.	*Mayflower* Compact signed (Nov. 11, Julian calendar), 1620 • Composer Henry Purcell died, 1695	*Rinse,*
22	D	25th. S. af. P. • British clipper *Cutty Sark* launched, 1869 • {9.0 9.4	*repeat—*
23	M.	St. Clement • ☌♆☾ • Pathologist Walter Reed died, 1902 • {8.9 9.1	*Hey,*
24	Tu.	14.04-lb. saugeye caught, Antrim Lake, Ohio, 2004 • Tides {9.0 9.0	*let's*
25	W.	☾ on eq. • ☌♂☾ • Industrialist Andrew Carnegie born, 1835 • Tides {9.2 8.9	*eat!*
26	Th.	Thanksgiving Day • ☾ at apo. • *Gratitude preserves old friendship and procures new.*	*Autumn*
27	Fr.	☌♅☾ • C.A.R.E. founded, 1945 • Tides {9.6 9.0	*lingers*
28	Sa.	Navigator Ferdinand Magellan reached Pacific, emerging from what is now Strait of Magellan, 1520	*with*
29	D	1st. S. of Advent • ♆ stat. • 1st helicopter hoist rescue, Penfield Reef, Conn., 1945	*cold,*
30	M.	St. Andrew • Full Beaver ○ • Eclipse ☾ • {10.1 9.0	*gray fingers.*

Farmer's Calendar

When the new woodstove arrived, it sat unevenly until the deliveryman supplied a quarter and a nickel and stacked them under the stove's short foot. His 30 cents endures, even as the steady stove's been dark and cold for months, serving as an overbuilt pedestal for vases displaying the summer's array, from aconite to zinnias. Once, on an excessively sultry day, I caught the cat draped across its soapstone top. Not anymore: Now orange flames flicker within and both the cat and the dog have succumbed to its heat, basking before it, on the floor. I'm keeping the fire alive by feeding it pages of old notebooks full of my expired ideas and crossed out scrawl. Later I'll shovel these ashes into a wide tin pail, the one I'll carry out to the snow-fleeced pasture. There, I'll scatter and dump these soots to sweeten the grasses' roots, which will bring on lavish clovers later, when the snow is over and the coin-size Sun again burns steady in the sky and finds me lugging buckets of water out to the grazing lambs. Then an idea might spark my mind and I'll dash back to the desk beside the chilly stove to scribble new lines on a white page.

DECEMBER

SKY WATCH: We welcome winter with the "Great Conjunction," which unfolds every two decades and has been celebrated since ancient times. The Moon is near the two giant worlds of Jupiter and Saturn on the 16th and 17th. Then Jupiter passes extremely close to Saturn from the 20th to the 22nd, coming closest on the 21st—the solstice. So close are the two planets that they merge almost into a single "star," near enough to fit together in the same telescope field of view and very much visible with the naked eye. Look for them 45 minutes after local sunset, low in fading evening twilight, roughly 14 degrees above the southwestern horizon. Often too close to the Sun to be observable (as in 2000), this conjunction is truly great and not to be missed!

| ◗ LAST QUARTER | 7th day | 7:37 P.M. | ◖ FIRST QUARTER | 21st day | 6:41 P.M. |
| ● NEW MOON | 14th day | 11:17 A.M. | ○ FULL MOON | 29th day | 10:28 P.M. |

All times are given in Eastern Standard Time.

GET THESE PAGES WITH TIMES SET TO YOUR ZIP CODE AT ALMANAC.COM/ACCESS.

DAY OF YEAR	DAY OF MONTH	DAY OF WEEK	☀ RISES H.M.	RISE KEY	☀ SETS H.M.	SET KEY	LENGTH OF DAY H.M.	SUN FAST M.	SUN DECLINATION ° '	HIGH TIDE TIMES BOSTON		☾ RISES H.M.	RISE KEY	☾ SETS H.M.	SET KEY	ASTRON. PLACE	☾ AGE
336	1	Tu.	6:54	E	4:12	A	9 18	26	21 s. 56	11½	—	5:12	B	8:01	E	TAU	16
337	2	W.	6:55	E	4:12	A	9 17	26	22 s. 05	12¼	12¼	6:00	B	8:59	E	GEM	17
338	3	Th.	6:56	E	4:12	A	9 16	26	22 s. 13	12¾	12¾	6:56	B	9:52	E	GEM	18
339	4	Fr.	6:57	E	4:12	A	9 15	25	22 s. 21	1½	1½	7:59	B	10:38	E	GEM	19
340	5	Sa.	6:58	E	4:12	A	9 14	25	22 s. 28	2¼	2¼	9:06	B	11:18	E	CAN	20
341	6	**D**	6:59	E	4:12	A	9 13	24	22 s. 35	3	3¼	10:16	C	11:52	E	LEO	21
342	7	M.	7:00	E	4:11	A	9 11	24	22 s. 42	4	4¼	11:27	C	12:22	E	LEO	22
343	8	Tu.	7:01	E	4:11	A	9 10	24	22 s. 48	4¾	5¼	—	-	12:50	D	LEO	23
344	9	W.	7:02	E	4:11	A	9 09	23	22 s. 54	5¾	6¼	12:39	D	1:16	D	VIR	24
345	10	Th.	7:03	E	4:12	A	9 09	23	22 s. 59	6¾	7¼	1:53	E	1:43	C	VIR	25
346	11	Fr.	7:04	E	4:12	A	9 08	22	23 s. 04	7¾	8¼	3:08	E	2:12	C	VIR	26
347	12	Sa.	7:04	E	4:12	A	9 08	22	23 s. 08	8½	9¼	4:26	E	2:46	B	LIB	27
348	13	**D**	7:05	E	4:12	A	9 07	21	23 s. 12	9½	10	5:45	E	3:26	B	LIB	28
349	14	M.	7:06	E	4:12	A	9 06	21	23 s. 15	10¼	11	7:01	E	4:15	B	OPH	0
350	15	Tu.	7:07	E	4:12	A	9 05	20	23 s. 18	11¼	11¾	8:12	E	5:12	B	SAG	1
351	16	W.	7:07	E	4:13	A	9 06	20	23 s. 21	12	—	9:12	E	6:17	B	SAG	2
352	17	Th.	7:08	E	4:13	A	9 05	19	23 s. 22	12¾	12¾	10:01	E	7:26	B	CAP	3
353	18	Fr.	7:09	E	4:14	A	9 05	19	23 s. 24	1½	1¾	10:40	E	8:34	C	CAP	4
354	19	Sa.	7:09	E	4:14	A	9 05	18	23 s. 25	2½	2½	11:12	E	9:41	C	AQU	5
355	20	**D**	7:10	E	4:15	A	9 05	18	23 s. 26	3¼	3½	11:38	E	10:44	C	AQU	6
356	21	M.	7:10	E	4:15	A	9 05	17	23 s. 26	4¼	4½	12:02	D	11:46	D	AQU	7
357	22	Tu.	7:11	E	4:16	A	9 05	17	23 s. 25	5	5¼	12:23	D	—	-	PSC	8
358	23	W.	7:11	E	4:16	A	9 05	16	23 s. 24	6	6¼	12:45	C	12:46	D	CET	9
359	24	Th.	7:12	E	4:17	A	9 05	16	23 s. 23	6¾	7¼	1:07	C	1:46	E	PSC	10
360	25	Fr.	7:12	E	4:17	A	9 05	15	23 s. 21	7½	8¼	1:31	B	2:46	E	ARI	11
361	26	Sa.	7:12	E	4:18	A	9 06	15	23 s. 19	8½	9	1:58	B	3:47	E	ARI	12
362	27	**D**	7:13	E	4:19	A	9 06	14	23 s. 16	9	9¾	2:30	B	4:49	E	TAU	13
363	28	M.	7:13	E	4:19	A	9 06	14	23 s. 13	9¾	10½	3:08	B	5:51	E	TAU	14
364	29	Tu.	7:13	E	4:20	A	9 07	13	23 s. 10	10½	11¼	3:54	B	6:51	E	TAU	15
365	30	W.	7:13	E	4:21	A	9 08	13	23 s. 05	11¼	11¾	4:49	B	7:47	E	GEM	16
366	31	Th.	7:13	E	4:22	A	9 09	13	23 s. 01	11¾	—	5:51	B	8:36	E	GEM	17

THE TWELFTH MONTH • 2020 **DECEMBER** DECEMBER HATH 31 DAYS

Look! the massy trunks are cased in the pure crystal;
Each light spray nodding and tinkling in the breath of heaven.
–**William Cullen Bryant, of trees glazed with ice**

DAY OF MONTH	DAY OF WEEK	DATES, FEASTS, FASTS, ASPECTS, TIDE HEIGHTS, AND WEATHER	
1	Tu.	☾ AT ☊ • Astronaut Bob Thirsk returned to Earth after 6 mos. on ISS, 2009 • {10.2 / —	*Two-*
2	W.	St. Viviana • ☾ RIDES HIGH • Environmental Protection Agency (EPA) began operation, 1970	*faced—*
3	Th.	*If snowflakes increase in size, a thaw will follow.* • Tides {8.9 / 10.1	*snow's*
4	Fr.	Historian Thomas Carlyle born, 1795 • Tides {8.8 / 10.0	*erased*
5	Sa.	1st large hydroponicum established, Montebello, Calif., 1935 • Tides {8.8 / 9.9	*by*
6	**D**	**2nd. S. of Advent** • **St. Nicholas** • {8.8 / 9.8	*rain*
7	M.	St. Ambrose • **National Pearl Harbor Remembrance Day** • {9.0 / 9.7	*and*
8	Tu.	Inventor Eli Whitney born, 1765 • Tides {9.3 / 9.7	*southern*
9	W.	☾ ON EQ. • 1st Heisman Trophy, awarded to Jay Berwanger, 1935 • {9.7 / 9.7	*breezes.*
10	Th.	St. Eulalia • Chanukah begins at sundown • Tides {10.3 / 9.9	*Flakefest,*
11	Fr.	2.1" rain, Vancouver, B.C., 1925 • Conservationist Benton MacKaye died, 1975	*then*
12	Sa.	**Our Lady of Guadalupe** • ☾ AT PERIG. • OCCN. ♀☾ • {11.4 / 10.2	*a*
13	**D**	**3rd. S. of Advent** • **St. Lucia** • Tides {11.8 / 10.4	*rest*
14	M.	Halcyon Days begin. • **NEW** ● • **ECLIPSE** ⊙ • ☾ AT ☋ • ☌☿☾	*(still,*
15	Tu.	☾ RUNS LOW • *He who prizes little things is worthy of great ones.* • Tides {12.0 / 10.3	*it*
16	W.	Ember Day • ☌♃☾ • ☌♇☾ • 2nd Cape Hatteras, N.C., lighthouse likely 1st lit, 1870	*freezes).*
17	Th.	☌♄☾ • Composer Ludwig van Beethoven baptized, 1770 • Tides {10.1 / 11.4	*Polar*
18	Fr.	Ember Day • Great Comet reached perihelion, 1680 • Tides {9.8 / 10.9	*pelting,*
19	Sa.	Ember Day • ☿ IN SUP. ☌ • Beware the Pogonip. • Tides {9.5 / 10.3	*followed*
20	**D**	**4th. S. of Advent** • ☌♆☾ • Mo. imposed $1 tax on bachelors, 1820	*by*
21	M.	St. Thomas • **WINTER SOLSTICE** • ☌♃♄ • Tides {9.0 / 9.2	*melting,*
22	Tu.	☾ ON EQ. • Writer George Eliot died, 1880 • {8.9 / 8.7	*Santa*
23	W.	☌♂☾ • Reginald Fessenden 1st to transmit voice over wireless radio, 1900 • {8.9 / 8.5	*can't a-*
24	Th.	☾ AT APO. • ☌⛢☾ • CONAD (later NORAD) began to track Santa Claus, 1955 • {9.0 / 8.4	*bide.*
25	Fr.	**Christmas** • Bytown (Ottawa) and Prescott Rwy. opened, Ont., 1854 • {9.1 / 8.4	*Such*
26	Sa.	St. Stephen • **Boxing Day (Canada)** • **First day of Kwanzaa** • {9.4 / 8.5	*contrasting*
27	**D**	**1st. S. af. Ch.** • *The more haste, the worse speed.* • Tides {9.6 / 8.6	*forecasting*
28	M.	Holy Innocents • ☾ AT ☊ • Writer Theodore Dreiser died, 1945 • {9.9 / 8.7	*means*
29	Tu.	St. John[T] • **FULL COLD** ○ • Texas statehood, 1845 • {10.1 / 8.8	*a*
30	W.	☾ RIDES HIGH • 1st photo of Earth's curvature exhibited, Cleveland, Ohio, 1930 • {10.3 / 9.0	*bumpy*
31	Th.	St. Sylvester • Gymnast Gabby Douglas born, 1995 • {10.4 / —	*ride!*

Farmer's Calendar

Clues #1 and #2: The room stank with a funky musk, and the cat hunched, its full attention given to the heating vent. When I snapped on the lamp, A-ha! Eye-shine glimmered from the open vent, and then a flash of white as something dashed under the dresser. After extracting the cat and shutting the door, I made an ignominious phone call to someone I'd heard was handy with these sort of predicaments. Hello, I greeted the person and got straight to the point: There's a weasel in my bedroom.

"Ermine" is the winter word for this creature whose brownish coat has turned pure white, a camouflage in snowy environs. Shouldn't I have been grateful for a lithe carnivore to feed on the unseen things constantly scrabbling in the walls—Mice? Squirrels? Chipmunks? Every night, I bang to quiet them. Futilely. But whose bedroom is big enough to host both cats and weasels? After the Good Samaritan arrived and set up his trap, I expected a prolonged scuffle—so I closed the door and wished him luck. But before 5 minutes had elapsed, my uninvited roommate was caged and leaving the premises, on his way to a spacious field that matched his hue.

HOLIDAYS AND OBSERVANCES

2020 HOLIDAYS
FEDERAL HOLIDAYS ARE LISTED IN BOLD.

JAN. 1: New Year's Day

JAN. 20: Martin Luther King Jr.'s Birthday, observed

FEB. 2: Groundhog Day

FEB. 12: Abraham Lincoln's Birthday

FEB. 14: Valentine's Day

FEB. 15: Susan B. Anthony's Birthday *(Fla.)*

FEB. 17: Presidents' Day

FEB. 22: George Washington's Birthday

FEB. 25: Mardi Gras *(Baldwin & Mobile counties, Ala.; La.)*

FEB. 29: Leap Day

MAR. 2: Texas Independence Day

MAR. 3: Town Meeting Day *(Vt.)*

MAR. 8: International Women's Day

MAR. 17: St. Patrick's Day
Evacuation Day *(Suffolk Co., Mass.)*

MAR. 30: Seward's Day *(Alaska)*

MAR. 31: César Chávez Day

APR. 2: Pascua Florida Day

APR. 20: Patriots Day *(Maine, Mass.)*

APR. 21: San Jacinto Day *(Tex.)*

APR. 22: Earth Day

APR. 24: National Arbor Day

MAY 5: Cinco de Mayo

MAY 8: Truman Day *(Mo.)*

MAY 10: Mother's Day

MAY 16: Armed Forces Day

MAY 18: Victoria Day *(Canada)*

MAY 22: National Maritime Day

MAY 25: Memorial Day, observed

JUNE 5: World Environment Day

JUNE 11: King Kamehameha I Day *(Hawaii)*

JUNE 14: Flag Day

JUNE 17: Bunker Hill Day *(Suffolk Co., Mass.)*

JUNE 19: Emancipation Day *(Tex.)*

JUNE 20: West Virginia Day

JUNE 21: Father's Day

JULY 1: Canada Day

JULY 4: Independence Day

JULY 24: Pioneer Day *(Utah)*

JULY 25: National Day of the Cowboy

AUG. 1: Colorado Day

AUG. 3: Civic Holiday *(parts of Canada)*

AUG. 16: Bennington Battle Day *(Vt.)*

AUG. 19: National Aviation Day

AUG. 26: Women's Equality Day

SEPT. 7: Labor Day

SEPT. 9: Admission Day *(Calif.)*

SEPT. 11: Patriot Day

SEPT. 13: Grandparents Day

SEPT. 17: Constitution Day

SEPT. 21: International Day of Peace

OCT. 5: Child Health Day

OCT. 9: Leif Eriksson Day

OCT. 12: Columbus Day, observed
Indigenous Peoples' Day *(parts of U.S.)*
Thanksgiving Day *(Canada)*

OCT. 18: Alaska Day

OCT. 24: United Nations Day

OCT. 30: Nevada Day

OCT. 31: Halloween

NOV. 3: Election Day

NOV. 4: Will Rogers Day *(Okla.)*

NOV. 10: U.S. Marine Corps Birthday

NOV. 11: Veterans Day
Remembrance Day *(Canada)*

NOV. 19: Discovery of Puerto Rico Day

Love calendar lore? See page 152 and visit Almanac.com/Calendar.

NOV. 26: Thanksgiving Day	**DEC. 17:** Wright Brothers Day
NOV. 27: Acadian Day *(La.)*	**DEC. 25:** Christmas Day
DEC. 7: National Pearl Harbor Remembrance Day	**DEC. 26:** Boxing Day *(Canada)* First day of Kwanzaa
DEC. 15: Bill of Rights Day	

Movable Religious Observances

FEB. 9: Septuagesima Sunday	**MAY 21:** Ascension Day
FEB. 25: Shrove Tuesday	**MAY 31:** Whitsunday–Pentecost
FEB. 26: Ash Wednesday	**JUNE 7:** Trinity Sunday
APR. 5: Palm Sunday	**JUNE 14:** Corpus Christi
APR. 8: Passover begins at sundown	**SEPT. 18:** Rosh Hashanah begins at sundown
APR. 10: Good Friday	
APR. 12: Easter	**SEPT. 27:** Yom Kippur begins at sundown
APR. 19: Orthodox Easter	
APR. 23: Ramadan begins at sundown	**NOV. 29:** First Sunday of Advent
MAY 17: Rogation Sunday	**DEC. 10:** Chanukah begins at sundown

CHRONOLOGICAL CYCLES

Dominical Letter **ED**

Epact **5**

Golden Number (Lunar Cycle) **7**

Roman Indiction **13**

Solar Cycle **13**

Year of Julian Period **6733**

–Beth Krommes

ERAS

ERA	YEAR	BEGINS
Byzantine	7529	September 14
Jewish (A.M.)*	5781	September 18
Chinese (Lunar) [Year of the Rat]	4718	January 25
Roman (A.U.C.)	2773	January 14
Nabonassar	2769	April 18
Japanese	2680	January 1
Grecian (Seleucidae)	2332	September 14 (or October 14)
Indian (Saka)	1942	March 21
Diocletian	1737	September 11
Islamic (Hegira)* [FCNA date]	1442	August 19
Bahá'í*	177	March 19

*Year begins at sundown.

Natural device stops a cold before it starts

New research shows you can stop a cold in its tracks if you take one simple step with a new device when you feel a cold about to start.

Colds start after cold viruses get in your nose. Viruses multiply fast. If you don't stop them early, they spread and cause misery.

But scientists have found a quick way to kill a virus. Touch it with copper. Researchers at labs and universities agree, copper is "antimicrobial." It kills microbes, such as viruses and bacteria, just by touch.

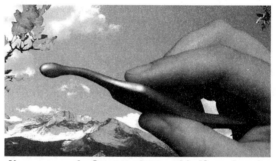

New research: Copper stops colds if used early.

That's why ancient Greeks and Egyptians used copper to purify water and heal wounds. They didn't know about viruses and bacteria, but now we do.

Scientists say the high conductance of copper disrupts the electrical balance in a microbe cell and destroys the cell in seconds.

Tests by the EPA (Environmental Protection Agency) show germs die fast on copper. So some hospitals tried copper for touch surfaces like faucets and doorknobs. This cut the spread of MRSA and other illnesses by over half, and saved lives.

The strong scientific evidence gave inventor Doug Cornell an idea. When he felt a cold about to start he fashioned a smooth copper probe and rubbed it gently in his nose for 60 seconds.

"It worked!" he exclaimed. "The cold never got going." It worked again every time. He has not had a single cold for 7 years since.

He asked relatives and friends to try it. They said it worked for them, too, so he patented CopperZap™ and put it on the market.

Soon hundreds of people had tried it. Nearly 100% said the copper stops their colds if used within 3 hours after the first sign. Even up to 2 days, if they still get the cold it is milder and they feel better.

Users wrote things like, "It stopped my cold right away," and "Is it supposed to work that fast?"

"What a wonderful thing," wrote Physician's Assistant Julie. "Now I have this little magic wand, no more colds for me!"

Pat McAllister, age 70, received one for Christmas and called it "one of the best presents ever. This little jewel really works." Now thousands have simply stopped getting colds.

Copper can also stop flu that starts in the nose if used right away and for several days. In a lab test, scientists placed 25 million live flu viruses on a CopperZap. No viruses were found still alive soon after.

People often use CopperZap preventively. Frequent flier Karen Gauci used to get colds after crowded flights. Though skeptical, she tried it several times a day on travel days for 2 months. "Sixteen flights and not a sniffle!" she exclaimed.

Businesswoman Rosaleen says when people are sick around her she uses CopperZap morning and night. "It saved me last holidays," she said. "The kids had colds going round and round, but not me."

Some users say it also helps with sinuses. Attorney Donna Blight had a 2-day sinus headache. She tried CopperZap. "I am shocked!" she said. "My head cleared, no more headache, no more congestion."

One man suffered seasonal sinus problems for years. It ruined family vacations and even dinners out with friends. His wife Judy bought CopperZaps for both of them. He was so skeptical he said, "Oh Judy, you are such a whack job!" But he finally tried it and the copper cleared up his sinuses right away. Judy and their daughter both said, "It has changed our lives."

Some users say copper stops nighttime stuffiness, too, if they use it just before bed. One man said, "Best sleep I've had in years."

People have used it on cold sores and say it can completely prevent outbreaks. You can also use it on cuts, or lesions to combat infections.

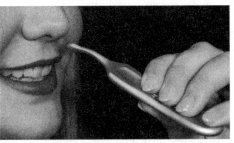

Sinus trouble, cold sores, stuffiness.

Copper even kills deadly germs that have become resistant to antibiotics. If you are near sick people, a moment of handling it may keep serious infection away. It may even save a life.

The EPA says copper still works even when tarnished. It kills hundreds of different disease germs so it can prevent serious illness.

CopperZap is made in the U.S. of pure copper. It has a 90-day full money back guarantee when used as directed to stop a cold. It is $69.95. Get $10 off each CopperZap with code **OFMA** at www.CopperZap.com or call toll-free 1-888-411-6114. Buy once, use forever.

GLOSSARY OF ALMANAC ODDITIES

Many readers have expressed puzzlement over the rather obscure entries that appear on our **Right-Hand Calendar Pages, 121–147.** These "oddities" have long been fixtures in the Almanac, and we are pleased to provide some definitions. Once explained, they may not seem so odd after all!

EMBER DAYS: These are the Wednesdays, Fridays, and Saturdays that occur in succession following (1) the First Sunday in Lent; (2) Whitsunday–Pentecost; (3) the Feast of the Holy Cross, September 14; and (4) the Feast of St. Lucia, December 13. The word *ember* is perhaps a corruption of the Latin *quatuor tempora,* "four times." The four periods are observed by some Christian denominations for prayer, fasting, and the ordination of clergy.

Folklore has it that the weather on each of the 3 days foretells the weather for the next 3 months; that is, in September, the first Ember Day, Wednesday, forecasts the weather for October; Friday predicts November; and Saturday foretells December.

DISTAFF DAY (JANUARY 7): This was the day after Epiphany, when women were expected to return to their spinning following the Christmas holiday. A distaff is the staff that women used for holding the flax or wool in spinning. (Hence the term "distaff" refers to women's work or the maternal side of the family.)

PLOUGH MONDAY (JANUARY): Traditionally, the first Monday after Epiphany was called Plough Monday because it was the day when men returned to their plough, or daily work, following the Christmas holiday. (Every few years, Plough Monday and Distaff Day fall on the same day.) It was customary at this time for farm laborers to draw a plough through the village, soliciting money for a "plough light,"

–Beth Krommes

which was kept burning in the parish church all year. This traditional verse captures the spirit of it:

> *Yule is come and Yule is gone,*
> *and we have feasted well;*
> *so Jack must to his flail again*
> *and Jenny to her wheel.*

THREE CHILLY SAINTS (MAY): Mamertus, Pancras, and Gervais were three early Christian saints whose feast days, on May 11, 12, and 13, respectively, are traditionally cold; thus they have come to be known as the Three Chilly Saints. An old French saying translates to "St. Mamertus, St. Pancras, and St. Gervais do not pass without a frost."

MIDSUMMER DAY (JUNE 24): To the farmer, this day is the midpoint of the growing season, halfway between planting and harvest. The Anglican Church considered it a "Quarter Day," one of the four major divisions of the liturgical year. It also marks the feast day of St. John the Baptist. (Midsummer Eve is an occasion for festivity and celebrates fertility.)

CORNSCATEOUS AIR (JULY): First used by early almanac makers, this term signifies warm, damp air. Although it signals ideal climatic conditions for growing corn, warm, damp air poses

Break Free from Neuropathy with a New Supportive Care Cream

A patented relief cream stands to help millions of Americans crippled from the side effects of neuropathy by increasing sensation and blood flow wherever it's applied

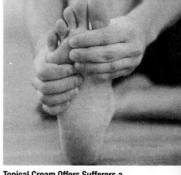

Topical Cream Offers Sufferers a Safer, More Effective Avenue of Relief: Diabasens increases sensation and blood flow wherever its applied. It's now being used to relieve painful legs and feet.

Raymond Wilson
The Associated Heath Press

AHP — A recent breakthrough stands to help millions of Americans plagued by burning, tingling and numb legs and feet.

But this time it comes in the form of a cream, not a pill, suggesting the medical community may have been going about the problem all wrong.

The breakthrough, called *Diabasens*, is a new relief cream developed for managing the relentless discomfort caused by neuropathy.

When applied directly to the legs and feet, it causes arteries and blood vessels to expand, increasing the flow of warm, nutrient rich blood to damaged tissue.

However, what's most remarkable about the cream...and what makes it so brilliant...is that it contains one of the only natural substances known to activate a special sensory pathway right below the surface of the skin.

This pathway is called TRPA1 and it controls the sensitivity of nerves. In laymen terms, it determines whether you feel pins and needles or soothing relief.

Studies show that symptoms of neuropathy arise when the nerves in your legs deteriorate and blood flow is lost to the areas which surround them.

As the nerves begins to die, sensation is lost. This lack of sensation is what causes the feelings of burning, tingling and numbness.

This is why the makers of *Diabasens* say their cream has performed so well in a recent clinical use survey trial: it increases sensation and blood flow where ever its applied.

No Pills or Prescriptions

Until now, many doctors have failed to consider a topical cream as an effective way to manage neuropathy. *Diabasens* is proving it may be the only way going forward.

"Most of today's treatment methods have focused on minimizing discomfort instead of attacking its underlining cause. That's why millions of adults are still in excruciating pain every single day, and are constantly dealing with side effects" explains Dr. Esber, the creator of *Diabasens*.

"*Diabasens* is different. Since the most commonly reported symptoms — burning, tingling and numb legs and feet — are caused by lack of sensation of the nerves, we've designed the formula increase their sensitivity.

And since these nerves are located right below the skin, we've chosen to formulate it as a cream. This allows for the ingredients to get to them faster and without any drug like side effects" he adds.

Study Finds Restoring Sensation the Key To Relief

With the conclusion of their latest human clinical use survey trial, Dr. Esber and his team are now offering *Diabasens* nationwide. And regardless of the market, its sales are exploding.

Men and women from all over the country are eager to get their hands on the new cream and, according to the results initial users reported, they should be.

Diabasens is shown to provide relief from:

- Burning
- Swelling
- Tingling
- Heaviness
- Numbness
- Cold extremities

In the trial above, as compared to baseline, participants taking *Diabasens* saw a staggering 51% increase sensitivity in just one week. This resulted in significant relief from burning, tingling and nubmness throughout their legs.

Many participants taking *Diabasens*

described feeling much more balanced and comfortable throughout the day. They also noticed that after applying, there was a pleasant warming sensation that was remarkably soothing.

Targets Nerve Damage Right Below the Skins Surface

Diabasens is a topical cream that is to be applied to your legs and feet twice a day for the first two weeks then once a day after. It does not require a prescription.

Studies show that neuropathy is caused when the peripheral nerves break down and blood is unable to circulate into your legs and feet.

As these nerves deteriorate, sensation is lost. This is why you may not feel hot or cold and your legs and feet may burn, tingle and go numb.

Additionally, without proper blood flow, tissues and cells in these areas start to die, causing unbearable pain.

An ingredient called cinnamaldehyde in *Diabasens* is one of the only compounds in existence that can activate TRPA1, a special sensory pathway that runs through your entire body.

According to research, activating this pathway (which can only be done with a cream) increases the sensitivity of nerves, relieving feelings of tingling and numbness in your legs and feet.

Supporting ingredients boost blood flow, supplying the nerves with the nutrients they need for increased sensation.

How to Get *Diabasens*

In order to get the word out about *Diabasens*, the company is offering special introductory discounts to all who call. Discounts will automatically be applied to all callers, but don't wait. This offer may not last forever. **Call toll-free: 1-800-516-6923.**

a danger to those affected by asthma and other respiratory problems.

DOG DAYS (JULY 3–AUGUST 11): These 40 days are traditionally the year's hottest and unhealthiest. They once coincided with the year's heliacal (at sunrise) rising of the Dog Star, Sirius. Ancient folks thought that the "combined heat" of Sirius and the Sun caused summer's swelter.

LAMMAS DAY (AUGUST 1): Derived from the Old English *hlaf maesse,* meaning "loaf mass," Lammas Day marked the beginning of the harvest. Traditionally, loaves of bread were baked from the first-ripened grain and brought to the churches to be consecrated. In Scotland, Lammastide fairs became famous as the time when trial marriages could be made. These marriages could end after a year with no strings attached.

CAT NIGHTS COMMENCE (AUGUST 17): This term harks back to the days when people believed in witches. An Irish legend says that a witch could turn into a cat and regain herself eight times, but on the ninth time (August 17), she couldn't change back and thus began her final life permanently as a cat. Hence the saying "A cat has nine lives."

HARVEST HOME (SEPTEMBER): In Britain and other parts of Europe, this marked the conclusion of the harvest and a period of festivals for feasting and thanksgiving. It was also a time to hold elections, pay workers, and collect rents. These festivals usually took place around the autumnal equinox. Certain groups in the United States, e.g., the Pennsylvania Dutch, have kept the tradition alive.

ST. LUKE'S LITTLE SUMMER (OCTOBER): This is a period of warm weather that occurs on or near St. Luke's feast day (usually October 18) and is sometimes called Indian summer.

INDIAN SUMMER (NOVEMBER): A period of warm weather following a cold spell or a hard frost, Indian summer can occur between St. Martin's Day (November 11) and November 20. Although there are differing dates for its occurrence, for more than 225 years the Almanac has adhered to the saying "If All Saints' [November 1] brings out winter, St. Martin's brings out Indian summer." The term may have come from early Native Americans, some of whom believed that the condition was caused by a warm wind sent from the court of their southwestern god, Cautantowwit.

HALCYON DAYS (DECEMBER): This period of about 2 weeks of calm weather often follows the blustery winds at autumn's end. Ancient Greeks and Romans experienced this weather at around the time of the winter solstice, when the halcyon, or kingfisher, was thought to brood in a nest floating on the sea. The bird was said to have charmed the wind and waves so that waters were especially calm at this time.

BEWARE THE POGONIP (DECEMBER): The word *pogonip* refers to frozen fog and was coined by Native Americans to describe the frozen fogs of fine ice needles that occur in the mountain valleys of the western United States and Canada. According to tradition, breathing the fog is injurious to the lungs. ∎

–Beth Krommes

LEAPIN' Leap Day!

A CELEBRATION OF LEAPS AND BOUNDS

by Heidi Stonehill

L eap years occur almost every 4 years—and this is one. To qualify, the year number must be divisible by 4 and a century year must be divisible by 400 (e.g., 1700, 1800, and 1900 were not leap years). In a leap year, the calendar gets an extra day—February 29, aka Leap Day.

Why all the fuss? Earth takes a fraction longer than the Gregorian calendar's 365 days to complete its orbit around the Sun—about .2422 of a day more. Adding an extra day to the calendar every 4 years or so keeps it synchronized with the four seasons. Without Leap Days, the calendar would be off by about 5 hours, 48 minutes, 45 seconds each year.

While it may not always be cause for invoking Little Orphan Annie's "Leapin' lizards!," February 29 does call to mind a number of other "leaps" of the imagination.

Leaping Amphibians

In 1865, Mark Twain wrote "The Celebrated Jumping Frog of Calaveras County," set in a mining camp based on Angels Camp, California. In 1928, the story inspired that city to hold the first modern frog jump. Today, the Jumping Frog Jubilee occurs every year in the third weekend of May. Professional frog teams travel from all over to participate. A world record jump was made in 1986, when Lee Giudici's frog Rosie the Ribeter leaped 21 feet 5.75 inches.

LEAPING IN LINE

Who remembers Leap Frog, a game in which players in turn vault with parted legs over other players who are stooped in a froglike pose? Each leaper then assumes the frog pose and others leap over him/her in succession.

Leaping "Legumes"

Some seedpods from the Mexican shrub *Sebastiania pavoniana* contain a moth caterpillar *(Cydia deshaisiana)*. When a pod gets too warm, such as when held in the hand, the yellowish larva jumps or twitches, possibly in an effort to move the seed to a cooler spot. The activity led to these pods' nickname: Mexican jumping beans. *(continued)*

A High Leap

On February 5, 1949, Huaso, a jittery, 16-year-old horse in Viña del Mar, Chile, leaped 8 feet 1 inch, setting a high-jump world record. His rider and trainer, Capt. Alberto Larraguibel of the Chilean army, had worked with him 2 years in anticipation of that triumphant moment.

A SECOND-LONG LEAP

A leap second is sometimes added to or removed from Coordinated Universal Time (UTC)—the time scale that everyday clocks use that is based on atomic time—to keep in sync with Earth's variable and slowing rotation. If needed, leap seconds are added or subtracted, usually at the end of either June or December. The first leap second was added on June 30, 1972.

A QUANTUM LEAP

In physics, the sudden jump of a particle—for example, an electron—from one energy level to another is a quantum leap. In general usage, this can mean an abrupt change, sudden increase, or dramatic advance; a breakthrough.

The Giant Leap

On July 20, 1969, astronaut and commander of the *Apollo 11* spacecraft Neil Armstrong placed one foot onto the Moon's surface and was heard to say by a half-billion people watching on television, "That's one small step for a man, one giant leap for mankind."

Heartfelt Leaps

"Lovers' leap" is a term used for cliffs or other high locations from which, legends say, despairing lovers have plummeted, either by accident or on purpose.

A Welcome Leap

Humpback whales breach, or leap, partway into the air and crash back down into the sea. Scientists think that the sound of this splash traveling through the water to other whales may be a whale's way of saying "Hello!" The longest recorded sustained series of breaches by a humpback whale was 130 leaps in less than 90 minutes in the West Indies.

A LEAP OUT OF THIS WORLD

On October 14, 2012, Austrian skydiver Felix Baumgartner leaped out of a pressurized space capsule 24 miles above Earth's surface. He set a world record for the highest parachute jump (127,852.4 feet), the greatest free-fall distance (119,431.1 feet) and fastest unaided speed (843.6 mph, or Mach 1.25—1.25 times the speed of sound). Baumgartner was also the first skydiver to break the sound barrier. Two years later, Google vice president Alan Eustace broke the altitude record, plunging 135,890 feet above Roswell, New Mexico. ■

FELIX BAUMGARTNER

JUMP OVER TO ALMANAC.COM/LEAP FOR MORE FUN FACTS.

Heidi Stonehill, a senior editor at *The Old Farmer's Almanac,* leaped for joy one day when her newly acquired shy cat, Joey, who had hidden from the world for weeks, came up to her for a pat. Now they are best buddies.

Your hens are the most profitable stock you have if you treat them rightly.
–Facts for Farmers, *1865*

Join the movement for . . .

A CHICKEN IN EVERY PLOT!

Here's how to benefit from some real "hens and chicks" in your garden, plus bring some order to their pecking.

BY LISA STEELE

One of the reasons most commonly cited for raising a flock of backyard chickens is for the delicious, fresh eggs that they lay—and it's a good reason. But chickens offer many other benefits to the home gardener: Happy hens will till, aerate, weed, and fertilize your plot while they rid it of pesky insects!

Japanese beetles or tomato hornworms! To make the most of your fowls' play, you need to let your chickens know that you rule their roost. And you do that with supervision and timing.

PREPARE YOUR PROPERTY

Before you let your chickens roam free, prepare your property for their presence. Controlling your

roots. Look around your yard and identify any flower beds, bushes, or shrubs that you want to be off-limits. Surround the bases of large plants with bricks, stones, or pavers to protect the roots. Shield smaller plants (annual flowers or seedlings) with a cloche of chicken wire: Shape the wire into a generous tube to surround the plants. Before you put down mulch on flower beds, lay chicken wire flat on the ground, cutting holes in it for established plants or cutting it to fit between plants. The wire should encourage the chickens to move to a different area.

Once your plants are safe, you can start letting your chickens assist you in the garden. There is work for them to do year-round.

THE SCOOP ON THE POOP

Chicken manure is wonderful fertilizer, and chickens are natural spreaders: They poop while they roam. Gather large amounts from the garden and/or coop and set it all aside to age for several months. Or, compost it over 5 to 6 weeks. Either way, it should not be used in the garden for at least 90 days.

The thing is, chickens aren't picky about what they peck: Along with invasive weeds, they eat vegetable seeds and seedlings, and they tuck into toads as easily as they devour destructive bugs. In fact, chickens can wreak far more havoc on a vegetable garden than can an army of

chickens' access to your vegetables is critical to keeping your plants safe, so enclose your vegetable garden behind a fence that's at least 4 feet high.

Hens will eat the leaves and flowers of almost any plant within a beak's reach, and their kicking and scratching can lay waste to plant

SPRING

This is the ideal time to give chickens free rein in the garden. They love to scratch in the soil for weed seeds, bugs that overwintered, and insect larvae. As they dig their long, sharp toenails into the soil, they loosen and turn over the top few inches—but much more gently than a traditional tiller does (and chickens never run out of gas!). Let your hens rove the garden plot right up until you plant your seeds.

SUMMER

After you plant your seeds and seedlings, temporarily ban your flock from the garden. (Later, you can reward your brood's good behavior with a few of the seedlings that you pull while thinning.) When plants stand a foot or more tall, invite your chickens back for short supervised visits. A few hens can (and will) eat your plants down to the dirt when you're not looking, but under your watchful eye, they can be encouraged to nibble on weeds and eat bugs. (They'll devour "good" as well as "bad" bugs, so be ready to scoot them in a different direction, if necessary.) Chickens will also gobble up toads that hop into their sights. Carry a bucket to scoop up any that you see. When the chickens are

Happy hens will till, aerate, weed, and fertilize your plot while they rid it of pesky insects!

safely penned up, return the toads to your plot.

If you don't trust your chickens in the garden, handpick bugs off your plants and collect them in a bucket, along with any weeds that you might pull and any bug-eaten produce or wilted leaves. Feed these to the chickens later.

Depending on the size of your flock—and your garden—supervising chickens can occasionally be a challenge. For these times, you need a simple wooden frame chicken "tractor," or movable pen. This can be any size, but it may be most useful at about 2 feet high by 6 feet long and no wider than the paths in your garden. Cover the frame top and sides with chicken wire; leave the bottom open. It will confine three chickens yet still be small and light enough to move.

With the tractor positioned between your plants, you can tuck a few chickens underneath and move it along the rows, encouraging the hens to move with it. Bear in mind that this pen is not completely predator-proof (against a fox or dog, for example), but it will keep your chickens safe from aerial enemies such as hawks and eagles. And, yes, you can use it anywhere on your property!

FALL

After you've harvested your produce, let the chickens back into the garden. They'll chow down on any remaining vegetables, eating stems and leaves; consume any remaining bugs; and scratch at stalks and roots, tearing—even shredding—them into the soil. All the while, poop will be dropping to eventually

You can continue to give your chickens access to the garden throughout the winter.

fertilize the soil.

Chickens generally know what's good for them, but it's important that you know, too: Plants in the nightshade family—tomatoes, eggplants, white (not sweet) potatoes, and peppers—contain toxins that can be harmful to chickens. Remove these plants from your garden to be composted or discarded before letting in chickens. Rhubarb leaves also are toxic to chickens.

WINTER

When you clean your coop to get it ready for winter, rake the soiled bedding (pine shavings or straw, including feathers) into your garden. It will decompose over the winter, providing wonderful organic matter. If you've been saving eggshells (and you should!), crush them and add them to the soiled bedding mix. Next year's tomatoes and peppers will benefit from the calcium. You can continue to give your chickens access to the garden throughout the winter. They'll enjoy scratching in the dirt and fertilizer.

Putting your chickens to work in the garden has many benefits. Oh, and this one: Their eating on the job will reduce your feed bill a bit—and that's a way to feather *your* nest! ■

Lisa Steele is a Master Gardener, fifth-generation chicken keeper, and the founder of fresheggsdaily .com. Her latest book is *Gardening With Chickens: Plans and Plants for You and Your Hens* (Voyageur Press, 2016). She writes and gardens in Maine.

20/20

FOR 2020

EYE-CATCHING INSIGHTS
IN THIS OPTICAL YEAR

COMPILED BY TIM CLARK

The eye hath ever been thought the pearl of the face.
–JOHN LYLY, ENGLISH WRITER (C. 1554–1606)

Try this: On a clear night, look up at the sky and find the Big Dipper. In autumn and winter, you'll find it close to the horizon; in spring and summer, it sits high in the sky. Using only the naked eye, spot the second star from the end of the handle, Mizar. Now, spot the star that appears next to it, Alcor. (They are actually not near each other but instead light-years apart.)

If you can distinguish the two stars separately, you have passed the world's oldest eye test and have approximately 20/20 vision—or average acuity, which is the ability to discern detail. In the ancient Middle East and among some Native Americans, you might have qualified as an elite warrior!

As enthusiasm for telescopes increased through the years, so did the idea of testing eyes—and correcting vision with lenses. In 1623, Spaniard Benito Daza de Valdés, who wrote the first book on optometry, placed mustard seeds at measured distances and asked subjects to count them. Later he presented small print to be read at different distances. The results guided him in deciding whether and how much to make eyeglass lenses convex or concave.

In 1843, German ophthalmologist Heinrich Georg Küchler created the first eye chart using symbols. He cut images—frogs, birds, farm tools, weapons—from calendars and almanacs and glued them to a piece of paper, arranged from the largest to the smallest. He also used a chart of alphabet letters in graduated sizes.

Others contributed to the advance of optometry, but none had the impact of Herman Snellen of the Netherlands. In 1862, he designed a type font for the optotypes (letters or figures for testing) in a chart of specifically calibrated letters in 11 rows. The top row contained the largest letter (E), and each successive row decreased in size. Snellen designed it to be read from a distance of 6 meters, or about 20 feet. You've probably seen it if you've ever had your vision checked; Snellen's chart has become an icon and is still in use today.

Thus, normal, or standard (not "perfect"!), vision came to be described as the ratio 20/20, an arithmetical expression of the distance from the chart over the distance from which normal vision can read the chart. A 20/30 reading suggests problems with vision: Only at 20 feet can the individual see what a person with standard vision can see at 30 feet; 20/40 vision means that the viewer needs to be 20 feet away from something to see what a normal viewer can see at 40 feet. A reading of 20/10 indicates that the viewer has higher acuity than average: He or she can see at 20 feet what a normal viewer can see only at 10 feet.

Someone whose visual acuity is 20/200 or less, when using eyeglasses or contact lenses, is considered legally blind, which is not the same as sightless.

Some 35 percent of adults have unaided or uncorrected 20/20 vision. Athletes are among the most sharp-eyed individuals. Olympic-level archers and sharpshooters have an average uncorrected visual acuity of 20/16; baseball players, about 20/13 (on average)—pretty close to a human's personal best, which experts say is 20/8. An anonymous Australian aboriginal man holds the record for the sharpest eyesight ever measured: He had 20/5 vision.

Your spelling is terrible, Doc!

Nearly 30 percent of North Americans have been found to be nearsighted, or myopic; that is, they can see relatively close objects clearly while those at a distance—for example, a television screen or classroom black/white board—appear blurred.

This number is expected to rise, according to a study released in 2016. Nearly half of the world's population could be nearsighted by 2050. The reason for this, some researchers say, is too much screen time and not enough time outdoors—which brings us back to the Big Dipper. Can you see it? ∎

ONE FOR A MAN, TWO FOR A HORSE

*Folk remedies linking us with our
beasts are as ancient—and mysterious—
as our mutual dependence.*

BY ERIKA BRADY

For centuries, mankind has been sharing and swapping folk remedies with animals. These practices remain common in rural agricultural regions but may even occur in today's (sub)urban areas.

FARM ANIMAL FORMULAS

The most conspicuous contemporary examples of animal–human crossover care relate to skin and cosmetic aids.

A healing balm invented by a Vermont pharmacist in 1899 to soothe sore cow udders has claimed long since then that "It's not just for cows anymore!" In fact, usage cuts straight across species boundaries: Bag Balm's Web site describes the ointment as "ready to moisturize . . . every member of the household . . . right down to the family dog."

In 1970, Phillip and Bonnie Katzev, owners of a horse farm in New Jersey, created an equine shampoo and conditioner. They branded it "Mane 'n Tail," and by the 1980s, it had become a personal favorite of groomers, who admired their steeds' flowing manes. Today, son Devon is president of the brand's parent firm, Straight Arrow. Even though product lines for both equines and

In a scene from *Theatrum Sanitatis,* a medieval medical handbook encouraging practical hygiene over magic or spiritual beliefs, boars eat acorns alongside a shepherd.

humans have expanded, customers continue the crossover use of many of them.

NANNY NOSTRUMS

Historically, however, the crossover pattern runs much deeper. Ailments have been more serious than chapped hands and udders or lusterless horse manes and human ponytails.

The Kentucky Folklife Archives at Western Kentucky University in Bowling Green contain many recent references—some from the 1990s—to a tea made of sheep dung and used to treat measles and childhood respiratory ailments. Aka "nanny tea," the brew was sometimes varied with dried manure from other animals. The practice is corroborated widely in such collections throughout North America but is most commonly cited in the American South. (The writer Alice Walker uses the belief powerfully in her short story "Strong Horse Tea.")

Another practice involves coaxing a stallion to breathe down your throat or sipping water out of a trough from which a white horse has just drunk—all to gain relief from whooping cough.

PLUCKY CHARMS

Over the years, ordinary threats to animal health have given rise to nonscientific beliefs and practices, some of which have spiritual or cosmological implications:

• According to one book of Ohio folk medical practice, ashes sprinkled over a creature on Ash Wednesday will prevent lice.

• Many contemporary farmers carefully consult their Almanac to avoid castrating stock when the Moon is in Scorpio, the sign of the loins, lest the poor beast bleed out.

• It has been reported by 19th- and 20th-century collectors of folk belief in North Carolina, Georgia, and Wisconsin that one must not count

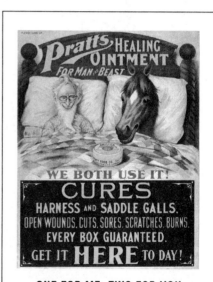

ONE FOR ME, TWO FOR YOU

The slogan "One for a man, two for a horse" describes the dosage for Pratts Healing Ointment, a popular 19th-century nostrum that claimed to be "good for cuts, burns, galls, scratches, or other diseases on either man or beast." Pratts is no longer available, but other products claiming to benefit both humans and animals are.

hens, turkeys, horses, or cattle, lest evil spirits overhear and take action.
• In parts of Texas, it is still considered bad manners to ask a rancher how many head of cattle he or she owns. Perhaps this is because giving a number can appear to be bragging or perhaps it is due to the survival of an earlier belief: To call attention to one's assets can bring ill fortune.

9TH-CENTURY EFFICACY

Many beliefs connected with animals may have both natural and supernatural underlying explanations.

Wherever the origin of maladies such as parasites, arthritis, or intestinal problems was poorly understood, the use of herbs and ointments suggests careful observation of cause-and-effect. Take the 9th-century English manuscript titled *Bald's Leechbook,* a collection of charms and remedies. (Bald was the tome's owner, and "leech" was a word for "physician" at that time.) It deals briskly with many shared animal and human woes that would be familiar to any present-day farmer and his family: aching joints, sore muscles, diarrhea, constipation, worms, and other vermin. Ailments could be addressed by applications of herbs, sometimes enhanced with magical spells, some of which may have hearkened back to pre-Christian religious beliefs.

Ancient, yes, but not obscure: The restorative powers of the potions giv-

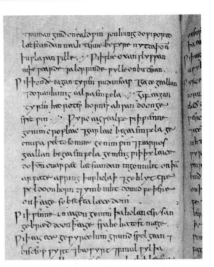

This *Bald's Leechbook* remedy for an eye infection was tested in 2015— with "astonishing" results.

en in Bald's book should not be underestimated. In 2015, British scientists concocted the *Leechbook* remedy for an eye infection—garlic, onion or leeks, wine, and cow bile pounded well and chilled for 9 days—as a curative for methicillin-resistant *Staphylococcus aureus* (MRSA, or staph infection). They pronounced its results "astonishing."

ELFIN AFFLICTIONS

Threats thought to be from the supernatural brought further distress to our ancestors. Particularly dreadful was the threat of elf shot, dangerous to both humans and beasts and treated similarly in both instances.

Elf shot was believed to be caused by small, invisible, malevolent beings—elves. A 12th-century illustration accompanying a psalm depicts an unhappy gentleman pierced (or shot) with arrows wielded by little flying manikins sporting pointy hats. To be "elfshotten" was no joke; manifestations ran from ague (fever and shivering) to cramps to madness. Cures for humans and animals involved both religious spells and (often) a strenuous course of purgatives to bring out the internal poisons through sweating, vomiting, or defecation.

A 12th-century depiction of elf shot

OMINOUS NOTIONS

Concern over a curse affecting your livestock is still reflected in practices found in 20th-century collections of traditional remedies.

The Frank C. Brown Collection of North Carolina Folklore cites one source as recommending burial of a dime under a hog pen to keep witches away. The same source recommends throwing a handful of salt on the fire if your turkeys are bewitched, although it provides no guidance on how to discern this condition beforehand.

Frogs and toads appear in a surprising number of warnings and remedies. In some communities, to kill a frog is to endanger your cattle. And if you are afflicted with malaria, one treatment reported from Indiana suggests placing a toad under a pot and walking around it three times. You hope that the toad is then allowed to hop away to freedom, carrying with it the human ailment.

HOME AND HUSBANDRY

It may seem a stretch to go from frogs and toads to our beloved pet dogs, cats, horses, and other animals, but the curious folklore that weaves our well-being with theirs through the swapping of cures and remedies suggests that we still feel an interdependence.

In fact, it may be more than a feeling. A study by the University of Wisconsin School of Medicine and Public Health, published in September 2017, claims to be the first to show a correlation between dairy farm exposure and reduced respiratory illnesses. So, what is good for animals may indeed be good for us, and their healthy presence in our lives does make us feel better. ∎

Erika Brady is a professor of folk studies at Western Kentucky University and host of a radio show featuring American roots music.

Why Viagra Is Failing Men

Soaring demand expected for new scientific advance made just for older men. Works on both men's physical ability and their desire in bed.

By Harlan S. Waxman
Health News Syndicate

New York – If you're like the rest of us guys over 50; you probably already know the truth… Prescription ED pills don't work! Simply getting an erection doesn't fix the problem" says Dr. Bassam Damaj, chief scientific officer at the world famous Innovus Pharma Laboratories.

As we get older, we need more help in bed. Not only does our desire fade; but erections can be soft or feeble, one of the main complaints with prescription pills. Besides, they're expensive… costing as much as $50.00 each

Plus, it does nothing to stimulate your brain to want sex. "I don't care what you take, if you aren't interested in sex, you can't get or keep an erection. It's physiologically impossible," said Dr. Damaj.

MADE JUST FOR MEN OVER 50

But now, for the first time ever, there's a pill made just for older men. It's called Vesele®. A new pill that helps you get an erection by stimulating your body and your brainwaves. So Vesele® can work even when nothing else worked before.

The new men's pill is not a drug. It's something completely different Because you don't need a prescription for Vesele®, sales are exploding. The maker just can't produce enough of it to keep up with demand. Even doctors are having a tough time getting their hands on it. So what's all the fuss about?

WORKS ON YOUR HEAD AND YOUR BODY

The new formula takes on erectile problems with a whole new twist. It doesn't just address the physical problems of getting older; it works on the mental part of sex too. Unlike the expensive prescriptions, the new

pill stimulates your sexual brain chemistry as well. Actually helping you regain the passion and burning desire you had for your partner again.

THE BRAIN/ERECTION CONNECTION

Vesele takes off where Viagra® only begins. Thanks to a discovery made by 3 Nobel-Prize winning scientists; Vesele® has become the first ever patented supplement to harden you and your libido. So you regain your desire as well as the ability to act on it.

JAW-DROPPING CLINICAL PROOF

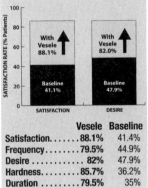

	Vesele	Baseline
Satisfaction	88.1%	41.4%
Frequency	79.5%	44.9%
Desire	82%	47.9%
Hardness	85.7%	36.2%
Duration	79.5%	35%
Ability to Satisfy	83.3%	44.1%

In a 16-week clinical study; scientists from the U.S.A. joined forces to prove Nitric Oxide's effects on the cardio vascular system. They showed that Nitric Oxide could not only increase your ability to get an erection, it would also work on your brainwaves to stimulate your desire for sex. The results were remarkable and published in the world's most respected medical journals.

THE SCIENCE OF SEX

The study asked men, 45 to 65 years old to take the main ingredient in

New men's pill overwhelms your senses with sexual desire as well as firmer, long-lasting erections. There's never been anything like it before.

Vesele® once a day. Then they were instructed not to change the way they eat or exercise but to take Vesele® twice a day. What happened next was remarkable. Virtually every man in the study who took Vesele® twice a day reported a huge difference in their desire for sex. They also experienced harder erections that lasted for almost 20 minutes. The placebo controlled group (who received sugar pills) mostly saw no difference.

The study results even showed an impressive increase in the energy, brain-power and memory of the participants.

"VESELE® PASSED THE TEST"

"As an expert in the development of sexual dysfunction, I've studied the effectiveness of Nitric Oxide on the body and the brain. I'm impressed by the way it increases cerebral and penile blood flow. The result is evident in the creation of Vesele®. It's sure-fire proof that the mind/body connection is unbeatable when achieving and maintaining an erection and the results are remarkable" said Dr. Damaj.

HOW TO GET VESELE®

In order to get the word out about Vesele®, Innovus Pharma is offering special introductory discounts to all who call. Discounts will automatically be applied to all callers, but don't wait. This offer may not last forever. **Call toll-free: 1-800-611-1445.**

How DOGS TRAIN People

TO BEST TRAIN A CANINE, SOMETIMES YOU NEED TO BE TRAINED FIRST.

by **Stephanie Gibeault**

A secret among dog trainers is that we train owners just as much as we train dogs. After all, people and their pets learn in many of the same ways and share many of the same emotions. We can all learn a lesson from man's best friend. So grab some treats and start reading.

Sit Tight

John's Labrador retriever, Bailey, would sit only after being asked six times. John regularly repeated his cues without waiting for Bailey to respond, so Bailey knew that she didn't need to respond the first time—or the fourth or the fifth—because John would reliably ask again. His behavior was the same as nagging his teenager to mow the lawn. The lawn might eventually get cut, but both of them would be exhausted by the process. To get the response he wanted, John needed to ask Bailey to sit only once. Then wait. Initially, he had to lure her with a treat, but once she sat, he praised and rewarded her.

Bailey quickly learned how to make good things happen. The same is true with people. If we encourage the behavior that we want and reward it when we get it, we're far more likely to get it again in the future.

Stay the Course

Allison's Yorkshire terrier puppy, Charlie, refused to obey her "stay" cue because right after cuing Charlie, Allison would walk away. Charlie had no idea yet what the word "stay" meant, so, naturally, he followed her. I suggested that Allison's 16-year-old daughter would not be expected to have a driving lesson on a busy highway if the girl had not mastered the controls on a quiet side street.

To help Charlie learn, Allison stood directly in front of him and gave the command. After only a second, she rewarded him with a treat for being still. Once he understood what was expected, Allison could slowly increase how long she asked him to stay. Only later did she try walking away from him. Breaking complex tasks into smaller, simpler steps helps both dogs and people to learn successfully.

Getting Barking Mad?

Erica's anxious dog, Molly, barked continually while in the backyard. To fix this unwanted habit, Erica installed an antibarking device on the porch. Whenever Molly barked, the device emitted a high-pitch sound that

she did not like. Erica achieved her goal: Molly stopped barking—but she developed a new unwanted behavior: She started avoiding the yard altogether. Like a person who calls in sick to work to avoid a disapproving boss, Molly avoided Erica's punishment (the noise). Not only did the quick-fix device worsen the underlying issue, but also it risked damaging the canine–owner bond. Erica had to remove the device and build Molly's confidence by exposing her to more sights, sounds, and smells so that the world was less overwhelming.

Looking for Trouble

General, a German shepherd owned by Bill, spent most of dog training class staring at other dogs. This is rude and threatening behavior in canine culture. The more General stared, the more agitated he became. Bill could have punished his dog, but General would have learned nothing about what to

do instead. Bill needed to think of General as an unmannered child: He was bound to make social blunders until he learned alternative behaviors.

General needed something else to focus on, so Bill taught him to make eye contact with him. After all, General could not stare at both Bill and another dog at the same time! When General complied, Bill praised him and gave him a treat. Eventually,

BREAKING COMPLEX TASKS INTO SMALLER, SIMPLER STEPS HELPS BOTH DOGS AND PEOPLE TO LEARN SUCCESSFULLY.

General saw other dogs as a chance to look at Bill and earn a reward.

Just Reward

When Karen adopted Max, an adult Pekingese, he experienced a significant change in his environment and, as a result, began acting out. Karen decided that adjustment time and a little praise were all he needed. Praise is wonderful, but more tangible rewards can keep pets—and people—truly motivated.

Karen needed to use Max's favorite food and new toys as rewards to help Max associate the new aspects of his life with those things that he already loved. For example, Karen fed Max his preferred treat in his new crate, which soon became a favorite place.

When you watch what you say and how you say it, your dog will better understand you. This improved communication always leads to more effective training and a better relationship with your furry friend. ■

Stephanie Gibeault is a certified professional dog trainer from Pickering, Ontario.

177

DOUBLE-ACTION
NATURAL PAIN RELIEVERS

Soothe body ailments and give your wallet
a rest at the same time.

BY MARGARET BOYLES

EASE ACHY MUSCLES

Many over-the-counter products designed to relieve pain—such as from arthritis, muscle pulls and aches, sprains, and shingles—contain capsaicin, the source of the "heat" that you feel when you eat a hot pepper. Scientists theorize that the burning sensation produced by capsaicinoids triggers the release of endorphins, the body's natural painkillers. Cayenne is commonly available, so why not make your own capsaicin oil or cream?

You will need ...

2 tablespoons cayenne powder

2 cups olive or canola oil

**2 ounces grated beeswax or
   beeswax beads (optional)**

cheesecloth

Combine the cayenne and oil in a pan (used only for this purpose). Heat on low, stirring occasionally, for 10 to 12 minutes. Set aside for a few days, then rewarm the mixture. Add beeswax, if using, and stir to dissolve. Strain the mixture through the cheesecloth into a large glass jar with a lid. Cover and store in a cool place.

To use, wearing kitchen gloves or using a cotton swab, rub the oil or cream into the sore or chronically inflamed area several times a day. Do not apply it to broken skin or burned areas; avoid using immediately after a hot bath or shower and/or with a heating pad.

Consult a health care professional before using capsaicin or hot peppers for therapeutic use; do not use on children, and be aware that capsaicin may interact with a number of prescriptions or commercial products.

CALM UNCOMFORTABLE JOINTS

Perhaps you have a heat pack or bag that you heat in the microwave before applying it to sore muscles or joints? Often these are filled with rice, which dries out and can develop an unpleasant odor after repeated heating. Whole corn is wholly different: It produces a slightly moist heat that penetrates more deeply into the painful areas, and corn kernels hold heat longer than rice does. Here's how to make a corn warmer.

You will need . . .

4 cups whole raw corn kernels (not popping corn), often available at animal feed and hardware stores

1 cotton knee-length or tube sock

Pour the corn kernels into the sock. Tie off the end of the sock or stitch it closed. Microwave the filled sock for up to a minute at full power or in increments of 30 seconds to get it as hot as you like it. (Don't worry; the corn will not pop, although it may release a subtle popcorn aroma.) Lay the corn warmer on achy or tired joints.

TAKE THE STING OUT OF A CANKER

The exact cause of canker sores—those whitish, red-edged spots inside the mouth—is not known, but they may be brought on by vitamin or mineral deficiencies, hormonal changes, allergies, or even gluten sensitivity. They may last a week or two if no treatment is applied, but why endure the pain any longer than you need to? Here are a few easy remedies.

■ Steep a cup of sage or chamomile tea and, as you sip it, swoosh it around your mouth and on the sore.

■ Dissolve 1 teaspoon of baking soda in ½ cup of warm water and rinse your mouth with it.

■ Chip some ice cubes, then put the pieces into your mouth and let them dissolve slowly.

Don't confuse cankers with cold sores—aka "fever blisters"—caused by the *Herpes simplex* virus; these usually appear on or around the lips or the outside of the mouth.

FOR PAIN IN THE NECK

Your body's immune system often responds to a viral or bacterial infection by giving you a sore throat. Drinking fluids helps to keep the swollen mucous membranes moist, which helps the healing process. Water is excellent, right out of the tap. Or try packaged herbal teas, such as echinacea, peppermint, and chamomile. Then there are these centuries-old palliatives:

■ Combine 1 cup of warm water with 1 teaspoon of salt and stir to dissolve. Gargle with a mouthful of this for 30 seconds once every hour.

■ Before going to bed, take 1 tablespoon of concentrated lemon juice immediately followed by 1 tablespoon of honey.

■ Mix 1 tablespoon of apple cider vinegar and 1 tablespoon of honey in 1 cup of warm water. Drink, sipping.

■ Grate 1 tablespoon of fresh ginger. Boil 4 cups of water. Turn off the heat, add the ginger, and cover the pan for 10 minutes. Drink the beverage hot or cool. Reheat as desired. ■

New Hampshire's **Margaret Boyles** is the author of Almanac.com's popular "Living Naturally" blog.

HORSESHOES

A Game Conceived on the Hoof

BY ALICE CARY

∪ ∪ ∪ ∪ ∪ ∪

People have been pitching horseshoes for hundreds of years. Many scholars believe that the sport originated with the ancient Greek Olympics, at which athletes popularized the throwing of metal and stone discuses for distance. People who didn't have discuses took up the sport of heaving old horseshoes bent into circles.

At some point in the 1st millennium, the notion of throwing objects onto a stake came along. English peasants in the 16th century played what we know as horseshoes, as well as a closely related game called quoits, which involved a metal disk with a hole in the middle.

"Pitchers of Horse Hardware"

Both games spread to the New World, where American Revolutionary War soldiers played horseshoes so much that the Duke of Wellington observed: "The war was won by the pitchers of horse hardware."

Years later, the game was particularly popular among Union soldiers in the Civil War, who tossed mule horseshoes. Returning soldiers introduced the game to their families, and eventually horseshoe courts were built across the United States and then Canada.

The first official rules were established in England in 1869 (they were used in America as well, with regional differences). A "world championship" tournament was held at a 1910 horse show in Bronson, Kansas. The winner was Frank Jackson, who went on to win more tournaments with a custom-made pair of horseshoes.

The Grand League of American Horseshoe Pitchers Association, established in Kansas City, Kansas, in 1914, nailed down precise rules concerning everything from the weight of horseshoes to distances on the court. Later, another national organization was formed and the two groups eventually merged, becoming the National Horseshoe Pitchers Association of America.

The Dominion of Canada Horseshoe Pitchers Association, Canada's first, came into being in 1929 largely through the efforts of Walter Kane, an active player and the Association's unanimously elected first president.

(continued)

Tournaments come and go, but a ringer is always a ringer.

–Southern California Horseshoe Pitching Association

Tournament champions, including Kane, were celebrated across the provinces, often on the front page of newspapers.

Courting Farms and Clubs

Kane was a keen promoter, once proclaiming, "Every farm should have a court, every village a club, and every county a league." During a visit to Regina, Saskatchewan, in 1930 to encourage interest, he demonstrated his horseshoe-pitching skill with different tosses: through a man's legs, over a boy's head, and onto a stake concealed by a blanket. After several name changes, the organization emerged as Horseshoe Canada Association in 1979.

By the 1920s, the sport was so popular that games attracted spectators and were regularly covered in the sports pages. Doc Kerr, a sports-writer in Akron, Ohio, called the game "barnyard golf" because it was such a hit in rural regions. However, according to the *Richmond* [Virginia] *Times-Dispatch* in January 1929, "men of the city are quite as much given to it as their brothers in the country." By the end of the decade, it had become hailed as good exercise, and indoor playing courts ("in connection with bowling alleys") were predicted as a trend.

Today, over 15 million players across the United States and Canada pitch horseshoes in tournaments, leagues, parks, and backyards. The beauty of the game is that almost anyone can play.

The Dueling Duo

In 1930 in Hayward, Minnesota, R. E. Dewey and J. C. Hanson challenged each other to a game of horseshoes. Their

◡◡◡◡◡◡ REINING IN THE RULES ◡◡◡◡◡◡

An official horseshoe court is 50 feet long by 10 feet wide and made of clay. Iron stakes 14 or 15 inches high are planted 40 feet apart for men's competition and 30 feet apart for women. Two or four players take turns throwing two horseshoes as close as possible to the opposite stake. (Officially, horseshoes are "swung" rather than pitched or tossed.) Good delivery depends on a variety of factors, including the grip of the horseshoe, finger placement, release, stance, and movement of the feet and rest of the body.

Scoring is simple:
• A horseshoe that encircles the stake (determined when the straight edge of one shoe can be placed across both tips of the encircling shoe without touching the stake) is called a ringer and counts for 3 points.
• Ringers thrown by both players are called "dead ringers" and cancel each other out.
• The shoe closest to the stake gets 1 point, as long as it's within one horseshoe's width of the stake. If both shoes are closer than the opponent's, 2 points are awarded.
• A ringer plus closest shoe counts for 4 points.
• Formal games are played to a winning score of 40 points; informal games go to 21.

Horseshoes are usually made of iron or steel and must weigh no more than 2 pounds, 10 ounces. They must be less than 7⅝ inches long, with an opening no larger than 3½ inches wide.

The wise
horseshoe
pitcher plays
her own game
and does not
compete
against her
opponent.

−SCHPA

plan was to play to 5,000 points. The contest began on March 6, with an average of five 50-point games played each day. Dewey reached 5,000 first, but Hanson was so close, with 4,972 points, that the men agreed to continue.

On August 9, they called it quits. Dewey had 25,000 points and Hanson had 24,949. The pair was well matched: Just 3 days earlier, each had stood at 181 games won, with a score of 23,961 points.

The Natural

When Clifton Jones saw Shernetta Edwards pitch horseshoes at an employee appreciation outing, he knew that she was a natural ringer. Jones had competed in national championships and urged Edwards to do so herself. The pair began practicing and competing together, and Jones built a regulation horseshoe pit in Edwards's backyard. His encouragement and efforts soon paid off. Edwards won the Women's Class C Championship in the 2011 World Horseshoe Tournament.

The Road to Sensible Shoes

Alexander the Great once marched his troops and animals until the shoeless hooves of his horses were broken.

Ancient people in Asia put socks or booties on horses' hooves in snow.

The earliest horseshoes were made of leather. Later, horses' hooves were placed inside metal shoes, sometimes attached with leather straps. The mules that pulled Roman Emperor Nero's chariot had silver shoes, while those that pulled his wife's chariot wore shoes of gold.

By the 6th and 7th centuries, Europeans were nailing metal shoes onto their horses' feet.

During the Crusades, horseshoes served as currency to pay taxes.

The Industrial Revolution made horseshoe production a snap. In 1835, Henry Burden, a Scottish inventor in Troy, New York, patented a horseshoe machine. During the Civil War, his machine made most of the horseshoes for the Union cavalry, at a peak production of 51 million a year.

Whether on the hoof or in the hand, horseshoes continue to be an integral part of North American culture. ∎

Alice Cary, a longtime Almanac contributor from Groton, Massachusetts, hasn't thrown a ringer in a very long time.

∪∪∪∪∪∪∪∪ LUCK AND LORE ∪∪∪∪∪∪∪∪

According to ancient Celtic folklore, goblins fear the iron used in weapons, prompting superstitious people to hang horseshoes over their doorways to ward off evil spirits.

Legend says that England's St. Dunstan managed to horseshoe the devil's cloven hoof; thereafter, Satan pledged never to enter a doorway over which a horseshoe is hung.

Some say that a horseshoe's ends should point up to collect good luck; others believe that ends pointing down pour good luck onto those who pass underneath. Undecided? Play it safe and hang two.

Superstition holds that found horseshoes have 10 times the power of those acquired in other ways, while one that is bought is useless.

Photo: National Archives and Records Administration

**Learn
to see only
the stake.**
–SCHPA

(continued from page 41) reminding me of a twisty, newfangled roller coaster. They also tend to be a darker, deeper green than those of most regular varieties, but this can vary.

At first glance, dwarfs seem like stumpier determinates, and technically many of them are: one crop, and they're done. Many of the long-standing favorites tend to be determinate dwarfs. I'm partial to 'Hahms Gelbe Topftomate', a German variety that sounds a bit like a location in Middle Earth but is really just a description: a tomato bearing yellow fruit that can be grown in a pot. For a plant that tops off at 8 inches, Hahms is an enthusiastic producer. In the years that I've been growing it, I've enjoyed some incredible harvests from the 1-foot-deep sap buckets in which I grow them. Plants grow laden and top-heavy with masses of fruit. Again, this is due to that intensely dense foliage, which also makes for a very attractive plant.

'Red Robin' is a fantastic red cherry option that is of a size similar to that of 'Hahms' and as generous, too. Both plants are very early producers, coming in at around 50 to 60 days.

If you're looking for a plant that can be grown in a really small pot (1 gallon, or 6 to 7 inches deep), try the micro- or ultra-dwarfs. There are

'LIME GREEN SALAD'

lots of popular, accessible hybrid options out there with names like 'Micro Tom' and 'Tiny Tim'. I much prefer a teeny, open-pollinated variety ("open-pollinated" means that you can save seed for next year that will be true to form) called 'Mohamed'. Unlike many other micro-minis, 'Mohamed' produces sweet and melt-in-your-mouth, delicious, red cherry tomatoes. Kids love a diminutive plant that suits their size, and I like that I can grow it just about anywhere. I've even had success during the winter on a windowsill, which can be a challenge with other varieties.

Not all dwarfs produce tiny *red* fruit. 'Goldilox' is a little-known determinate dwarf that yields loads of sweet, golden-orange "saladette" fruit that are about 2½ inches in diameter. 'Lime Green Salad' makes tangy, olive-green ovals of a similar size with a shocking lime-green interior. If you're really looking for flash, 'Cherokee Tiger Large' is a newer determinate cross with colorful, orange-stripe, 3½-inch, beefsteak fruit on a stunning chartreuse plant. There's really nothing like it!

Dwarf varieties can carry indeterminate traits, growing off a main stem and continuing with new growth and fruit until the season reaches an end. Most of these

THE DWARF TOMATO PROJECT

Seeing a hole in the range of high-quality patio and container varieties, tomato-growing enthusiasts Craig LeHoullier of North Carolina and Patrina Nuske Small

'ROSELLA PURPLE'

of Australia came up with a plan to crossbreed favorite indeterminate heirlooms with short and stocky dwarfs. The goal of the Dwarf Tomato Project was to create nonhybrid, compact, tree types with the full scope of color, shape, and flavor diversity found in the large heirlooms. Imagine the gorgeous and sizable, mouthwatering fruit of 'Cherokee Purple' or 'Brandywine' on manageable, 3- to 5-foot-tall plants suitable for growing in midsize containers!

It seems unthinkable that such a small plant could support large, delicious fruit, but the tree type's ability is due to the high ratio of foliage to fruit that results from its stocky build and dense, rugose foliage.

It can take years to stabilize a new cross so that plants grown from seed come out reliably true to—or close to—the characteristics of the variety. Wisely, LeHoullier and Small used their seasonal separation by hemisphere to advantage and rallied volunteer growers on both sides of the globe. This allowed them to grow out two crops per year instead of just one, speeding up the process.

They began the endeavor in 2006 and by 2010 released their first varieties. This collaborative growing initiative has resulted in approximately 70 breathtaking varieties—with more on the way!

I've grown about a dozen and recommend sweet and prolific, yellow-fruiting 'Dwarf Sweet Sue'; rich, smoky, and dark 'Dwarf Wild Fred'; and the complex flavors of 'Rosella Purple'. With so many different varieties, there's something to suit every palette, space, and taste.

'DWARF WILD FRED'

Photos, from left: Heritage Tomato Seed/Tatiana'sTOMATObase; Tatiana Kouchnareva/Tatiana'sTOMATObase

indeterminates, or "tree types," are newly created varieties, resulting from a fantastic breeding program called the Dwarf Tomato Project.

GROWING CONCERNS

Like all other tomatoes, dwarf varieties can be grown in a container or in the ground. I grow most of my dwarf plants in pots; they were made for it! As long as you drill or cut drainage holes in the bottom, pretty much any old thing of a certain depth/size can qualify as a suitable container. I shop yard sales, thrift stores—even scour the curbsides of my city—looking for cheap and cheerful objects to repurpose. Lately, I've been experimenting with cloth pots. They're affordable and easy to move and can be washed and put away for the winter. Plant roots grow differently inside cloth than they do in plastic or metal. They cut themselves off when they hit the edges rather than wind tightly around the bottom, and I have found that this results in plants that thrive despite less available root space.

Whatever sort of pot you choose, use one appropriate to each variety's potential maximum size.

Micro-dwarfs are fine in 6- to 8-inch pots, although I tend to go larger since a bigger pot means less maintenance and less chance that the plant will be subjected to stress caused by dry soil and a lack of nutrients.

A PASSION FOR "LOVE APPLES"

Centuries ago, tomatoes grew in berry-like clusters in their native South America. Later, in Mexico, the Aztecs called them *tomatl.* Spanish conquistadors brought the fruit to Europe where, noticing its heart-like shape, many people believed them to be an aphrodisiac. As a result, the French called them *pommes d'amour,* or "love apples."

Determinate dwarfs do well in 5-gallon pots that are around 10 to 12 inches deep. While indeterminate dwarfs can thrive in the same size, I prefer to go larger (7 gallons) because the heavy, larger fruit require slightly deeper staking to prevent the whole thing from toppling over.

Start your seeds alongside other varieties, or do as I do: Start dwarfs weeks earlier. This trick allows me to produce even earlier fruit. And since dwarf varieties stay small and manageable longer, they do not take up much extra space under lights.

Earlier fresh tomatoes and big, tasty yields on compact plants that can be grown just about anywhere you've got enough sunlight and room for a pot: What's not to love about these "love apples"? ∎

Canadian gardener, author, and photographer **Gayla Trail** has produced five books on gardening and growing food in small and challenging urban spaces. See more of her work at yougrowgirl.com.

Good News for Americans, Bad News for Pain Drugs

Millions are expected to benefit from a new technology that could relieve years of severe joint discomfort; reprograms the body to block slow burning inflammation instead of creating it

By Casey Law
Health News Correspondent

NATION — Several of the major drug companies behind popular pain relievers may take a financial hit as manufacturing of a new pill is now complete.

Using a new technology, the pill could be safer and more effective than many store bought brands.

The pill, VeraFlex, was developed in May of this year by a private company in Seattle.

The Science Behind Relief

Research shows that the joint stiffness, soreness and discomfort associated with arthritis is caused by inflammation which attacks healthy cartilage and protective tissue.

And according to leading medical scientists, this inflammation is caused by two inflammatory enzymes released by the body's immune system.

Remarkably, the active ingredients in VeraFlex help to block the production of both these enzymes, resulting in a dramatic decreasing in swelling, inflammation, and discomfort.

Right now, the leading over-the-counter pills are only able to block one of these enzymes!

"VeraFlex users can generally expect more flexibility in three days...their joint pain alleviated in five days...and in just seven days, a tremendous improvement in overall joint function that may help them move like they did years prior" explains Dr. Liza Leal, developer and spokesperson for VeraFlex.

"It's an incredibly powerful little pill. And with the addition of a patented absorption enhancer, it packs an even greater punch. That's why I'm so excited to be the first to share these results. It's giving sufferers their life back."

A Safer Avenue to Amazing Relief

Its widely accepted through the medical community that inflammatory enzymes are the primary cause of pain and suffering in millions of Americans. It's why most prescriptions and even nonprescription pills are designed to block them.

However, what most people don't know is that even the most advanced ones can't block both!

"Top pharma companies have struggled to create a drug that blocks COX and LOX; the medical names for the two inflammatory enzymes in the body. Consider the top seller Celebrex, it only blocks one variation of the COX enzyme" explains Leal.

"Every VeraFlex capsule contains an ultra-high dose of a patented plant extract which has been clinically shown to block both enzymes, bringing relief to every joint that hurts!

Piling on the Clinical Research

Remarkably, the key ingredient in VeraFlex is protected by 8 patents that spread from the US into Canada. And as would one guess, it's backed by an enormous amount of research, including two patient clinical trials.

In the first, 60 participants with rheumatoid arthritis and/or osteoarthritis were randomly placed into four groups.

Two groups were given the patented ingredient in VeraFlex, one was given the drug Celecoxib, and the last group a placebo. The results were monitored at 30, 60, and 90 days and were stunning.

The groups taking the VeraFlex ingredient saw staggering improvements in arthritis symptoms such as flexibility, discomfort and function.

And even more astonishing they experienced a dramatic reduction in pain by the 30-day mark that was even better than Celecoxib, a powerful drug!

A second study was conducted to ensure the data was accurate and again the results participants experienced taking the VeraFlex compound blew away researchers.

This time it beat out the drug Naproxen. Shockingly, both men and women experienced a reduction in joint stiffness two days faster than when using Naproxen.

Faster Delivery, Maximum Absorption

VeraFlex is mainly comprised of two patented ingredients: Univestin, a powerful immune modulator which blocks the enzymes which cause your joints to hurt and BiAloe, an absorption enhancer (accelerator) that ensures maximum potency.

Research shows that severe joint discomfort arises when the immune system goes haywire and releases COX and LOX into your blood stream, two enzymes that causes tremendous swelling and inflammation around cartilage and protective tissue.

Unfortunately, modern day pain pills are only able block only one of these enzymes, resulting in marginal relief and continued suffering.

The Univestin in VeraFlex is one of the only known substances which has been proven successful in blocking both enzymes, resulting in phenomenal relief from the worst kinds of discomfort.

The addition of BiAloe, a unique aloe vera extra, maximizes the delivery of the plant based Univestin extract to every joint in the body because it is proven to improve nutrient absorption for maximum results.

Claim a Free 3-Month Supply

This is the official nationwide release of VeraFlex, and so, the company is offering our readers up to 3 FREE bottles with their order.

All you have to do is call toll free 1-800-236-1961 and provide the operator with the Free Bottle Approval Code: VF350.

LARUE SWAMP IS SPRING-FED FROM THE LIMESTONE CLIFFS.

(continued from page 84)
(rust) between the rock particles; now the sandstone is bound together by them. This area is also one of the best places to experience a cuesta—a long, rocky ridge that in places resembles the back of a Stegosaurus.

Surrounding the Recreation Area

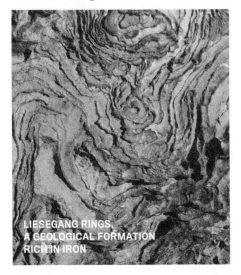

LIESEGANG RINGS, A GEOLOGICAL FORMATION RICH IN IRON

is the Garden of the Gods Wilderness Area, a rocky, 3,300-acre forested fortress of solitude. No motorized vehicles are allowed. If you want a glimpse into the geological and historical past of southern Illinois—with its cool, rocky streams; massive, mushroom-shape rocks; and overhanging cliffs likely once camped under by Native Americans—you'll have to walk.

Some 50 miles from Garden of the Gods lies LaRue–Pine Hills–Otter Pond Research Natural Area, a 5x2-mile strip of rugged forestland bordering a large swamp along the western edge of the Shawnee National Forest. Designated in 1970 as the National Forest Service's first Ecological Area and in 1991 as a National Research Natural Area by the Department of the Interior, LaRue–Pine Hills–Otter Pond contains diverse habitats.

A massive, gleaming limestone cliff abuts the swamp. Nearby, dense cove forests follow ravines carved into the highlands. Here, in only a few square miles, 1,200 plant species grow—40 percent of all known Illinois plant species and nearly as many as live in the Great Smoky Mountains! A florist's bounty of purple larkspur, trilliums, phacelia, cleft phlox, and celandine poppies grow along the bases of the bluffs and up the steep ravines. Ninety percent of Illinois's mammal species live here and 65 species of amphibians and snakes (including venomous copperheads and cottonmouths). Frogs, turtles, salamanders, and skinks and other lizards also call the area home.

It's the reptiles and amphibians, however, that hold a special place of honor: The road at the base of the bluff (officially LaRue Road #345, aka Snake Road) is closed from March 15–May 15 and September 1–October 30 for their migration from bluff to swamp and back again. It is the only road in the United States that is closed biannually for snake (and other reptile and am-phibian) migration. (You're welcome to walk it—if you dare!)

Snake Road straddles two vastly different ecological regions—the Ozark bluffs and the Mississippi River floodplain. Their juxtaposition provides the reptiles and amphibians with all of their life-cycle requirements: They forage and reproduce in the swamps during spring and summer and overwinter in the bluffs.

Whether Snake Road is so flooded or muddy that visitors walk it in knee boots or so dusty that shoes kick up miniature dust devils, tiny cricket frogs will often be found cloaking its surface. LaRue–Pine Hills–Otter Pond is truly Illinois's version of the Garden of Eden.

All sites in the Shawnee National Forest are easily accessible from both Interstate 57 and Interstate 24, 7 miles south of Marion. For more information, visit www.fs.usda.gov/shawnee. ■

Michael Jeffords and **Susan Post** are the authors of *Exploring Nature in Illinois: A Field Guide to the Prairie State* (University of Illinois Press, 2014).

SOUTHERN LEOPARD FROG

VENOMOUS COTTONMOUTH ON SNAKE ROAD

(continued from page 89)

Symbols of Peace, Loyalty, and Lore

Donkey history mirrors human history. Donkey remains discovered in Egypt and later in Mesopotamia and Iran date back 5,000 to 6,000 years. They are one of the few domesticated animals with African origins, bred from wild asses. However, their heritage is well documented by more than ancient bones; the donkey is also present in art, literature, and folklore.

Marguerite Henry's *Brighty of the Grand Canyon,* the 1953 children's book.

In music, donkeys figure only modestly in Christmas songs like Boswell's *Little Donkey* or *Dominick the Donkey* by Lou Monte.

Folklore has promoted some lingering beliefs, such as that eating the dark, cross-forming hair on donkeys' backs will cure various maladies and that wearing a donkey

Probably the most enduring symbols of this heritage are the many biblical references. Legend says that the dark dorsal and shoulder stripes that create a "cross" exist because the humble animal carried Jesus, but donkeys are also respected symbols in Islam and Hinduism.

More contemporary literature calls to mind Don Quixote: It wasn't the nobleman's horse Rocinante that carried his battered body but Sancho Panza's beloved donkey Dapple.

A burro discovered in the Grand Canyon in 1890 became a subject for

hair charm (or riding a donkey backward) will offer protection from ailments as well as help to avoid or cure toothaches.

The Democratic Party can thank Andrew Jackson for their mascot. When he was running for office in 1828, his opponents called him "A. Jack-ass," intending it as an insult, but Jackson embraced the symbol to portray himself as strong-willed and determined. In 1870, cartoonist Thomas Nast used the image to influence public opinion. By 1880, the donkey was the official Democratic symbol.

Photos: Sasha Fox Walters/Getty Images; corolanty/Getty Images

Unburdened Beasts

Donkeys are versatile and vital creatures whose virtues and utility are impressive. In developing countries, they are key means of transport and play critical socioeconomic roles. In more developed places, their roles are more discretionary. Harnessed to a cart, they are popular for pleasure driving. Their natural affinity with humans makes them excellent therapy animals, especially with children.

Need a livestock guardian? Choose a donkey. Unlike horses that flee danger, donkeys face it with loud braying and aggressive chasing to drive off predators.

Flat backs make them well-suited pack animals (although ideally they should be loaded with only about one-third of their own weight). A donkey of any size can be trained for light agricultural draft work, while the mammoth variety is a surefooted riding steed.

Donkey milk in cosmetics is not a new concept. It's said that Cleopatra bathed in it because of its unique anti-inflammatory and hydrating properties.

Burros as BFFs

The Wild and Free-Roaming Horses and Burros Act of 1971 afforded donkeys protection as ". . . living symbols of the historic and pioneer spirit of the West . . .," but the U.S. Bureau of Land Management (BLM) is tasked with establishing controversial inventories. "Excess" animals are collected and offered for adoption. BLM auctions present opportunities to obtain a reasonably priced new best friend. ∎

Karen L. Kirsch lives in Louisville, Ohio, with a menagerie that includes two donkeys.

Photos, from left: Schrempf2/Getty Images; cnx4004/Getty Images

THE ARCTIC PLUNGE

The temperature difference between the cold Arctic and warmer south affects the jet stream (a river of strong westerly winds in the upper atmosphere). When the Arctic warms faster than areas farther south, the difference in temperature is reduced. This weakens the jet stream, which then tends to take bigger swings to the north and south. This pattern allows warm air to penetrate farther north and cold air to plunge farther south than usual (see graphic on page 196). Large jet stream waves tend to move slowly, as do the surface weather systems that they create, causing more persistent weather. Read about this effect on last winter's weather on page 198.

Why Is
EXTREME WEATHER
on the Rise?
LOOK TO THE ARCTIC FOR ANSWERS.

by Jennifer Francis

Warming global temperatures are clearly making heat waves hotter, hurricanes more intense, downpours heavier, and droughts longer-lasting. It is no misperception that the number of natural catastrophes seems to be increasing. Now new research is finding other factors affecting our weather, such as the melting Arctic.

Just during the past 40 years, we have watched the Arctic's summer sea ice shrink to half the area that it typically covered during pre-industrial times, and total ice by volume has declined to only one-third of its long-term average.

These Arctic events are not occurring in isolation; other changes in the climate system—involving ocean, land, fresh water, plants, animals, the cryosphere (perennially frozen areas), and the atmosphere—are happening simultaneously. Indeed, some unknowns remain, but many impacts of a rapidly warming Arctic are coming into focus.

One of these is the impact of the Arctic meltdown on midlatitude weather systems, particularly on extreme events. The fundamental idea is that a warming Arctic will enable certain weather conditions to persist, leading to damaging droughts, prolonged heat waves and cold spells, and parades of storms—familiar headlines in recent years. Here are three examples.

1. WHY NORTH AMERICA HAS A WARM, DRY WEST AND A COLD, SNOWY EAST

Since late 2013, the predominant weather pattern over North America has featured a strong and persistent northward swing in the jet stream (aka a "ridge") in the West. Dubbed the "ridiculously resilient ridge," it has been responsible for persistent drought, heat waves, and extensive wildfires across western North America.

A jet stream ridge is usually accompanied by a downstream southward dip (aka a "trough"), a familiar pattern over eastern North America during recent winters (see below). Deep troughs allow cold Arctic air to plunge southward into regions unaccustomed to cold, often accompanied by a parade of destructive "bomb cyclones." This pattern has helped to drive a cooling trend in eastern North America, despite warming over the rest of the globe.

Recent studies are revealing how Arctic warming helps to promote this ridge/trough pattern and vice versa. When ocean temperatures along the west coast of North America are warmer than normal (as they have been since late 2013), a ridge tends to form there. The ridge's strength is bolstered by the new atmospheric heat source related to extreme ice loss north of Alaska. Much more of the Sun's energy is absorbed in the areas of newly exposed dark ocean, warming that open water.

As the autumn Sun sets over the Arctic to begin the long, dark winter,

HOW DOES ARCTIC WARMING AFFECT THE JET STREAM?

The difference in temperature between the Arctic and areas farther south fuels the west winds of the jet stream.

A large temperature difference fuels a strong jet stream that flows on a straighter eastward path and keeps cold air in.

When the jet stream weakens, it becomes wobblier, allowing cold Arctic air to move southward.

Illustration: Rob Schuster

the air temperature plummets. Much of this extra heat stored in the ocean then returns to the atmosphere, slowing the freeze-up process and contributing to abnormal Arctic warmth. Consequently, the natural fluctuation in Pacific Ocean temperature patterns, combined with the recent Arctic meltdown, favors the formation, intensification, and persistence of the western ridge/eastern trough pattern.

2. THE EURASIAN INFLUENCE
A ridge/trough pattern similar to that in North America has occurred with increasing frequency in Eurasia in recent decades. This pattern can become so intense that the resulting wave energy in the jet stream is transferred upward into the stratosphere, where the true polar vortex resides. This influx of wave energy can disrupt the normally circular flow of the vortex around the North Pole, causing it to plunge southward or even to split into two gyres.

When this occurs, large jet stream waves persist into late winter and even early spring, resulting in extended periods of unusual and stagnant weather patterns around the Northern Hemisphere. The winters of 2017–18 and 2018–19 provide clear examples of this, with large ridges and troughs causing both extreme cold spells and winter heat waves.

3. WHY SUMMER WEATHER STAGNATES
The Arctic meltdown may be contributing to summer heat waves and flooding over Northern Hemisphere continents, according to new research. The spring snow cover on high-latitude land areas has been disappearing much earlier in recent decades, leading to the strongest Arctic warming in late spring/early summer being located over northern continents. Snow loss during the season of most intense sunshine causes the soil to dry out and warm earlier, effectively giving summer heat a jump start.

The location of this warming also can create a double peak in the north-south temperature trend, which favors the formation of a split jet stream: one branch along the Arctic coast, the other farther south through the middle of a continent. Weather systems between the jet branches tend to become "stuck" and cause prolonged hot spells or rainy periods, depending on the location of the jet stream waves. Recent deadly heat waves, floods, drought, and wildfires in many parts of the Northern Hemisphere, especially during 2018, were likely exacerbated by this connection.

As the Arctic continues to surprise us with its rapid pace of change, researchers are scrambling to understand the myriad ways in which it will affect other parts of the climate system. But it's becoming ice-crystal-clear that change at the top of the globe will increasingly affect us all. ∎

Jennifer Francis, Ph.D., is a senior scientist at the Woods Hole Research Center in Falmouth, Massachusetts. In a 2012 study, she and Dr. Steve Vavrus first proposed the impact of Arctic meltdown on mid-latitude extreme weather systems.

WEATHER

LAST WINTER'S RECORD-BREAKING, WRATHFUL, AND WICKED WEATHER

Here's everything you were trying to remember—or forget!

NOVEMBER 2018

A plunge in the jet stream kickstarted winter in many parts of the Northeast, Midwest, Plains, and Rockies, with a midmonth storm bringing extreme cold and snow to some 74 cities. Burlington, Vermont, had 7 days of below-freezing temperatures and got almost three times its average season-to-date snowfall. New York City's Central Park measured 6.4 inches of snow—enough to topple leafy trees a few blocks away. The storm brought an unseasonable chill to parts of the South: Monroe (Louisiana) Regional Airport recorded 0.4 inch of snow. Light snow was seen in Greenville, Mississippi, and Tupelo got sleet mixed with drizzle. Memphis had its snowiest November day in 27 years, picking up 0.6 inch.

The St. Louis metro area got 2 to 5 inches, while areas beyond it got 6 to 9. Louisville, Kentucky, saw nearly a quarter-inch of ice accumulation on trees and elevated surfaces. Parts of Cincinnati and Dayton, Ohio, got a coating of that much or slightly more. Up to a half-inch of ice was reported near Boone, North Carolina. On Black Friday (the 23rd), a blizzard arrived in the Cascade mountains of the Pacific Northwest. Over the next 5 days or so, it brought high winds, heavy snow, and treacherous conditions to the Rockies, across the middle of the country, and into northern New England.

DECEMBER 2018

Yet another change in the jet stream brought relative calm to most areas.

Temperatures were warmer than average in much of the country, and these mild conditions spawned more wet than white: Some 378 U.S. cities (mostly east of the Mississippi) experienced one of their Top 10 wettest Decembers on record, while 47 cities, including Asheville, Pensacola, and Tallahassee, broke a record for rain. The wettest place was Quillayute, Washington, with 22.92 inches for the month.

Enhanced Fujita scale category 3 (EF3) tornadoes struck in both Georgia and Illinois—two such events among 66 twisters this month in the U.S. (16 more than the average). Meanwhile, 2-inch-diameter hail rained down on Bracketville, Texas. The snow queen was Marquette, Michigan, which got 39 inches—an awesome accumulation but not a record.

JANUARY 2019

The new year brought an array of extreme conditions, beginning on Day 1. Albuquerque, New Mexico, said good-bye to a major winter storm that had left 3- to 5-foot-tall drifts amid bitter cold temperatures. Intense rainfall in areas near Malibu, California, resulted in mudslides and debris flows, while a lack of precipitation in Hawaii expanded drought conditions. Caribou, Maine, picked up 59.8 inches of snow, for its record-snowiest January, while low snowfall in Alaska forced cancellation of several sled dog races.

While no state's monthly average temperature was below normal, frigid temps did occur. Most arrived in the final days of the month, when a polar vortex shattered records, primarily in the Midwest but also extending across into the Northeast: Chicago, Illinois, dropped to –23°F on January 30 (part of a 52-hour below-zero streak for the Windy City), while Cotton, Minnesota, experienced a frigid –56°F on the next day. How cold was it? The difference between

WEATHER

Key West, Florida, and Key West, Iowa, was 94 degrees on January 30.

FEBRUARY 2019

The snow and ice forecast for Atlanta, Georgia, in advance of the Super Bowl (on the 3rd) did not occur, but weather events elsewhere made headlines: For the first time in February since records began (in 1877), high temperatures in Los Angeles did not reach or exceed 70°F, while the nearby Sierra Nevada mountains measured more than 17 feet of snow. A Snowpocalypse struck Seattle with a total of 20.2 inches, making this the snowiest month there since 1916. Eau Claire, Wisconsin, crushed its monthly record, with 53.7 inches of snow. Omaha, Nebraska, got 27 inches, raising its record stakes. Rainfall records were also broken this month: Nashville, Tennessee, beat its February 1880 record with 13.47 inches, and Tupelo, Mississippi, surpassed its 2018 record of 12.98 inches with 15.61 inches.

A number of temperature records were smashed around the country: Aberdeen, South Dakota, was below zero for 24 days; Rapid City, for 20; and Billings, Montana, for 19. Several Florida cities had hottest-ever days, and Hatteras, North Carolina, recorded a record-warm month for the second year in a row.

MARCH 2019

Thanks to a bend in the jet stream, Alaska recorded its warmest March ever, but these same upper-level

Photo: clintspencer/Getty Images

winds also pushed bitter Arctic cold into the northern Rockies, Plains, and Midwest. Montana took a beating. On the 3rd, the mean temperature in Great Falls was 50 degrees colder than average. Not only the ground but also the water pipes froze in several Montana cities, and in Bozeman, the weight of the snow caused two roofs to collapse. At midmonth, a bomb cyclone brought heavy snow and rain to the U.S. interior, causing widespread damaging flooding as the Missouri, Platte, and Mississippi rivers breached their banks.

Violent storms ravaged the South, spawning deadly tornadoes (97 warnings in 1 day). Worst hit: Lee County, Alabama, with an EF4 that took at least 23 lives.

Meanwhile, California was declared to be drought-free for the first time since December 2011. ■

–Almanac editors

HOW WE PREDICT THE WEATHER

We derive our weather forecasts from a secret formula that was devised by the founder of this Almanac, Robert B. Thomas, in 1792. Thomas believed that weather on Earth was influenced by sunspots, which are magnetic storms on the surface of the Sun.

Over the years, we have refined and enhanced this formula with state-of-the-art technology and modern scientific calculations. We employ three scientific disciplines to make our long-range predictions: solar science, the study of sunspots and other solar activity; climatology, the study of prevailing weather patterns; and meteorology, the study of the atmosphere. We predict weather trends and events by comparing solar patterns and historical weather conditions with current solar activity.

Our forecasts emphasize temperature and precipitation deviations from averages, or normals. These are based on 30-year statistical averages prepared by government meteorological agencies and updated every 10 years. The most-recent tabulations span the period 1981 through 2010.

The borders of the 16 weather regions of the contiguous states (page 205) are based primarily on climatology and the movement of weather systems. For example, while the average weather in Richmond, Virginia, and Boston, Massachusetts, is very different (although both are in Region 2), both areas tend to be affected by the same storms and high-pressure centers and have weather deviations from normal that are similar.

We believe that nothing in the universe happens haphazardly, that there is a cause-and-effect pattern to all phenomena. However, although neither we nor any other forecasters have as yet gained sufficient insight into the mysteries of the universe to predict the weather with total accuracy, our results are almost always very close to our traditional claim of 80%.

WEATHER PHOBIAS

FEAR OF	PHOBIA
Clouds	Nephophobia
Cold	Cheimatophobia
	Frigophobia
	Psychrophobia
Dampness, moisture	Hygrophobia
Daylight, sunshine	Heliophobia
	Phengophobia
Extreme cold, frost, ice	Cryophobia
	Pagophobia
Floods	Antlophobia
Fog	Homichlophobia
	Nebulaphobia
Heat	Thermophobia
Hurricanes, tornadoes	Lilapsophobia
Lightning, thunder	Astraphobia
	Brontophobia
	Keraunophobia
Northern lights, southern lights	Auroraphobia
Rain	Ombrophobia
	Pluviophobia
Snow	Chionophobia
Thunder	Ceraunophobia
	Tonitrophobia
Wind	Ancraophobia
	Anemophobia

HOW ACCURATE WAS OUR FORECAST LAST WINTER?

Our overall accuracy rate in forecasting the direction of the change in temperature compared with the previous winter season across the 18 regions of the United States was 88.9%, while our accuracy rate in precipitation was 72.2%. So, our overall accuracy rate was 80.5%, which is slightly above our traditional average rate of 80%. Our forecasts were even more accurate for the heart of the winter season: In the period from December through February, our accuracy rate for both temperature and precipitation deviations from normal was 94.4% for some of the cities shown on each regional map. The only regions in which the December–February forecasts were incorrect were the Pacific Northwest (for temperatures) and the Upper Midwest (for precipitation).

Nearly all of the areas in which we forecast above-normal snowfall received more snow than normal, although a small portion of the Intermountain region did not. Most of the area in which we forecast below-normal snowfall received less snow than normal, with the chief exception being much of the Upper Midwest, Heartland, and northern High Plains. Other areas that received more snow than we forecast included northern New England, a few areas from central North Carolina northward to central Pennsylvania, most of the Pacific Northwest, parts of the Intermountain and Desert Southwest regions, and portions of western Alaska.

The table below shows how the actual average temperature differed from our forecast for November through March for one city in each region. On average, these actual winter temperatures differed from our forecasts by 1.18 degrees F.

REGION/ CITY	Nov.-Mar. Temp Variations From Normal (degrees) PREDICTED	ACTUAL	REGION/ CITY	Nov.-Mar. Temp Variations From Normal (degrees) PREDICTED	ACTUAL
1. Albany, NY	0.6	0.7	10. St. Louis, MO	2.2	−2.0
2. Washington, DC	2.6	1.0	11. Houston, TX	4.0	0.1
3. Asheville, NC	1.6	1.7	12. Amarillo, TX	2.0	0.2
4. Savannah, GA	3.8	2.7	13. Salt Lake City, UT	1.8	0.4
5. Orlando, FL	2.4	2.4	14. Albuquerque, NM	−0.6	−0.2
6. Rochester, NY	2.4	0.1	15. Seattle, WA	1.2	1.0
7. Charleston, WV	2.8	0.6	16. San Francisco, CA	−0.2	0.9
8. Montgomery, AL	2.8	2.5	17. Juneau, AK	1.6	1.6
9. Green Bay, WI	0.4	0.0	18. Honolulu, HI	0.8	0.7

WEATHER REGIONS

Local 7-day weather forecasts for postal codes in the United States and Canada, as well as long-range weather predictions and weather history, are available at Almanac.com/Weather.

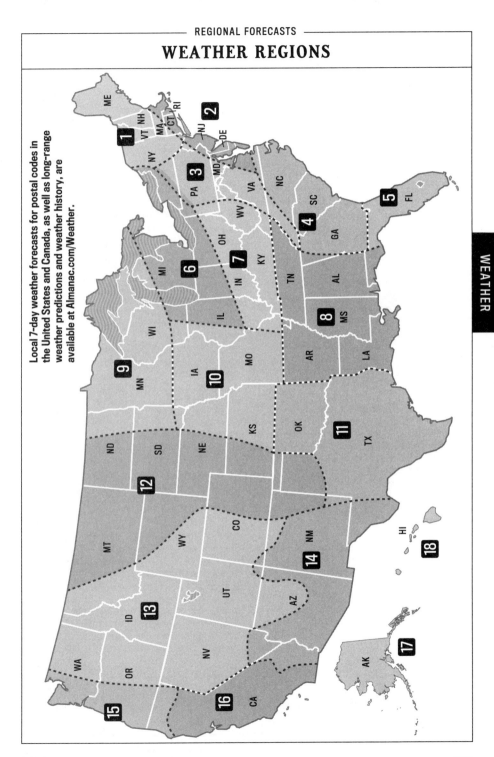

WEATHER

Illustrations of U.S. map and regional maps 1–16: Rob Schuster

NORTHEAST

SUMMARY: Winter will be milder than normal, on average, with above-normal precipitation and near- or below-normal snowfall. The coldest periods will be in early to mid-January, late January, and early February. The snowiest periods will be in mid-November, mid- to late December, and early and late January. **April** and **May** will have above-normal temperatures, with below-normal rainfall. **Summer** temperatures will be hotter than normal, with the hottest periods in mid-June, mid- to late July, and early August. Rainfall will be below normal in the north and above normal in the south. **September** and **October** will be warmer and rainier than normal, with a tropical storm threat in mid-October.

NOV. 2019: Temp. 37° (2° below avg.); precip. 4" (0.5" above avg.). 1–3 Sunny, cool. 4–7 Rainy, mild. 8–12 Snow showers, then sunny, mild. 13–16 Rain to snow, then sunny, cold. 17–25 Snowstorm, then flurries, cold. 26–30 Snow, then sunny, cold.

DEC. 2019: Temp. 33° (5° above avg.); precip. 2.5" (0.5" below avg.). 1–2 Rainy, mild. 3–6 Rain and snow showers, mild. 7–9 Snow showers, cold. 10–17 Snow, then showers, mild. 18–22 Snow, then sunny, mild. 23–26 Snowy, mild. 27–31 Snow showers, cold.

JAN. 2020: Temp. 24.5° (1° below avg. north, 4° above south); precip. 3.5" (0.5" above avg.). 1–6 Snow, then showers, mild. 7–15 Snow showers, cold. 16–20 Snow north, rain south; turning mild. 21–29 Snow north, rain south, then sunny, cold. 30–31 Snowstorm.

FEB. 2020: Temp. 25° (2° above avg.); precip. 2.5" (avg.). 1–8 Snow showers, very cold. 9–15 Rain and snow showers, mild. 16–19 Rainy, quite mild. 20–23 Rain and snow showers, mild. 24–29 Snow showers, cold.

MAR. 2020: Temp. 32° (2° below avg.); precip. 4" (1" above avg.). 1–8 Snow showers, then sunny, cold. 9–12 Rain to snow, then colder. 13–22 Snowstorm, then flurries, cold. 23–28 Showers, warm. 29–31 Rain and wet snow.

APR. 2020: Temp. 44° (2° below avg.); precip. 2" (1" below avg.). 1–4 Rain and snow showers, chilly. 5–11 Sunny, turning mild. 12–16 Rain, then sunny, cool. 17–23 Showers, then sunny,

cool. 24–30 A few showers; cool, then mild.

MAY 2020: Temp. 59° (4° above avg.); precip. 3.5" (avg.). 1–4 Sunny, turning warm. 5–10 Showers, warm. 11–18 Showers north, sunny south; warm. 19–25 Rainy periods, warm. 26–31 Showers, cool.

JUNE 2020: Temp. 67° (2° above avg.); precip. 2.5" (1" below avg.). 1–9 A few showers, cool. 10–17 Sunny, turning hot. 18–30 Isolated t-storms, warm.

JULY 2020: Temp. 74° (4° above avg.); precip. 5" (1" above avg.). 1–9 A few t-storms, warm. 10–13 Sunny, hot. 14–18 T-storms, warm. 19–22 A few t-storms, cool. 23–26 Sunny, hot. 27–31 T-storms, warm.

AUG. 2020: Temp. 65° (1° below avg.); precip. 3.5" (2" below avg. north, 1" above south). 1–3 Sunny, warm north; t-storms south. 4–7 Scattered t-storms, hot. 8–13 Sunny, cold. 14–17 Showers, cool. 18–20 T-storms, warm. 21–25 Sunny north, showers south; cool. 26–31 Showers, cool.

SEPT. 2020: Temp. 59° (avg.); precip. 4" (avg.). 1–4 Sunny, cool. 5–14 A few showers, cool. 15–21 Rainy periods, warm. 22–24 Sunny, warm. 25–30 Sunny, cool.

OCT. 2020: Temp. 51° (1° above avg. north, 5° above south); precip. 4.5" (1" above avg.). 1–3 Sunny, cool. 4–10 Showers; cool north, warm south. 11–13 Tropical rainstorm. 14–22 Sunny, then showers, warm. 23–31 A few showers; cool, then mild.

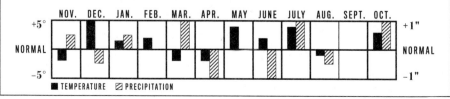

ATLANTIC CORRIDOR

SUMMARY: Winter temperatures will be much above normal, on average, with the coldest periods in mid- and late January and early and late February. Precipitation will be above normal, with below-normal snowfall. The snowiest periods will occur in mid- and late January and early February. **April** and **May** will be warmer than normal, with precipitation near normal in the north and above normal in the south. **Summer** will be hotter and rainier than normal, with the hottest periods in mid-July and early to mid-August. **September** and **October** will be warmer and rainier than normal, with a tropical storm threat in early to mid-October.

NOV. 2019: Temp. 46° (1° below avg.); precip. 2.5" (1" below avg.). 1–4 Sunny, cool. 5–10 Showers; warm, then cool. 11–16 Showers, then sunny, cool. 17–23 Rain to wet snow, then sunny, cold. 24–29 Heavy rain, then sunny, cold. 30 Rain.

DEC. 2019: Temp. 43° (4° above avg.); precip. 2.5" (0.5" below avg.). 1–4 Rain, then sunny, mild. 5–7 Showers, mild. 8–13 Heavy rain, then sunny, cool. 14–18 Rainy periods, mild. 19–23 Sunny, mild. 24–27 Rain and snow, then sunny, mild. 28–31 Rain and wet snow, mild.

JAN. 2020: Temp. 39° (4° above avg.); precip. 5.5" (2" above avg.). 1–5 Rainy, mild. 6–10 Rain to snow, then sunny, cold. 11–16 Rain to snow, then sunny, cold. 17–23 Rainy periods, mild. 24–28 Snow showers, cold. 29–31 Snow north, rain south.

FEB. 2020: Temp. 36° (2° below avg.); precip. 2" (1" above avg.). 1–7 Snow north, rain south; then sunny, cold. 8–12 Rainy periods, mild. 13–15 Sunny, quite mild. 16–20 Rain, then sunny, mild. 21–27 Rain, then sunny, cold. 28–29 Rain.

MAR. 2020: Temp. 42° (2° below avg.); precip. 5.5" (1.5" above avg.). 1–8 Periods of rain and snow, chilly. 9–11 Sunny north, rain south. 12–18 Rainy periods, mild. 19–21 Sunny, cold. 22–27 Rainy periods, chilly. 28–31 Rain and snow north, sunny south; cool.

APR. 2020: Temp. 50° (2° below avg.); precip. 3.5" (1" below avg. north, 1" above south). 1–6 Sunny, cool. 7–13 Rainy periods, turning warm. 14–16 Sunny, cool. 17–23 Rain, then sunny, cool. 24–30 Rainy periods, cool.

MAY 2020: Temp. 67° (5° above avg.); precip. 4" (1" above avg.). 1–3 Sunny, cool. 4–14 Scattered t-storms, turning quite warm. 15–19 Sunny, cool north; t-storms, warm south. 20–26 A few t-storms, cool. 27–31 Rainy, cool.

JUNE 2020: Temp. 72° (1° above avg.); precip. 3.5" (avg.). 1–5 Rainy periods, cool. 6–12 Scattered t-storms, turning hot. 13–17 Sunny, hot. 18–25 Showers, then sunny; cool. 26–30 Scattered t-storms; hot north, cool south.

JULY 2020: Temp. 77° (1° above avg.); precip. 8" (4" above avg.). 1–8 Scattered t-storms, hot, then cool. 9–12 Sunny, hot. 13–18 Scattered t-storms, hot. 19–26 Sunny; cool, then hot. 27–31 Rainy periods, cool.

AUG. 2020: Temp. 74.5° (1° below avg. north, 2° above south); precip. 4" (avg.). 1–8 Scattered t-storms, turning hot. 9–18 Isolated t-storms; cool north, hot south. 19–21 Sunny, warm. 22–27 Rain, then sunny, cool. 28–31 Showers, cool.

SEPT. 2020: Temp. 65° (2° below avg.); precip. 6.5" (3" above avg.). 1–10 Showers, then sunny, cool. 11–20 Rain, some heavy; mild. 21–30 Sunny; cool, then warm.

OCT. 2020: Temp. 62° (6° above avg.): precip. 3.5" (avg.). 1–8 Rain, then sunny, warm. 9–12 Tropical rains, warm. 13–17 Sunny, warm. 18–24 Isolated showers, turning cool. 25–31 Sunny, warm.

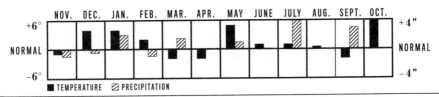

APPALACHIANS

Elmira
Scranton
Harrisburg
Frederick
Roanoke
Asheville

SUMMARY: Winter will be warmer than normal, with above-normal precipitation. Snowfall will be below normal in the north and above normal in the south. The coldest periods will be in mid-January and from late February into early March. The snowiest periods will be in late November, mid- and late January, early February, and early March. **April** and **May** will be warmer and rainier than normal. **Summer** will be warmer than normal, with the hottest periods in mid-June, mid- to late July, and mid-August. Rainfall will be below normal in the north and above normal in the south. **September** and **October** will be warmer and rainier than normal.

NOV. 2019: Temp. 42° (2° below avg.); precip. 3" (0.5" below avg.). 1–4 Sunny, mild. 5–8 Rain, then wet snow, turning cold. 9–13 Showers, mild. 14–17 Snow showers, then sunny, cold. 18–22 Flurries, cold. 23–30 Snow, then sunny, cold.

DEC. 2019: Temp. 40° (4° above avg.); precip. 2" (1" below avg.). 1–7 Rainy periods, mild. 8–12 Snow showers, cold. 13–22 Rain and snow showers, mild. 23–31 Occasional rain and snow, mild.

JAN. 2020: Temp. 35° (5° above avg.); precip. 4.5" (2" above avg.). 1–5 Rainy periods, quite mild. 6–10 Snow, then sunny, cold. 11–12 Snow showers, cold north; sunny, mild south. 13–17 Snow, then flurries, mild. 18–26 Rainy periods, mild. 27–31 Snowy periods.

FEB. 2020: Temp. 32° (2° above avg.); precip. 2.5" (1" above avg. north, 1" below south). 1–6 Snowy periods, cold north; rainy, mild south. 7–18 Rainy periods, mild. 19–29 Snow showers, cold.

MAR. 2020: Temp. 37° (3° below avg.); precip. 5.5" (1" above avg. north, 4" above south). 1–7 Snowy periods, cold. 8–12 Sunny north, rain south; chilly. 13–18 Rainy periods north, sunny south; mild. 19–27 Rain and snow north, rainy periods south; chilly. 28–31 Flurries, cold.

APR. 2020: Temp. 48° (2° below avg.); precip. 1.5" (1" below avg.). 1–3 Sunny, cool. 4–12 Showers, turning warmer. 13–15 Sunny, cool. 16–23 Rain, then sunny, cool. 24–30 Rainy periods, mild.

MAY 2020: Temp. 64° (4° above avg.); precip. 6.5" (2" above avg.). 1–3 Sunny, warm. 4–10 Rainy periods, warm. 11–14 Sunny, hot. 15–19 T-storms, hot. 20–22 Sunny, warm. 23–31 A few t-storms, turning cool.

JUNE 2020: Temp. 68° (1° above avg.); precip. 3" (1" below avg.). 1–3 Sunny, cool. 4–6 Rainy periods, cool. 7–16 Sunny, turning hot. 17–21 T-storms, cool. 22–26 Sunny, warm. 27–30 Sunny north, t-storms south; hot.

JULY 2020: Temp. 74° (1° above avg.); precip. 5" (1.5" above avg.). 1–8 A few t-storms; warm north, cool south. 9–17 Scattered t-storms, very warm. 18–23 Sunny, comfortable. 24–29 Sunny north, t-storms south; hot. 30–31 Rainy, cool.

AUG. 2020: Temp. 71.5° (1° below avg. north, 2° below south); precip. 3.5" (1" below avg. north, 1" above south). 1–9 A few t-storms, turning warm. 10–14 Sunny, cool. 15–19 T-storms, hot. 20–22 Sunny, nice. 23–25 Showers, cool. 26–31 A few t-storms, warm.

SEPT. 2020: Temp. 62° (2° below avg.); precip. 5.5" (2" above avg.). 1–5 Rainy, cool north; sunny, warm south. 6–9 Sunny, cool. 10–19 Rainy periods, mild. 20–24 Sunny, mild. 25–30 T-storms, then sunny, cool.

OCT. 2020: Temp. 59° (6° above avg.); precip. 2.5" (0.5" below avg.). 1–3 Rainy, mild. 4–6 Rain north, sunny south; mild. 7–9 Sunny, warm. 10–13 Rainy periods, cool. 14–21 Sunny, warm. 22–25 Showers, then sunny, cold. 26–31 Sunny, warm.

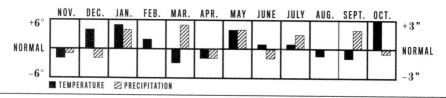

SUMMARY: Winter will be warmer and rainier than normal, with below-normal snowfall. The coldest periods will be in mid- to late November, early to mid-December, and early and late February. The best chance for snow will be in late February in the north. **April** and **May** will be warmer than normal, with rainfall below normal in the north and above normal in the south. **Summer** will be cooler and rainier than normal, with the hottest periods in late July and mid- and late August. A tropical storm will threaten in mid- to late June. **September** and **October** will be warmer and rainier than normal, with a hurricane threat in mid-September and tropical storm threats in mid-October.

Raleigh

Columbia

• Atlanta

Savannah

WEATHER

NOV. 2019: Temp. 52° (3° below avg.); precip. 3.5" (0.5" above avg.). 1–3 Sunny, cool. 4–13 Rainy periods; cool, then mild. 14–17 Sunny, cool. 18–22 Showers, then sunny, cold. 23–29 Rain, then sunny, cold. 30 Rainy, cool.

DEC. 2019: Temp. 50° (3° above avg.); precip. 4" (0.5" above avg.). 1–4 Rain, then sunny, cold. 5–11 Rain, then sunny, cold. 12–15 Rainy, cold. 16–18 Sunny, warm. 19–25 Rainy periods, quite mild. 26–31 Rainy periods, cool.

JAN. 2020: Temp. 48° (5° above avg.); precip. 7.5" (3" above avg.). 1–6 Rainy periods, mild. 7–11 Sunny, cold. 12–15 Rain, then sunny, cold. 16–19 Rainy, mild. 20–25 Sunny, warm. 26–31 Rain, then sunny, cold.

FEB. 2020: Temp. 47° (1° above avg.); precip. 4" (1" below avg. north, 1" above south). 1–8 Showers; cold, then mild. 9–17 Rainy periods, mild. 18–20 Sunny, cool. 21–27 Rain, then sunny, cold. 28–29 Rainy, mild.

MAR. 2020: Temp. 53° (2° below avg.); precip. 6.5" (2" above avg.). 1–2 Sunny, cold. 3–7 Rainy; cold north, mild south. 8–17 Rainy periods, turning warm. 18–21 Sunny, cool. 22–27 Rainy periods, cool. 28–31 Sunny, cool.

APR. 2020: Temp. 63° (avg.); precip. 4" (1" below avg. north, 3" above south). 1–2 Sunny, cool. 3–8 Rainy, cool. 9–17 Sunny, turning warm. 18–27 Scattered t-storms, warm. 28–30 Sunny, warm.

MAY 2020: Temp. 73° (2° above avg.); precip. 3.5" (avg.). 1–6 Sunny, warm. 7–11 T-storms, warm. 12–16 Sunny, hot. 17–25 Scattered t-storms, warm. 26–31 Sunny, north, t-storms south; warm.

JUNE 2020: Temp. 77° (1° below avg.); precip. 3.5" (1" below avg.). 1–4 Scattered t-storms, cool. 5–14 A few t-storms, warm. 15–19 Sunny, warm north; showers, cool south. 20–23 Tropical storm threat. 24–30 Scattered t-storms, cool.

JULY 2020: Temp. 80° (2° below avg.); precip. 8.5" (4" above avg.). 1–11 Daily t-storms, cool. 12–19 Scattered t-storms; cool north, warm south. 20–25 A few t-storms, cool. 26–31 Sunny north, t-storms south; hot.

AUG. 2020: Temp. 81° (1° above avg.); precip. 3" (2" below avg.). 1–4 Scattered t-storms, cool. 5–9 Sunny, hot. 10–20 Isolated t-storms, hot. 21–31 A few t-storms; cool, then hot.

SEPT. 2020: Temp. 73° (2° below avg. north, avg. south); precip. 5.5" (1" above avg.). 1–5 Scattered t-storms, hot. 6–8 Sunny, cool. 9–16 A few t-storms, turning warm. 17–20 Hurricane threat. 21–26 Sunny, turning cool. 27–30 Showers, warm.

OCT. 2020: Temp. 68° (4° above avg.); precip. 4" (avg.). 1–7 T-storms, then sunny, warm. 8–10 Tropical storm threat. 11–18 Sunny; cool, then warm. 19–22 Tropical storm threat. 23–31 Sunny, turning warm.

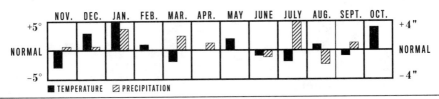

NOV. DEC. JAN. FEB. MAR. APR. MAY JUNE JULY AUG. SEPT. OCT.

+5°   +4"

NORMAL   NORMAL

-5°   -4"

■ TEMPERATURE ▨ PRECIPITATION

FLORIDA

Jacksonville

Orlando

Tampa

Miami

SUMMARY: Winter will be milder and drier than normal, with the coldest temperatures in mid- and late January into early February and the second half of February. **April** and **May** will be hotter than normal, with rainfall above normal in the north and below normal in the south. **Summer** will be slightly cooler and drier than normal, with the hottest periods in late June, mid-July, and mid-August. Watch for tropical storm threats in mid-June and mid- to late July. **September** and **October** will be warmer and drier than normal. Watch for a hurricane threat in mid-September and a tropical storm threat in mid- to late October.

NOV. 2019: Temp. 65° (4° below avg.); precip. 2.5" (avg.). 1–5 A few showers, cool. 6–12 Sunny, turning warm. 13–23 Isolated showers, cool. 24–30 Sunny, cool.

DEC. 2019: Temp. 66° (3° above avg.); precip. 2.5" (0.5" below avg.). 1–4 Scattered showers, cool. 5–8 T-storms, warm. 9–12 Sunny, cool. 13–15 T-storms, warm. 16–22 Sunny, warm. 23–31 Scattered showers; turning cool north, warm south.

JAN. 2020: Temp. 65° (5° above avg.); precip. 2.5" (avg.). 1–5 A few t-storms, warm. 6–9 Sunny, cool. 10–19 Scattered t-storms, warm. 20–26 A few showers, warm. 27–31 Showers, turning cool.

FEB. 2020: Temp. 63° (2° above avg.); precip. 1.5" (1" below avg.). 1–3 Sunny, cool. 4–17 Scattered showers, mild. 18–22 Sunny, cool. 23–29 Rainy periods, chilly.

MAR. 2020: Temp. 68° (1° above avg.); precip. 1" (2" below avg.). 1–7 Sunny, turning warm. 8–15 A few showers, cool. 16–23 Scattered t-storms, warm. 24–31 Sunny, cool.

APR. 2020: Temp. 73° (2° above avg.); precip. 3" (3" above avg. north, 2" below south). 1–8 Scattered t-storms; cool north, warm south. 9–13 Sunny, warm. 14–17 A few showers, cool. 18–23 Sunny, warm. 24–30 Scattered t-storms, warm.

MAY 2020: Temp. 78° (1° above avg.); precip.

4.5" (3" above avg. north, 2" below south). 1–11 Scattered t-storms, warm. 12–17 Sunny, warm. 18–31 Scattered t-storms, warm.

JUNE 2020: Temp. 81° (1° below avg.); precip. 7.5" (1" above avg.). 1–12 Several t-storms, warm. 13–20 A few t-storms, cool. 21–23 Tropical storm threat. 24–30 A few t-storms; cool, then hot.

JULY 2020: Temp. 82° (1° below avg.); precip. 6.5" (avg.). 1–12 Daily t-storms, cool. 13–17 Sunny, warm. 18–22 Scattered t-storms, cool. 23–25 Tropical storm threat. 26–31 Scattered t-storms, seasonable.

AUG. 2020: Temp. 82° (avg.); precip. 4.5" (3" below avg.). 1–9 A few t-storms, humid. 10–18 Scattered t-storms, hot. 19–25 Daily t-storms, humid. 26–31 Scattered t-storms, warm.

SEPT. 2020: Temp. 80.5° (0.5° above avg.); precip. 4.5" (1" below avg.). 1–8 Scattered t-storms, warm. 9–16 A few t-storms, turning hot. 17–19 Hurricane threat. 20–30 Scattered t-storms, warm.

OCT. 2020: Temp. 76.5° (3° above avg. north, avg. south); precip. 3" (1" below avg.). 1–10 Scattered t-storms, warm. 11–15 Sunny, cool north; t-storms south. 16–18 Sunny, warm. 19–21 Tropical storm threat. 22–31 Scattered showers, warm.

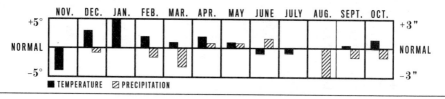

| | NOV. | DEC. | JAN. | FEB. | MAR. | APR. | MAY | JUNE | JULY | AUG. | SEPT. | OCT. | |

+5°

NORMAL

-5°

+3"

NORMAL

-3"

■ TEMPERATURE ◩ PRECIPITATION

WEATHER

LOWER LAKES

SUMMARY: Winter will be warmer than normal, with above-normal precipitation. The coldest periods will be in early December and early to mid-January, from late January into early February, and in late February. Snowfall will be above normal in Ohio and below normal in most other areas. The snowiest periods will be in early to mid-January, from late January into early February and late February into early March, and in late March. **April** and **May** will be warmer than normal, with precipitation below normal in the east and above normal in the west. **Summer** will be hotter and rainier than normal. The hottest periods will be in mid-June, mid- to late July, and mid-August. **September** and **October** will be warmer than normal, with below-normal precipitation.

WEATHER

NOV. 2019: Temp. 39° (2° below avg.); precip. 2.5" (1" above avg. east, 1" below west). 1–3 Sunny, mild. 4–9 Rain to snow. 10–13 Rainy periods, mild. 14–25 Periods of rain and snow, cold. 26–29 Rain, then sunny, cold. 30 Rain.

DEC. 2019: Temp. 36° (4° above avg.); precip. 2.5" (0.5" below avg.). 1–9 Snow showers; cold, then mild. 10–18 Rain and snow showers, mild. 19–23 Showers, quite mild. 24–27 Snowy periods, colder. 28–31 Showers, mild.

JAN. 2020: Temp. 32° (5° above avg.); precip. 3.5" (0.5" below avg. east, 2" above west). 1–5 Rain, then sunny, warm. 6–10 Snow showers, cold. 11–13 Rain and snow. 14–22 Rainy periods, quite mild. 23–27 Flurries, colder. 28–31 Snowy periods, cold.

FEB. 2020: Temp. 28° (3° above avg. east, 1° below west); precip. 3" (1" above avg.). 1–3 Lake snows, very cold. 4–7 Snow showers, cold. 8–12 Periods of rain and snow, mild. 13–17 Rainy, quite mild. 18–25 Snow showers, cold. 26–29 Rain and snow, mild.

MAR. 2020: Temp. 35° (3° below avg.); precip. 3" (avg.). 1–4 Snow showers, cold. 5–9 Rain, then flurries, cold. 10–13 Sunny, then rain; mild. 14–17 Showers, mild. 18–25 Snow showers, cold. 26–31 Snowstorm, then flurries, cold.

APR. 2020: Temp. 46° (2° below avg.); precip. 3.5" (1" below avg. east, 1" above west). 1–6 Sunny, cold. 7–12 A few showers, turning warm. 13–23 A few showers east, t-storms

west; mild. 24–30 Rainy periods, cool.

MAY 2020: Temp. 63° (5° above avg.); precip. 3.5" (avg.). 1–4 Sunny, warm. 5–10 T-storms, then sunny; warm east, cool west. 11–19 Scattered t-storms, very warm. 20–22 Sunny, warm. 23–31 T-storms, turning cool.

JUNE 2020: Temp. 69° (3° above avg.); precip. 4" (0.5" above avg.). 1–6 Scattered t-storms, turning cool. 7–12 T-storms, warm. 13–16 Sunny, hot. 17–25 T-storms, then sunny, turning hot. 26–30 Scattered t-storms, warm.

JULY 2020: Temp. 72.5° (2° above avg.); precip. 2.5" (1" below avg.). 1–6 Scattered t-storms, cool. 7–10 Sunny, hot. 11–17 Scattered t-storms, warm. 18–22 Isolated t-storms; cool east, hot west. 23–26 Sunny, hot. 27–31 T-storms, then sunny, cool.

AUG. 2020: Temp. 71° (avg. east, 4° above west); precip. 6" (2" above avg.). 1–2 Sunny, warm. 3–10 Scattered t-storms, warm. 11–19 T-storms, turning hot. 20–31 Scattered t-storms, cool.

SEPT. 2020: Temp. 60° (2° below avg.); precip. 3.5" (1" below avg.). 1–3 Sunny, cool. 4–8 T-storms, then sunny, cool. 9–14 Rainy periods, cool. 15–20 Showers, cool. 21–24 Sunny, warm. 25–30 Showers, then sunny, cool.

OCT. 2020: Temp. 57° (5° above avg.); precip. 2" (0.5" below avg.). 1–13 Rainy periods, mild. 14–18 Sunny, warm. 19–24 Showers, then sunny, cool. 25–31 Rainy periods, quite mild.

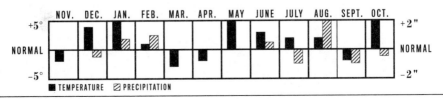

OHIO VALLEY

SUMMARY: Winter will have slightly above-normal temperatures and precipitation, on average. The coldest periods will be in early to mid- and late January, early February, mid- to late February, and early March. Snowfall will be above normal in the east and near to below normal elsewhere, with the snowiest periods in late November, early January, and early March. **April** and **May** will be warmer than normal, with above-normal rainfall. **Summer** will be hotter than normal, with the hottest periods in early to mid-June, early to mid- and mid- to late July, and mid- and late August. Rainfall will be above normal in the east and below normal in the west. **September** and **October** will be warmer and rainier than normal.

WEATHER

NOV. 2019: Temp. 43° (3° below avg.); precip. 3.5" (avg.). 1–3 Sunny, cool. 4–11 Rain, then flurries, cold. 12–16 Rain, then flurries, cold. 17–22 Rain to snow, then flurries, cold. 23–29 Snowstorm, then sunny, cold. 30 Rain.

DEC. 2019: Temp. 39° (2° above avg.); precip. 2.5" (0.5" below avg.). 1–4 Rain and snow showers, cold. 5–7 Showers, mild. 8–15 Occasional rain and snow, colder. 16–25 Rainy periods, mild. 26–31 Snow, then showers, mild.

JAN. 2020: Temp. 38° (5° above avg.); precip. 4.5" (1.5" above avg.). 1–4 Rainy periods, quite mild. 5–10 Snowstorm, then flurries, cold. 11–14 Rain to snow, then flurries, cold. 15–17 Sunny, mild. 18–22 Snow, then rainy periods, turning warm. 23–29 Periods of rain and snow, mild. 30–31 Snow showers, cold.

FEB. 2020: Temp. 34° (avg.); precip. 3.5" (2" above avg. north, 1" below south). 1–3 Snow showers, very cold. 4–7 Rain and snow, then sunny, cold. 8–11 Rainy, quite mild. 12–16 Flurries, then rainy, mild. 17–21 Snow, then flurries, cold. 22–26 Snow showers, very cold. 27–29 Rainy, mild.

MAR. 2020: Temp. 43° (2° below avg.); precip. 6" (2" above avg.). 1–4 Snow, then flurries, cold. 5–9 Rain to snow, then flurries, cold. 10–17 Rainy periods, mild. 18–24 Periods of rain and wet snow, cold. 25–31 Rain, then snow showers, cold.

APR. 2020: Temp. 53° (2° below avg.); precip. 4.5" (1" above avg.). 1–6 Sunny, cool. 7–9

Showers, cool. 10–12 Rainy, warm. 13–21 Rainy periods, cool. 22–30 A few showers, mild.

MAY 2020: Temp. 67° (4° above avg.); precip. 3.5" (avg.). 1–4 Sunny, warm. 5–11 Showers, cool. 12–21 A few t-storms, warm. 22–27 Rainy periods, turning cool. 28–31 T-storms, then sunny, cool.

JUNE 2020: Temp. 74° (2° above avg.); precip. 4" (avg.). 1–3 Sunny, cool. 4–13 A few t-storms, turning hot. 14–18 Sunny, warm. 19–25 T-storms, then sunny, warm. 26–30 Scattered t-storms, warm.

JULY 2020: Temp. 76° (1° above avg.); precip. 3.5" (0.5" below avg.). 1–6 A few t-storms, cool. 7–10 Sunny, hot. 11–17 Scattered t-storms, warm. 18–26 Sunny, hot. 27–31 T-storms, then sunny, cool.

AUG. 2020: Temp. 76° (3° above avg.); precip. 5" (1" above avg.). 1–2 Sunny, warm. 3–11 T-storms, warm. 12–17 Sunny, hot. 18–25 Scattered t-storms, turning cool. 26–31 T-storms; hot, then cool.

SEPT. 2020: Temp. 63° (4° below avg.); precip. 4" (1" above avg.). 1–8 A few t-storms, cool. 9–17 Rainy periods, cool. 18–23 Sunny, chilly. 24–30 Rain, then sunny, cool.

OCT. 2020: Temp. 63° (6° above avg.); precip. 3.5" (1" above avg.). 1–7 Rain, then sunny, turning warm. 8–13 Rainy, cool. 14–21 Sunny, warm. 22–24 T-storms, then sunny, cool. 25–31 Sunny, quite warm.

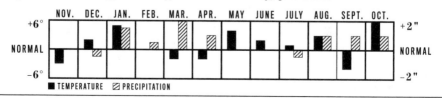

■ TEMPERATURE ▨ PRECIPITATION

DEEP SOUTH

SUMMARY: Winter will be warmer than normal, on average, with the coldest periods in early December, late January, and early to mid-February. Rainfall will be below normal near the Gulf but above normal elsewhere, with the best chance for snowfall in mid- to late November and early January. **April** and **May** will be warmer and rainier than normal. **Summer** will have slightly above-normal temperatures, on average, with rainfall below normal in Tennessee and above normal elsewhere. The hottest periods will be in mid- to late June and mid- and late August. Watch for a tropical storm threat in mid- to late July. **September** and **October** will be warmer and rainier than normal. Watch for a tropical storm threat in early to mid-October.

WEATHER

NOV. 2019: Temp. 53° (2° below avg.); precip. 5" (avg.). 1–6 Rain, then sunny, cold. 7–13 Rainy periods, turning warm. 14–21 Occasional rain, turning cold. 22–25 Snow north, rain south. 26–28 Sunny, cold. 29–30 Rainy.

DEC. 2019: Temp. 51° (3° above avg.); precip. 4" (1" below avg.). 1–4 Rainy, cold. 5–7 Sunny, mild. 8–12 Rain, then sunny, cold. 13–24 Rainy periods, quite mild. 25–28 Sunny, cool. 29–31 Showers, mild.

JAN. 2020: Temp. 51° (6° above avg.); precip. 7" (2" above avg.). 1–4 Rainy, mild. 5–8 Snow, then sunny, cold. 9–12 Rainy, mild. 13–15 Sunny, cold. 16–19 Rainy, mild. 20–29 Rainy periods, quite mild. 30–31 Flurries, cold.

FEB. 2020: Temp. 48° (1° above avg.); precip. 4" (1" below avg.). 1–5 Rainy periods, turning mild. 6–7 Sunny, cold. 8–11 Rainy, mild. 12–16 Rainy periods; cold, then mild. 17–21 Sunny, cold. 22–26 Rain, then sunny, cold. 27–29 Rainy, mild.

MAR. 2020: Temp. 55° (1° below avg.); precip. 8" (5" above avg. north, 1" below south). 1–2 Sunny, cold. 3–5 Rainy, turning mild. 6–12 Rainy periods, chilly. 13–16 Sunny, warm. 17–19 T-storms, then sunny, cool. 20–25 Rainy; warm, then cool. 26–31 Sunny, chilly.

APR. 2020: Temp. 65° (2° above avg.); precip. 5" (0.5" above avg.). 1–7 Rainy periods, cool. 8–11 Sunny, turning warm. 12–16 T-storms, then sunny, cool. 17–23 Scattered t-storms, warm. 24–30 Sunny, cool, then t-storms, warm.

MAY 2020: Temp. 72° (3° above avg. north, 1° below south); precip. 6" (1" above avg.). 1–6 T-storms, then sunny, cool. 7–10 Rain and heavy t-storms, warm. 11–17 Sunny, very warm. 18–24 A few t-storms, cooler. 25–31 Sunny, then t-storms, warm.

JUNE 2020: Temp. 78° (avg.); precip. 7" (2" below avg. northeast, 6" above southwest). 1–10 A few t-storms, warm. 11–16 Sunny north, t-storms south; very warm. 17–28 Isolated t-storms north, several t-storms south; hot. 29–30 T-storms, cool.

JULY 2020: Temp. 80° (0.5° below avg.); precip. 9" (3" above avg. north, 6" above south). 1–4 Sunny north, t-storms south; turning cooler. 5–9 Sunny, cool. 10–22 Scattered t-storms, warm. 23–25 Tropical storm threat. 26–31 T-storms, cool.

AUG. 2020: Temp. 81° (1° above avg.); precip. 4" (0.5" below avg.). 1–8 T-storms, then sunny, warm. 9–12 T-storms. 13–21 Sunny, hot north; scattered t-storms, warm south. 22–28 T-storms, then sunny, hot. 29–31 T-storms, cool.

SEPT. 2020: Temp. 73° (3° below avg.); precip. 5.5" (1" above avg.). 1–4 T-storms, warm. 5–8 Sunny, cool. 9–17 Rainy periods, cool. 18–23 Sunny, cool. 24–30 Rain, then sunny, cool.

OCT. 2020: Temp. 70° (5° above avg.); precip. 5" (2" above avg.). 1–7 Scattered showers, turning warm. 8–11 Tropical storm threat. 12–17 Sunny; cool, then warm. 18–22 Rainy periods, cool. 23–31 Sunny, turning warm.

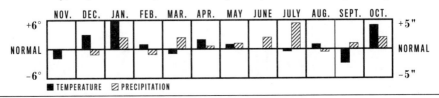

UPPER MIDWEST

International Falls
Marquette
Duluth
Minneapolis
Green Bay

SUMMARY: Winter temperatures will be above normal, on average, with slightly below-normal precipitation and near- to above-normal snowfall. The coldest periods will be in early and mid-January, from late January into early February, in late February, and in early and mid- to late March. The snowiest periods will be in early and mid-January, early February, and early and mid-March. **April** and **May** will be slightly warmer and rainier than normal. **Summer** will be hotter and rainier than normal, with the hottest periods in late June, early to mid-July, mid- to late July, and mid-August. **September** and **October** will have above-normal temperatures and below-normal precipitation.

NOV. 2019: Temp. 32° (3° above avg.); precip. 1" (1" below avg.). 1–4 Rainy periods, mild. 5–8 Snow showers, cold. 9–15 Showers, mild. 16–21 Snow showers, mild. 22–25 Sunny, cold. 26–30 Flurries, mild.

DEC. 2019: Temp. 24° (8° above avg.); precip. 0.5" (0.5" below avg.). 1–4 Sunny, mild. 5–17 Snow showers, mild. 18–24 Sunny, mild. 25–31 Snow showers, mild.

JAN. 2020: Temp. 14° (1° above avg.); precip. 2" (1" above avg.). 1–4 Snowstorm. 5–9 Flurries, cold. 10–15 Snowy periods, cold. 16–23 Snowy periods; mild, then cold. 24–28 Snow showers, mild. 29–31 Flurries, very cold.

FEB. 2020: Temp. 11.5° (2° above avg. east, 3° below west); precip. 1" (avg.). 1–6 Snowy periods, very cold. 7–15 Snow showers, mild. 16–19 Snowy; mild east, cold west. 20–29 Snow showers, cold.

MAR. 2020: Temp. 24° (4° below avg.); precip. 1.5" (avg.). 1–8 Snowy periods, then sunny, cold. 9–12 Sunny, mild. 13–15 Snow showers, mild. 16–24 Snowstorm, then snow showers, very cold. 25–31 Sunny, cold.

APR. 2020: Temp. 40° (2° below avg.); precip. 4" (2" above avg.). 1–6 Snow, then sunny, cold. 7–10 Rainy periods, mild. 11–14 Snow, then sunny, cool. 15–24 Rainy periods, cool. 25–30 Showers, turning warmer.

MAY 2020: Temp. 58° (3° above avg.); precip. 3" (avg.). 1–5 Sunny, cool. 6–9 Rainy periods, cool. 10–17 Scattered t-storms, warm. 18–31 A few t-storms, turning cool.

JUNE 2020: Temp. 67° (4° above avg.); precip. 7" (2" above avg. east, 4" above west). 1–3 Showers, cool. 4–10 Rainy periods, cool. 11–20 Scattered t-storms, warm. 21–30 Sunny east, a few t-storms west; turning hot.

JULY 2020: Temp. 70° (2° above avg.); precip. 2.5" (1" below avg.). 1–7 Scattered t-storms, cool. 8–11 Sunny, hot. 12–18 Scattered t-storms, cool. 19–24 Sunny, hot. 25–31 T-storms, then sunny, cool.

AUG. 2020: Temp. 65° (1° below avg.); precip. 3.5" (avg.). 1–4 Sunny, warm. 5–15 Scattered t-storms, cool. 16–23 Isolated t-storms; hot, then cool. 24–31 Showers, cool.

SEPT. 2020: Temp. 57° (1° below avg.); precip. 2" (1" below avg.). 1–4 Rainy periods, cool. 5–9 Sunny, turning warm. 10–16 Showers, cool. 17–22 Sunny, turning warm. 23–30 Sunny, warm.

OCT. 2020: Temp. 53° (6° above avg.); precip. 1.5" (1" below avg.). 1–9 Showers, turning cool. 10–14 Sunny, mild. 15–21 Rain, then sunny; mild east, chilly west. 22–31 Sunny, turning warm.

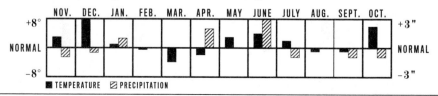

HEARTLAND

SUMMARY: Winter temperatures will be below normal, on average, with above-normal snowfall and slightly above-normal precipitation. The coldest periods will be in early to mid-January, early and mid-February, and early March. The snowiest periods will be in early to mid-December, early to mid-January, and mid-February. **April** and **May** will be warmer and slightly drier than normal. **Summer** will be slightly warmer and rainier than normal, with the hottest periods in mid- and late June, mid-July, and mid- and late August. **September** and **October** will bring above-normal temperatures and below-normal rainfall.

NOV. 2019: Temp. 42° (1° below avg.); precip. 1.5" (1" below avg.). 1–7 Rain, then snow showers, turning cold. 8–15 Sunny, mild. 16–21 Showers, then sunny, cold. 22–28 Snow, then flurries, cold. 29–30 Rainy, mild.

DEC. 2019: Temp. 35° (3° above avg.); precip. 1" (0.5" below avg.). 1–2 Sunny, cold. 3–7 Rainy periods, mild. 8–14 Snow, then flurries, cold. 15–17 Sunny, mild. 18–20 Snow showers. 21–31 Rainy periods, mild.

JAN. 2020: Temp. 32° (3° above avg.); precip. 3" (2" above avg.). 1–3 Rainy, mild. 4–10 Snow, then sunny, cold. 11–13 Rain and wet snow. 14–20 Showers, mild. 21–28 Rainy periods, mild. 29–31 Snow, then sunny, cold.

FEB. 2020: Temp. 28° (3° below avg.); precip. 2.5" (1" above avg.). 1–7 Periods of snow, then sunny, frigid. 8–14 Rain and snow, then sunny, mild. 15–18 Rain to heavy snow. 19–25 Flurries, very cold. 26–29 Snow north, rain south.

MAR. 2020: Temp. 40° (4° below avg.); precip. 2.5" (avg.). 1–9 Periods of rain and snow, then sunny, very cold. 10–14 Sunny, warm. 15–21 Snow north, rain south; cold. 22–26 Sunny, cold. 27–31 Snow, then sunny, cool.

APR. 2020: Temp. 55° (1° above avg.); precip. 3.5" (avg.). 1–5 Rain, then sunny, cool. 6–17 Showers, turning warm. 18–23 Scattered t-storms, warm. 24–30 Scattered t-storms; cool, then warm.

MAY 2020: Temp. 66° (2° above avg.); precip. 3.5" (1" below avg.). 1–10 Isolated t-storms, cool. 11–12 Sunny, hot. 13–23 A few t-storms, warm. 24–31 Scattered t-storms; cool, then warm.

JUNE 2020: Temp. 73° (1° above avg.); precip. 6.5" (2" above avg.). 1–5 Rainy periods, cool. 6–12 A few t-storms, warm. 13–15 Sunny, hot. 16–20 T-storms, warm. 21–27 Sunny, hot. 28–30 T-storms, warm.

JULY 2020: Temp. 75° (2° below avg.); precip. 2" (2" below avg.). 1–8 A few showers, turning cool. 9–14 Sunny, hot north; scattered t-storms south. 15–21 Isolated t-storms, hot. 22–26 Sunny, hot north; t-storms south. 27–31 Showers, cool.

AUG. 2020: Temp. 77° (2° above avg.); precip. 5.5" (2" above avg.). 1–3 Sunny; hot north, cool south. 4–12 A few t-storms; hot, then cool. 13–17 Sunny, hot. 18–23 Heavy t-storms, warm. 24–27 Sunny, hot. 28–31 Showers, cool.

SEPT. 2020: Temp. 63° (4° below avg.); precip. 3.5" (avg.). 1–4 T-storms, warm. 5–12 Rain, then sunny, cool. 13–17 Sunny, warm. 18–27 Rain, then sunny, cool. 28–30 Sunny, warm.

OCT. 2020: Temp. 62° (6° above avg.); precip. 1" (2" below avg.). 1–7 Rain, then sunny, very warm. 8–13 Rain, then sunny, cool. 14–18 Sunny, warm. 19–20 Showers, cool. 21–31 Occasional rain, turning warm.

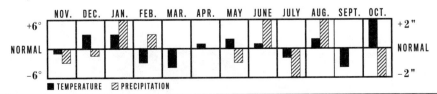

TEXAS–OKLAHOMA

SUMMARY: Winter will be milder and drier than normal, with below-normal snowfall in places that normally receive snow. The coldest periods will be in mid- to late November and early January and from late January into early February. The best chances for snow are in early December, early to mid-January, and mid-February. **April** and **May** will be warmer than normal (expect a hot spell in late May), with near-normal rainfall. **Summer** will be cooler and rainier than normal, with the hottest periods in mid-June and mid-August. Watch for a hurricane in mid- to late July and a tropical storm threat in mid- to late August. **September** and **October** will be cooler and drier than normal.

NOV. 2019: Temp. 55° (2° below avg.); precip. 3" (avg.). 1–8 Rain, then sunny, cool. 9–15 Rain, then sunny, warm. 16–21 Rain, then sunny, cool. 22–26 Rain, then sunny, cold. 27–30 Rainy, mild.

DEC. 2019: Temp. 54° (1° above avg.); precip. 2" (0.5" below avg.). 1–4 Snow north, rain south; cold. 5–11 Sunny; mild, then cold. 12–17 Scattered showers, turning warm. 18–26 Rainy periods; cool, then mild. 27–31 Sunny; cool, then mild.

JAN. 2020: Temp. 55° (5° above avg.); precip. 3" (1" above avg.). 1–2 Sunny, mild. 3–7 Rain to snow, turning cold. 8–15 Showers, then sunny; mild. 16–22 Rain, then sunny, warm. 23–28 Rainy, turning cooler. 29–31 Sunny, cold.

FEB. 2020: Temp. 50.5° (2° below avg. north, 3° above south); precip. 0.5" (1.5" below avg.). 1–6 Showers, turning mild. 7–11 Rain and snow, cold north; showers, mild south. 12–14 Sunny, mild. 15–19 Rain and snow north, sunny south. 20–23 Sunny, mild. 24–29 Showers; cool, then mild.

MAR. 2020: Temp. 59.5° (1° below avg. north, 2° above south); precip. 1.5" (1" below avg.). 1–5 Rainy periods; cold north, warm south. 6–11 Showers, cool. 12–18 Sunny, warm. 19–28 Rain, then sunny, chilly. 29–31 T-storms.

APR. 2020: Temp. 69° (3° above avg.); precip. 2" (1" below avg.). 1–6 Rainy periods, cool. 7–10 Scattered t-storms, warm. 11–19 Sunny, warm. 20–30 Scattered t-storms, warm.

MAY 2020: Temp. 72° (1° below avg.); precip. 6" (1" above avg.). 1–8 T-storms; warm, then cooler. 9–15 Scattered t-storms, warm. 16–22 A few t-storms; cool north, warm south. 23–31 Isolated t-storms; cool, then hot.

JUNE 2020: Temp. 78° (1° below avg.); precip. 5" (1" below avg. northwest, 3" above southeast). 1–8 Rain, then sunny; warm. 9–17 Rainy periods, cool north; sunny, hot south. 18–27 Scattered t-storms, warm. 28–30 Sunny, warm.

JULY 2020: Temp. 79° (2° below avg.); precip. 7" (4" above avg.). 1–12 A few t-storms, cool. 13–16 Sunny, warm. 17–22 A few t-storms, humid. 23–26 Hurricane threat. 27–31 Sunny, cool north; t-storms south.

AUG. 2020: Temp. 80° (1° below avg.); precip. 1.5" (1" below avg.). 1–4 Sunny north, t-storms south; warm. 5–14 Scattered t-storms, warm. 15–19 Sunny north, t-storms south; hot. 20–24 Tropical storm threat. 25–31 Scattered t-storms, warm.

SEPT. 2020: Temp. 72° (4° below avg.); precip. 0.5" (3" below avg.). 1–14 A few showers; turning chilly north, warm south. 15–21 Sunny, cool. 22–30 Sunny; warm, then cool.

OCT. 2020: Temp. 70° (3° above avg.); precip. 2" (2" below avg.). 1–6 Sunny, warm. 7–16 Rain, then sunny, warm. 17–25 T-storms, then sunny, warm. 26–31 Showers, warm.

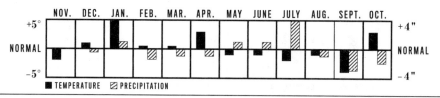

Get your local forecast at Almanac.com/Weather.

HIGH PLAINS

SUMMARY: Winter will be milder than normal in the north and colder than normal in the south, with slightly above-normal precipitation. The coldest periods will be in mid-December and early January and from late January into mid-February. Snowfall will be above normal in the north and below normal in the south, with the snowiest periods in early January, early to mid-February, and early March. **April** and **May** will be cooler than normal, with precipitation mostly above normal. **Summer** temps will be above normal in the north and below normal in the south, with the hottest spells in late June, mid- and late July, and mid-August. It will be drier than normal. **September** and **October** will have above-normal temperatures and below-normal precipitation.

NOV. 2019: Temp. 39° (3° above avg.); precip. 0.5" (0.5" below avg.). 1–5 Showers, mild. 6–14 Snow, then sunny, warm. 15–20 Showers, then sunny, cold. 21–27 Snow, then sunny, mild. 28–30 Rain and snow showers.

DEC. 2019: Temp. 32.5° (6° above avg. north, 1° below south); precip. 0.5" (avg.). 1–3 Sunny, mild. 4–8 Snow showers, cold. 9–11 Sunny, mild. 12–18 Rain and snow showers, turning cold. 19–31 A few snow showers, mild.

JAN. 2020: Temp. 27.5° (1.5° below avg. northwest, 1.5° above southeast); precip. 1" (0.5" above avg.). 1–5 Snowy periods, frigid. 6–17 Snow showers, mild. 18–22 Snow north, sunny south. 23–27 Sunny; frigid north, mild south. 28–31 Snow showers, frigid.

FEB. 2020: Temp. 25° (3° below avg.); precip. 0.5" (avg.). 1–11 Snow showers, cold. 12–16 Sunny north, snow south; cold. 17–23 Sunny, mild. 24–29 Snow showers, turning cold north; sunny, mild south.

MAR. 2020: Temp. 35° (4° below avg.); precip. 2" (1" above avg.). 1–7 Snow north, rain south; then sunny, cold. 8–14 Sunny north, showers south; mild. 15–27 Snowy periods, very cold. 28–31 Snow north, rain south.

APR. 2020: Temp. 47° (1° below avg.); precip. 2.5" (2" above avg. north, 1" below south). 1–7 Snow north, rain south. 8–13 Rain and snow showers north, sunny south; cool. 14–19 Rainy periods north, sunny south; mild. 20–23 Showers north, sunny south. 24–27 Sunny,

warm. 28–30 Rain north, sunny south.

MAY 2020: Temp. 57° (1° below avg.); precip. 3" (avg. north, 1" above south). 1–11 Showers, warm. 12–18 Rain and wet snow north; sunny, warm south. 19–27 A few showers north, rainy south; cool. 28–31 Showers, cool.

JUNE 2020: Temp. 66° (1° below avg.); precip. 2.5" (avg.). 1–3 Rainy, cool. 4–12 Showers; cool north, warm south. 13–23 Scattered t-storms, warm. 24–30 A few t-storms, hot.

JULY 2020: Temp. 71° (1° above avg. north, 3° below south); precip. 1.5" (0.5" below avg.) 1–9 Isolated t-storms; turning hot north, warm south. 10–15 A few t-storms, warm. 16–19 Sunny, hot north; t-storms south. 20–23 Scattered t-storms, hot. 24–28 Sunny north, t-storms south; cool. 29–31 Sunny, hot.

AUG. 2020: Temp. 72° (1° below avg.); precip. 1" (1" below avg.). 1–5 Sunny, warm. 6–11 Rainy periods, cool. 12–19 A few showers, cool north; sunny, hot south. 20–31 Sunny, hot east; scattered t-storms, cool west.

SEPT. 2020: Temp. 60° (1° below avg.); precip. 0.5" (1" below avg.). 1–2 Sunny, hot. 3–10 A few t-storms, cool. 11–18 Sunny; warm north, cool south. 19–24 Showers, cool. 25–30 Sunny, warm.

OCT. 2020: Temp. 53° (4° above avg.); precip. 1" (avg.). 1–7 Rain and snow showers, chilly north; sunny, warm south. 8–12 Sunny, warm. 13–16 Rain and snow. 17–23 Sunny, mild. 24–25 Sunny north, rain south; mild. 26–31 Sunny, warm.

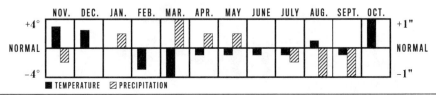

INTERMOUNTAIN

SUMMARY: Winter temperatures will be above normal, on average, in the north and below average in central and southern portions of the region, with the coldest periods in mid- to late December and early January and from late January through the first half of February. Precipitation and snowfall will be above normal, with the snowiest periods in mid- to late December, early and late January, early February, and early and late March. **April** and **May** will be cooler than normal, with near-normal precipitation. **Summer** will be slightly cooler and rainier than normal, with the hottest period from late June through early July. **September** and **October** will be warmer than normal, with below-normal precipitation.

NOV. 2019: Temp. 43° (3° above avg.); precip. 1" (0.5" below avg.). 1–9 Rain, then sunny; cool north, warm south. 10–18 Rainy periods north, sunny south; mild. 19–24 Snow showers, then sunny, mild. 25–30 Periods of rain and snow north, sunny south; chilly.

DEC. 2019: Temp. 33° (3° above avg. north, 3° below south); precip. 1.5" (avg.). 1–10 Periods of rain and snow north, sunny south; mild. 11–15 Rain and snow showers, mild. 16–25 Snowy periods, cold. 26–31 Snowy north, sunny south; turning milder.

JAN. 2020: Temp. 30° (2° below avg.); precip. 1.5" (1" above avg. north, 0.5" below south). 1–7 Snowstorm, then flurries, cold. 8–13 Sunny, mild. 14–19 Snowy periods north, sunny south; mild. 20–24 Snow showers, cold. 25–31 Snowy periods, cold.

FEB. 2020: Temp. 35° (1° above avg.); precip. 2" (0.5" above avg.). 1–9 Snowy periods, cold. 10–15 Snow showers, very cold. 16–22 Rainy periods, mild. 23–29 Sunny, cold north; rain and snow showers south.

MAR. 2020: Temp. 39° (4° below avg.); precip. 2.5" (1" above avg.). 1–10 Snowy periods, cold. 11–14 Rain and snow showers north; sunny, mild south. 15–16 Sunny north, showers south. 17–25 Snow showers, cold. 26–28 Snow north, sunny south; cold. 29–31 Snowy periods.

APR. 2020: Temp. 45° (4° below avg.); precip. 1.5" (0.5" above avg.). 1–6 Flurries north, snowstorm south, then sunny, chilly. 7–13 Rainy periods north, snow south; cool. 14–17 Showers, cool. 18–24 Snowstorm central, showers elsewhere, then sunny, cool. 25–30 Periods of rain and snow.

MAY 2020: Temp. 57° (avg.); precip. 0.5" (0.5" below avg.). 1–8 Isolated t-storms, turning warm. 9–19 Periods of rain and wet snow, then sunny; chilly. 20–25 Scattered t-storms, turning warm. 26–31 Showers, then sunny, cool.

JUNE 2020: Temp. 65° (1° below avg.); precip. 0.5" (avg.). 1–8 Sunny, warm. 9–17 Showers, cool. 18–22 Scattered t-storms; cool north, hot south. 23–30 A few showers, hot.

JULY 2020: Temp. 75° (2° above avg.); precip. 0.8" (0.3" above avg.). 1–7 Scattered t-storms, hot. 8–18 Sunny, turning warm. 19–26 T-storms, then sunny, cool. 27–31 Sunny, warm.

AUG. 2020: Temp. 70° (2° below avg.); precip. 1.2" (0.2" above avg.). 1–7 Sunny north, scattered t-storms south; warm. 8–16 Showers, cool. 17–20 Sunny, warm. 21–28 A few showers; cool north, warm south. 29–31 Sunny, warm north; rainy, cool south.

SEPT. 2020: Temp. 65° (3° above avg.); precip. 0.5" (avg. north, 1" below south). 1–9 Sunny, warm north; showers south. 10–13 Sunny, cool north; showers, warm south. 14–25 Sunny, warm. 26–30 Showers, turning cool.

OCT. 2020: Temp. 51° (avg.); precip. 0.5" (0.5" below avg.). 1–9 Showers, then sunny, cool. 10–15 Rainy periods, cool. 16–20 Snowy periods, cold. 21–29 Showers, then sunny, turning warm. 30–31 Rainy, cool.

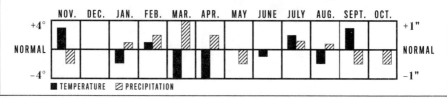

SUMMARY: Winter will be colder than normal, with cold weather predominant from mid-December to mid-January and in mid-February. Precipitation and snowfall will be above normal in the east and below normal in the west. The snowiest periods will be in mid- to late December, mid-January, and mid-February. **April** and **May** will be cooler than normal, on average, with rainfall below normal in the east and above normal in the west. **Summer** will be slightly cooler and drier than normal. The hottest periods will occur in early to mid-June and early and late July. **September** and **October** will be cooler and drier than normal in the east and near normal in the west.

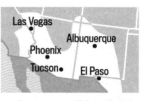

NOV. 2019: Temp. 57° (1° above avg.); precip. 1" (avg.). 1–6 Rain, then sunny, cool east; sunny, warm west. 7–15 Sunny, warm. 16–20 Showers, then sunny, cool. 21–25 Scattered showers, then sunny, cool. 26–30 Showers, warm.

DEC. 2019: Temp. 45° (3° below avg.); precip. 0.2" (0.3" below avg.). 1–8 Showers, then sunny, chilly. 9–16 Sunny; mild, then cold. 17–20 Snow east, sunny west; cold. 21–26 Periods of rain and snow, cold. 27–31 Sunny, cold.

JAN. 2020: Temp. 46° (2° below avg.); precip. 0.5" (0.5" above avg. east, 0.5" below west). 1–7 Rain and snow showers, then sunny, cold. 8–14 Sunny; cold east, mild west. 15–16 Snow east, sunny west; cold. 17–20 Sunny, warm. 21–27 Rainy periods, mild east; sunny, cold west. 28–31 Flurries, cold.

FEB. 2020: Temp. 50° (1° below avg.); precip. 0.2" (0.3" below avg.). 1–4 Sunny, mild. 5–13 Showers, then sunny, cool. 14–17 Snow, then sunny east; sunny west; cold. 18–24 Sunny, turning mild. 25–29 Showers, mild.

MAR. 2020: Temp. 54° (4° below avg.); precip. 1" (0.5" above avg.). 1–6 Showers, cool. 7–14 Rain and snow, then sunny, turning warmer. 15–18 Scattered showers, mild. 19–23 Snow showers east, sunny west; cold. 24–31 Showers west, sunny east; cool.

APR. 2020: Temp. 61° (4° below avg.); precip. 0.5" (0.2" below avg. east, 0.2" above west). 1–6 Rainy periods, cool. 7–9 Sunny; warm east, cool west. 10–17 Isolated showers, then

sunny, cool. 18–23 Isolated showers, cool. 24–30 Sunny, cool.

MAY 2020: Temp. 73° (1° below avg.); precip. 0.5" (avg.). 1–8 Scattered showers, then sunny, warm. 9–16 Showers, then sunny, cool. 17–20 Sunny, warm. 21–31 Isolated t-storms; cool, then hot.

JUNE 2020: Temp. 82° (1° below avg.); precip. 0.3" (0.2" below avg.). 1–9 Sunny, turning hot. 10–19 Isolated showers, warm. 20–24 Sunny, warm. 25–30 Scattered t-storms, warm.

JULY 2020: Temp. 87° (avg.); precip. 1" (0.5" below avg.). 1–7 T-storms, warm east; sunny, hot west. 8–12 Isolated t-storms, warm. 13–20 Scattered t-storms east, sunny west; hot. 21–31 Isolated t-storms; warm, then hot.

AUG. 2020: Temp. 84° (1° below avg.); precip. 1" (0.5" below avg.). 1–12 Scattered t-storms east, sunny west; warm. 13–15 T-storms, cooler. 16–26 Isolated t-storms; hot east, warm west. 27–31 T-storms; cool east; sunny, warm west.

SEPT. 2020: Temp. 78° (3° below avg. east, 1° above west); precip. 1.5" (0.5" above avg.). 1–3 Showers, warm. 4–7 Rainy, cool east; sunny west. 8–13 Scattered t-storms, warm. 14–27 Sunny; cool east, warm west. 28–30 Sunny, cool.

OCT. 2020: Temp. 68° (1° above avg. east, 1° below west); precip. 0.5" (0.5" below avg.). 1–6 Sunny; warm east, cool west. 7–11 Sunny, cool. 12–19 T-storms, then sunny, chilly. 20–25 Scattered showers, cool. 26–31 Sunny, warm.

WEATHER

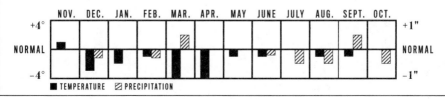

PACIFIC NORTHWEST

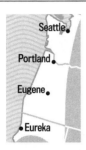

Seattle●
Portland●
Eugene●
●Eureka

SUMMARY: Winter will be warmer and rainier than normal, with below-normal snowfall. The coldest periods will occur in mid- to late December, early and mid- to late January, mid-February, and mid- to late March. The snowiest periods will occur in mid-December and early and mid- to late January. **April** and **May** will have near-normal temperatures, with below-normal rainfall. **Summer** will have slightly above-normal temperatures, on average, with above-normal precipitation. The hottest periods will be in late June, mid-July, and late August. **September** and **October** will be warmer and rainier than normal. The hottest periods will be in early and mid-September.

NOV. 2019: Temp. 52° (5° above avg.); precip. 5.5" (1" below avg.). 1–5 Rainy periods, mild. 6–9 Sunny, mild. 10–18 Rainy, mild. 19–23 Sunny; cool, then mild. 24–30 Rainy periods, mild.

DEC. 2019: Temp. 48° (5° above avg.); precip. 8.5" (2" above avg.). 1–6 Rainy, mild. 7–13 Rain, some heavy; mild. 14–17 Sunny, cool. 18–20 Stormy, heavy rain and snow. 21–24 Sunny, cold. 25–31 Rainy periods; cool north, mild south.

JAN. 2020: Temp. 44° (3° below avg. north, 5° above south); precip. 6" (avg.). 1–4 Rain and snow, cold. 5–9 Rain, some heavy; cold north, mild south. 10–17 Rainy periods, mild. 18–24 Rain to snow, then sunny, cold. 25–31 Rainy periods, cool.

FEB. 2020: Temp. 44° (avg.); precip. 6" (2" above avg. north, avg. south). 1–6 Rainy periods; cold north, mild south. 7–10 Rain and wet snow, chilly. 11–15 Rain, then sunny, cold. 16–23 Rainy periods, mild. 24–29 Sunny, cool.

MAR. 2020: Temp. 44° (3° below avg.); precip. 5" (1" below avg. north, 3" above south). 1–7 Rain, then sunny, cool. 8–19 Rainy periods, cool. 20–22 Sunny, cold. 23–31 Rainy periods, chilly.

APR. 2020: Temp. 48° (2° below avg.); precip. 3" (avg.). 1–5 Sunny, mild. 6–12 Rainy periods, cool. 13–14 Sunny, cool. 15–20 Rainy periods, cool. 21–24 Sunny, warm. 25–30 Rainy periods, cool.

MAY 2020: Temp. 57° (2° above avg.); precip. 0.5" (1.5" below avg.). 1–2 Sunny, warm. 3–7 Showers, then sunny, warm. 8–20 Showers, cool. 21–25 Sunny, turning hot. 26–31 Showers, then sunny, cool.

JUNE 2020: Temp. 61.5° (1.5° above avg.); precip. 1" (0.5" below avg.). 1–7 Sunny, very warm. 8–10 Showers, cool. 11–15 Sunny, cool. 16–25 Rainy periods, cool. 26–30 Sunny, hot.

JULY 2020: Temp. 66° (1° above avg.); precip. 0.3" (0.2" below avg.). 1–3 Sunny, warm. 4–11 Scattered showers, cool. 12–20 Sunny, turning hot. 21–28 Scattered showers, warm. 29–31 Showers, cool.

AUG. 2020: Temp. 64° (2° below avg.); precip. 2.5" (1.5" above avg.). 1–8 Sunny, warm. 9–23 Showers and t-storms, cool. 24–31 Sunny, turning hot.

SEPT. 2020: Temp. 64° (3° above avg.); precip. 1" (0.5" below avg.). 1–7 Sunny, hot. 8–15 Showers, then sunny, hot. 16–24 Sunny; cool, then warm. 25–30 Rainy periods, warm.

OCT. 2020: Temp. 55° (1° above avg.); precip. 5" (2" above avg.). 1–6 Rainy periods, cool. 7–13 Rainy periods, mild. 14–23 Rain, some heavy; cool. 24–31 Rainy periods; cool, then mild.

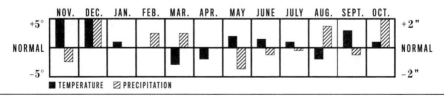

WEATHER

SUMMARY: Winter will be cooler than normal. Rainfall will be below normal in the north and above normal in the south, with below-normal mountain snows. The coolest temperatures will occur in mid- and late December, mid- to late January, early to mid-February, and early and late March. The stormiest periods will be in late November, mid- to late December, and early February; from late February into early March; and in mid- and late March. **April** and **May** will be cooler than normal, on average, with rainfall below normal in the north and above normal in the south. **Summer** will be cooler than normal, with rainfall slightly above normal. The hottest periods will be in mid-July and late August. **September** and **October** will be slightly cooler than normal, on average, with rainfall above normal in the north and below normal in the south.

NOV. 2019: Temp. 59° (1° above avg.); precip. 1.5" (1" below avg. north, 1" above south). 1–6 Sunny, warm. 7–12 Scattered showers north, sunny south; cool. 13–17 Scattered showers, warm. 18–24 Sunny, cool. 25–30 Rain, then sunny, cool.

DEC. 2019: Temp. 52° (2° below avg.); precip. 1" (1" below avg.). 1–4 Sunny, cool. 5–12 Isolated showers, turning warm. 13–19 Sunny, cool. 20–24 Rainy, cool. 25–31 Sunny, then rain; cool.

JAN. 2020: Temp. 53° (1° below avg.); precip. 2" (1" below avg.). 1–3 Showers, cool. 4–17 Sunny; cool coast, warm inland. 18–20 Sunny, cool. 21–28 Rainy periods, cool. 29–31 Showers, mild.

FEB. 2020: Temp. 54° (1° below avg.); precip. 2.5" (1" above avg. north, avg. south). 1–7 Rainy periods; mild, then cool. 8–11 Sunny, cool. 12–19 Rain, then sunny, cool. 20–24 Showers, mild. 25–29 Rain, some heavy; mild.

MAR. 2020: Temp. 54° (3° below avg.); precip. 4.5" (2" above avg.). 1–9 Rainy periods, cool. 10–13 Showers, cool north; sunny, mild south. 14–18 Rainy periods, cool. 19–23 Sunny, cool. 24–31 Rainy periods, cool.

APR. 2020: Temp. 56° (4° below avg.); precip. 1.3" (0.5" below avg. north, 1" above south). 1–6 Sunny, cool. 7–10 Rainy, cool. 11–15 Sunny, cool. 16–25 Rain, then sunny, cool. 26–30 Scattered showers, cool.

MAY 2020: Temp. 65.5° (2° above avg.); precip. 0.4" (0.1" below avg.). 1–4 Sunny, warm inland; A.M. sprinkles, P.M. sun coast. 5–6 Sunny; warm coast, hot inland. 7–12 Sunny, hot inland; A.M. sprinkles, cool coast. 13–23 Sunny, turning hot. 24–31 Sunny inland; A.M. sprinkles, P.M. sun coast; warm.

JUNE 2020: Temp. 67° (1° below avg.); precip. 0.15" (0.05" above avg.). 1–7 Sunny, warm. 8–17 Sunny inland; A.M. sprinkles, P.M. sun coast; cool. 18–30 Sunny, cool.

JULY 2020: Temp. 71° (avg.); precip. 0" (avg.). 1–14 Sunny inland; A.M. sprinkles, P.M. sun coast; warm, then cool. 15–20 Sunny, turning hot. 21–23 Sunny inland; A.M. clouds, P.M. sun coast; cool. 24–31 Sunny, warm.

AUG. 2020: Temp. 69° (2° below avg.); precip. 0.2" (0.2" above avg. north, avg. south). 1–8 Sunny, seasonable. 9–11 Scattered showers north, sunny south; cool. 12–16 Sunny, warm. 17–25 Sunny inland; A.M. clouds, P.M. sun coast; cool. 26–31 Sunny, warm.

SEPT. 2020: Temp. 71° (1° above avg.); precip. 0.2" (avg.). 1–3 Showers, cool. 4–8 Sunny inland; A.M. sprinkles, P.M. sun coast; cool. 9–15 Sunny; hot inland, cool coast. 16–18 Sunny, hot. 19–27 Sunny, warm. 28–30 Showers, cool.

OCT. 2020: Temp. 63° (2° below avg.); precip. 0.8" (1" above avg. north, 0.5" below south). 1–4 Rainy periods, cool. 5–12 Sunny, turning warm. 13–17 Showers, then sunny, cool. 18–23 Rainy periods, cool. 24–31 Sunny, cool.

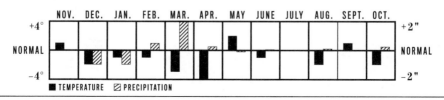

ALASKA

SUMMARY: Winter temperatures will be milder than normal, with the coldest period from late December into early January. Precipitation and snowfall will be mostly above normal. The snowiest periods will occur in early November N+C (see Key below), mid- to late December and mid- to late January S, and early to mid-February P. **April** and **May** will be warmer than normal, with slightly above-normal precipitation. **Summer** will be slightly warmer than normal, with the hottest period in early July. Precipitation will be above normal N and below normal S. **September** and **October** will be colder than normal, with precipitation near normal S and below normal EW. Snowfall will be below normal (except above normal C), with the snowiest period in mid-October.

KEY: north (N), central (C), south (S), panhandle (P), elsewhere (EW).

NOV. 2019: Temp. -3° N, 41° S (5° below avg. N, 5° above S); precip. 0.9" N, 5.5" S (0.5" above avg.). 1–9 Snowy periods; cold, then mild. 10–14 Flurries, cold. 15–27 Flurries, cold N; snowy periods, mild S. 28–30 Sunny, cold.

DEC. 2019: Temp. -13° N, 36° S (6° below avg. N, 5° above S); precip. 0.7" N, 5.5" S (0.5" above avg.). 1–8 Snow showers; cold N, mild S. 9–14 Flurries, cold. 15–19 Flurries, cold N; snow showers, mild S. 20–25 Flurries, cold N, snowy periods, mild S. 26–31 Clear, frigid.

JAN. 2020: Temp. -4° N, 37° S (8° above avg.); precip. 0.9" N, 5.7" S (0.7" above avg.). 1–6 Clear, cold. 7–15 Snow showers, turning mild. 16–21 Snowy periods, mild. 22–31 Snowy periods, mild N+C; clear, cold S.

FEB. 2020: Temp. -8° N, 37° S (6° above avg.); precip. 0.2" N, 4" S (avg.). 1–6 Clear, cold. 7–12 Snow showers, cold N+C; snowy periods, mild S. 13–23 Snowy periods, mild. 24–29 Flurries, quite mild.

MAR. 2020: Temp. -7° N, 32° S (6° above avg. N, 2° below S); precip. 0.5" N, 5" S (avg.). 1–6 Snow showers, quite mild. 7–11 Clear, mild. 12–18 Flurries, mild N; snowy periods, cold S. 19–24 Snowy periods, mild. 25–31 Flurries, cool.

APR. 2020: Temp. 2° N, 41° S (avg.); precip. 1" N, 3.3" S (0.3" above avg.). 1–5 Sunny, cold N; snow to rain S. 6–14 Sunny, cold, then mild N; snowy periods, cold C; rain, then sunny, cool S. 15–18 Sunny, mild. 19–22 Flurries N, sunny S; mild. 23–30 Sunny N, showers C+S.

MAY 2020: Temp. 23° N, 49° EW (2° above avg.); precip. 0.4" N, 2.8" S (0.2" below avg.). 1–8 Sunny, warm. 9–18 Snow showers N, rain showers C+S; mild. 19–31 Sprinkles, mild N; a few showers, warm C+S.

JUNE 2020: Temp. 37° N, 57° EW (2° above avg.); precip. 0.7" N, 3" S (avg.). 1–8 Showers; warm C, cool EW. 9–16 Showers, cool. 17–21 Showers N; sunny, warm S. 22–30 Showers, warm.

JULY 2020: Temp. 44° N, 59° EW (2° above avg.); precip. 1.6" N, 4.4" S (0.4" above avg.). 1–8 Showers; turning hot C, warm EW. 9–12 Sunny, warm. 13–21 Scattered showers; cool N, warm EW. 22–31 Rainy periods, cool.

AUG. 2020: Temp. 39° N, 55° EW (1° below avg.); precip. 0.7" N, 4.5" S (0.5" below avg.). 1–4 Showers, cool. 5–13 Rainy periods, cool. 14–17 Sunny N, showers C+S; cool. 18–21 Showers, cool. 22–31 Snow showers, cold N; rainy periods, mild EW.

SEPT. 2020: Temp. 35° N, 57° EW (3° above avg.); precip. 2.1" N, 8" S (1" above avg.). 1–5 A few showers N+C, rainy S; cool. 6–15 Rain, then snow showers, cold N; rainy periods, mild C+S. 16–24 Flurries, cold N; sunny, cool C; rainy, mild S. 25–30 Snow showers N, sunny C, showers S; mild.

OCT. 2020: Temp. 12° N, 37° S (5° below avg.); precip. 0.2" N, 6.7" S (0.3" below avg.). 1–10 Snow showers, cold N; rain and snow showers C; rainy, mild S. 11–17 Flurries N, periods of rain and snow C, showers S; mild. 18–26 Flurries, cold N+C; sunny, turning cold S. 27–31 Snow showers N+C, sunny S; cold.

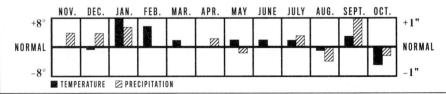

HAWAII

SUMMARY: Winter temperatures will be near or slightly below normal, on average, with the coolest periods in late January and mid-February. Rainfall will be above normal in the east and below normal in the west, with the stormiest periods in mid-December, mid- to late January, and early and mid- to late March. **April** and **May** will be slightly cooler and drier than normal. **Summer** will be cooler and drier than normal, on average, with the warmest period in mid-July. **September** and **October** will be cooler and drier than normal, with the rainiest periods in mid- and late October.

KEY: east (E), central (C), west (W). Note: Temperature and precipitation are substantially based upon topography. The detailed forecast focuses on the Honolulu–Waikiki area and provides general trends elsewhere.

NOV. 2019: Temp. 77.2° (avg. E, 1.5° below C, 1.5° above W); precip. 1.3" (avg. C, 2" below E+W). 1–11 A few showers, cool. 12–16 Rainy periods, cool. 17–28 Sunny, pleasant. 29–30 Showers.

DEC. 2019: Temp. 76° (1° above avg.); precip. 5.3" (10" above avg. E, 6" below W). 1–11 A few showers, warm. 12–19 Daily showers, warm. 20–26 Sunny, cool. 27–31 A few showers, warm.

JAN. 2020: Temp. 72° (1° below avg.); precip. 7" (1" below avg. E, 10" above W). 1–7 Showers, cool. 8–16 Sunny, cool. 17–22 A few showers, cool. 23–26 Showers and heavy t-storms. 27–31 Sunny, cool.

FEB. 2020: Temp. 73° (avg.); precip. 0.5" (avg. E, 3" below W). 1–9 Showers, turning very warm. 10–15 A few showers, cool. 16–24 Rainy periods E, a few showers C, sunny W; warm. 25–29 Showers, seasonable.

MAR. 2020: Temp. 73° (1° below avg.); precip. 2.5" (0.5" above avg.). 1–8 Heavy rain E, a few showers C+W. 9–15 Showers, warm. 16–19 Sunny C, showers E+W. 20–24 Rainy periods, some heavy; cool E+C, warm W. 25–31 Showers, warm.

APR. 2020: Temp. 75° (0.5° below avg.); precip. 0.5" (0.2" below avg.). 1–10 Rainy periods, warm E; a few showers, cool C+W. 11–23 Sunny C, rainy periods E+W; warm. 24–30 Daily showers, seasonable.

MAY 2020: Temp. 76.5° (0.5° below avg.); precip. 0.5" (0.2" below avg.). 1–5 Showers E+W, sunny C; cool. 6–14 A few showers, cool. 15–27 Showers, warm E; sunny, seasonable C+W. 28–31 Scattered showers, warm.

JUNE 2020: Temp. 78.5° (1° below avg.); precip. 0.2" (0.2" below avg.). 1–9 Daily showers E, isolated showers C+W; warm. 10–18 Showers E+W, sunny C; warm. 19–24 Showers, cool. 25–30 Showers E+W, sunny C; warm.

JULY 2020: Temp. 80° (1° below avg.); precip. 0.3" (2.5" below avg. E, 2" above W). 1–4 A few showers, cool. 5–9 Showers E+W, sunny C; cool. 10–18 Daily showers, warm. 19–31 Showers E+W, sunny C; seasonable.

AUG. 2020: Temp. 79.5° (2° below avg.); precip. 0.3" (0.3" below avg.). 1–13 Rainy periods, cool E+W; sprinkles, warm C. 14–23 Showers E+W, sunny C; cool. 24–31 Sunny, seasonable.

SEPT. 2020: Temp. 79.5° (2° below avg.); precip. 0.4" (0.4" below avg.). 1–7 A few showers, cool. 8–21 A few showers E+C, daily showers W; cool. 22–30 A few showers, warm.

OCT. 2020: Temp. 79° (1° below avg.); precip. 1" (1" below avg.). 1–10 Showers E, sunny C+W; seasonable. 11–21 Daily showers E, a few showers C+W; cool. 22–26 A few showers E+W, sunny C; cool. 27–31 Daily showers, warm.

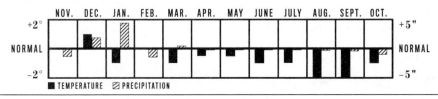

	NOV.	DEC.	JAN.	FEB.	MAR.	APR.	MAY	JUNE	JULY	AUG.	SEPT.	OCT.	
+2°													+5"
NORMAL													NORMAL
-2°													-5"

■ TEMPERATURE ▨ PRECIPITATION

SECRETS OF THE ZODIAC

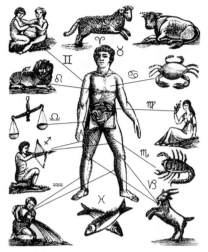

The Man of the Signs

Ancient astrologers believed that each astrological sign influenced a specific part of the body. The first sign of the zodiac—Aries—was attributed to the head, with the rest of the signs moving down the body, ending with Pisces at the feet.

Sign	Body Part	Abbr.	Dates
♈ Aries	head	ARI	*Mar. 21–Apr. 20*
♉ Taurus	neck	TAU	*Apr. 21–May 20*
♊ Gemini	arms	GEM	*May 21–June 20*
♋ Cancer	breast	CAN	*June 21–July 22*
♌ Leo	heart	LEO	*July 23–Aug. 22*
♍ Virgo	belly	VIR	*Aug. 23–Sept. 22*
♎ Libra	reins	LIB	*Sept. 23–Oct. 22*
♏ Scorpio	secrets	SCO	*Oct. 23–Nov. 22*
♐ Sagittarius	thighs	SAG	*Nov. 23–Dec. 21*
♑ Capricorn	knees	CAP	*Dec. 22–Jan. 19*
♒ Aquarius	legs	AQU	*Jan. 20–Feb. 19*
♓ Pisces	feet	PSC	*Feb. 20–Mar. 20*

ASTROLOGY VS. ASTRONOMY

Astrology is a tool we use to plan events according to the placements of the Sun, the Moon, and the planets in the 12 signs of the zodiac. In astrology, the planetary movements do not cause events; rather, they explain the path, or "flow," that events tend to follow. *The Moon's astrological place is given on the next page.* **Astronomy** is the study of the actual placement of the known planets and constellations. The Moon's astronomical place is given in the **Left-Hand Calendar Pages, 120–146.** *(The placement of the planets in the signs of the zodiac is not the same astrologically and astronomically.)*

The dates in the **Best Days** table, **pages 226–227,** are based on the astrological passage of the Moon.

WHEN MERCURY IS RETROGRADE

Sometimes the other planets appear to be traveling backward through the zodiac; this is an illusion. We call this illusion *retrograde motion.*

Mercury's retrograde periods can cause our plans to go awry. However, intuition is high during these periods and coincidences can be extraordinary.

When Mercury is retrograde, stay flexible, allow more time for travel, and don't sign contracts. Review projects and plans but wait until Mercury is direct again to make final decisions.

In 2020, Mercury will be retrograde during **February 17–March 10, June 18–July 12,** and **October 14–November 3.**

—Celeste Longacre

GARDENING BY THE MOON'S SIGN

USE CHART ON NEXT PAGE TO FIND THE BEST DATES FOR THE FOLLOWING GARDEN TASKS . . .

PLANT, TRANSPLANT, AND GRAFT: Cancer, Scorpio, Pisces, or Taurus
HARVEST: Aries, Leo, Sagittarius, Gemini, or Aquarius
BUILD/FIX FENCES OR GARDEN BEDS: Capricorn

CONTROL INSECT PESTS, PLOW, AND WEED: Aries, Gemini, Leo, Sagittarius, or Aquarius
PRUNE: Aries, Leo, or Sagittarius. During a waxing Moon, pruning encourages growth; during a waning Moon, it discourages it.

SETTING EGGS BY THE MOON'S SIGN

Chicks take about 21 days to hatch. Those born under a waxing Moon in Cancer, Scorpio, or Pisces are healthier and mature faster. To ensure that chicks are born during these times, "set eggs" (place eggs in an incubator or under a hen) 21 days before the desired hatching dates.

EXAMPLE:
The Moon is new on March 24 and full on April 7 (EDT). Between these dates, the Moon is in the sign of Cancer on March 31 and April 1 and 2. To have chicks born on April 2, count back 21 days; set eggs on March 12.

Below are the best days to set eggs in 2020, using only the fruitful dates between the new and full Moons, and counting back 21 days:

JAN.: 6, 7, 16, 17   **APR.:** 6–8, 15, 16   **JULY:** 6, 7   **OCT.:** 5, 6
FEB.: 2–4, 12, 13   **MAY:** 4, 5, 12–14, 31   **AUG.:** 2, 3, 11, 12, 30, 31   **NOV.:** 1, 2, 28–30
MAR.: 10–12   **JUNE:** 1, 9, 10, 29   **SEPT.:** 7–9, 26, 27   **DEC.:** 8, 26, 27

The Moon's Astrological Place, 2019–20

	NOV.	DEC.	JAN.	FEB.	MAR.	APR.	MAY	JUNE	JULY	AUG.	SEPT.	OCT.	NOV.	DEC.
1	CAP	AQU	PSC	TAU	TAU	CAN	LEO	LIB	SCO	CAP	PSC	ARI	TAU	GEM
2	CAP	AQU	ARI	TAU	GEM	CAN	VIR	SCO	SAG	CAP	PSC	ARI	GEM	CAN
3	AQU	PSC	ARI	GEM	GEM	LEO	VIR	SCO	SAG	AQU	PSC	TAU	GEM	CAN
4	AQU	PSC	TAU	GEM	CAN	LEO	LIB	SCO	CAP	AQU	ARI	TAU	GEM	LEO
5	AQU	ARI	TAU	GEM	CAN	VIR	LIB	SAG	CAP	PSC	ARI	TAU	CAN	LEO
6	PSC	ARI	TAU	CAN	LEO	VIR	SCO	SAG	AQU	PSC	TAU	GEM	CAN	LEO
7	PSC	ARI	GEM	CAN	LEO	LIB	SCO	CAP	AQU	ARI	TAU	GEM	LEO	VIR
8	ARI	TAU	GEM	LEO	VIR	LIB	SAG	CAP	AQU	ARI	TAU	CAN	LEO	VIR
9	ARI	TAU	CAN	LEO	VIR	SCO	SAG	AQU	PSC	ARI	GEM	CAN	VIR	LIB
10	ARI	GEM	CAN	VIR	LIB	SCO	CAP	AQU	PSC	TAU	GEM	CAN	VIR	LIB
11	TAU	GEM	LEO	VIR	LIB	SAG	CAP	PSC	ARI	TAU	CAN	LEO	LIB	SCO
12	TAU	GEM	LEO	LIB	SCO	SAG	AQU	PSC	ARI	GEM	CAN	LEO	LIB	SCO
13	GEM	CAN	VIR	LIB	SCO	CAP	AQU	PSC	TAU	GEM	LEO	VIR	SCO	SAG
14	GEM	CAN	VIR	SCO	SAG	CAP	AQU	ARI	TAU	GEM	LEO	VIR	SCO	SAG
15	CAN	LEO	LIB	SCO	SAG	AQU	PSC	ARI	TAU	CAN	LEO	LIB	SAG	CAP
16	CAN	LEO	LIB	SAG	CAP	AQU	PSC	TAU	GEM	CAN	VIR	LIB	SAG	CAP
17	CAN	VIR	LIB	SAG	CAP	AQU	ARI	TAU	GEM	LEO	VIR	SCO	CAP	AQU
18	LEO	VIR	SCO	CAP	CAP	PSC	ARI	TAU	CAN	LEO	LIB	SCO	CAP	AQU
19	LEO	LIB	SCO	CAP	AQU	PSC	ARI	GEM	CAN	VIR	LIB	SAG	CAP	PSC
20	VIR	LIB	SAG	CAP	AQU	ARI	TAU	GEM	CAN	VIR	SCO	SAG	AQU	PSC
21	VIR	SCO	SAG	AQU	PSC	ARI	TAU	CAN	LEO	LIB	SCO	CAP	AQU	PSC
22	LIB	SCO	CAP	AQU	PSC	ARI	GEM	CAN	LEO	LIB	SAG	CAP	PSC	ARI
23	LIB	SAG	CAP	PSC	PSC	TAU	GEM	LEO	VIR	SCO	SAG	AQU	PSC	ARI
24	SCO	SAG	AQU	PSC	ARI	TAU	GEM	LEO	VIR	SCO	CAP	AQU	ARI	TAU
25	SCO	SAG	AQU	PSC	ARI	GEM	CAN	VIR	LIB	SAG	CAP	AQU	ARI	TAU
26	SAG	CAP	AQU	ARI	TAU	GEM	CAN	VIR	LIB	SAG	AQU	PSC	ARI	TAU
27	SAG	CAP	PSC	ARI	TAU	CAN	LEO	VIR	SCO	SAG	AQU	PSC	TAU	GEM
28	CAP	AQU	PSC	TAU	TAU	CAN	LEO	LIB	SCO	CAP	PSC	ARI	TAU	GEM
29	CAP	AQU	ARI	TAU	GEM	CAN	VIR	LIB	SAG	CAP	PSC	ARI	GEM	CAN
30	CAP	PSC	ARI	—	GEM	LEO	VIR	SCO	SAG	AQU	PSC	ARI	GEM	CAN
31	—	PSC	ARI	—	CAN	—	LIB	—	CAP	AQU	—	TAU	—	CAN

BEST DAYS FOR 2020

This chart is based on the Moon's sign and shows the best days each
month for certain activities. –*Celeste Longacre*

	JAN.	FEB.	MAR.	APR.	MAY	JUNE	JULY	AUG.	SEPT.	OCT.	NOV.	DEC.
Quit smoking	6, 11	3, 7	7, 16	3, 13	1, 10	7, 11	4, 9, 31	5, 9, 27	1, 5, 28	7, 26	3, 26	5, 28
Bake	9, 10	6, 7	4, 5, 31	1, 2, 27–29	25, 26	21, 22	18–20	15, 16	11, 12	8, 9	5, 6	2, 3, 29–31
Brew	18, 19	14, 15	12, 13	9, 10	6, 7	2–4, 30	1, 27, 28	23, 24	20, 21	17, 18	13, 14	11, 12
Dry fruit, vegetables, or meat	11, 12	16, 17	14, 15	20, 21	8, 9	14, 15	11, 12	7–9	4, 5	11, 12	24–26	4–6
Make jams or jellies	1, 27, 28	23–25	21–23	18, 19	15, 16	11–13	9, 10	5, 6	1–3, 28–30	26, 27	22, 23	19–21
Can, pickle, or make sauerkraut	18, 19	14, 15	12, 13	9, 10	15, 16	11–13	9, 10	5, 6	11, 12	9, 10	5, 6	2, 3, 30, 31
Begin diet to lose weight	14, 19	11, 15	13, 23	10, 19	16, 21	18	10, 15	5, 11	3, 8	5, 14	1, 11	8, 12
Begin diet to gain weight	6, 28	2, 7, 29	1, 28	6, 24	3, 31	4, 27	1, 28	20, 24	21, 30	18, 27	23, 28	19, 26
Cut hair to encourage growth	27, 28	23–25	26–28	23, 24	4, 5	1, 28, 29	25, 26	21, 22	18, 19	26, 27, 31	22, 23	24, 25
Cut hair to discourage growth	15, 16	12, 13	10, 11	8, 18, 19	20, 21	11–13	9, 10	5, 6	6–8	3–5	1, 11, 12	9, 10
Perm hair	24–26	21, 22	19, 20	15–17	12–14	9, 10	6–8	3, 4, 30, 31	26, 27	23–25	20, 21	17, 18
Color hair	4–6	1, 2, 28, 29	1, 26–28	23, 24	20, 21	16–18	13–15	10, 11	6–8	3–5, 31	1, 27, 28	24–26
Straighten hair	20, 21	16, 17	14, 15	11, 12	8, 9	5, 6	2, 3, 29, 30	25–27	22, 23	19, 20	15, 16	13, 14
Have dental care	13, 14	10, 11	8, 9	5, 6	2, 3, 29, 30	25–27	23, 24	19, 20	16, 17	13, 14	9, 10	7, 8
Start projects	25	24	25	23	23	22	21	19	18	17	16	15
End projects	23	22	23	21	21	20	19	17	16	15	14	13
Demolish	18, 19	14, 15	12, 13	9, 10	6, 7	2–4, 30	1, 27, 28	23, 24	20, 21	17, 18	13, 14	11, 12
Lay shingles	11, 12	8, 9	6, 7	3, 4, 30	1, 27, 28	23, 24	21, 22	17, 18	13–15	11, 12	7, 8	4–6
Paint	15–17	12, 13	10, 11	7, 8	4, 5, 31	1, 28, 29	25, 26	21, 22	18, 19	15, 16	11, 12	9, 10
Wash windows	2, 3, 29–31	26, 27	24, 25	20–22	17–19	14, 15	11, 12	7–9	4, 5	1, 2, 28–30	24–26	22, 23
Wash floors	1, 27, 28	23–25	21–23	18, 19	15, 16	11–13	9, 10	5, 6	1–3, 28–30	26, 27	22, 23	19–21
Go camping	20, 21	16, 17	14, 15	11, 12	8, 9	5, 6	2, 3, 29, 30	25–27	22, 23	19, 20	15, 16	13, 14

	JAN.	FEB.	MAR.	APR.	MAY	JUNE	JULY	AUG.	SEPT.	OCT.	NOV.	DEC.
Entertain	11, 12	8, 9	6, 7	3, 4, 30	1, 27, 28	23, 24	21, 22	17, 18	13–15	11, 12	7, 8	4–6
Travel for pleasure	11, 12	8, 9	6, 7	3, 4, 30	1, 27, 28	23, 24	21, 22	17, 18	13–15	11, 12	7, 8	4–6
Get married	15–17	12, 13	10, 11	7, 8	4, 5, 31	1, 28, 29	25, 26	21, 22	18, 19	15, 16	11, 12	9, 10
Ask for a loan	14, 19	11, 15	13, 23	19	16, 21	11, 18	10, 15	5, 11	3, 8	5, 14	1, 11	8, 12
Buy a home	6, 28	2, 7	1, 28	6, 24	3, 31	4, 27	1, 28	20, 24	21, 30	18, 27	23, 28	19, 26
Move (house/household)	7, 8	3–5	2, 3, 29, 30	25, 26	22–24	19, 20	16, 17	12–14	9, 10	6, 7	2–4, 29, 30	1, 27, 28
Advertise to sell	5, 6	28, 29	26–28	23, 24	6, 28	2, 3	1, 27, 28	23, 24	20, 21	17, 18	22, 28	24, 25
Mow to promote growth	2, 3, 29–31	26, 27	24, 25	1, 2, 24	6, 28	3, 4, 30	1, 22	23, 24	20, 21	17, 18	24, 25	22, 23
Mow to slow growth	18, 19	14, 15	12, 13	9, 10	18, 19	14, 15	11, 12	7–9	4, 5	2, 11	8, 14	11, 12
Plant aboveground crops	5, 6, 9, 27, 28	23–25	4, 5, 31	1, 2, 27–29	25, 26	2–4	1, 27, 28	23, 24	1, 20, 21, 29, 30	17, 18	22, 23	20, 21, 29
Plant belowground crops	18, 19	14, 15	12, 13, 21–23	9, 10, 18, 19	15, 16	11–13	9, 10, 19	5, 6	11, 12	8–10	5, 6	2, 3, 11, 12
Destroy pests and weeds	2, 3, 29–31	26, 27	24, 25	20–22	17–19	14, 15	11, 12	7–9	4, 5	1, 2, 28–30	24–26	22, 23
Graft or pollinate	9, 10	6, 7	4, 5, 31	1, 2, 27–29	25, 26	21, 22	18–20	15, 16	20, 21	8–10	5, 6	2, 3, 29–31
Prune to encourage growth	2, 3, 29–31	26, 27	24, 25	3, 4, 22	1, 27, 28	23, 24	21, 22	25–27	22, 23	19, 20	15, 16	22, 23
Prune to discourage growth	11, 12	16, 17	14, 15	11, 12	8, 9	14, 15	11, 12	7–9	4, 5	11, 12	7, 8	4–6
Pick fruit	13, 14	10, 11	8, 9	5, 6	2, 3, 29, 30	25–27	23, 24	19, 20	16, 17	13, 14	9, 10	7, 8
Harvest above-ground crops	5, 6	28, 29	26–28	23, 24	2, 3, 29, 30	25–27	23, 24	19, 20	17, 24, 25	21, 22, 31	18, 19, 27, 28	15, 16
Harvest below-ground crops	13, 14	10, 11	17, 18	13, 14	20, 21	7, 8	14, 15	10, 11	6–8	4, 5	1, 9, 10	7, 8
Cut hay	2, 3, 29–31	26, 27	24, 25	20–22	17–19	14, 15	11, 12	7–9	4, 5	1, 2, 28–30	24–26	22, 23
Begin logging, set posts, pour concrete	22, 23	18–20	16–18	13, 14	10, 11	7, 8	4, 5, 31	1, 2, 28, 29	24, 25	21, 22	17–19	15, 16
Purchase animals	9, 10	6, 7	4, 5, 31	1, 2, 27–29	25, 26	21, 22	18–20	15, 16	11, 12	8, 9	5, 6	2, 3, 29–31
Breed animals	18, 19	14, 15	12, 13	9, 10	6, 7	2–4, 30	1, 27, 28	23, 24	20, 21	17, 18	13, 14	11, 12
Wean children or animals	6, 11	3, 7	7, 16	3, 13	1, 10	7, 11	4, 9, 31	5, 9, 27	1, 5, 28	7, 26	3, 26	5, 28
Castrate animals	24–26	21, 22	19, 20	15–17	12–14	9, 10	6–8	3, 4, 30, 31	26, 27	23–25	20, 21	17, 18
Slaughter livestock	18, 19	14, 15	12, 13	9, 10	6, 7	2–4, 30	1, 27, 28	23, 24	20, 21	17, 18	13, 14	11, 12

BEST FISHING DAYS AND TIMES

The best times to fish are when the fish are naturally most active. The Sun, Moon, tides, and weather all influence fish activity. For example, fish tend to feed more at sunrise and sunset, and also during a full Moon (when tides are higher than average). However, most of us go fishing simply when we can get the time off. But there are best times, according to fishing lore:

■ One hour before and one hour after high tides, and one hour before and one hour after low tides. The times of high tides for Boston are given on **pages 120–146;** also see **pages 236–237.** (Inland, the times for high tides correspond with the times when the Moon is due south. Low tides are halfway between high tides.)

GET TIDE TIMES AND HEIGHTS NEAREST TO YOUR LOCATION AT ALMANAC.COM/TIDES.

■ During the "morning rise" (after sunup for a spell) and the "evening rise" (just before sundown and the hour or so after).

■ During the rise and set of the Moon.

■ When the barometer is steady or on the rise. (But even during stormy periods, the fish aren't going to give up feeding. The clever angler will find just the right bait.)

■ When there is a hatch of flies—caddis flies or mayflies, commonly.

■ When the breeze is from a westerly quarter, rather than from the north or east.

■ When the water is still or slightly rippled, rather than during a wind.

THE BEST FISHING DAYS FOR 2020, WHEN THE MOON IS BETWEEN NEW AND FULL

January 1–10
January 24–February 9
February 23–March 9
March 24–April 7
April 22–May 7
May 22–June 5
June 21–July 5
July 20–August 3
August 18–September 2
September 17–October 1
October 16–31
November 15–30
December 14–29

Dates based on Eastern Time.

HOW TO ESTIMATE THE WEIGHT OF A FISH

Measure the fish from the tip of its nose to the tip of its tail. Then measure its girth at the thickest portion of its midsection.

The weight of a fat-bodied fish (bass, salmon) =
(length x girth x girth)/800

SALMON

The weight of a slender fish (trout, northern pike) =
(length x girth x girth)/900

EXAMPLE: If a trout is 20 inches long and has a 12-inch girth, its estimated weight is
(20 x 12 x 12)/900 =
2,880/900 = 3.2 pounds

TROUT

CATFISH

GESTATION AND MATING TABLES

	PROPER AGE OR WEIGHT FOR FIRST MATING	PERIOD OF FERTILITY (YRS.)	NUMBER OF FEMALES FOR ONE MALE	PERIOD OF GESTATION (DAYS) AVERAGE	RANGE
CATTLE: Cow	15–18 mos.[1]	10–14		283	279–290[2] 262–300[3]
Bull	1 yr., well matured	10–12	50[4] / thousands[5]		
GOAT: Doe	10 mos. or 85–90 lbs.	6		150	145–155
Buck	well matured	5	30		
HORSE: Mare	3 yrs.	10–12		336	310–370
Stallion	3 yrs.	12–15	40–45[4] / record 252[5]		
PIG: Sow	5–6 mos. or 250 lbs.	6		115	110–120
Boar	250–300 lbs.	6	50[6] / 35–40[7]		
RABBIT: Doe	6 mos.	5–6		31	30–32
Buck	6 mos.	5–6	30		
SHEEP: Ewe	1 yr. or 90 lbs.	6		147 / 151[8]	142–154
Ram	12–14 mos., well matured	7	50–75[6] / 35–40[7]		
CAT: Queen	12 mos.	6		63	60–68
Tom	12 mos.	6	6–8		
DOG: Bitch	16–18 mos.	8		63	58–67
Male	12–16 mos.	8	8–10		

[1]Holstein and beef: 750 lbs.; Jersey: 500 lbs. [2]Beef; 8–10 days shorter for Angus. [3]Dairy. [4]Natural. [5]Artificial. [6]Hand-mated. [7]Pasture. [8]For fine wool breeds.

INCUBATION PERIOD OF POULTRY (DAYS)

Chicken	21
Duck	26–32
Goose	30–34
Guinea	26–28
Turkey	28

AVERAGE LIFE SPAN OF ANIMALS IN CAPTIVITY (YEARS)

Cat (domestic)	14	Goose (domestic)	20
Chicken (domestic)	8	Horse	22
Dog (domestic)	13	Pig	12
Duck (domestic)	10	Rabbit	6
Goat (domestic)	14	Turkey (domestic)	10

	ESTRAL/ESTROUS CYCLE (INCLUDING HEAT PERIOD) AVERAGE	RANGE	LENGTH OF ESTRUS (HEAT) AVERAGE	RANGE	USUAL TIME OF OVULATION	WHEN CYCLE RECURS IF NOT BRED
Cow	21 days	18–24 days	18 hours	10–24 hours	10–12 hours after end of estrus	21 days
Doe goat	21 days	18–24 days	2–3 days	1–4 days	Near end of estrus	21 days
Mare	21 days	10–37 days	5–6 days	2–11 days	24–48 hours before end of estrus	21 days
Sow	21 days	18–24 days	2–3 days	1–5 days	30–36 hours after start of estrus	21 days
Ewe	16½ days	14–19 days	30 hours	24–32 hours	12–24 hours before end of estrus	16½ days
Queen cat		15–21 days	3–4 days, if mated	9–10 days, in absence of male	24–56 hours after coitus	Pseudo-pregnancy
Bitch	24 days	16–30 days	7 days	5–9 days	1–3 days after first acceptance	Pseudo-pregnancy

PLANTING BY THE MOON'S PHASE

ACCORDING TO THIS AGE-OLD PRACTICE, CYCLES OF THE MOON AFFECT PLANT GROWTH.

Plant annual flowers and vegetables that bear crops above ground during the light, or waxing, of the Moon: from the day the Moon is new to the day it is full.

Plant flowering bulbs, biennial and perennial flowers, and vegetables that bear crops below ground during the dark, or waning, of the Moon: from the day after it is full to the day before it is new again.

The Planting Dates columns give the safe periods for planting in areas that receive frost. (See **page 232** for frost dates in your area.) The Moon Favorable columns give the best planting days within the Planting Dates based on the Moon's phases for 2020. (See **pages 120–146** for the exact days of the new and full Moons.)

The dates listed in this table are meant as general guidelines only. For seed-sowing dates based on frost dates in your local area, go to **Almanac.com/PlantingTable.**

Aboveground crops are marked *.
(E) means early; (L) means late.

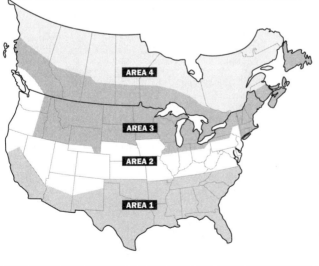

* Barley	(E)
* Beans	(E)
	(L)
Beets	(E)
	(L)
* Broccoli plants	(E)
	(L)
* Brussels sprouts	
* Cabbage plants	
Carrots	(E)
	(L)
* Cauliflower plants	(E)
	(L)
* Celery plants	(E)
	(L)
* Collards	(E)
	(L)
* Corn, sweet	(E)
	(L)
* Cucumbers	
* Eggplant plants	
* Endive	(E)
	(L)
* Kale	(E)
	(L)
Leek plants	
* Lettuce	
* Muskmelons	
* Okra	
Onion sets	
* Parsley	
Parsnips	
* Peas	(E)
	(L)
* Pepper plants	
Potatoes	
* Pumpkins	
Radishes	(E)
	(L)
* Spinach	(E)
	(L)
* Squashes	
Sweet potatoes	
* Swiss chard	
* Tomato plants	
Turnips	(E)
	(L)
* Watermelons	
* Wheat, spring	
* Wheat, winter	

AREA 1		AREA 2		AREA 3		AREA 4	
PLANTING DATES	MOON FAVORABLE	PLANTING DATES	MOON FAVORABLE	PLANTING DATES	MOON FAVORABLE	PLANTING DATES	MOON FAVORABLE
2/15-3/7	2/23-3/7	3/15-4/7	3/24-4/7	5/15-6/21	5/22-6/5, 6/21	6/1-30	6/1-5, 6/21-30
3/15-4/7	3/24-4/7	4/15-30	4/22-30	5/7-6/21	5/7, 5/22-6/5, 6/21	5/30-6/15	5/30-6/5
8/7-31	8/18-31	7/1-31	7/1-5, 7/20-21	6/15-7/15	6/21-7/5	—	—
2/7-29	2/10-22	3/15-4/3	3/15-23	5/1-15	5/8-15	5/25-6/10	6/6-10
9/1-30	9/3-16	8/15-31	8/15-17	7/15-8/15	7/15-19, 8/4-15	6/15-7/8	6/15-20, 7/6-8
2/15-3/15	2/23-3/9	3/7-31	3/7-9, 3/24-31	5/15-31	5/22-31	6/1-25	6/1-5, 6/21-25
9/7-30	9/17-30	8/1-20	8/1-3, 8/18-20	6/15-7/7	6/21-7/5	—	—
2/11-3/20	2/23-3/9	3/7-4/15	3/7-9, 3/24-4/7	5/15-31	5/22-31	6/1-25	6/1-5, 6/21-25
2/11-3/20	2/23-3/9	3/7-4/15	3/7-9, 3/24-4/7	5/15-31	5/22-31	6/1-25	6/1-5, 6/21-25
2/15-3/7	2/15-22	3/7-31	3/10-23	5/15-31	5/15-21	5/25-6/10	6/6-10
8/1-9/7	8/4-17, 9/3-7	7/7-31	7/7-19	6/15-7/21	6/15-20, 7/6-19	6/15-7/8	6/15-20, 7/6-8
2/15-3/7	2/23-3/7	3/15-4/7	3/24-4/7	5/15-31	5/22-31	6/1-25	6/1-5, 6/21-25
8/7-31	8/18-31	7/1-8/7	7/1-5, 7/20-8/3	6/15-7/21	6/21-7/5, 7/20-21	—	—
2/15-29	2/23-29	3/7-31	3/7-9, 3/24-31	5/15-6/30	5/22-6/5, 6/21-30	6/1-30	6/1-5, 6/21-30
9/15-30	9/17-30	8/15-9/7	8/18-9/2	7/15-8/15	7/20-8/3	—	—
2/11-3/20	2/23-3/9	3/7-4/7	3/7-9, 3/24-4/7	5/15-31	5/22-31	6/1-25	6/1-5, 6/21-25
9/7-30	9/17-30	8/15-31	8/18-31	7/1-8/7	7/1-5, 7/20-8/3	—	—
3/15-31	3/24-31	4/1-17	4/1-7	5/10-6/15	5/22-6/5	5/30-6/20	5/30-6/5
8/7-31	8/18-31	7/7-21	7/20-21	6/15-30	6/21-30	—	—
3/7-4/15	3/7-9, 3/24-4/7	4/7-5/15	4/7, 4/22-5/7	5/7-6/20	5/7, 5/22-6/5	5/30-6/15	5/30-6/5
3/7-4/15	3/7-9, 3/24-4/7	4/7-5/15	4/7, 4/22-5/7	6/1-30	6/1-5, 6/21-30	6/15-30	6/21-30
2/15-3/20	2/23-3/9	4/7-5/15	4/7, 4/22-5/7	5/15-31	5/22-31	6/1-25	6/1-5, 6/21-25
8/15-9/7	8/18-9/2	7/15-8/15	7/20-8/3	6/7-30	6/21-30	—	—
2/11-3/20	2/23-3/9	3/7-4/7	3/7-9, 3/24-4/7	5/15-31	5/22-31	6/1-15	6/1-5
9/7-30	9/17-30	8/15-31	8/18-31	7/1-8/7	7/1-5, 7/20-8/3	6/25-7/15	6/25-7/5
2/15-4/15	2/15-22, 3/10-23, 4/8-15	3/7-4/7	3/10-23	5/15-31	5/15-21	6/1-25	6/6-20
2/15-3/7	2/23-3/7	3/1-31	3/1-9, 3/24-31	5/15-6/30	5/22-6/5, 6/21-30	6/1-30	6/1-5, 6/21-30
3/15-4/7	3/24-4/7	4/15-5/7	4/22-5/7	5/15-6/30	5/22-6/5, 6/21-30	6/1-30	6/1-5, 6/21-30
4/15-6/1	4/22-5/7, 5/22-6/1	5/25-6/15	5/25-6/5	6/15-7/10	6/21-7/5	6/25-7/7	6/25-7/5
2/1-29	2/10-22	3/1-31	3/10-23	5/15-6/7	5/15-21, 6/6-7	6/1-25	6/6-20
2/20-3/15	2/23-3/9	3/1-31	3/1-9, 3/24-31	5/15-31	5/22-31	6/1-15	6/1-5
1/15-2/4	1/15-23	3/7-31	3/10-23	4/1-30	4/8-21	5/10-31	5/10-21
1/15-2/7	1/24-2/7	3/7-31	3/7-9, 3/24-31	4/15-5/7	4/22-5/7	5/15-31	5/22-31
9/15-30	9/17-30	8/7-31	8/18-31	7/15-31	7/20-31	7/10-25	7/20-25
3/1-20	3/1-9	4/1-30	4/1-7, 4/22-30	5/15-6/30	5/22-6/5, 6/21-30	6/1-30	6/1-5, 6/21-30
2/10-29	2/10-22	4/1-30	4/8-21	5/1-31	5/8-21	6/1-25	6/6-20
3/7-20	3/7-9	4/23-5/15	4/23-5/7	5/15-31	5/22-31	6/1-30	6/1-5, 6/21-30
1/21-3/1	1/21-23, 2/10-22	3/7-31	3/10-23	4/15-30	4/15-21	5/15-6/5	5/15-21
10/1-21	10/2-15	9/7-30	9/7-16	8/15-31	8/15-17	7/10-31	7/10-19
2/7-3/15	2/7-9, 2/23-3/9	3/15-4/20	3/24-4/7	5/15-31	5/22-31	6/1-25	6/1-5, 6/21-25
10/1-21	10/1, 10/16-21	8/1-9/15	8/1-3, 8/18-9/2	7/17-9/7	7/20-8/3, 8/18-9/2	7/20-8/5	7/20-8/3
3/15-4/15	3/24-4/7	4/15-30	4/22-30	5/15-6/15	5/22-6/5	6/1-30	6/1-5, 6/21-30
3/23-4/6	3/23	4/21-5/9	4/21, 5/8-9	5/15-6/15	5/15-21, 6/6-15	6/1-30	6/6-20
2/7-3/15	2/7-9, 2/23-3/9	3/15-4/15	3/24-4/7	5/1-31	5/1-7, 5/22-31	5/15-31	5/22-31
3/7-20	3/7-9	4/7-30	4/7, 4/22-30	5/15-31	5/22-31	6/1-15	6/1-5
1/20-2/15	1/20-23, 2/10-15	3/15-31	3/15-23	4/7-30	4/8-21	5/10-31	5/10-21
9/1-10/15	9/3-16, 10/2-15	8/1-20	8/4-17	7/1-8/15	7/6-19, 8/4-15	—	—
3/15-4/7	3/24-4/7	4/15-5/7	4/22-5/7	5/15-6/30	5/22-6/5, 6/21-30	6/1-30	6/1-5, 6/21-30
2/15-29	2/23-29	3/1-20	3/1-9	4/7-30	4/7, 4/22-30	5/15-6/10	5/22-6/5
10/15-12/7	10/16-31, 11/15-30	9/15-10/20	9/17-10/1, 10/16-20	8/11-9/15	8/18-9/2	8/5-30	8/18-30

FROSTS AND GROWING SEASONS

Dates given are normal averages for a light freeze; local weather and topography may cause considerable variations. The possibility of frost occurring after the spring dates and before the fall dates is 30 percent. The classification of freeze temperatures is usually based on their effect on plants. **Light freeze:** 29° to 32°F—tender plants killed. **Moderate freeze:** 25° to 28°F—widely destructive to most plants. **Severe freeze:** 24°F and colder—heavy damage to most plants. –dates courtesy of National Centers for Environmental Information

STATE	CITY	GROWING SEASON (DAYS)	LAST SPRING FROST	FIRST FALL FROST	STATE	CITY	GROWING SEASON (DAYS)	LAST SPRING FROST	FIRST FALL FROST
AK	Juneau	142	May 8	Sept. 28	ND	Bismarck	122	May 19	Sept. 19
AL	Mobile	267	Mar. 6	Nov. 29	NE	Omaha	160	Apr. 27	Oct. 5
AR	Pine Bluff	226	Mar. 26	Nov. 8	NE	North Platte	146	May 6	Sept. 30
AZ	Phoenix	341	Jan. 20	Dec. 27	NH	Concord	127	May 19	Sept. 24
AZ	Tucson	271	Mar. 3	Nov. 30	NJ	Newark	209	Apr. 8	Nov. 4
CA	Eureka	222	Apr. 6	Nov. 15	NM	Carlsbad	209	Apr. 5	Nov. 1
CA	Sacramento	263	Mar. 1	Nov. 20	NM	Los Alamos	146	May 10	Oct. 4
CA	San Francisco	*	*	*	NV	Las Vegas	301	Feb. 6	Dec. 4
CO	Denver	145	May 7	Sept. 30	NY	Albany	153	May 4	Oct. 5
CT	Hartford	159	May 1	Oct. 8	NY	Syracuse	156	May 4	Oct. 8
DE	Wilmington	194	Apr. 14	Oct. 26	OH	Akron	165	May 2	Oct. 15
FL	Orlando	332	Jan. 31	Dec. 29	OH	Cincinnati	175	Apr. 23	Oct. 16
FL	Tallahassee	224	Mar. 29	Nov. 9	OK	Lawton	211	Apr. 3	Nov. 1
GA	Athens	214	Apr. 3	Nov. 4	OK	Tulsa	210	Apr. 4	Nov. 1
GA	Savannah	249	Mar. 15	Nov. 20	OR	Pendleton	152	May 2	Oct. 2
IA	Atlantic	136	May 8	Sept. 22	OR	Portland	226	Mar. 25	Nov. 7
IA	Cedar Rapids	157	Apr. 30	Oct. 5	PA	Franklin	156	May 10	Oct. 14
ID	Boise	152	May 7	Oct. 7	PA	Williamsport	162	May 3	Oct. 13
IL	Chicago	186	Apr. 18	Oct. 22	RI	Kingston	142	May 12	Oct. 2
IL	Springfield	168	Apr. 23	Oct. 9	SC	Charleston	247	Mar. 17	Nov. 20
IN	Indianapolis	171	Apr. 25	Oct. 14	SC	Columbia	235	Mar. 23	Nov. 14
IN	South Bend	162	May 3	Oct. 13	SD	Rapid City	128	May 17	Sept. 23
KS	Topeka	173	Apr. 22	Oct. 13	TN	Memphis	225	Mar. 27	Nov. 8
KY	Lexington	183	Apr. 20	Oct. 21	TN	Nashville	198	Apr. 12	Oct. 28
LA	Monroe	234	Mar. 17	Nov. 7	TX	Amarillo	179	Apr. 21	Oct. 18
LA	New Orleans	310	Feb. 9	Dec. 16	TX	Denton	227	Mar. 27	Nov. 10
MA	Worcester	167	Apr. 28	Oct. 13	TX	San Antonio	257	Mar. 10	Nov. 23
MD	Baltimore	187	Apr. 18	Oct. 23	UT	Cedar City	122	May 28	Sept. 28
ME	Portland	152	May 5	Oct. 5	UT	Spanish Fork	158	May 4	Oct. 10
MI	Lansing	147	May 9	Oct. 4	VA	Norfolk	234	Mar. 28	Nov. 18
MI	Marquette	155	May 11	Oct. 14	VA	Richmond	202	Apr. 10	Oct. 30
MN	Duluth	119	May 25	Sept. 22	VT	Burlington	145	May 10	Oct. 3
MN	Willmar	146	May 5	Sept. 29	WA	Seattle	239	Mar. 18	Nov. 13
MO	Jefferson City	189	Apr. 14	Oct. 21	WA	Spokane	148	May 6	Oct. 2
MS	Columbia	234	Mar. 20	Nov. 10	WI	Green Bay	140	May 11	Sept. 29
MS	Tupelo	211	Apr. 3	Nov. 1	WI	Sparta	138	May 12	Sept. 28
MT	Fort Peck	129	May 15	Sept. 22	WV	Parkersburg	179	Apr. 23	Oct. 20
MT	Helena	123	May 19	Sept. 20	WY	Casper	107	May 31	Sept. 16
NC	Fayetteville	208	Apr. 8	Nov. 3	*Frosts do not occur every year.				

PHENOLOGY: NATURE'S CALENDAR

Study nature, love nature, stay close to nature. It will never fail you.
–FRANK LLOYD WRIGHT, AMERICAN ARCHITECT (1867–1959)

For centuries, farmers and gardeners have looked to events in nature to tell them when to plant vegetables and flowers and when to expect insects. Making such observations is called "phenology," the study of phenomena. Specifically, this refers to the life cycles of plants and animals as they correlate to weather and temperature, or nature's calendar.

VEGETABLES

- Plant peas when forsythias bloom.
- Plant potatoes when the first dandelion blooms.
- Plant beets, carrots, cole crops (broccoli, brussels sprouts, collards), lettuce, and spinach when lilacs are in first leaf or dandelions are in full bloom.
- Plant corn when oak leaves are the size of a squirrel's ear (about ½ inch in diameter). Or, plant corn when apple blossoms fade and fall.
- Plant bean, cucumber, and squash seeds when lilacs are in full bloom.
- Plant tomatoes when lilies-of-the-valley are in full bloom.
- Transplant eggplants and peppers when bearded irises bloom.
- Plant onions when red maples bloom.

FLOWERS

- Plant morning glories when maple trees have full-size leaves.
- Plant zinnias and marigolds when black locusts are in full bloom.
- Plant pansies, snapdragons, and other hardy annuals when aspens and chokecherries have leafed out.

INSECTS

- When purple lilacs bloom, grasshopper eggs hatch.
- When chicory blooms, beware of squash vine borers.
- When Canada thistles bloom, protect susceptible fruit; apple maggot flies are at peak.
- When foxglove flowers open, expect Mexican beetle larvae.
- When crabapple trees are in bud, eastern tent caterpillars are hatching.
- When morning glory vines begin to climb, Japanese beetles appear.
- When wild rocket blooms, cabbage root maggots appear.

If the signal plants are not growing in your area, notice other coincident events; record them and watch for them in ensuing seasons.

TABLE OF MEASURES

LINEAR

1 hand = 4 inches
1 link = 7.92 inches
1 span = 9 inches
1 foot = 12 inches
1 yard = 3 feet
1 rod = 5½ yards
1 mile = 320 rods = 1,760 yards = 5,280 feet
1 international nautical mile = 6,076.1155 feet
1 knot = 1 nautical mile per hour
1 fathom = 2 yards = 6 feet
1 furlong = ⅛ mile = 660 feet = 220 yards
1 league = 3 miles = 24 furlongs
1 chain = 100 links = 22 yards

SQUARE

1 square foot = 144 square inches
1 square yard = 9 square feet
1 square rod = 30½ square yards = 272½ square feet = 625 square links

1 square chain = 16 square rods
1 acre = 10 square chains = 160 square rods = 43,560 square feet
1 square mile = 640 acres = 102,400 square rods

CUBIC

1 cubic foot = 1,728 cubic inches
1 cubic yard = 27 cubic feet
1 cord = 128 cubic feet
1 U.S. liquid gallon = 4 quarts = 231 cubic inches
1 imperial gallon = 1.20 U.S. gallons = 0.16 cubic foot
1 board foot = 144 cubic inches

DRY

2 pints = 1 quart
4 quarts = 1 gallon
2 gallons = 1 peck
4 pecks = 1 bushel

LIQUID

4 gills = 1 pint
63 gallons = 1 hogshead
2 hogsheads = 1 pipe or butt
2 pipes = 1 tun

KITCHEN

3 teaspoons = 1 tablespoon
16 tablespoons = 1 cup
1 cup = 8 ounces
2 cups = 1 pint
2 pints = 1 quart
4 quarts = 1 gallon

AVOIRDUPOIS

(for general use)

1 ounce = 16 drams
1 pound = 16 ounces
1 short hundredweight = 100 pounds
1 ton = 2,000 pounds
1 long ton = 2,240 pounds

APOTHECARIES'

(for pharmaceutical use)

1 scruple = 20 grains
1 dram = 3 scruples
1 ounce = 8 drams
1 pound = 12 ounces

METRIC CONVERSIONS

LINEAR

1 inch = 2.54 centimeters
1 centimeter = 0.39 inch
1 meter = 39.37 inches
1 yard = 0.914 meter
1 mile = 1.61 kilometers
1 kilometer = 0.62 mile

SQUARE

1 square inch = 6.45 square centimeters
1 square yard = 0.84 square meter
1 square mile = 2.59 square kilometers

1 square kilometer = 0.386 square mile
1 acre = 0.40 hectare
1 hectare = 2.47 acres

CUBIC

1 cubic yard = 0.76 cubic meter
1 cubic meter = 1.31 cubic yards

HOUSEHOLD

½ teaspoon = 2 mL
1 teaspoon = 5 mL
1 tablespoon = 15 mL
¼ cup = 60 mL

⅓ cup = 75 mL
½ cup = 125 mL
⅔ cup = 150 mL
¾ cup = 175 mL
1 cup = 250 mL
1 liter = 1.057 U.S. liquid quarts
1 U.S. liquid quart = 0.946 liter
1 U.S. liquid gallon = 3.78 liters
1 gram = 0.035 ounce
1 ounce = 28.349 grams
1 kilogram = 2.2 pounds
1 pound = 0.45 kilogram

TO CONVERT CELSIUS AND FAHRENHEIT: $°C = (°F - 32)/1.8$; $°F = (°C × 1.8) + 32$

There's more of everything at Almanac.com.

TIDAL GLOSSARY

APOGEAN TIDE: A monthly tide of decreased range that occurs when the Moon is at apogee (farthest from Earth).

CURRENT: Generally, a horizontal movement of water. Currents may be classified as tidal and nontidal. Tidal currents are caused by gravitational interactions between the Sun, Moon, and Earth and are part of the same general movement of the sea that is manifested in the vertical rise and fall, called tide. Nontidal currents include the permanent currents in the general circulatory systems of the sea as well as temporary currents arising from more pronounced meteorological variability.

DIURNAL TIDE: A tide with one high water and one low water in a tidal day of approximately 24 hours.

MEAN LOWER LOW WATER: The arithmetic mean of the lesser of a daily pair of low waters, observed over a specific 19-year cycle called the National Tidal Datum Epoch.

NEAP TIDE: A tide of decreased range that occurs twice a month, when the Moon is in quadrature (during its first and last quarters, when the Sun and the Moon are at right angles to each other relative to Earth).

PERIGEAN TIDE: A monthly tide of increased range that occurs when the Moon is at perigee (closest to Earth).

RED TIDE: Toxic algal blooms caused by several genera of dinoflagellates that usually turn the sea red or brown. These pose a serious threat to marine life and may be harmful to humans.

RIP CURRENT: A potentially dangerous, narrow, intense, surf-zone current flowing outward from shore.

SEMIDIURNAL TIDE: A tide with one high water and one low water every half-day. East Coast tides, for example, are semidiurnal, with two highs and two lows during a tidal day of approximately 24 hours.

SLACK WATER (SLACK): The state of a tidal current when its speed is near zero, especially the moment when a reversing current changes direction and its speed is zero.

SPRING TIDE: A tide of increased range that occurs at times of syzygy each month. Named not for the season of spring but from the German *springen* ("to leap up"), a spring tide also brings a lower low water.

STORM SURGE: The local change in the elevation of the ocean along a shore due to a storm, measured by subtracting the astronomic tidal elevation from the total elevation. It typically has a duration of a few hours and is potentially catastrophic, especially on low-lying coasts with gently sloping offshore topography.

SYZYGY: The nearly straight-line configuration that occurs twice a month, when the Sun and the Moon are in conjunction (on the same side of Earth, at the new Moon) and when they are in opposition (on opposite sides of Earth, at the full Moon). In both cases, the gravitational effects of the Sun and the Moon reinforce each other, and tidal range is increased.

TIDAL BORE: A tide-induced wave that propagates up a relatively shallow and sloping estuary or river with a steep wave front.

TSUNAMI: Commonly called a tidal wave, a tsunami is a series of long-period waves caused by an underwater earthquake or volcano. In open ocean, the waves are small and travel at high speed; as they near shore, some may build to more than 30 feet high, becoming a threat to life and property.

VANISHING TIDE: A mixed tide of considerable inequality in the two highs and two lows, so that the lower high (or higher low) may appear to vanish. ■

TIDE CORRECTIONS

Many factors affect tides, including the shoreline, time of the Moon's southing (crossing the meridian), and the Moon's phase. The High Tide Times column on the **Left-Hand Calendar Pages, 120–146,** lists the times of high tide at Commonwealth Pier in Boston (MA) Harbor. The heights of some of these tides, reckoned from Mean Lower Low Water, are given on the **Right-Hand Calendar Pages, 121–147.** Use the table below to calculate the approximate times and heights of high tide at the places shown. Apply the time difference to the times of high tide at Boston and the height difference to the heights at Boston. A more detailed and accurate tide calculator for the United States and Canada can be found at **Almanac.com/Tides.**

EXAMPLE:

The conversion of the times and heights of the tides at Boston to those at Cape Fear, North Carolina, is given below:

High tide at Boston	11:45 A.M.
Correction for Cape Fear	- 3 55
High tide at Cape Fear	7:50 A.M.
Tide height at Boston	11.6 ft.
Correction for Cape Fear	- 5.0 ft.
Tide height at Cape Fear	6.6 ft.

Estimations derived from this table are *not* meant to be used for navigation. *The Old Farmer's Almanac* accepts no responsibility for errors or any consequences ensuing from the use of this table.

TIDAL SITE	TIME (H. M.)	HEIGHT (FT.)	TIDAL SITE	TIME (H. M.)	HEIGHT (FT.)
CANADA			Cape Cod Canal		
Alberton, PE	*–5 45	–7.5	East Entrance	–0 01	–0.8
Charlottetown, PE	*–0 45	–3.5	West Entrance	–2 16	–5.9
Halifax, NS	–3 23	–4.5	Chatham Outer Coast	+0 30	–2.8
North Sydney, NS	–3 15	–6.5	Inside	+1 54	**0.4
Saint John, NB	+0 30	+15.0	Cohasset	+0 02	–0.07
St. John's, NL	–4 00	–6.5	Cotuit Highlands	+1 15	**0.3
Yarmouth, NS	–0 40	+3.0	Dennis Port	+1 01	**0.4
MAINE			Duxbury–Gurnet Point	+0 02	–0.3
Bar Harbor	–0 34	+0.9	Fall River	–3 03	–5.0
Belfast	–0 20	+0.4	Gloucester	–0 03	–0.8
Boothbay Harbor	–0 18	–0.8	Hingham	+0 07	0.0
Chebeague Island	–0 16	–0.6	Hull	+0 03	–0.2
Eastport	–0 28	+8.4	Hyannis Port	+1 01	**0.3
Kennebunkport	+0 04	–1.0	Magnolia–Manchester	–0 02	–0.7
Machias	–0 28	+2.8	Marblehead	–0 02	–0.4
Monhegan Island	–0 25	–0.8	Marion	–3 22	–5.4
Old Orchard	0 00	–0.8	Monument Beach	–3 08	–5.4
Portland	–0 12	–0.6	Nahant	–0 01	–0.5
Rockland	–0 28	+0.1	Nantasket	+0 04	–0.1
Stonington	–0 30	+0.1	Nantucket	+0 56	**0.3
York	–0 09	–1.0	Nauset Beach	+0 30	**0.6
NEW HAMPSHIRE			New Bedford	–3 24	–5.7
Hampton	+0 02	–1.3	Newburyport	+0 19	–1.8
Portsmouth	+0 11	–1.5	Oak Bluffs	+0 30	**0.2
Rye Beach	–0 09	–0.9	Onset–R.R. Bridge	–2 16	–5.9
MASSACHUSETTS			Plymouth	+0 05	0.0
Annisquam	–0 02	–1.1	Provincetown	+0 14	–0.4
Beverly Farms	0 00	–0.5	Revere Beach	–0 01	–0.3

TIDAL SITE	TIME (H. M.)	HEIGHT (FT.)	TIDAL SITE	TIME (H. M.)	HEIGHT (FT.)
Rockport	–0 08	–1.0	**PENNSYLVANIA**		
Salem	0 00	–0.5	Philadelphia	+2 40	–3.5
Scituate	–0 05	–0.7	**DELAWARE**		
Wareham	–3 09	–5.3	Cape Henlopen	–2 48	–5.3
Wellfleet	+0 12	+0.5	Rehoboth Beach	–3 37	–5.7
West Falmouth	–3 10	–5.4	Wilmington	+1 56	–3.8
Westport Harbor	–3 22	–6.4	**MARYLAND**		
Woods Hole			Annapolis	+6 23	–8.5
Little Harbor	–2 50	**0.2	Baltimore	+7 59	–8.3
Oceanographic			Cambridge	+5 05	–7.8
Institute	–3 07	**0.2	Havre de Grace	+11 21	–7.7
RHODE ISLAND			Point No Point	+2 28	–8.1
Bristol	–3 24	–5.3	Prince Frederick–		
Narragansett Pier	–3 42	–6.2	Plum Point	+4 25	–8.5
Newport	–3 34	–5.9	**VIRGINIA**		
Point Judith	–3 41	–6.3	Cape Charles	–2 20	–7.0
Providence	–3 20	–4.8	Hampton Roads	–2 02	–6.9
Sakonnet	–3 44	–5.6	Norfolk	–2 06	–6.6
Watch Hill	–2 50	–6.8	Virginia Beach	–4 00	–6.0
CONNECTICUT			Yorktown	–2 13	–7.0
Bridgeport	+0 01	–2.6	**NORTH CAROLINA**		
Madison	–0 22	–2.3	Cape Fear	–3 55	–5.0
New Haven	–0 11	–3.2	Cape Lookout	–4 28	–5.7
New London	–1 54	–6.7	Currituck	–4 10	–5.8
Norwalk	+0 01	–2.2	Hatteras		
Old Lyme–			Inlet	–4 03	–7.4
Highway Bridge	–0 30	–6.2	Kitty Hawk	–4 14	–6.2
Stamford	+0 01	–2.2	Ocean	–4 26	–6.0
Stonington	–2 27	–6.6	**SOUTH CAROLINA**		
NEW YORK			Charleston	–3 22	–4.3
Coney Island	–3 33	–4.9	Georgetown	–1 48	**0.36
Fire Island Light	–2 43	**0.1	Hilton Head	–3 22	–2.9
Long Beach	–3 11	–5.7	Myrtle Beach	–3 49	–4.4
Montauk Harbor	–2 19	–7.4	St. Helena–		
New York City–Battery	–2 43	–5.0	Harbor Entrance	–3 15	–3.4
Oyster Bay	+0 04	–1.8	**GEORGIA**		
Port Chester	–0 09	–2.2	Jekyll Island	–3 46	–2.9
Port Washington	–0 01	–2.1	St. Simon's Island	–2 50	–2.9
Sag Harbor	–0 55	–6.8	Savannah Beach		
Southampton–			River Entrance	–3 14	–5.5
Shinnecock Inlet	–4 20	**0.2	Tybee Light	–3 22	–2.7
Willets Point	0 00	–2.3	**FLORIDA**		
NEW JERSEY			Cape Canaveral	–3 59	–6.0
Asbury Park	–4 04	–5.3	Daytona Beach	–3 28	–5.3
Atlantic City	–3 56	–5.5	Fort Lauderdale	–2 50	–7.2
Bay Head–Sea Girt	–4 04	–5.3	Fort Pierce Inlet	–3 32	–6.9
Beach Haven	–1 43	**0.24	Jacksonville–		
Cape May	–3 28	–5.3	Railroad Bridge	–6 55	**0.1
Ocean City	–3 06	–5.9	Miami Harbor Entrance	–3 18	–7.0
Sandy Hook	–3 30	–5.0	St. Augustine	–2 55	–4.9
Seaside Park	–4 03	–5.4			

*VARIES WIDELY; ACCURATE ONLY TO WITHIN 1½ HOURS. CONSULT LOCAL TIDE TABLES FOR PRECISE TIMES AND HEIGHTS.
**WHERE THE DIFFERENCE IN THE HEIGHT COLUMN IS SO MARKED, THE HEIGHT AT BOSTON SHOULD BE MULTIPLIED BY THIS RATIO.

TIME CORRECTIONS

Astronomical data for Boston (42°22' N, 71°3' W) is given on **pages 104, 108–109, and 120–146.** Use the Key Letters shown on those pages with this table to find the number of minutes that you must add to or subtract from Boston time to get the correct time for your city. (Times are approximate.) For more information on the use of Key Letters, see **How to Use This Almanac, page 116.**

GET TIMES SIMPLY AND SPECIFICALLY: Download astronomical times calculated for your zip code and presented as Left-Hand Calendar Pages at **Almanac.com/Access.**

TIME ZONES CODES represent standard time. Atlantic is –1, Eastern is 0, Central is 1, Mountain is 2, Pacific is 3, Alaska is 4, and Hawaii-Aleutian is 5.

STATE	CITY	NORTH LATITUDE °	NORTH LATITUDE '	WEST LONGITUDE °	WEST LONGITUDE '	TIME ZONE CODE	A	B	C	D	E
AK	Anchorage	61	10	149	59	4	–46	+27	+71	+122	+171
AK	Cordova	60	33	145	45	4	–55	+13	+55	+103	+149
AK	Fairbanks	64	48	147	51	4	–127	+2	+61	+131	+205
AK	Juneau	58	18	134	25	4	–76	–23	+10	+49	+86
AK	Ketchikan	55	21	131	39	4	–62	–25	0	+29	+56
AK	Kodiak	57	47	152	24	4	0	+49	+82	+120	+154
AL	Birmingham	33	31	86	49	1	+30	+15	+3	–10	–20
AL	Decatur	34	36	86	59	1	+27	+14	+4	–7	–17
AL	Mobile	30	42	88	3	1	+42	+23	+8	–8	–22
AL	Montgomery	32	23	86	19	1	+31	+14	+1	–13	–25
AR	Fort Smith	35	23	94	25	1	+55	+43	+33	+22	+14
AR	Little Rock	34	45	92	17	1	+48	+35	+25	+13	+4
AR	Texarkana	33	26	94	3	1	+59	+44	+32	+18	+8
AZ	Flagstaff	35	12	111	39	2	+64	+52	+42	+31	+22
AZ	Phoenix	33	27	112	4	2	+71	+56	+44	+30	+20
AZ	Tucson	32	13	110	58	2	+70	+53	+40	+24	+12
AZ	Yuma	32	43	114	37	2	+83	+67	+54	+40	+28
CA	Bakersfield	35	23	119	1	3	+33	+21	+12	+1	–7
CA	Barstow	34	54	117	1	3	+27	+14	+4	–7	–16
CA	Fresno	36	44	119	47	3	+32	+22	+15	+6	0
CA	Los Angeles-Pasadena-Santa Monica	34	3	118	14	3	+34	+20	+9	–3	–13
CA	Palm Springs	33	49	116	32	3	+28	+13	+1	–12	–22
CA	Redding	40	35	122	24	3	+31	+27	+25	+22	+19
CA	Sacramento	38	35	121	30	3	+34	+27	+21	+15	+10
CA	San Diego	32	43	117	9	3	+33	+17	+4	–9	–21
CA	San Francisco-Oakland-San Jose	37	47	122	25	3	+40	+31	+25	+18	+12
CO	Craig	40	31	107	33	2	+32	+28	+25	+22	+20
CO	Denver-Boulder	39	44	104	59	2	+24	+19	+15	+11	+7
CO	Grand Junction	39	4	108	33	2	+40	+34	+29	+24	+20
CO	Pueblo	38	16	104	37	2	+27	+20	+14	+7	+2
CO	Trinidad	37	10	104	31	2	+30	+21	+13	+5	0
CT	Bridgeport	41	11	73	11	0	+12	+10	+8	+6	+4
CT	Hartford-New Britain	41	46	72	41	0	+8	+7	+6	+5	+4
CT	New Haven	41	18	72	56	0	+11	+8	+7	+5	+4
CT	New London	41	22	72	6	0	+7	+5	+4	+2	+1
CT	Norwalk-Stamford	41	7	73	22	0	+13	+10	+9	+7	+5
CT	Waterbury-Meriden	41	33	73	3	0	+10	+9	+7	+6	+5
DC	Washington	38	54	77	1	0	+35	+28	+23	+18	+13
DE	Wilmington	39	45	75	33	0	+26	+21	+18	+13	+10

Get local rise, set, and tide times at Almanac.com/Astronomy.

STATE	CITY	NORTH LATITUDE °	NORTH LATITUDE ′	WEST LONGITUDE °	WEST LONGITUDE ′	TIME ZONE CODE	KEY LETTERS (MINUTES) A	B	C	D	E
FL	Fort Myers	26	38	81	52	0	+87	+63	+44	+21	+4
FL	Jacksonville	30	20	81	40	0	+77	+58	+43	+25	+11
FL	Miami	25	47	80	12	0	+88	+57	+37	+14	−3
FL	Orlando	28	32	81	22	0	+80	+59	+42	+22	+6
FL	Pensacola	30	25	87	13	1	+39	+20	+5	−12	−26
FL	St. Petersburg	27	46	82	39	0	+87	+65	+47	+26	+10
FL	Tallahassee	30	27	84	17	0	+87	+68	+53	+35	+22
FL	Tampa	27	57	82	27	0	+86	+64	+46	+25	+9
FL	West Palm Beach	26	43	80	3	0	+79	+55	+36	+14	−2
GA	Atlanta	33	45	84	24	0	+79	+65	+53	+40	+30
GA	Augusta	33	28	81	58	0	+70	+55	+44	+30	+19
GA	Macon	32	50	83	38	0	+79	+63	+50	+36	+24
GA	Savannah	32	5	81	6	0	+70	+54	+40	+25	+13
HI	Hilo	19	44	155	5	5	+94	+62	+37	+7	−15
HI	Honolulu	21	18	157	52	5	+102	+72	+48	+19	−1
HI	Lanai City	20	50	156	55	5	+99	+69	+44	+15	−6
HI	Lihue	21	59	159	23	5	+107	+77	+54	+26	+6
IA	Davenport	41	32	90	35	1	+20	+19	+17	+16	+15
IA	Des Moines	41	35	93	37	1	+32	+31	+30	+28	+27
IA	Dubuque	42	30	90	41	1	+17	+18	+18	+18	+18
IA	Waterloo	42	30	92	20	1	+24	+24	+24	+25	+25
ID	Boise	43	37	116	12	2	+55	+58	+60	+62	+64
ID	Lewiston	46	25	117	1	3	−12	−3	+2	+10	+17
ID	Pocatello	42	52	112	27	2	+43	+44	+45	+46	+46
IL	Cairo	37	0	89	11	1	+29	+20	+12	+4	−2
IL	Chicago-Oak Park	41	52	87	38	1	+7	+6	+6	+5	+4
IL	Danville	40	8	87	37	1	+13	+9	+6	+2	0
IL	Decatur	39	51	88	57	1	+19	+15	+11	+7	+4
IL	Peoria	40	42	89	36	1	+19	+16	+14	+11	+9
IL	Springfield	39	48	89	39	1	+22	+18	+14	+10	+6
IN	Fort Wayne	41	4	85	9	0	+60	+58	+56	+54	+52
IN	Gary	41	36	87	20	1	+7	+6	+4	+3	+2
IN	Indianapolis	39	46	86	10	0	+69	+64	+60	+56	+52
IN	Muncie	40	12	85	23	0	+64	+60	+57	+53	+50
IN	South Bend	41	41	86	15	0	+62	+61	+60	+59	+58
IN	Terre Haute	39	28	87	24	0	+74	+69	+65	+60	+56
KS	Fort Scott	37	50	94	42	1	+49	+41	+34	+27	+21
KS	Liberal	37	3	100	55	1	+76	+66	+59	+51	+44
KS	Oakley	39	8	100	51	1	+69	+63	+59	+53	+49
KS	Salina	38	50	97	37	1	+57	+51	+46	+40	+35
KS	Topeka	39	3	95	40	1	+49	+43	+38	+32	+28
KS	Wichita	37	42	97	20	1	+60	+51	+45	+37	+31
KY	Lexington-Frankfort	38	3	84	30	0	+67	+59	+53	+46	+41
KY	Louisville	38	15	85	46	0	+72	+64	+58	+52	+46
LA	Alexandria	31	18	92	27	1	+58	+40	+26	+9	−3
LA	Baton Rouge	30	27	91	11	1	+55	+36	+21	+3	−10
LA	Lake Charles	30	14	93	13	1	+64	+44	+29	+11	−2
LA	Monroe	32	30	92	7	1	+53	+37	+24	+9	−1
LA	New Orleans	29	57	90	4	1	+52	+32	+16	−1	−15
LA	Shreveport	32	31	93	45	1	+60	+44	+31	+16	+4
MA	Brockton	42	5	71	1	0	0	0	0	0	−1
MA	Fall River-New Bedford	41	42	71	9	0	+2	+1	0	0	−1
MA	Lawrence-Lowell	42	42	71	10	0	0	0	0	0	+1
MA	Pittsfield	42	27	73	15	0	+8	+8	+8	+8	+8
MA	Springfield-Holyoke	42	6	72	36	0	+6	+6	+6	+5	+5
MA	Worcester	42	16	71	48	0	+3	+2	+2	+2	+2

STATE	CITY	NORTH LATITUDE		WEST LONGITUDE		TIME ZONE CODE	KEY LETTERS (MINUTES)				
		°	'	°	'		A	B	C	D	E
MD	Baltimore	39	17	76	37	0	+32	+26	+22	+17	+13
MD	Hagerstown	39	39	77	43	0	+35	+30	+26	+22	+18
MD	Salisbury	38	22	75	36	0	+31	+23	+18	+11	+6
ME	Augusta	44	19	69	46	0	−12	−8	−5	−1	0
ME	Bangor	44	48	68	46	0	−18	−13	−9	−5	−1
ME	Eastport	44	54	67	0	0	−26	−20	−16	−11	−8
ME	Ellsworth	44	33	68	25	0	−18	−14	−10	−6	−3
ME	Portland	43	40	70	15	0	−8	−5	−3	−1	0
ME	Presque Isle	46	41	68	1	0	−29	−19	−12	−4	+2
MI	Cheboygan	45	39	84	29	0	+40	+47	+53	+59	+64
MI	Detroit-Dearborn	42	20	83	3	0	+47	+47	+47	+47	+47
MI	Flint	43	1	83	41	0	+47	+49	+50	+51	+52
MI	Ironwood	46	27	90	9	1	0	+9	+15	+23	+29
MI	Jackson	42	15	84	24	0	+53	+53	+53	+52	+52
MI	Kalamazoo	42	17	85	35	0	+58	+57	+57	+57	+57
MI	Lansing	42	44	84	33	0	+52	+53	+53	+54	+54
MI	St. Joseph	42	5	86	26	0	+61	+61	+60	+60	+59
MI	Traverse City	44	46	85	38	0	+49	+54	+57	+62	+65
MN	Albert Lea	43	39	93	22	1	+24	+26	+28	+31	+33
MN	Bemidji	47	28	94	53	1	+14	+26	+34	+44	+52
MN	Duluth	46	47	92	6	1	+6	+16	+23	+31	+38
MN	Minneapolis-St. Paul	44	59	93	16	1	+18	+24	+28	+33	+37
MN	Ortonville	45	19	96	27	1	+30	+36	+40	+46	+51
MO	Jefferson City	38	34	92	10	1	+36	+29	+24	+18	+13
MO	Joplin	37	6	94	30	1	+50	+41	+33	+25	+18
MO	Kansas City	39	1	94	20	1	+44	+37	+33	+27	+23
MO	Poplar Bluff	36	46	90	24	1	+35	+25	+17	+8	+1
MO	St. Joseph	39	46	94	50	1	+43	+38	+35	+30	+27
MO	St. Louis	38	37	90	12	1	+28	+21	+16	+10	+5
MO	Springfield	37	13	93	18	1	+45	+36	+29	+20	+14
MS	Biloxi	30	24	88	53	1	+46	+27	+11	−5	−19
MS	Jackson	32	18	90	11	1	+46	+30	+17	+1	−10
MS	Meridian	32	22	88	42	1	+40	+24	+11	−4	−15
MS	Tupelo	34	16	88	34	1	+35	+21	+10	−2	−11
MT	Billings	45	47	108	30	2	+16	+23	+29	+35	+40
MT	Butte	46	1	112	32	2	+31	+39	+45	+52	+57
MT	Glasgow	48	12	106	38	2	−1	+11	+21	+32	+42
MT	Great Falls	47	30	111	17	2	+20	+31	+39	+49	+58
MT	Helena	46	36	112	2	2	+27	+36	+43	+51	+57
MT	Miles City	46	25	105	51	2	+3	+11	+18	+26	+32
NC	Asheville	35	36	82	33	0	+67	+55	+46	+35	+27
NC	Charlotte	35	14	80	51	0	+61	+49	+39	+28	+19
NC	Durham	36	0	78	55	0	+51	+40	+31	+21	+13
NC	Greensboro	36	4	79	47	0	+54	+43	+35	+25	+17
NC	Raleigh	35	47	78	38	0	+51	+39	+30	+21	+12
NC	Wilmington	34	14	77	55	0	+52	+38	+27	+15	+5
ND	Bismarck	46	48	100	47	1	+41	+50	+58	+66	+73
ND	Fargo	46	53	96	47	1	+24	+34	+42	+50	+57
ND	Grand Forks	47	55	97	3	1	+21	+33	+43	+53	+62
ND	Minot	48	14	101	18	1	+36	+50	+59	+71	+81
ND	Williston	48	9	103	37	1	+46	+59	+69	+80	+90
NE	Grand Island	40	55	98	21	1	+53	+51	+49	+46	+44
NE	Lincoln	40	49	96	41	1	+47	+44	+42	+39	+37
NE	North Platte	41	8	100	46	1	+62	+60	+58	+56	+54
NE	Omaha	41	16	95	56	1	+43	+40	+39	+37	+36
NH	Berlin	44	28	71	11	0	−7	−3	0	+3	+7
NH	Keene	42	56	72	17	0	+2	+3	+4	+5	+6

Get local rise, set, and tide times at Almanac.com/Astronomy.

STATE	CITY	NORTH LATITUDE °	NORTH LATITUDE '	WEST LONGITUDE °	WEST LONGITUDE '	TIME ZONE CODE	KEY LETTERS (MINUTES) A	B	C	D	E
NH	Manchester-Concord	42	59	71	28	0	0	0	+1	+2	+3
NH	Portsmouth	43	5	70	45	0	−4	−2	−1	0	0
NJ	Atlantic City	39	22	74	26	0	+23	+17	+13	+8	+4
NJ	Camden	39	57	75	7	0	+24	+19	+16	+12	+9
NJ	Cape May	38	56	74	56	0	+26	+20	+15	+9	+5
NJ	Newark-East Orange	40	44	74	10	0	+17	+14	+12	+9	+7
NJ	Paterson	40	55	74	10	0	+17	+14	+12	+9	+7
NJ	Trenton	40	13	74	46	0	+21	+17	+14	+11	+8
NM	Albuquerque	35	5	106	39	2	+45	+32	+22	+11	+2
NM	Gallup	35	32	108	45	2	+52	+40	+31	+20	+11
NM	Las Cruces	32	19	106	47	2	+53	+36	+23	+8	−3
NM	Roswell	33	24	104	32	2	+41	+26	+14	0	−10
NM	Santa Fe	35	41	105	56	2	+40	+28	+19	+9	0
NV	Carson City-Reno	39	10	119	46	3	+25	+19	+14	+9	+5
NV	Elko	40	50	115	46	3	+3	0	−1	−3	−5
NV	Las Vegas	36	10	115	9	3	+16	+4	−3	−13	−20
NY	Albany	42	39	73	45	0	+9	+10	+10	+11	+11
NY	Binghamton	42	6	75	55	0	+20	+19	+19	+18	+18
NY	Buffalo	42	53	78	52	0	+29	+30	+30	+31	+32
NY	New York	40	45	74	0	0	+17	+14	+11	+9	+6
NY	Ogdensburg	44	42	75	30	0	+8	+13	+17	+21	+25
NY	Syracuse	43	3	76	9	0	+17	+19	+20	+21	+22
OH	Akron	41	5	81	31	0	+46	+43	+41	+39	+37
OH	Canton	40	48	81	23	0	+46	+43	+41	+38	+36
OH	Cincinnati-Hamilton	39	6	84	31	0	+64	+58	+53	+48	+44
OH	Cleveland-Lakewood	41	30	81	42	0	+45	+43	+42	+40	+39
OH	Columbus	39	57	83	1	0	+55	+51	+47	+43	+40
OH	Dayton	39	45	84	10	0	+61	+56	+52	+48	+44
OH	Toledo	41	39	83	33	0	+52	+50	+49	+48	+47
OH	Youngstown	41	6	80	39	0	+42	+40	+38	+36	+34
OK	Oklahoma City	35	28	97	31	1	+67	+55	+46	+35	+26
OK	Tulsa	36	9	95	60	1	+59	+48	+40	+30	+22
OR	Eugene	44	3	123	6	3	+21	+24	+27	+30	+33
OR	Pendleton	45	40	118	47	3	−1	+4	+10	+16	+21
OR	Portland	45	31	122	41	3	+14	+20	+25	+31	+36
OR	Salem	44	57	123	1	3	+17	+23	+27	+31	+35
PA	Allentown-Bethlehem	40	36	75	28	0	+23	+20	+17	+14	+12
PA	Erie	42	7	80	5	0	+36	+36	+35	+35	+35
PA	Harrisburg	40	16	76	53	0	+30	+26	+23	+19	+16
PA	Lancaster	40	2	76	18	0	+28	+24	+20	+17	+13
PA	Philadelphia-Chester	39	57	75	9	0	+24	+19	+16	+12	+9
PA	Pittsburgh-McKeesport	40	26	80	0	0	+42	+38	+35	+32	+29
PA	Reading	40	20	75	56	0	+26	+22	+19	+16	+13
PA	Scranton-Wilkes-Barre	41	25	75	40	0	+21	+19	+18	+16	+15
PA	York	39	58	76	43	0	+30	+26	+22	+18	+15
RI	Providence	41	50	71	25	0	+3	+2	+1	0	0
SC	Charleston	32	47	79	56	0	+64	+48	+36	+21	+10
SC	Columbia	34	0	81	2	0	+65	+51	+40	+27	+17
SC	Spartanburg	34	56	81	57	0	+66	+53	+43	+32	+23
SD	Aberdeen	45	28	98	29	1	+37	+44	+49	+54	+59
SD	Pierre	44	22	100	21	1	+49	+53	+56	+60	+63
SD	Rapid City	44	5	103	14	2	+2	+5	+8	+11	+13
SD	Sioux Falls	43	33	96	44	1	+38	+40	+42	+44	+46
TN	Chattanooga	35	3	85	19	0	+79	+67	+57	+45	+36
TN	Knoxville	35	58	83	55	0	+71	+60	+51	+41	+33
TN	Memphis	35	9	90	3	1	+38	+26	+16	+5	−3
TN	Nashville	36	10	86	47	1	+22	+11	+3	−6	−14

STATE/PROVINCE	CITY	NORTH LATITUDE °	NORTH LATITUDE '	WEST LONGITUDE °	WEST LONGITUDE '	TIME ZONE CODE	KEY LETTERS (MINUTES) A	B	C	D	E
TX	Amarillo	35	12	101	50	1	+85	+73	+63	+52	+43
TX	Austin	30	16	97	45	1	+82	+62	+47	+29	+15
TX	Beaumont	30	5	94	6	1	+67	+48	+32	+14	0
TX	Brownsville	25	54	97	30	1	+91	+66	+46	+23	+5
TX	Corpus Christi	27	48	97	24	1	+86	+64	+46	+25	+9
TX	Dallas–Fort Worth	32	47	96	48	1	+71	+55	+43	+28	+17
TX	El Paso	31	45	106	29	2	+53	+35	+22	+6	−6
TX	Galveston	29	18	94	48	1	+72	+52	+35	+16	+1
TX	Houston	29	45	95	22	1	+73	+53	+37	+19	+5
TX	McAllen	26	12	98	14	1	+93	+69	+49	+26	+9
TX	San Antonio	29	25	98	30	1	+87	+66	+50	+31	+16
UT	Kanab	37	3	112	32	2	+62	+53	+46	+37	+30
UT	Moab	38	35	109	33	2	+46	+39	+33	+27	+22
UT	Ogden	41	13	111	58	2	+47	+45	+43	+41	+40
UT	Salt Lake City	40	45	111	53	2	+48	+45	+43	+40	+38
UT	Vernal	40	27	109	32	2	+40	+36	+33	+30	+28
VA	Charlottesville	38	2	78	30	0	+43	+35	+29	+22	+17
VA	Danville	36	36	79	23	0	+51	+41	+33	+24	+17
VA	Norfolk	36	51	76	17	0	+38	+28	+21	+12	+5
VA	Richmond	37	32	77	26	0	+41	+32	+25	+17	+11
VA	Roanoke	37	16	79	57	0	+51	+42	+35	+27	+21
VA	Winchester	39	11	78	10	0	+38	+33	+28	+23	+19
VT	Brattleboro	42	51	72	34	0	+4	+5	+5	+6	+7
VT	Burlington	44	29	73	13	0	0	+4	+8	+12	+15
VT	Rutland	43	37	72	58	0	+2	+5	+7	+9	+11
VT	St. Johnsbury	44	25	72	1	0	−4	0	+3	+7	+10
WA	Bellingham	48	45	122	29	3	0	+13	+24	+37	+47
WA	Seattle-Tacoma-Olympia	47	37	122	20	3	+3	+15	+24	+34	+42
WA	Spokane	47	40	117	24	3	−16	−4	+4	+14	+23
WA	Walla Walla	46	4	118	20	3	−5	+2	+8	+15	+21
WI	Eau Claire	44	49	91	30	1	+12	+17	+21	+25	+29
WI	Green Bay	44	31	88	0	1	0	+3	+7	+11	+14
WI	La Crosse	43	48	91	15	1	+15	+18	+20	+22	+25
WI	Madison	43	4	89	23	1	+10	+11	+12	+14	+15
WI	Milwaukee	43	2	87	54	1	+4	+6	+7	+8	+9
WI	Oshkosh	44	1	88	33	1	+3	+6	+9	+12	+15
WI	Wausau	44	58	89	38	1	+4	+9	+13	+18	+22
WV	Charleston	38	21	81	38	0	+55	+48	+42	+35	+30
WV	Parkersburg	39	16	81	34	0	+52	+46	+42	+36	+32
WY	Casper	42	51	106	19	2	+19	+19	+20	+21	+22
WY	Cheyenne	41	8	104	49	2	+19	+16	+14	+12	+11
WY	Sheridan	44	48	106	58	2	+14	+19	+23	+27	+31
CANADA											
AB	Calgary	51	5	114	5	2	+13	+35	+50	+68	+84
AB	Edmonton	53	34	113	25	2	−3	+26	+47	+72	+93
BC	Vancouver	49	13	123	6	3	0	+15	+26	+40	+52
MB	Winnipeg	49	53	97	10	1	+12	+30	+43	+58	+71
NB	Saint John	45	16	66	3	−1	+28	+34	+39	+44	+49
NS	Halifax	44	38	63	35	−1	+21	+26	+29	+33	+37
NS	Sydney	46	10	60	10	−1	+1	+9	+15	+23	+28
ON	Ottawa	45	25	75	43	0	+6	+13	+18	+23	+28
ON	Peterborough	44	18	78	19	0	+21	+25	+28	+32	+35
ON	Thunder Bay	48	27	89	12	0	+47	+61	+71	+83	+93
ON	Toronto	43	39	79	23	0	+28	+30	+32	+35	+37
QC	Montreal	45	28	73	39	0	−1	+4	+9	+15	+20
SK	Saskatoon	52	10	106	40	1	+37	+63	+80	+101	+119

GENERAL STORE CLASSIFIEDS

For advertising information and rates, go to Almanac.com/Advertising
or call RJ Media at 212-986-0016. The 2021 edition closes on May 1, 2020.

ASTROLOGY

REV. ROSE, HEALER. Miracle Powerful Prayers. Solves all problems. Removes Pain, Evil Influences. Guaranteed! 1-252-458-5937.

SEEKING LUCK, LOVE, MONEY? With Spiritual Cleansing, achieve goals! FREE Tarot Reading! 811 Saluda Street, Rockville, SC 29730. 1-803-371-7711.

BILINGUAL ASTROLOGER. Spiritualist—Tarot Readings! Changes life direction! Achieve Love, Financial, Career, Family Stability. 1-402-519-3199.

BOOKS/MAGAZINES/CATALOGS

FREE BOOKLETS: Life, Immortality, Soul, Pollution, Crisis, Judgment Day, Restitution, sample magazine. Bible Standard (OFA), 1156 St. Matthews Road, Chester Springs PA 19425; visit www.biblestandard.com.

FREE BOOKLET: Pro and Con assessment of Jehovah's Witnesses teachings. Bible Standard (OFA), 1156 St. Matthews Road, Chester Springs PA 19425; www.biblestandard.com.

BUSINESS OPPORTUNITIES

$800 WEEKLY POTENTIAL! Process HUD/FHA refunds from home. Free information available. 1-860-357-1599.

EXCHANGE IDEAS

**I WANT TO EXCHANGE IDEAS
ON EVERYTHING!**
Energy-Efficiency, Self-Sufficiency,
Meta-Psychical Concepts, Money-Making
Opportunities, Anything of Interest
Orville Hill • PO Box 375 • Toledo OH 43697

HEALTH

**HOW TO REVERSE
MACULAR DEGENERATION**
Free book describes how.
Call: 1-650-780-9900
Visit us:
www.bettereyehealth.com/free-book-download

JEWELRY

WWW.AZUREGREEN.NET. Jewelry, Amulets, Incense, Oils, Statuary, Gifts, Herbs, Candles, Gemstones. 8,000 Items. Wholesale inquiries welcome.

PERSONAL

ASIAN WOMEN! Overseas Penpals. Romance! Free brochure. P.I.C., Box 4601-OFA, Thousand Oaks CA 91359. 1-805-492-8040. www.pacisl.com.

PSYCHIC

ALANA, Psychic Spiritualist. Helps all problems: Love, Business, Family. Reunites Lovers, Twin Flames! FREE QUESTION. 1-469-585-5000.

REAL ESTATE/RETIREMENT LIVING

RETIRE TO EASTPORT, MAINE
Affordable Coastal Living
Gorgeous Views. Lively Arts & Social Scene
Health Center
Contact: Kevin Raye, Realtor®,
Due East Real Estate
kevin@kevinraye.com

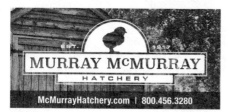

2019 ESSAY CONTEST WINNERS
"Kids Say the Funniest Things!"

First Prize: $300

When her new brother was born, my 4-year-old daughter was reluctant to relinquish her "only child" throne. She frequently attempted to give her brother away to his numerous and very vocal admirers. Once, when he was a few months old and the three of us were in a hair salon, the ladies were all gushing over his adorableness. Olivia was obviously feeling left out and perhaps a little jealous. She told one of the ladies that if she needed a crying baby at her house, she could have Turner.

The woman picked up my son in his baby carrier and pretended she was going to leave with him. When she reached the door, my daughter jumped up and yelled, "Wait!" The woman stopped, smirking because she thought that she had called Olivia's bluff; surely now she would be able to tease Olivia about how she truly loved her baby brother. "What?" she asked, with eyebrows raised. Olivia replied, "You forgot his diaper bag!"

–Kelly Thompson, Joplin, Missouri

Second Prize: $200

Children are uniquely brilliant in their non sequiturs. When my eldest was 6 years old and grappling with the concept of time, she asked, lisping through the new gap in her teeth, "If Grammy and Pop Pop were born in the olden days, and I was born in the new days, does that mean you and Daddy are from the Middle Ages?"

–J. C. Elkin, Annapolis, Maryland

Third Prize: $100

Overheard from the stall next to mine in a restaurant ladies' room:
Preschooler: "How long 'til we see Grandma?"
Mother: "Nine days. Here, let's count it on your fingers."
Preschooler: "One, two, three, four, five, six, seven, eight, nine!"
Mother: "Yes! And when you get bigger, you won't use your fingers."
Preschooler: "But how can I pick things up?"

–Kate Moloney, Frederick, Maryland

Honorable Mentions

"Nana," 5-year-old Brent said, "my friend Tommy's Mommy and Daddy are getting divorced. Does that mean his Mommy has to go to church and walk down the aisle backwards?"

–Marilyn Long, Milton Mills, New Hampshire

I was pregnant with Child Number Three when I took two sons, John, 7, and Jim, 5, to the pediatrician for their regular checkup. As we were ready to leave, the pediatrician said, "I understand you are going to get a new brother or sister." Son John asked, "When the new one comes out, can we put Jimmy back in?"

–Willma C. Gore, Sedona, Arizona

When my daughter was young, she spent most Saturday nights at Grandma's house. One evening, as they were getting ready for bed, my daughter watched as my mother applied her face cream, a ritual of Mom's for as long as I can remember. "What is that stuff?" my daughter asked. "Oh, just wrinkle cream," Mom said. After several moments of intense study, my daughter declared, "It works good, Gram. You've got lots of wrinkles."

–Bobbi Miller, Waynesburg, Pennsylvania

As many youth groups or schools do, my son's was selling candy bars. I followed my son along one day as he pulled his little red wagon with a couple of boxes of candy bars and his envelope. As he peddled, he came upon a fellow working under his car in his driveway. Only his feet were sticking out. This did not deter Matthew. He quietly walked up with his squeaky wagon, stooped down as if investigating, and asked, "Mister, would you like to buy a candy bar?" "Not right now—maybe later," the man replied. Matthew peered on and replied, "OK, I'll wait." At that, the man chuckled, rolled out from the car with a big grin on his face, and bought two bars from the little salesman.

–Tom McGowan, Shawnee, Kansas ∎

**ANNOUNCING THE 2020 ESSAY CONTEST TOPIC:
WHAT WORN-OUT POSSESSION IS DEAREST
TO YOU, AND WHY?**
SEE CONTEST RULES ON PAGE 251.

MADDENING MIND-MANGLERS

Tennessee Teasers

1. What is the total of the number of months that have 30 days and the number of months that have 31 days?

2. What is unique about the number 8,549,176,320?

In #3 and #4, each letter represents a digit in a number (example: XZ might be the number 58, where X = 5 and Z = 8).

3. AA x AA = ABA. What is the total of A + B?

4. AB x AB = CAB. What is the total of A + B + C?

Find a word that is related to both key words listed (example: Left, wine = Port).

5. Write, tree_____

6. Baseball, cake_____

7. Poker, feline_____

8. Plod, wood_____

9. Money, river_____

10. Abandon, color_____

11. Toss, tar _____

12. Metal, press_____

13. Canal, key_____

14. Spice, spring_____

Find two rhyming words that answer the question (example: Rabbit fur? Hare hair).

15. Man with a sprayer?_____

16. Deer on a dollar bill?

_____

17. Naked grizzly?_____

18. Flying rodent's stick?

_____

19. Improved gambler?

_____

20. Entire opening?

_____

21. Good monetary punishment?

_____

22. Sphere at a dance?

_____

23. Playing cards on a porch?

_____

–courtesy of Morris Bowles, Cane Ridge, Tennessee

Movie Tickets

Two grandfathers, four fathers, and four sons went to the movies. What is the minimum number of tickets that they might need to buy?

–courtesy of E. R., Portage la Prairie, Manitoba

The Ship's Ladder

The good ship *Potiphar* lay at anchor in Portsmouth Harbor. An interested spectator observed that a ladder was dangling from her deck; that the bottom four rungs of the ladder were submerged; that each rung was 2 inches thick; and that the rungs were 11 inches apart. The tide was rising at the rate of 18 inches per hour. At the end of 2 hours, how many rungs would be submerged?

–The Old Farmer's Almanac, 1940

ANSWERS:

Tennessee Teasers: **1.** 18. (11 + 7 = 18). **2.** All 10 digits are in alphabetical order. **3.** 3. (A = 1, B = 2). **4.** 13. (A = 2, B = 5, C = 6). **5.** Log. **6.** Batter. **7.** Kitty. **8.** Lumber. **9.** Bank. **10.** Maroon. **11.** Pitch. **12.** Iron. **13.** Lock. **14.** Season. **15.** Mister mister. **16.** Buck buck. **17.** Bare bear. **18.** Bat bat. **19.** Better bettor. **20.** Whole hole. **21.** Fine fine. **22.** Ball ball. **23.** Deck deck.

Movie Tickets: Answer: Four. Two men (sons themselves) are grandfathers and thus fathers. Two other men (also sons) are fathers but not grandfathers.

The Ship's Ladder: Answer: Exactly the same number of rungs as before, as naturally the ladder rose with the ship.

ESSAY AND RECIPE CONTEST RULES

Cash prizes (first, $300; second, $200; third, $100) will be awarded for the best essays in 200 words or less on the subject "What worn-out possession is dearest to you, and why?" and the best recipes in the category "Appetizers." Entries must be yours, original, and unpublished. Amateur cooks only, please. One recipe per person. All entries become the property of Yankee Publishing, which reserves all rights to the material. The deadline for entries is Friday, January 24, 2020. Enter at Almanac.com/EssayContest or at Almanac.com/RecipeContest or label "Essay Contest" or "Recipe Contest" and mail to The Old Farmer's Almanac, P.O. Box 520, Dublin, NH 03444. Include your name, mailing address, and email address. Winners will appear in *The 2021 Old Farmer's Almanac* and on Almanac.com. ∎

ANECDOTES & PLEASANTRIES

A sampling from the thousands of letters, clippings,
articles, and emails sent to us during the past year by our
Almanac family all over the United States and Canada.

ILLUSTRATIONS BY TIM ROBINSON

True Kid Emergencies

• From Ireland, a 6-year-old lass wrote NASA that she needed Pluto upgraded back to full planet status (not that NASA would be in charge of this anyway) because she wanted to be an astronaut and "work for ye but you need to fix this problem."

• In Fort Collins, Colorado, a young 9-1-1 caller pleaded for help with 71 divided by 3,052.

• A fifth-grader in Lafayette, Indiana, got guidance on fractions from a helpful emergency operator. Bemoaned the beleaguered boy: "I just have tons of homework, and it's *so* hard."

• Ontario Provincial Police added a 7-year-old to the "naughty list" for his Christmas morning 9-1-1 call to complain about his gift of snow pants, which he described as "not appreciated."

–courtesy of Irish Times, *Minnesota Public Radio,* New York Post

CHICKEN COATING

On a bitterly cold day, a man goes into a farmers' supply store and asks if they have any hens.

"Of course," responds the clerk, as he leads the man outside. "These are Rhode Island Reds, our top egg producers."

"Perfect!" says the customer. "So, how do I put them on?"

"Put them on?"

"Sure," answers the shivering man. "They always say, 'The best way to stay warm in this weather is to dress in layers.'"

–courtesy of M. D., Three Lakes, Michigan

The Toes Knows

Don't look now, but your downstairs digits can tell a lot about your personality.

If your.../You are (a)...
- *first three toes are about the same length, with two smaller ones on the outside:* sociable, outgoing, balanced, traveler, great public speaker
- *toes are all about the same length:* caring, reliable, practical, good friend, careful decision-maker
- *toes descend in length from big toe to little toe:* private, moody, secretive, needful of own space, hider of emotions
- *second toe is longer than your first toe:* stress-prone, impulsive, active, athletic, creative, enthusiastic, good leader
- *second toe bends toward your big toe:* nostalgic, sentimental
- *big toe extends way beyond the rest:* creative, sharp thinker
- *little toe can be wiggled by itself:* adventurous, flirty, restless, unconventional, in need of constant change
- *little toe can't be wiggled by itself:* loyal
- *little toe tucks under or sticks out at an angle:* rebellious, unconventional, demanding
- *little toe is unusually small:* childlike, playful, fun to be around

–courtesy of The Telegraph *(UK)*

THE CHANGE IN YOUR POCKET

A man with an uncanny mania for juggling with figures produced pencil and paper and said to a friend:

"Put down your age. Multiply it by 2. Add 5. Multiply by 50. Add the change in your pocket. Subtract the number of days in a non–leap year, 365. Add 115 for good measure."

The friend did it.

"Now," said the other with a cunning smile, "the two left-hand figures will show your age, and the two right-hand figures, the amount of change in your pocket."

–The Old Farmer's Almanac, *1937*

WEIRD STUFF ABOUT CANADIAN MONEY

True or false? (Answers on page 255.)

1. The Bank of Canada once printed the Devil's face in Queen Elizabeth II's hair.
2. The Canadian "loonie" $1 coin was originally meant to show a hockey puck, not a loon.

–courtesy of Thecanadaguide.com

SS *WARRIMOO* ENTERS THE TWILIGHT ZONE

On December 30, 1899, the passenger steamer SS *Warrimoo* was quietly slicing through the waters of the mid-Pacific on its way from Vancouver to Australia.

The navigator had worked out a star fix and brought the master, Captain John Phillips, the result: The *Warrimoo*'s position was 0°31' N, 179°30' W. Ever alert, the first mate then pointed out that they were only a few miles from the intersection of the Equator and the International Date Line.

The captain was prankish enough to take full advantage of the opportunity to achieve the navigational freak of a lifetime. He called all of his navigators to the bridge to double-check the ship's position and then changed course slightly to bear directly on his mark. Then he adjusted the engine speed.

The calm weather and clear night worked in his favor. At midnight, the *Warrimoo* lay on the Equator at exactly the point where it crossed the International Date Line!

The consequences of this bizarre position were many. The forward part of the ship was in the Southern Hemisphere and the middle of summer. The stern was in the Northern Hemisphere and in the middle of winter. The date in the aft part of the ship was December 31, 1899. Forward, it was January 1, 1900.

Thus the *Warrimoo* was not only in two different days, two different months, two different seasons, and two different years, but also in two different centuries—all at the same time.

–courtesy of Company of Master Mariners of Australia

When Pets Go Trick-or-Treating

Top 10 costumes for pets? (And please don't call us, because we don't understand #5 and #6 either.)

1. Pumpkin
2. Hot dog
3. Bumblebee
4. Devil
5. Cat
6. Dog
7. Lion
8. *Star Wars* character
9. Superhero
10. Ghost

–courtesy of National Retail Federation

"NOW THEY TELL ME!" DEPT.

- In Luzerne County, Pennsylvania, the alleged thief of a pot of meatballs was apprehended after being spotted with red sauce all over his face and clothes.
- As if its voracious appetite hadn't been enough of a clue, the supposed Tibetan mastiff puppy adopted by a family in southwest China definitely raised eyebrows at age 2 when it started walking on its hind legs—and was correctly identified as an Asiatic black bear.

–courtesy of AP, IFLScience

Blankets of Snow

Blankets of snow cover the fields
today,
The orchard, the pond, the rutted
roadway.
Limbs hang heavy, some touching
the ground;
Many have broken with cracking
sounds.

Swirling flakes bring chilling designs;
Now barn and coop are hard to find.
Trees are coated to the windward
side;
A few lonely leaves seem to jump
and slide.

In the distance, a wall of white;
Before it, saplings appear so slight.
Hemlocks sway, together in song;
Pines stand tall, anchored strong.

Roofs feel heavy, coated in waves;
Drifts render doors tight to stay.
Windows are painted in fanciful art;
Houses are dressed a color apart.

Blankets of snow cover the land today;
Who ventures forth, one could not say.
Time to reflect, to work past the storm;
Time to collect, to think a new dawn.
–Donald E. Webber, Exeter, New Hampshire

Answers to Weird Stuff About Canadian Money:

1. *True.* Sort of. Part of the queen's curls on the faces of 1954 paper currency was said by some to resemble the Devil's face (or head), a phenomenon attributable not to design, but to bad lighting for the 1951 portrait from which the image was taken. The backlash led to a redesign in 1956 that cleaned up the troubling tresses.

2. *False* . . . but the original plan was to have it show a *voyageur*, not a loon. However, when the dies for the voyageur coin got lost in transit to the Royal Canadian Mint in Winnipeg in 1986, the government switched the design to a loon to protect the integrity of the coinage system.

Send your contribution for
The 2021 Old Farmer's Almanac
by January 24, 2020, to "A & P,"
The Old Farmer's Almanac,
P.O. Box 520, Dublin, NH 03444, or email
it to AlmanacEditors@yankeepub.com
(subject: A & P).

Why Diet? Try Vinegar!
Eat and lose pounds the healthy way.

If you want to lose weight and keep it off -- hate dieting and are tired of taking pills, buying costly diet foods or gimmick "fast loss" plans that don't work-- *you'll love the easy Vinegar way to lose all the pounds you want to lose. And keep them off!*

Today, the natural Vinegar weight loss plan is a reality after years of research by noted vinegar authority Emily Thacker. Her just published book "Vinegar Anniversary" will help you attain your ideal weight the healthiest and most enjoyable way ever.

You'll never again have to count calories. Or go hungry. Or go to expensive diet salons. Or buy pills, drugs.

You'll eat foods you like and get a trimmer, slimmer figure-- free of fat and flab-- as the pounds fade away.

To prove that you can eat great and feel great while losing ugly, unhealthy pounds the natural Vinegar way, you're invited to try the program for up to 3 months on a *"You Must Be Satisfied Trial."*

Let your bathroom scale decide if the plan works for you. You must be satisfied. You never risk one cent. Guaranteed.

What's the secret? Modern research combined with nature's golden elixir.

Since ancient times apple cider vinegar has been used in folk remedies to help control weight and speed-up the metabolism to burn fat. And to also aid overall good health.

Now-- for the first time-- Emily has combined the latest scientific findings and all the weight loss benefits of vinegar into a program with lifetime benefits-- to melt away pounds for health and beauty.

If you like food and hate dieting, you'll love losing pounds and inches the Vinegar way.

Suddenly your body will be energized with new vigor and zest as you combine nature's most powerful, nutritional foods with vinegar to trim away pounds while helping the body to heal itself.

You'll feel and look years younger shed-ding unhealthy pounds that make one look older than their age.

According to her findings, staying trim and fit the Vinegar way also provides preventive health care against the curses of mankind-- cancer, heart disease, diabetes, high cholesterol and blood pressure and other maladies.

In fact, the book's program is so complete that it also helps you:
* Learn secrets of ageless beauty and glowing skin
* Help build the immune system, to fight arthritis and disease
* Speed the metabolism to use natural thermogenesis to burn fat

PLUS so much more that you simply must use the book's easy Vinegar way to lose all the weight you want to lose--and enjoy all its other benefits-- before deciding if you want to keep it.

To Lose Pounds and Enjoy a 90-Day No-Risk Trial... Do This Now To Get Your Personal Copy of the Book:

Simply write "Vinegar Anniversary" on a piece of paper and send it with your check or money order of only $12.95 plus $3.98 shipping and handling (total of $16.93, OH residents please add 6.5% sales tax) to: James Direct Inc., Dept. VA3157, 500 S. Prospect Ave., Box 980, Hartville, Ohio 44632.

You can charge to your VISA, MasterCard, Discover or American Express by mail. Be sure to include your card number, expiration date and signature.

Remember: You're protected by the publisher's 90-Day Money Back Guarantee if you are not delighted.

WANT TO SAVE MORE? Do a favor for a relative or friend and get 2 books for the low introductory price of $20 postpaid. You save $13.86.

Special Bonus - Act promptly to also receive "The Very Best Old-Time Remedies" booklet absolutely FREE. Supplies are limited so order now.   ©2019 JDI VA188S03

http://www.jamesdirect.com

A Reference Compendium

REFERENCE

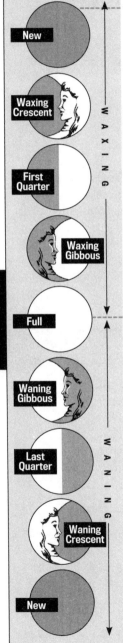

PHASES OF THE MOON

New

Waxing Crescent

First Quarter

Waxing Gibbous

Full

Waning Gibbous

Last Quarter

Waning Crescent

New

WAXING

WANING

WHEN WILL THE MOON RISE?

Use the following saying to remember the time of moonrise on a day when a Moon phase occurs. Keep in mind that the phase itself may happen earlier or later that day, depending on location.

The new Moon always rises near sunrise;

The first quarter, near noon;

The full Moon always rises near sunset;

The last quarter, near midnight.

Moonrise occurs about 50 minutes later each day.

FULL MOON NAMES

NAME	MONTH	VARIATIONS
Full Wolf Moon	JANUARY	Full Old Moon
Full Snow Moon	FEBRUARY	Full Hunger Moon
Full Worm Moon	MARCH	Full Crow Moon Full Crust Moon Full Sugar Moon Full Sap Moon
Full Pink Moon	APRIL	Full Sprouting Grass Moon Full Egg Moon Full Fish Moon
Full Flower Moon	MAY	Full Corn Planting Moon Full Milk Moon
Full Strawberry Moon	JUNE	Full Rose Moon Full Hot Moon
Full Buck Moon	JULY	Full Thunder Moon Full Hay Moon
Full Sturgeon Moon	AUGUST	Full Red Moon Full Green Corn Moon
Full Harvest Moon*	SEPTEMBER	Full Corn Moon Full Barley Moon
Full Hunter's Moon	OCTOBER	Full Travel Moon Full Dying Grass Moon
Full Beaver Moon	NOVEMBER	Full Frost Moon
Full Cold Moon	DECEMBER	Full Long Nights Moon

*The Harvest Moon is always the full Moon closest to the autumnal equinox. If the Harvest Moon occurs in October, the September full Moon is usually called the Corn Moon.

THE ORIGIN OF FULL MOON NAMES

Historically, some Native Americans who lived in the area that is now the United States kept track of the seasons by giving a distinctive name to each recurring full Moon. (This name was applied to the entire month in which it occurred.) The names were used by various tribes and/or by colonial Americans, who also brought their own traditions.

Meanings of Full Moon Names

JANUARY'S full Moon was called the **Wolf Moon** because wolves were more often heard at this time.

FEBRUARY'S full Moon was called the **Snow Moon** because it was a time of heavy snow. It was also called the **Hunger Moon** because hunting was difficult and hunger often resulted.

MARCH'S full Moon was called the **Worm Moon** because, as the Sun increasingly warmed the soil, earthworms became active and their castings (excrement) began to appear.

APRIL'S full Moon was called the **Pink Moon** because it heralded the appearance of the moss pink, or wild ground phlox—one of the first spring flowers.

MAY'S full Moon was called the **Flower Moon** because blossoms were abundant everywhere at this time.

JUNE'S full Moon was called the **Strawberry Moon** because it appeared when the strawberry harvest took place.

JULY'S full Moon was called the **Buck Moon;** it arrived when a male deer's antlers were in full growth mode.

AUGUST'S full Moon was called the **Sturgeon Moon** because this large fish, which is found in the Great Lakes and Lake Champlain, was caught easily at this time.

SEPTEMBER'S full Moon was called the **Corn Moon** because this was the time to harvest corn.

The **Harvest Moon** is the full Moon that occurs closest to the autumnal equinox. It can occur in either September or October. At this time, crops such as corn, pumpkins, squash, and wild rice were ready for gathering.

OCTOBER'S full Moon was called the **Hunter's Moon** because this was the time to hunt in preparation for winter.

NOVEMBER'S full Moon was called the **Beaver Moon** because it was the time to set beaver traps, before the waters froze over.

DECEMBER'S full Moon was called the **Cold Moon.** It was also called the **Long Nights Moon** because nights at this time of year were the longest.

REFERENCE

THE ORIGIN OF MONTH NAMES

JANUARY. For the Roman god Janus, protector of gates and doorways. Janus is depicted with two faces, one looking into the past, the other into the future.

FEBRUARY. From the Latin *februa*, "to cleanse." The Roman Februalia was a festival of purification and atonement that took place during this time of year.

MARCH. For the Roman god of war, Mars. This was the time of year to resume military campaigns that had been interrupted by winter.

APRIL. From the Latin *aperio*, "to open (bud)," because plants begin to grow now.

MAY. For the Roman goddess Maia, who oversaw the growth of plants. Also from the Latin *maiores*, "elders," who were celebrated now.

JUNE. For the Roman goddess Juno, patroness of marriage and the well-being of women. Also from the Latin *juvenis*, "young people."

JULY. To honor Roman dictator Julius Caesar (100 B.C.–44 B.C.). In 46 B.C., with the help of Sosigenes, he developed the Julian calendar.

AUGUST. To honor the first Roman emperor (and grandnephew of Julius Caesar), Augustus Caesar (63 B.C.–A.D. 14).

SEPTEMBER. From the Latin *septem*, "seven," because this was the seventh month of the early Roman calendar.

OCTOBER. From the Latin *octo*, "eight," because this was the eighth month of the early Roman calendar.

NOVEMBER. From the Latin *novem*, "nine," because this was the ninth month of the early Roman calendar.

DECEMBER. From the Latin *decem*, "ten," because this was the tenth month of the early Roman calendar.

Easter Dates (2020–23)

Christian churches that follow the Gregorian calendar celebrate Easter on the first Sunday after the paschal full Moon on or just after the vernal equinox.

YEAR	EASTER
2020	April 12
2021	April 4
2022	April 17
2023	April 9

The Julian calendar is used by some churches, including many Eastern Orthodox. The dates below are Julian calendar dates for Easter converted to Gregorian dates.

YEAR	EASTER
2020	April 19
2021	May 2
2022	April 24
2023	April 16

FRIGGATRISKAIDEKAPHOBIA TRIVIA

Here are a few facts about Friday the 13th:

In the 14 possible configurations for the annual calendar (see any perpetual calendar), the occurrence of Friday the 13th is this:

6 of 14 years have one Friday the 13th.
6 of 14 years have two Fridays the 13th.
2 of 14 years have three Fridays the 13th.

No year is without one Friday the 13th, and no year has more than three.

Months that have a Friday the 13th begin on a Sunday.

2020 has a Friday the 13th in March and November.

CALENDAR

THE ORIGIN OF DAY NAMES

The days of the week were named by ancient Romans with the Latin words for the Sun, the Moon, and the five known planets. These names have survived in European languages, but English names also reflect Anglo-Saxon and Norse influences.

ENGLISH	LATIN	FRENCH	ITALIAN	SPANISH	ANGLO-SAXON AND NORSE
SUNDAY	dies Solis (Sol's day)	dimanche	domenica	domingo	Sunnandaeg (Sun's day)
		from the Latin for "Lord's day"			
MONDAY	dies Lunae (Luna's day)	lundi	lunedì	lunes	Monandaeg (Moon's day)
TUESDAY	dies Martis (Mars's day)	mardi	martedì	martes	Tiwesdaeg (Tiw's day)
WEDNESDAY	dies Mercurii (Mercury's day)	mercredi	mercoledì	miércoles	Wodnesdaeg (Woden's day)
THURSDAY	dies Jovis (Jupiter's day)	jeudi	giovedì	jueves	Thursdaeg (Thor's day)
FRIDAY	dies Veneris (Venus's day)	vendredi	venerdì	viernes	Frigedaeg (Frigga's day)
SATURDAY	dies Saturni (Saturn's day)	samedi	sabato	sábado	Saeterndaeg (Saturn's day)
		from the Latin for "Sabbath"			

REFERENCE

How to Find the Day of the Week for Any Given Date

To compute the day of the week for any given date as far back as the mid–18th century, proceed as follows:

Add the last two digits of the year to one-quarter of the last two digits (discard any remainder), the day of the month, and the month key from the key box below. Divide the sum by 7; the remainder is the day of the week (1 is Sunday, 2 is Monday, and so on). If there is no remainder, the day is Saturday. If you're searching for a weekday prior to 1900, add 2 to the sum before dividing; prior to 1800, add 4. The formula doesn't work for days prior to 1753. From 2000 through 2099, subtract 1 from the sum before dividing.

Example:

THE DAYTON FLOOD WAS ON MARCH 25, 1913.

Last two digits of year:	13
One-quarter of these two digits:	3
Given day of month:	25
Key number for March:	4
Sum:	45

45 ÷ 7 = 6, with a remainder of 3. The flood took place on Tuesday, the third day of the week.

KEY

JANUARY	1
LEAP YEAR	0
FEBRUARY	4
LEAP YEAR	3
MARCH	4
APRIL	0
MAY	2
JUNE	5
JULY	0
AUGUST	3
SEPTEMBER	6
OCTOBER	1
NOVEMBER	4
DECEMBER	6

ANIMAL SIGNS OF THE CHINESE ZODIAC

The animal designations of the Chinese zodiac follow a 12-year cycle and are always used in the same sequence. The Chinese year of 354 days begins 3 to 7 weeks into the western 365-day year, so the animal designation changes at that time, rather than on January 1. This year, the Chinese New Year starts on January 25.

RAT

Ambitious and sincere, you can be generous with your money. Compatible with the dragon and the monkey. Your opposite is the horse.

1924	1936	1948
1960	1972	1984
1996	2008	2020

OX OR BUFFALO

A leader, you are bright, patient, and cheerful. Compatible with the snake and the rooster. Your opposite is the sheep.

1925	1937	1949
1961	1973	1985
1997	2009	2021

TIGER

Forthright and sensitive, you possess great courage. Compatible with the horse and the dog. Your opposite is the monkey.

1926	1938	1950
1962	1974	1986
1998	2010	2022

RABBIT OR HARE

Talented and affectionate, you are a seeker of tranquility. Compatible with the sheep and the pig. Your opposite is the rooster.

1927	1939	1951
1963	1975	1987
1999	2011	2023

DRAGON

Robust and passionate, your life is filled with complexity. Compatible with the monkey and the rat. Your opposite is the dog.

1928	1940	1952
1964	1976	1988
2000	2012	2024

SNAKE

Strong-willed and intense, you display great wisdom. Compatible with the rooster and the ox. Your opposite is the pig.

1929	1941	1953
1965	1977	1989
2001	2013	2025

HORSE

Physically attractive and popular, you like the company of others. Compatible with the tiger and the dog. Your opposite is the rat.

1930	1942	1954
1966	1978	1990
2002	2014	2026

SHEEP OR GOAT

Aesthetic and stylish, you enjoy being a private person. Compatible with the pig and the rabbit. Your opposite is the ox.

1931	1943	1955
1967	1979	1991
2003	2015	2027

MONKEY

Persuasive, skillful, and intelligent, you strive to excel. Compatible with the dragon and the rat. Your opposite is the tiger.

1932	1944	1956
1968	1980	1992
2004	2016	2028

ROOSTER OR COCK

Seeking wisdom and truth, you have a pioneering spirit. Compatible with the snake and the ox. Your opposite is the rabbit.

1933	1945	1957
1969	1981	1993
2005	2017	2029

DOG

Generous and loyal, you have the ability to work well with others. Compatible with the horse and the tiger. Your opposite is the dragon.

1934	1946	1958
1970	1982	1994
2006	2018	2030

PIG OR BOAR

Gallant and noble, your friends will remain at your side. Compatible with the rabbit and the sheep. Your opposite is the snake.

1935	1947	1959
1971	1983	1995
2007	2019	2031

REFERENCE

A Table Foretelling the Weather Through All the Lunations of Each Year, or Forever

This table is the result of many years of actual observation and shows what sort of weather will probably follow the Moon's entrance into any of its quarters. For example, the table shows that the week following January 2, 2020, will be fair and frosty, because the Moon enters the first quarter on that day at 11:45 P.M. EST. (See the **Left-Hand Calendar Pages, 120–146,** for Moon phases.)

EDITOR'S NOTE: Although the data in this table is taken into consideration in the year-long process of compiling the annual long-range weather forecasts for *The Old Farmer's Almanac*, we rely far more on our projections of solar activity.

TIME OF CHANGE	SUMMER	WINTER
Midnight to 2 A.M.	Fair	Hard frost, unless wind is south or west
2 A.M. to 4 A.M.	Cold, with frequent showers	Snow and stormy
4 A.M. to 6 A.M.	Rain	Rain
6 A.M. to 8 A.M.	Wind and rain	Stormy
8 A.M. to 10 A.M.	Changeable	Cold rain if wind is west; snow, if east
10 A.M. to noon	Frequent showers	Cold with high winds
Noon to 2 P.M.	Very rainy	Snow or rain
2 P.M. to 4 P.M.	Changeable	Fair and mild
4 P.M. to 6 P.M.	Fair	Fair
6 P.M. to 10 P.M.	Fair if wind is northwest; rain if wind is south or southwest	Fair and frosty if wind is north or northeast; rain or snow if wind is south or southwest
10 P.M. to midnight	Fair	Fair and frosty

This table was created more than 180 years ago by Dr. Herschell for the Boston Courier; *it first appeared in* The Old Farmer's Almanac *in 1834.*

SAFE ICE THICKNESS*

ICE THICKNESS	PERMISSIBLE LOAD	ICE THICKNESS	PERMISSIBLE LOAD
3 inches	Single person on foot	12 inches	Heavy truck (8-ton gross)
4 inches	Group in single file	15 inches	10 tons
7½ inches	Passenger car (2-ton gross)	20 inches	25 tons
8 inches	Light truck (2½-ton gross)	30 inches	70 tons
10 inches	Medium truck (3½-ton gross)	36 inches	110 tons

*Solid, clear, blue/black pond and lake ice

The strength value of river ice is 15 percent less. Slush ice has only half the strength of blue ice.

HEAT INDEX °F (°C)

TEMP. °F (°C)	RELATIVE HUMIDITY (%)								
	40	45	50	55	60	65	70	75	80
100 (38)	109 (43)	114 (46)	118 (48)	124 (51)	129 (54)	136 (58)			
98 (37)	105 (41)	109 (43)	113 (45)	117 (47)	123 (51)	128 (53)	134 (57)		
96 (36)	101 (38)	104 (40)	108 (42)	112 (44)	116 (47)	121 (49)	126 (52)	132 (56)	
94 (34)	97 (36)	100 (38)	103 (39)	106 (41)	110 (43)	114 (46)	119 (48)	124 (51)	129 (54)
92 (33)	94 (34)	96 (36)	99 (37)	101 (38)	105 (41)	108 (42)	112 (44)	116 (47)	121 (49)
90 (32)	91 (33)	93 (34)	95 (35)	97 (36)	100 (38)	103 (39)	105 (41)	109 (43)	113 (45)
88 (31)	88 (31)	89 (32)	91 (33)	93 (34)	95 (35)	98 (37)	100 (38)	103 (39)	106 (41)
86 (30)	85 (29)	87 (31)	88 (31)	89 (32)	91 (33)	93 (34)	95 (35)	97 (36)	100 (38)
84 (29)	83 (28)	84 (29)	85 (29)	86 (30)	88 (31)	89 (32)	90 (32)	92 (33)	94 (34)
82 (28)	81 (27)	82 (28)	83 (28)	84 (29)	84 (29)	85 (29)	86 (30)	88 (31)	89 (32)
80 (27)	80 (27)	80 (27)	81 (27)	81 (27)	82 (28)	82 (28)	83 (28)	84 (29)	84 (29)

EXAMPLE: *When the temperature is 88°F (31°C) and the relative humidity is 60 percent, the heat index, or how hot it feels, is 95°F (35°C).*

THE UV INDEX FOR MEASURING ULTRAVIOLET RADIATION RISK

The U.S. National Weather Service's daily forecasts of ultraviolet levels use these numbers for various exposure levels:

UV INDEX NUMBER	EXPOSURE LEVEL	ACTIONS TO TAKE
0, 1, 2	Low	Wear UV-blocking sunglasses on bright days. In winter, reflection off snow can nearly double UV strength. If you burn easily, cover up and apply SPF 30+ sunscreen.
3, 4, 5	Moderate	Apply SPF 30+ sunscreen; wear a hat and sunglasses. Stay in shade when sun is strongest.
6, 7	High	Apply SPF 30+ sunscreen; wear a hat, sunglasses, and protective clothing; limit midday exposure.
8, 9, 10	Very High	Apply SPF 30+ sunscreen; wear a hat, sunglasses, and protective clothing; limit midday exposure. Seek shade. Unprotected skin will be damaged and can burn quickly.
11 or higher	Extreme	Apply SPF 30+ sunscreen; wear a hat, sunglasses, and protective clothing; avoid midday exposure; seek shade. Unprotected skin can burn in minutes.

REFERENCE

85	90	95	100
135 (57)			
126 (52)	131 (55)		
117 (47)	122 (50)	127 (53)	132 (56)
110 (43)	113 (45)	117 (47)	121 (49)
102 (39)	105 (41)	108 (42)	112 (44)
96 (36)	98 (37)	100 (38)	103 (39)
90 (32)	91 (33)	93 (34)	95 (35)
85 (29)	86 (30)	86 (30)	87 (31)

What Are Cooling/Heating Degree Days?

In an attempt to measure the need for air-conditioning, each degree of a day's mean temperature that is above a base temperature, such as 65°F (U.S.) or 18°C (Canada), is considered one cooling degree day. If the daily mean temperature is 75°F, for example, that's 10 cooling degree days.

Similarly, to measure the need for heating fuel consumption, each degree of a day's mean temperature that is below 65°F (18°C) is considered one heating degree. For example, a day with a high of 60°F and low of 40°F results in a mean of 50°, or 15 degrees less than 65°. Hence, that day had 15 heating degree days.

HOW TO MEASURE HAIL

The **TORRO HAILSTORM INTENSITY SCALE** was introduced by Jonathan Webb of Oxford, England, in 1986 as a means of categorizing hailstorms. The name derives from the private and mostly British research body named the TORnado and storm Research Organisation.

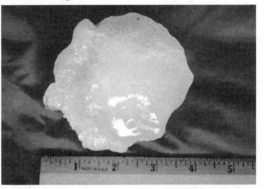

INTENSITY/DESCRIPTION OF HAIL DAMAGE

H0	True hail of pea size causes no damage
H1	Leaves and flower petals are punctured and torn
H2	Leaves are stripped from trees and plants
H3	Panes of glass are broken; auto bodies are dented
H4	Some house windows are broken; small tree branches are broken off; birds are killed
H5	Many windows are smashed; small animals are injured; large tree branches are broken off
H6	Shingle roofs are breached; metal roofs are scored; wooden window frames are broken away
H7	Roofs are shattered to expose rafters; autos are seriously damaged
H8	Shingle and tile roofs are destroyed; small tree trunks are split; people are seriously injured
H9	Concrete roofs are broken; large tree trunks are split and knocked down; people are at risk of fatal injuries
H10	Brick houses are damaged; people are at risk of fatal injuries

HOW TO MEASURE WIND SPEED

The **BEAUFORT WIND FORCE SCALE** is a common way of estimating wind speed. It was developed in 1805 by Admiral Sir Francis Beaufort of the British Navy to measure wind at sea. We can also use it to measure wind on land.

Admiral Beaufort arranged the numbers 0 to 12 to indicate the strength of the wind from calm, force 0, to hurricane, force 12. Here's a scale adapted to land.

"Used Mostly at Sea but of Help to All Who Are Interested in the Weather"

BEAUFORT FORCE	DESCRIPTION	WHEN YOU SEE OR FEEL THIS EFFECT	WIND SPEED (mph)	(km/h)
0	CALM	Smoke goes straight up	less than 1	less than 2
1	LIGHT AIR	Wind direction is shown by smoke drift but not by wind vane	1–3	2–5
2	LIGHT BREEZE	Wind is felt on the face; leaves rustle; wind vanes move	4–7	6–11
3	GENTLE BREEZE	Leaves and small twigs move steadily; wind extends small flags straight out	8–12	12–19
4	MODERATE BREEZE	Wind raises dust and loose paper; small branches move	13–18	20–29
5	FRESH BREEZE	Small trees sway; waves form on lakes	19–24	30–39
6	STRONG BREEZE	Large branches move; wires whistle; umbrellas are difficult to use	25–31	40–50
7	NEAR GALE	Whole trees are in motion; walking against the wind is difficult	32–38	51–61
8	GALE	Twigs break from trees; walking against the wind is very difficult	39–46	62–74
9	STRONG GALE	Buildings suffer minimal damage; roof shingles are removed	47–54	75–87
10	STORM	Trees are uprooted	55–63	88–101
11	VIOLENT STORM	Widespread damage	64–72	102–116
12	HURRICANE	Widespread destruction	73+	117+

RETIRED ATLANTIC HURRICANE NAMES

These storms have been some of the most destructive and costly.

NAME	YEAR	NAME	YEAR	NAME	YEAR	NAME	YEAR
Rita	2005	Gustav	2008	Sandy	2012	Harvey	2017
Stan	2005	Ike	2008	Ingrid	2013	Irma	2017
Wilma	2005	Paloma	2008	Erika	2015	Maria	2017
Dean	2007	Igor	2010	Joaquin	2015	Nate	2017
Felix	2007	Tomas	2010	Matthew	2016	Florence	2018
Noel	2007	Irene	2011	Otto	2016	Michael	2018

WEATHER

ATLANTIC TROPICAL (AND SUBTROPICAL) STORM NAMES FOR 2020			EASTERN NORTH-PACIFIC TROPICAL (AND SUBTROPICAL) STORM NAMES FOR 2020		
Arthur	Hanna	Omar	Amanda	Iselle	Rachel
Bertha	Isaias	Paulette	Boris	Julio	Simon
Cristobal	Josephine	Rene	Cristina	Karina	Trudy
Dolly	Kyle	Sally	Douglas	Lowell	Vance
Edouard	Laura	Teddy	Elida	Marie	Winnie
Fay	Marco	Vicky	Fausto	Norbert	Xavier
Gonzalo	Nana	Wilfred	Genevieve	Odalys	Yolanda
			Herman	Polo	Zeke

The lists above are used in rotation and recycled every 6 years, e.g., the 2020 list will be used again in 2026.

How to Measure Hurricane Strength

The SAFFIR-SIMPSON HURRICANE WIND SCALE assigns a rating from 1 to 5 based on a hurricane's intensity. It is used to give an estimate of the potential property damage from a hurricane landfall. Wind speed is the determining factor in the scale, as storm surge values are highly dependent on the slope of the continental shelf in the landfall region. Wind speeds are measured at a height of 33 feet (10 meters) using a 1-minute average.

CATEGORY ONE. Average wind: 74–95 mph. Significant damage to mobile homes. Some damage to roofing and siding of well-built frame homes. Large tree branches snap and shallow-rooted trees may topple. Power outages may last a few to several days.

CATEGORY TWO. Average wind: 96–110 mph. Mobile homes may be destroyed. Major roof and siding damage to frame homes. Many shallow-rooted trees snap or topple, blocking roads. Widespread power outages could last from several days to weeks. Potable water may be scarce.

CATEGORY THREE. Average wind: 111–129 mph. Most mobile homes destroyed.

Frame homes may sustain major roof damage. Many trees snap or topple, blocking numerous roads. Electricity and water may be unavailable for several days to weeks.

CATEGORY FOUR. Average wind: 130–156 mph. Mobile homes destroyed. Frame homes severely damaged or destroyed. Windborne debris may penetrate protected windows. Most trees snap or topple. Residential areas isolated by fallen trees and power poles. Most of the area uninhabitable for weeks to months.

CATEGORY FIVE. Average wind: 157+ mph. Most homes destroyed. Nearly all windows blown out of high-rises. Most of the area uninhabitable for weeks to months.

REFERENCE

HOW TO MEASURE A TORNADO

The original **FUJITA SCALE** (or F Scale) was developed by Dr. Theodore Fujita to classify tornadoes based on wind damage. All tornadoes, and other severe local windstorms, were assigned a number according to the most intense damage caused by the storm. An enhanced F (EF) scale was implemented in the United States on February 1, 2007. The EF scale uses 3-second gust estimates based on a more detailed system for assessing damage, taking into account different building materials.

F SCALE		EF SCALE (U.S.)
F0 · 40-72 mph (64-116 km/h)	LIGHT DAMAGE	EF0 · 65-85 mph (105-137 km/h)
F1 · 73-112 mph (117-180 km/h)	MODERATE DAMAGE	EF1 · 86-110 mph (138-178 km/h)
F2 · 113-157 mph (181-253 km/h)	CONSIDERABLE DAMAGE	EF2 · 111-135 mph (179-218 km/h)
F3 · 158-207 mph (254-332 km/h)	SEVERE DAMAGE	EF3 · 136-165 mph (219-266 km/h)
F4 · 208-260 mph (333-419 km/h)	DEVASTATING DAMAGE	EF4 · 166-200 mph (267-322 km/h)
F5 · 261-318 mph (420-512 km/h)	INCREDIBLE DAMAGE	EF5 · over 200 mph (over 322 km/h)

Wind/Barometer Table

BAROMETER (REDUCED TO SEA LEVEL)	WIND DIRECTION	CHARACTER OF WEATHER INDICATED
30.00 to 30.20, and steady	WESTERLY	Fair, with slight changes in temperature, for one to two days
30.00 to 30.20, and rising rapidly	WESTERLY	Fair, followed within two days by warmer and rain
30.00 to 30.20, and falling rapidly	SOUTH TO EAST	Warmer, and rain within 24 hours
30.20 or above, and falling rapidly	SOUTH TO EAST	Warmer, and rain within 36 hours
30.20 or above, and falling rapidly	WEST TO NORTH	Cold and clear, quickly followed by warmer and rain
30.20 or above, and steady	VARIABLE	No early change
30.00 or below, and falling slowly	SOUTH TO EAST	Rain within 18 hours that will continue a day or two
30.00 or below, and falling rapidly	SOUTHEAST TO NORTHEAST	Rain, with high wind, followed within two days by clearing, colder
30.00 or below, and rising	SOUTH TO WEST	Clearing and colder within 12 hours
29.80 or below, and falling rapidly	SOUTH TO EAST	Severe storm of wind and rain imminent; in winter, snow or cold wave within 24 hours
29.80 or below, and falling rapidly	EAST TO NORTH	Severe northeast gales and heavy rain or snow, followed in winter by cold wave
29.80 or below, and rising rapidly	GOING TO WEST	Clearing and colder

NOTE: *A barometer should be adjusted to show equivalent sea-level pressure for the altitude at which it is to be used. A change of 100 feet in elevation will cause a decrease of 1/10 inch in the reading.*

WINDCHILL TABLE

As wind speed increases, your body loses heat more rapidly, making the air feel colder than it really is. The combination of cold temperature and high wind can create a cooling effect so severe that exposed flesh can freeze.

	Calm	35	30	25	20	15	10	5	0	–5	–10	–15	–20	–25	–30	–35
TEMPERATURE (°F)																
5		31	25	19	13	7	1	–5	–11	–16	–22	–28	–34	–40	–46	–52
10		27	21	15	9	3	–4	–10	–16	–22	–28	–35	–41	–47	–53	–59
15		25	19	13	6	0	–7	–13	–19	–26	–32	–39	–45	–51	–58	–64
20		24	17	11	4	–2	–9	–15	–22	–29	–35	–42	–48	–55	–61	–68
25		23	16	9	3	–4	–11	–17	–24	–31	–37	–44	–51	–58	–64	–71
30		22	15	8	1	–5	–12	–19	–26	–33	–39	–46	–53	–60	–67	–73
35		21	14	7	0	–7	–14	–21	–27	–34	–41	–48	–55	–62	–69	–76
40		20	13	6	–1	–8	–15	–22	–29	–36	–43	–50	–57	–64	–71	–78
45		19	12	5	–2	–9	–16	–23	–30	–37	–44	–51	–58	–65	–72	–79
50		19	12	4	–3	–10	–17	–24	–31	–38	–45	–52	–60	–67	–74	–81
55		18	11	4	–3	–11	–18	–25	–32	–39	–46	–54	–61	–68	–75	–82
60		17	10	3	–4	–11	–19	–26	–33	–40	–48	–55	–62	–69	–76	–84

WIND SPEED (mph)

FROSTBITE OCCURS IN ☐ 30 MINUTES ☐ 10 MINUTES ☐ 5 MINUTES

EXAMPLE: *When the temperature is 15°F and the wind speed is 30 miles per hour, the windchill, or how cold it feels, is –5°F. For a Celsius version of this table, visit Almanac.com/WindchillCelsius.*
–courtesy of National Weather Service

HOW TO MEASURE EARTHQUAKES

In 1979, seismologists developed a measurement of earthquake size called **MOMENT MAGNITUDE**. It is more accurate than the previously used Richter scale, which is precise only for earthquakes of a certain size and at a certain distance from a seismometer. All earthquakes can now be compared on the same magnitude scale.

MAGNITUDE	DESCRIPTION	EFFECT
LESS THAN 3	MICRO	GENERALLY NOT FELT
3–3.9	MINOR	OFTEN FELT, LITTLE DAMAGE
4–4.9	LIGHT	SHAKING, SOME DAMAGE
5–5.9	MODERATE	SLIGHT TO MAJOR DAMAGE
6–6.9	STRONG	DESTRUCTIVE
7–7.9	MAJOR	SEVERE DAMAGE
8 OR MORE	GREAT	SERIOUS DAMAGE

A GARDENER'S WORST PHOBIAS

NAME OF FEAR	OBJECT FEARED
Alliumphobia	Garlic
Anthophobia	Flowers
Apiphobia	Bees
Arachnophobia	Spiders
Batonophobia	Plants
Bufonophobia	Toads
Dendrophobia	Trees
Entomophobia	Insects
Lachanophobia	Vegetables
Melissophobia	Bees
Mottephobia	Moths
Myrmecophobia	Ants
Ornithophobia	Birds
Ranidaphobia	Frogs
Rupophobia	Dirt
Scoleciphobia	Worms
Spheksophobia	Wasps

PLANTS FOR LAWNS

Choose varieties that suit your soil and your climate. All of these can withstand mowing and considerable foot traffic.

Ajuga or bugleweed *(Ajuga reptans)*
Corsican mint *(Mentha requienii)*
Dwarf cinquefoil *(Potentilla tabernaemontani)*
English pennyroyal *(Mentha pulegium)*
Green Irish moss *(Sagina subulata)*
Pearly everlasting *(Anaphalis margaritacea)*
Roman chamomile *(Chamaemelum nobile)*
Rupturewort *(Herniaria glabra)*
Speedwell *(Veronica officinalis)*
Stonecrop *(Sedum ternatum)*
Sweet violets (*Viola odorata* or *V. tricolor*)
Thyme *(Thymus serpyllum)*
White clover *(Trifolium repens)*
Wild strawberries *(Fragaria virginiana)*
Wintergreen or partridgeberry *(Mitchella repens)*

Lawn-Growing Tips

• Test your soil: The pH balance should be 7.0 or more; 6.2 to 6.7 puts your lawn at risk for fungal diseases. If the pH is too low, correct it with liming, best done in the fall.

• The best time to apply fertilizer is just before it rains.

• If you put lime and fertilizer on your lawn, spread half of it as you walk north to south, the other half as you walk east to west to cut down on missed areas.

• Any feeding of lawns in the fall should be done with a low-nitrogen, slow-acting fertilizer.

• In areas of your lawn where tree roots compete with the grass, apply some extra fertilizer to benefit both.

• Moss and sorrel in lawns usually means poor soil, poor aeration or drainage, or excessive acidity.

• Control weeds by promoting healthy lawn growth with natural fertilizers in spring and early fall.

• Raise the level of your lawn-mower blades during the hot summer days. Taller grass resists drought better than short.

• You can reduce mowing time by redesigning your lawn, reducing sharp corners and adding sweeping curves.

• During a drought, let the grass grow longer between mowings and reduce fertilizer.

• Water your lawn early in the morning or in the evening.

Flowers and Herbs That Attract Butterflies

Allium . . . . *Allium*	Mallow . . . . *Malva*
Aster . . . . *Aster*	Mealycup sage . . . .*Salvia farinacea*
Bee balm . . . .*Monarda*	Milkweed . . . . *Asclepias*
Butterfly bush. . . . . *Buddleia*	Mint. . . . . *Mentha*
Catmint . . . .*Nepeta*	Oregano . . . . *Origanum vulgare*
Clove pink . . . .*Dianthus*	Pansy . . . . *Viola*
Cornflower. . . . .*Centaurea*	Parsley . . . . *Petroselinum*
Creeping thyme . . . . . . *Thymus serpyllum*	*crispum*
Daylily. . . . .*Hemerocallis*	Phlox. . . . .*Phlox*
Dill. . . . . *Anethum graveolens*	Privet . . . .*Ligustrum*
False indigo . . . . *Baptisia*	Purple coneflower . . *Echinacea purpurea*
Fleabane. . . . . *Erigeron*	Rock cress . . . .*Arabis*
Floss flower . . . .*Ageratum*	Sea holly. . . . . *Eryngium*
Globe thistle . . . .*Echinops*	Shasta daisy . . . . *Chrysanthemum*
Goldenrod . . . . *Solidago*	Snapdragon. . . . . *Antirrhinum*
Helen's flower . . . .*Helenium*	Stonecrop . . . .*Sedum*
Hollyhock. . . . .*Alcea*	Sweet alyssum . . . .*Lobularia*
Honeysuckle . . . . *Lonicera*	Sweet marjoram. . . . *Origanum majorana*
Lavender . . . . *Lavandula*	Sweet rocket. . . . . *Hesperis*
Lilac. . . . .*Syringa*	Tickseed. . . . . *Coreopsis*
Lupine. . . . .*Lupinus*	Verbena . . . .*Verbena*
Lychnis. *Lychnis*	Zinnia . . . . *Zinnia*

FLOWERS* THAT ATTRACT HUMMINGBIRDS

Beard tongue. . . . . *Penstemon*	Soapwort . . . .*Saponaria*
Bee balm . . . .*Monarda*	Summer phlox . . . . *Phlox paniculata*
Butterfly bush. . . . . *Buddleia*	Trumpet honeysuckle. . . . . *Lonicera*
Catmint . . . .*Nepeta*	*sempervirens*
Clove pink . . . .*Dianthus*	Verbena . . . .*Verbena*
Columbine . . . . *Aquilegia*	Weigela. . . . .*Weigela*
Coral bells . . . .*Heuchera*	
Daylily. . . . . *Hemerocallis*	
Desert candle . . . .*Yucca*	
Flag iris . . . .*Iris*	
Flowering tobacco . . . . . . *Nicotiana alata*	
Foxglove. . . . . *Digitalis*	
Larkspur . . . .*Delphinium*	
Lily. . . . . *Lilium*	
Lupine. . . . .*Lupinus*	
Petunia. *Petunia*	
Pincushion flower . . . . *Scabiosa*	
Red-hot poker . . . . *Kniphofia*	
Scarlet sage. . . . . *Salvia splendens*	

*NOTE: *Choose varieties in red and orange shades, if available.*

pH PREFERENCES OF TREES, SHRUBS, FLOWERS, AND VEGETABLES

An accurate soil test will indicate your soil pH and will specify the amount of lime or sulfur that is needed to bring it up or down to the appropriate level. A pH of 6.5 is just about right for most home gardens, since most plants thrive in the 6.0 to 7.0 (slightly acidic to neutral) range. Some plants (azaleas, blueberries) prefer more strongly acidic soil in the 4.0 to 6.0 range, while a few (asparagus, plums) do best in soil that is neutral to slightly alkaline. Acidic, or sour, soil (below 7.0) is counteracted by applying finely ground limestone, and alkaline, or sweet, soil (above 7.0) is treated with ground sulfur.

COMMON NAME	OPTIMUM pH RANGE	COMMON NAME	OPTIMUM pH RANGE	COMMON NAME	OPTIMUM pH RANGE
TREES AND SHRUBS		Bee balm	6.0–7.5	Snapdragon	5.5–7.0
Apple	5.0–6.5	Begonia	5.5–7.0	Sunflower	6.0–7.5
Azalea	4.5–6.0	Black-eyed Susan	5.5–7.0	Tulip	6.0–7.0
Beautybush	6.0–7.5	Bleeding heart	6.0–7.5	Zinnia	5.5–7.0
Birch	5.0–6.5	Canna	6.0–8.0		
Blackberry	5.0–6.0	Carnation	6.0–7.0	**VEGETABLES**	
Blueberry	4.0–5.0	Chrysanthemum	6.0–7.5	Asparagus	6.0–8.0
Boxwood	6.0–7.5	Clematis	5.5–7.0	Bean	6.0–7.5
Cherry, sour	6.0–7.0	Coleus	6.0–7.0	Beet	6.0–7.5
Crab apple	6.0–7.5	Coneflower, purple	5.0–7.5	Broccoli	6.0–7.0
Dogwood	5.0–7.0	Cosmos	5.0–8.0	Brussels sprout	6.0–7.5
Fir, balsam	5.0–6.0	Crocus	6.0–8.0	Cabbage	6.0–7.5
Hemlock	5.0–6.0	Daffodil	6.0–6.5	Carrot	5.5–7.0
Hydrangea, blue-flowered	4.0–5.0	Dahlia	6.0–7.5	Cauliflower	5.5–7.5
Hydrangea, pink-flowered	6.0–7.0	Daisy, Shasta	6.0–8.0	Celery	5.8–7.0
		Daylily	6.0–8.0	Chive	6.0–7.0
Juniper	5.0–6.0	Delphinium	6.0–7.5	Collard	6.5–7.5
Laurel, mountain	4.5–6.0	Foxglove	6.0–7.5	Corn	5.5–7.0
Lemon	6.0–7.5	Geranium	6.0–8.0	Cucumber	5.5–7.0
Lilac	6.0–7.5	Gladiolus	5.0–7.0	Eggplant	6.0–7.0
Maple, sugar	6.0–7.5	Hibiscus	6.0–8.0	Garlic	5.5–8.0
Oak, white	5.0–6.5	Hollyhock	6.0–8.0	Kale	6.0–7.5
Orange	6.0–7.5	Hyacinth	6.5–7.5	Leek	6.0–8.0
Peach	6.0–7.0	Iris, blue flag	5.0–7.5	Lettuce	6.0–7.0
Pear	6.0–7.5	Lily-of-the-valley	4.5–6.0	Okra	6.0–7.0
Pecan	6.4–8.0	Lupine	5.0–6.5	Onion	6.0–7.0
Plum	6.0–8.0	Marigold	5.5–7.5	Pea	6.0–7.5
Raspberry, red	5.5–7.0	Morning glory	6.0–7.5	Pepper, sweet	5.5–7.0
Rhododendron	4.5–6.0	Narcissus, trumpet	5.5–6.5	Potato	4.8–6.5
Willow	6.0–8.0	Nasturtium	5.5–7.5	Pumpkin	5.5–7.5
		Pansy	5.5–6.5	Radish	6.0–7.0
FLOWERS		Peony	6.0–7.5	Spinach	6.0–7.5
Alyssum	6.0–7.5	Petunia	6.0–7.5	Squash, crookneck	6.0–7.5
Aster, New England	6.0–8.0	Phlox, summer	6.0–8.0	Squash, Hubbard	5.5–7.0
Baby's breath	6.0–7.0	Poppy, oriental	6.0–7.5	Swiss chard	6.0–7.0
Bachelor's button	6.0–7.5	Rose, hybrid tea	5.5–7.0	Tomato	5.5–7.5
		Rose, rugosa	6.0–7.0	Watermelon	5.5–6.5

PRODUCE WEIGHTS AND MEASURES

VEGETABLES

ASPARAGUS: 1 pound = 3 cups chopped

BEANS (STRING): 1 pound = 4 cups chopped

BEETS: 1 pound (5 medium) = 2½ cups chopped

BROCCOLI: 1 pound = 6 cups chopped

CABBAGE: 1 pound = 4½ cups shredded

CARROTS: 1 pound = 3½ cups sliced or grated

CELERY: 1 pound = 4 cups chopped

CUCUMBERS: 1 pound (2 medium) = 4 cups sliced

EGGPLANT: 1 pound = 4 cups chopped = 2 cups cooked

GARLIC: 1 clove = 1 teaspoon chopped

LEEKS: 1 pound = 4 cups chopped = 2 cups cooked

MUSHROOMS: 1 pound = 5 to 6 cups sliced = 2 cups cooked

ONIONS: 1 pound = 4 cups sliced = 2 cups cooked

PARSNIPS: 1 pound = 1½ cups cooked, puréed

PEAS: 1 pound whole = 1 to 1½ cups shelled

POTATOES: 1 pound (3 medium) sliced = 2 cups mashed

PUMPKIN: 1 pound = 4 cups chopped = 2 cups cooked and drained

SPINACH: 1 pound = ¾ to 1 cup cooked

SQUASHES (SUMMER): 1 pound = 4 cups grated = 2 cups sliced and cooked

SQUASHES (WINTER): 2 pounds = 2½ cups cooked, puréed

SWEET POTATOES: 1 pound = 4 cups grated = 1 cup cooked, puréed

SWISS CHARD: 1 pound = 5 to 6 cups packed leaves = 1 to 1½ cups cooked

TOMATOES: 1 pound (3 or 4 medium) = 1½ cups seeded pulp

TURNIPS: 1 pound = 4 cups chopped = 2 cups cooked, mashed

FRUIT

APPLES: 1 pound (3 or 4 medium) = 3 cups sliced

BANANAS: 1 pound (3 or 4 medium) = 1¾ cups mashed

BERRIES: 1 quart = 3½ cups

DATES: 1 pound = 2½ cups pitted

LEMON: 1 whole = 1 to 3 tablespoons juice; 1 to 1½ teaspoons grated rind

LIME: 1 whole = 1½ to 2 tablespoons juice

ORANGE: 1 medium = 6 to 8 tablespoons juice; 2 to 3 tablespoons grated rind

PEACHES: 1 pound (4 medium) = 3 cups sliced

PEARS: 1 pound (4 medium) = 2 cups sliced

RHUBARB: 1 pound = 2 cups cooked

STRAWBERRIES: 1 quart = 4 cups sliced

REFERENCE

SOWING VEGETABLE SEEDS

SOW OR PLANT IN COOL WEATHER	Beets, broccoli, brussels sprouts, cabbage, lettuce, onions, parsley, peas, radishes, spinach, Swiss chard, turnips
SOW OR PLANT IN WARM WEATHER	Beans, carrots, corn, cucumbers, eggplant, melons, okra, peppers, squashes, tomatoes
SOW OR PLANT FOR ONE CROP PER SEASON	Corn, eggplant, leeks, melons, peppers, potatoes, spinach (New Zealand), squashes, tomatoes
RESOW FOR ADDITIONAL CROPS	Beans, beets, cabbage, carrots, kohlrabi, lettuce, radishes, rutabagas, spinach, turnips

A Beginner's Vegetable Garden

The vegetables suggested below are common, easy-to-grow crops. Make 11 rows, 10 feet long, with at least 18 inches between them. Ideally, the rows should run north and south to take full advantage of the sun. This garden, planted as suggested, can feed a family of four for one summer, with a little extra for canning and freezing or giving away.

ROW
1 Zucchini (4 plants)
2 Tomatoes (5 plants, staked)
3 Peppers (6 plants)
4 Cabbage

ROW
5 Bush beans
6 Lettuce
7 Beets
8 Carrots
9 Swiss chard
10 Radishes
11 Marigolds
(to discourage rabbits!)

SOIL FIXES

If you have **sandy** soil, amend with compost; humus; aged manure; sawdust with extra nitrogen; heavy, clay-rich soil

If your soil contains a lot of **silt**, amend with coarse sand (not beach sand) or gravel and compost, or aged horse manure mixed with fresh straw

If your soil is dense with **clay**, amend with coarse sand (not beach sand) and compost

TO IMPROVE YOUR SOIL, ADD THE PROPER AMENDMENT(S) . . .

bark, ground: made from various tree barks; improves soil structure

compost: an excellent conditioner

leaf mold: decomposed leaves, which add nutrients and structure to soil

lime: raises the pH of acidic soil and helps to loosen clay soil

manure: best if composted; never add fresh ("hot") manure; is a good conditioner

coarse sand (not beach sand): improves drainage in clay soil

topsoil: usually used with another amendment; replaces existing soil

REFERENCE

IN THE GARDEN

WHEN TO . . .

	. . . FERTILIZE	. . . WATER
BEANS	After heavy bloom and set of pods	Regularly, from start of pod to set
BEETS	At time of planting	Only during drought conditions
BROCCOLI	3 weeks after transplanting	Only during drought conditions
BRUSSELS SPROUTS	3 weeks after transplanting	At transplanting
CABBAGE	3 weeks after transplanting	2 to 3 weeks before harvest
CARROTS	In the fall for the following spring	Only during drought conditions
CAULIFLOWER	3 weeks after transplanting	Once, 3 weeks before harvest
CELERY	At time of transplanting	Once a week
CORN	When 8 to 10 inches tall, and when first silk appears	When tassels appear and cobs start to swell
CUCUMBERS	1 week after bloom, and 3 weeks later	Frequently, especially when fruits form
LETTUCE	2 to 3 weeks after transplanting	Once a week
MELONS	1 week after bloom, and again 3 weeks later	Once a week
ONION SETS	When bulbs begin to swell, and when plants are 1 foot tall	Only during drought conditions
PARSNIPS	1 year before planting	Only during drought conditions
PEAS	After heavy bloom and set of pods	Regularly, from start of pod to set
PEPPERS	After first fruit-set	Once a week
POTATO TUBERS	At bloom time or time of second hilling	Regularly, when tubers start to form
PUMPKINS	Just before vines start to run, when plants are about 1 foot tall	Only during drought conditions
RADISHES	Before spring planting	Once a week
SPINACH	When plants are one-third grown	Once a week
SQUASHES, SUMMER	Just before vines start to run, when plants are about 1 foot tall	Only during drought conditions
SQUASHES, WINTER	Just before vines start to run, when plants are about 1 foot tall	Only during drought conditions
TOMATOES	2 weeks before, and after first picking	Twice a week

HOW TO GROW HERBS

HERB	START SEEDS INDOORS (WEEKS BEFORE LAST SPRING FROST)	START SEEDS OUTDOORS (WEEKS BEFORE/AFTER LAST SPRING FROST)	HEIGHT/ SPREAD (INCHES)	SOIL	LIGHT**
BASIL*	6–8	Anytime after	12–24/12	Rich, moist	○
BORAGE*	Not recommended	Anytime after	12–36/12	Rich, well-drained, dry	○
CHERVIL	Not recommended	3–4 before	12–24/8	Rich, moist	◑
CHIVES	8–10	3–4 before	12–18/18	Rich, moist	○
CILANTRO/ CORIANDER	Not recommended	Anytime after	12–36/6	Light	○◑
DILL	Not recommended	4–5 before	36–48/12	Rich	○
FENNEL	4–6	Anytime after	48–80/18	Rich	○
LAVENDER, ENGLISH*	8–12	1–2 before	18–36/24	Moderately fertile, well-drained	○
LAVENDER, FRENCH	Not recommended	Not recommended	18–36/24	Moderately fertile, well-drained	○
LEMON BALM*	6–10	2–3 before	12–24/18	Rich, well-drained	○◑
LOVAGE*	6–8	2–3 before	36–72/36	Fertile, sandy	○◑
MINT	Not recommended	Not recommended	12–24/18	Rich, moist	◑
OREGANO*	6–10	Anytime after	12–24/18	Poor	○
PARSLEY*	10–12	3–4 before	18–24/6–8	Medium-rich	◑
ROSEMARY*	8–10	Anytime after	48–72/48	Not too acidic	○
SAGE	6–10	1–2 before	12–48/30	Well-drained	○
SORREL	6–10	2–3 after	20–48/12–14	Rich, organic	○
SUMMER SAVORY	4–6	Anytime after	4–15/6	Medium-rich	○
SWEET CICELY	6–8	2–3 after	36–72/36	Moderately fertile, well-drained	○◑
TARRAGON, FRENCH	Not recommended	Not recommended	24–36/12	Well-drained	○◑
THYME, COMMON*	6–10	2–3 before	2–12/7–12	Fertile, well-drained	○◑

*Recommend minimum soil temperature of 70°F to germinate

** ○ FULL SUN ◑ PARTIAL SHADE

GROWTH TYPE
Annual
Annual, biennial
Annual, biennial
Perennial
Annual
Annual
Annual
Perennial
Tender perennial
Perennial
Perennial
Perennial
Tender perennial
Biennial
Tender perennial
Perennial
Perennial
Annual
Perennial
Perennial
Perennial

DRYING HERBS

Before drying, remove any dead or diseased leaves or stems. Wash under cool water, shake off excess water, and put on a towel to dry completely. Air drying preserves an herb's essential oils; use for sturdy herbs. A microwave dries herbs more quickly, so mold is less likely to develop; use for moist, tender herbs.

HANGING METHOD: Gather four to six stems of fresh herbs in a bunch and tie with string, leaving a loop for hanging. Or, use a rubber band with a paper clip attached to it. Hang the herbs in a warm, well-ventilated area, out of direct sunlight, until dry. For herbs that have full seed heads, such as dill or coriander, use a paper bag. Punch holes in the bag for ventilation, label it, and put the herb bunch into the bag before you tie a string around the top of the bag. The average drying time is 1 to 3 weeks.

MICROWAVE METHOD: This is better for small quantities, such as a cup or two at a time. Arrange a single layer of herbs between two paper towels and put them in the microwave for 1 to 2 minutes on high power. Let the leaves cool. If they are not dry, reheat for 30 seconds and check again. Repeat as needed. Let cool. Do not overcook, or the herbs will lose their flavor.

STORING HERBS AND SPICES

FRESH HERBS: Dill and parsley will keep for about 2 weeks with stems immersed in a glass of water tented with a plastic bag. Most other fresh herbs (and greens) will keep for short periods unwashed and refrigerated in tightly sealed plastic bags with just enough moisture to prevent wilting. For longer storage, use moisture- and gas-permeable paper and cellophane. Plastic cuts off oxygen to the plants and promotes spoilage.

SPICES AND DRIED HERBS: Store in a cool, dry place.

COOKING WITH HERBS

A **BOUQUET GARNI** is usually made with bay leaves, thyme, and parsley tied with string or wrapped in cheesecloth. Use to flavor casseroles and soups. Remove after cooking.

FINES HERBES use equal amounts of fresh parsley, tarragon, chives, and chervil chopped fine. Commonly used in French cooking, they make a fine omelet or add zest to soups and sauces. Add to salads and butter sauces or sprinkle on noodles, soups, and stews.

HOW TO GROW BULBS

COMMON NAME	LATIN NAME	HARDINESS ZONE	SOIL	LIGHT*	SPACING (INCHES)
ALLIUM	*Allium*	3–10	Well-drained/moist	○	12
BEGONIA, TUBEROUS	*Begonia*	10–11	Well-drained/moist	◑●	12–15
BLAZING STAR/ GAYFEATHER	*Liatris*	7–10	Well-drained	○	6
CALADIUM	*Caladium*	10–11	Well-drained/moist	◑●	8–12
CALLA LILY	*Zantedeschia*	8–10	Well-drained/moist	○◑	8–24
CANNA	*Canna*	8–11	Well-drained/moist	○	12–24
CYCLAMEN	*Cyclamen*	7–9	Well-drained/moist	◑	4
DAHLIA	*Dahlia*	9–11	Well-drained/fertile	○	12–36
DAYLILY	*Hemerocallis*	3–10	Adaptable to most soils	○◑	12–24
FREESIA	*Freesia*	9–11	Well-drained/moist/sandy	○◑	2–4
GARDEN GLOXINIA	*Incarvillea*	4–8	Well-drained/moist	○	12
GLADIOLUS	*Gladiolus*	4–11	Well-drained/fertile	○◑	4–9
IRIS	*Iris*	3–10	Well-drained/sandy	○	3–6
LILY, ASIATIC/ORIENTAL	*Lilium*	3–8	Well-drained	○◑	8–12
PEACOCK FLOWER	*Tigridia*	8–10	Well-drained	○	5–6
SHAMROCK/SORREL	*Oxalis*	5–9	Well-drained	○◑	4–6
WINDFLOWER	*Anemone*	3–9	Well-drained/moist	○◑	3–6
BLUEBELL	*Hyacinthoides*	4–9	Well-drained/fertile	○◑	4
CHRISTMAS ROSE/ HELLEBORE	*Helleborus*	4–8	Neutral–alkaline	○◑	18
CROCUS	*Crocus*	3–8	Well-drained/moist/fertile	○◑	4
DAFFODIL	*Narcissus*	3–10	Well-drained/moist/fertile	○◑	6
FRITILLARY	*Fritillaria*	3–9	Well-drained/sandy	○◑	3
GLORY OF THE SNOW	*Chionodoxa*	3–9	Well-drained/moist	○◑	3
GRAPE HYACINTH	*Muscari*	4–10	Well-drained/moist/fertile	○◑	3–4
IRIS, BEARDED	*Iris*	3–9	Well-drained	○◑	4
IRIS, SIBERIAN	*Iris*	4–9	Well-drained	○◑	4
ORNAMENTAL ONION	*Allium*	3–10	Well-drained/moist/fertile	○	12
SNOWDROP	*Galanthus*	3–9	Well-drained/moist/fertile	○◑	3
SNOWFLAKE	*Leucojum*	5–9	Well-drained/moist/sandy	○◑	4
SPRING STARFLOWER	*Ipheion uniflorum*	6–9	Well-drained loam	○◑	3–6
STAR OF BETHLEHEM	*Ornithogalum*	5–10	Well-drained/moist	○◑	2–5
STRIPED SQUILL	*Puschkinia scilloides*	3–9	Well-drained	○◑	6
TULIP	*Tulipa*	4–8	Well-drained/fertile	○◑	3–6
WINTER ACONITE	*Eranthis*	4–9	Well-drained/moist/fertile	○◑	3

SPRING-PLANTED BULBS

FALL-PLANTED BULBS

REFERENCE

DEPTH (INCHES)	BLOOMING SEASON	HEIGHT (INCHES)	NOTES
3–4	Spring to summer	6–60	Usually pest-free; a great cut flower
1–2	Summer to fall	8–18	North of Zone 10, lift in fall
4	Summer to fall	8–20	An excellent flower for drying; north of Zone 7, plant in spring, lift in fall
2	Summer	8–24	North of Zone 10, plant in spring, lift in fall
1–4	Summer	24–36	Fragrant; north of Zone 8, plant in spring, lift in fall
Level	Summer	18–60	North of Zone 8, plant in spring, lift in fall
1–2	Spring to fall	3–12	Naturalizes well in warm areas; north of Zone 7, lift in fall
4–6	Late summer	12–60	North of Zone 9, lift in fall
2	Summer	12–36	Mulch in winter in Zones 3 to 6
2	Summer	12–24	Fragrant; can be grown outdoors in warm climates
3–4	Summer	6–20	Does well in woodland settings
3–6	Early summer to early fall	12–80	North of Zone 10, lift in fall
4	Spring to late summer	3–72	Divide and replant rhizomes every two to five years
4–6	Early summer	36	Fragrant; self-sows; requires excellent drainage
4	Summer	18–24	North of Zone 8, lift in fall
2	Summer	2–12	Plant in confined area to control
2	Early summer	3–18	North of Zone 6, lift in fall
3–4	Spring	8–20	Excellent for borders, rock gardens and naturalizing
1–2	Spring	12	Hardy, but requires shelter from strong, cold winds
3	Early spring	5	Naturalizes well in grass
6	Early spring	14–24	Plant under shrubs or in a border
3	Midspring	6–30	Different species can be planted in rock gardens, woodland gardens, or borders
3	Spring	4–10	Self-sows easily; plant in rock gardens, raised beds, or under shrubs
2–3	Late winter to spring	6–12	Use as a border plant or in wildflower and rock gardens; self-sows easily
4	Early spring to early summer	3–48	Naturalizes well; a good cut flower
4	Early spring to midsummer	18–48	An excellent cut flower
3–4	Late spring to early summer	6–60	Usually pest-free; a great cut flower
3	Spring	6–12	Best when clustered and planted in an area that will not dry out in summer
4	Spring	6–18	Naturalizes well
3	Spring	4–6	Fragrant; naturalizes easily
4	Spring to summer	6–24	North of Zone 5, plant in spring, lift in fall
3	Spring	4–6	Naturalizes easily; makes an attractive edging
4–6	Early to late spring	8–30	Excellent for borders, rock gardens, and naturalizing
2–3	Late winter to spring	2–4	Self-sows and naturalizes easily

SUBSTITUTIONS FOR COMMON INGREDIENTS

ITEM	QUANTITY	SUBSTITUTION
BAKING POWDER	1 teaspoon	¼ teaspoon baking soda plus ¼ teaspoon cornstarch plus ½ teaspoon cream of tartar
BUTTERMILK	1 cup	1 tablespoon lemon juice or vinegar plus milk to equal 1 cup; or 1 cup plain yogurt
CHOCOLATE, UNSWEETENED	1 ounce	3 tablespoons cocoa plus 1 tablespoon unsalted butter, shortening, or vegetable oil
CRACKER CRUMBS	¾ cup	1 cup dry bread crumbs; or 1 tablespoon quick-cooking oats (for thickening)
CREAM, HEAVY	1 cup	¾ cup milk plus ⅓ cup melted unsalted butter (this will not whip)
CREAM, LIGHT	1 cup	⅞ cup milk plus 3 tablespoons melted, unsalted butter
CREAM, SOUR	1 cup	⅞ cup buttermilk or plain yogurt plus 3 tablespoons melted, unsalted butter
CREAM, WHIPPING	1 cup	⅔ cup well-chilled evaporated milk, whipped; or 1 cup nonfat dry milk powder whipped with 1 cup ice water
EGG	1 whole	2 yolks plus 1 tablespoon cold water; or 3 tablespoons vegetable oil plus 1 tablespoon water (for baking); or 2 to 3 tablespoons mayonnaise (for cakes)
EGG WHITE	1 white	2 teaspoons meringue powder plus 3 tablespoons water, combined
FLOUR, ALL-PURPOSE	1 cup	1 cup plus 3 tablespoons cake flour (not advised for cookies or quick breads); or 1 cup self-rising flour (omit baking powder and salt from recipe)
FLOUR, CAKE	1 cup	1 cup minus 3 tablespoons sifted all-purpose flour plus 3 tablespoons cornstarch
FLOUR, SELF-RISING	1 cup	1 cup all-purpose flour plus 1½ teaspoons baking powder plus ¼ teaspoon salt
HERBS, DRIED	1 teaspoon	1 tablespoon fresh, minced and packed
HONEY	1 cup	1¼ cups sugar plus ½ cup liquid called for in recipe (such as water or oil); or 1 cup pure maple syrup
KETCHUP	1 cup	1 cup tomato sauce plus ¼ cup sugar plus 3 tablespoons apple-cider vinegar plus ½ teaspoon salt plus pinch of ground cloves combined; or 1 cup chili sauce
LEMON JUICE	1 teaspoon	½ teaspoon vinegar
MAYONNAISE	1 cup	1 cup sour cream or plain yogurt; or 1 cup cottage cheese (puréed)
MILK, SKIM	1 cup	⅓ cup instant nonfat dry milk plus ¾ cup water

ITEM	QUANTITY	SUBSTITUTION
MILK, TO SOUR	1 cup	1 tablespoon vinegar or lemon juice plus milk to equal 1 cup. Stir and let stand 5 minutes.
MILK, WHOLE	1 cup	½ cup evaporated whole milk plus ½ cup water; or ¾ cup 2 percent milk plus ¼ cup half-and-half
MOLASSES	1 cup	1 cup honey or dark corn syrup
MUSTARD, DRY	1 teaspoon	1 tablespoon prepared mustard less 1 teaspoon liquid from recipe
OAT BRAN	1 cup	1 cup wheat bran or rice bran or wheat germ
OATS, OLD-FASHIONED	1 cup	1 cup steel-cut Irish or Scotch oats
QUINOA	1 cup	1 cup millet or couscous (whole wheat cooks faster) or bulgur
SUGAR, DARK-BROWN	1 cup	1 cup light-brown sugar, packed; or 1 cup granulated sugar plus 2 to 3 tablespoons molasses
SUGAR, GRANULATED	1 cup	1 cup firmly packed brown sugar; or 1¾ cups confectioners' sugar (makes baked goods less crisp); or 1 cup superfine sugar
SUGAR, LIGHT-BROWN	1 cup	1 cup granulated sugar plus 1 to 2 tablespoons molasses; or ½ cup dark-brown sugar plus ½ cup granulated sugar
SWEETENED CONDENSED MILK	1 can (14 oz.)	1 cup evaporated milk plus 1¼ cups granulated sugar. Combine and heat until sugar dissolves.
VANILLA BEAN	1-inch bean	1 teaspoon vanilla extract
VINEGAR, APPLE-CIDER	—	malt, white-wine, or rice vinegar
VINEGAR, BALSAMIC	1 tablespoon	1 tablespoon red- or white-wine vinegar plus ½ teaspoon sugar
VINEGAR, RED-WINE	—	white-wine, sherry, champagne, or balsamic vinegar
VINEGAR, RICE	—	apple-cider, champagne, or white-wine vinegar
VINEGAR, WHITE-WINE	—	apple-cider, champagne, fruit (raspberry), rice, or red-wine vinegar
YEAST	1 cake (⅗ oz.)	1 package (¼ ounce) or 1 scant tablespoon active dried yeast
YOGURT, PLAIN	1 cup	1 cup sour cream (thicker; less tart) or buttermilk (thinner; use in baking, dressings, sauces)

REFERENCE

TYPES OF FAT

One way to minimize your total blood cholesterol is to manage the amount and types of fat in your diet. Aim for monounsaturated and polyunsaturated fats; avoid saturated and trans fats.

MONOUNSATURATED FAT lowers LDL (bad cholesterol) and may raise HDL (good cholesterol) or leave it unchanged; found in almonds, avocados, canola oil, cashews, olive oil, peanut oil, and peanuts.

POLYUNSATURATED FAT lowers LDL and may lower HDL; includes omega-3 and omega-6 fatty acids; found in corn oil, cottonseed oil, fish such as salmon and tuna, safflower oil, sesame seeds, soybeans, and sunflower oil.

SATURATED FAT raises both LDL and HDL; found in chocolate, cocoa butter, coconut oil, dairy products (milk, butter, cheese, ice cream), egg yolks, palm oil, and red meat.

TRANS FAT raises LDL and lowers HDL; a type of fat common in many processed foods, such as most margarines (especially stick), vegetable shortening, partially hydrogenated vegetable oil, many commercial fried foods (doughnuts, french fries), and commercial baked goods (cookies, crackers, cakes).

Calorie-Burning Comparisons

If you hustle through your chores to get to the fitness center, relax. You're getting a great workout already. The left-hand column lists "chore" exercises, the middle column shows the number of calories burned per minute per pound of body weight, and the right-hand column lists comparable "recreational" exercises. For example, a 150-pound person forking straw bales burns 9.45 calories per minute, the same workout he or she would get playing basketball.

Chopping with an ax, fast	0.135	Skiing, cross country, uphill
Climbing hills, with 44-pound load	0.066	Swimming, crawl, fast
Digging trenches	0.065	Skiing, cross country, steady walk
Forking straw bales	0.063	Basketball
Chopping down trees	0.060	Football
Climbing hills, with 9-pound load	0.058	Swimming, crawl, slow
Sawing by hand	0.055	Skiing, cross country, moderate
Mowing lawns	0.051	Horseback riding, trotting
Scrubbing floors	0.049	Tennis
Shoveling coal	0.049	Aerobic dance, medium
Hoeing	0.041	Weight training, circuit training
Stacking firewood	0.040	Weight lifting, free weights
Shoveling grain	0.038	Golf
Painting houses	0.035	Walking, normal pace, asphalt road
Weeding	0.033	Table tennis
Shopping for food	0.028	Cycling, 5.5 mph
Mopping floors	0.028	Fishing
Washing windows	0.026	Croquet
Raking	0.025	Dancing, ballroom
Driving a tractor	0.016	Drawing, standing position

REFERENCE

FREEZER STORAGE TIME
(freezer temperature 0°F or colder)

PRODUCT	MONTHS IN FREEZER

FRESH MEAT

Beef . . . . 6 to 12
Lamb . . . . 6 to 9
Veal . . . . 6 to 9
Pork . . . . 4 to 6
Ground beef, veal, lamb, pork . . . . 3 to 4
Frankfurters . . . . 1 to 2
Sausage, fresh pork . . . . 1 to 2
Cold cuts . . . . Not recommended

FRESH POULTRY

Chicken, turkey (whole) 12
Chicken, turkey (pieces) . . . . 6 to 9
Cornish game hen, game birds . . . 6 to 9
Giblets . . . . 3 to 4

COOKED POULTRY

Breaded, fried 4
Pieces, plain 4
Pieces covered with broth, gravy 6

FRESH FISH AND SEAFOOD

Clams, mussels, oysters, scallops,
  shrimp . . . . 3 to 6
Fatty fish (bluefish, mackerel, perch,
  salmon) . . . . 2 to 3
Lean fish (flounder, haddock, sole) 6

FRESH FRUIT (PREPARED FOR FREEZING)

All fruit except those
  listed below . . . . 10 to 12
Avocados, bananas, plantains 3
Lemons, limes, oranges . . . . 4 to 6

FRESH VEGETABLES (PREPARED FOR FREEZING)

Beans, beets, bok choy, broccoli,
  brussels sprouts, cabbage, carrots,
  cauliflower, celery, corn, greens,
  kohlrabi, leeks, mushrooms, okra,
  onions, peas, peppers, soybeans,
  spinach, summer squashes . . . 10 to 12
Asparagus, rutabagas, turnips . . 8 to 10
Artichokes, eggplant . . . . 6 to 8
Tomatoes (overripe or sliced) 2
Bamboo shoots, cucumbers, endive,
  lettuce, radishes, watercress . . . .
  . . . . Not recommended

PRODUCT	MONTHS IN FREEZER

CHEESE (except those listed below) . . . 6
Cottage cheese, cream cheese, feta,
  goat, fresh mozzarella, Neufchâtel,
  Parmesan, processed cheese (opened)
  . . . . Not recommended

DAIRY PRODUCTS

Margarine (not diet) 12
Butter . . . . 6 to 9
Cream, half-and-half 4
Milk 3
Ice cream . . . . 1 to 2

FREEZING HINTS

FOR MEALS, remember that a quart container holds four servings, and a pint container holds two servings.

TO PREVENT STICKING, spread the food to be frozen (berries, hamburgers, cookies, etc.) on a cookie sheet and freeze until solid. Then place in plastic bags and freeze.

LABEL FOODS for easy identification. Write the name of the food, number of servings, and date of freezing on containers or bags.

FREEZE FOODS as quickly as possible by placing them directly against the sides of the freezer.

ARRANGE FREEZER into sections for each food category.

IF POWER IS INTERRUPTED, or if the freezer is not operating normally, do not open the freezer door. Food in a loaded freezer will usually stay frozen for 2 days if the freezer door remains closed during that time period.

PLASTICS

In your quest to go green, use this guide to use and sort plastic. The number, usually found with a triangle symbol on a container, indicates the type of resin used to produce the plastic. Visit **EARTH911.COM** for recycling information in your state.

PETE

NUMBER 1 · *PETE or PET (polyethylene terephthalate)*
IS USED IN . . . . microwavable food trays; salad dressing, soft drink, water, and juice bottles
STATUS . . . . hard to clean; absorbs bacteria and flavors; avoid reusing
IS RECYCLED TO MAKE . . . carpet, furniture, new containers, Polar fleece

HDPE

NUMBER 2 · *HDPE (high-density polyethylene)*
IS USED IN . . . . household cleaner and shampoo bottles, milk jugs, yogurt tubs
STATUS . . . . transmits no known chemicals into food
IS RECYCLED TO MAKE . . . detergent bottles, fencing, floor tiles, pens

V

NUMBER 3 · *V or PVC (vinyl)*
IS USED IN . . . . cooking oil bottles, clear food packaging, mouthwash bottles
STATUS . . . . is believed to contain phalates that interfere with hormonal development; avoid
IS RECYCLED TO MAKE . . . cables, mudflaps, paneling, roadway gutters

LDPE

NUMBER 4 · *LDPE (low-density polyethylene)*
IS USED IN . . . . bread and shopping bags, carpet, clothing, furniture
STATUS . . . . transmits no known chemicals into food
IS RECYCLED TO MAKE . . . envelopes, floor tiles, lumber, trash-can liners

PP

NUMBER 5 · *PP (polypropylene)*
IS USED IN . . . . .ketchup bottles, medicine and syrup bottles, drinking straws
STATUS . . . . transmits no known chemicals into food
IS RECYCLED TO MAKE . . . battery cables, brooms, ice scrapers, rakes

PS

NUMBER 6 · *PS (polystyrene)*
IS USED IN . . . . disposable cups and plates, egg cartons, take-out containers
STATUS . . . . .is believed to leach styrene, a possible human carcinogen, into food; avoid
IS RECYCLED TO MAKE . . . foam packaging, insulation, light switchplates, rulers

OTHER

NUMBER 7 · *Other (miscellaneous)*
IS USED IN . . . . .3- and 5-gallon water jugs, nylon, some food containers
STATUS . . . . contains bisphenol A, which has been linked to heart disease and obesity; avoid
IS RECYCLED TO MAKE . . . .custom-made products

HOW MUCH DO YOU NEED?

WALLPAPER

Before choosing your wallpaper, keep in mind that wallpaper with little or no pattern to match at the seams and the ceiling will be the easiest to apply, thus resulting in the least amount of wasted wallpaper. If you choose a patterned wallpaper, a small repeating pattern will result in less waste than a large repeating pattern. And a pattern that is aligned horizontally (matching on each column of paper) will waste less than one that drops or alternates its pattern (matching on every other column).

TO DETERMINE THE AMOUNT OF WALL SPACE YOU'RE COVERING:

• Measure the length of each wall, add these figures together, and multiply by the height of the walls to get the area (square footage) of the room's walls.

• Calculate the square footage of each door, window, and other opening in the room. Add these figures together and subtract the total from the area of the room's walls.

• Take that figure and multiply by 1.15, to account for a waste rate of about 15 percent in your wallpaper project. You'll end up with a target amount to purchase when you shop.

• Wallpaper is sold in single, double, and triple rolls. Coverage can vary, so be sure to refer to the roll's label for the proper square footage. (The average coverage for a double roll, for example, is 56 square feet.) After choosing a paper, divide the coverage figure (from the label) into the total square footage of the walls of the room you're papering. Round the answer up to the nearest whole number. This is the number of rolls you need to buy.

• Save leftover wallpaper rolls, carefully wrapped to keep clean.

INTERIOR PAINT

Estimate your room size and paint needs before you go to the store. Running out of a custom color halfway through the job could mean disaster. For the sake of the following exercise, assume that you have a 10x15-foot room with an 8-foot ceiling. The room has two doors and two windows.

FOR WALLS

Measure the total distance (perimeter) around the room:

(10 ft. + 15 ft.) x 2 = 50 ft.

Multiply the perimeter by the ceiling height to get the total wall area:

50 ft. x 8 ft. = 400 sq. ft.

Doors are usually 21 square feet (there are two in this exercise):

21 sq. ft. x 2 = 42 sq. ft.

Windows average 15 square feet (there are two in this exercise):

15 sq. ft. x 2 = 30 sq. ft.

Take the total wall area and subtract the area for the doors and windows to get the wall surface to be painted:

400 sq. ft. (wall area)
– 42 sq. ft. (doors)
– 30 sq. ft. (windows)
328 sq. ft.

As a rule of thumb, one gallon of quality paint will usually cover 400 square feet. One quart will cover 100 square feet. Because you need to cover 328 square feet in this example, one gallon will be adequate to give one coat of paint to the walls. (Coverage will be affected by the porosity and texture of the surface. In addition, bright colors may require a minimum of two coats.)

METRIC CONVERSION

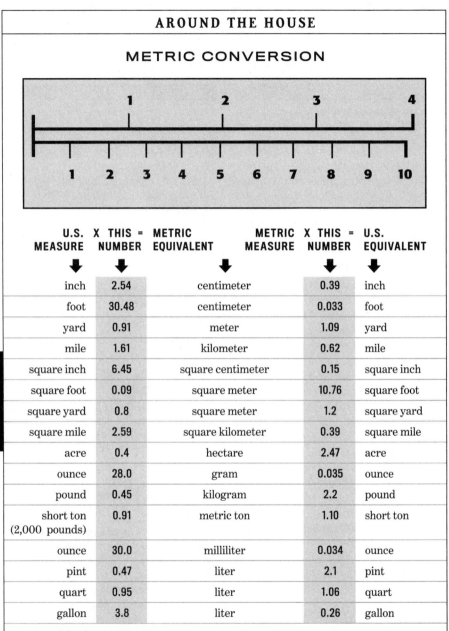

U.S. MEASURE	X THIS = NUMBER	METRIC EQUIVALENT	METRIC MEASURE	X THIS = NUMBER	U.S. EQUIVALENT
inch	2.54	centimeter		0.39	inch
foot	30.48	centimeter		0.033	foot
yard	0.91	meter		1.09	yard
mile	1.61	kilometer		0.62	mile
square inch	6.45	square centimeter		0.15	square inch
square foot	0.09	square meter		10.76	square foot
square yard	0.8	square meter		1.2	square yard
square mile	2.59	square kilometer		0.39	square mile
acre	0.4	hectare		2.47	acre
ounce	28.0	gram		0.035	ounce
pound	0.45	kilogram		2.2	pound
short ton (2,000 pounds)	0.91	metric ton		1.10	short ton
ounce	30.0	milliliter		0.034	ounce
pint	0.47	liter		2.1	pint
quart	0.95	liter		1.06	quart
gallon	3.8	liter		0.26	gallon

If you know the U.S. measurement and want to convert it to metric, multiply it by the number in the left shaded column (example: 1 inch equals 2.54 centimeters). If you know the metric measurement, multiply it by the number in the right shaded column (example: 2 meters equals 2.18 yards).

Where Do You Fit in Your Family Tree?

Technically it's known as consanguinity; that is, the quality or state of being related by blood or descended from a common ancestor. These relationships are shown below for the genealogy of six generations of one family. *–family tree information courtesy of Frederick H. Rohles*

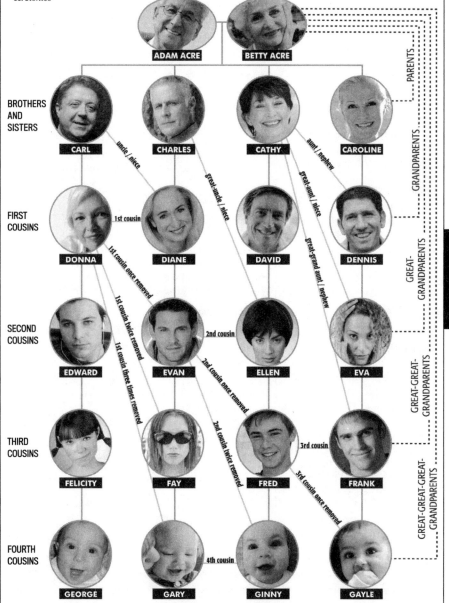

The Golden Rule
(It's true in all faiths.)

BRAHMANISM:
This is the sum of duty: Do naught unto others which would cause you pain if done to you.
Mahabharata 5:1517

BUDDHISM:
Hurt not others in ways that you yourself would find hurtful.
Udana-Varga 5:18

CHRISTIANITY:
All things whatsoever ye would that men should do to you, do ye even so to them; for this is the law and the prophets.
Matthew 7:12

CONFUCIANISM:
Surely it is the maxim of loving-kindness: Do not unto others what you would not have them do unto you.
Analects 15:23

ISLAM:
No one of you is a believer until he desires for his brother that which he desires for himself.
Sunnah

JUDAISM:
What is hateful to you, do not to your fellow man. That is the entire Law; all the rest is commentary.
Talmud, Shabbat 31a

TAOISM:
Regard your neighbor's gain as your own gain and your neighbor's loss as your own loss.
T'ai Shang Kan Ying P'ien

ZOROASTRIANISM:
That nature alone is good which refrains from doing unto another whatsoever is not good for itself.
Dadistan-i-dinik 94:5
–courtesy of Elizabeth Pool

FAMOUS LAST WORDS

Waiting, are they? Waiting, are they? Well—let 'em wait.
(To an attending doctor who attempted to comfort him by saying, "General, I fear the angels are waiting for you.")
–Ethan Allen, American Revolutionary general, d. February 12, 1789

A dying man can do nothing easy.
–Benjamin Franklin, American statesman, d. April 17, 1790

Now I shall go to sleep. Good night.
–Lord George Byron, English writer, d. April 19, 1824

Is it the Fourth?
–Thomas Jefferson, 3rd U.S. president, d. July 4, 1826

Thomas Jefferson—still survives . . .
(Actually, Jefferson had died earlier that same day.)
–John Adams, 2nd U.S. president, d. July 4, 1826

Friends, applaud. The comedy is finished.
–Ludwig van Beethoven, German-Austrian composer, d. March 26, 1827

Moose . . . Indian . . .
–Henry David Thoreau, American writer, d. May 6, 1862

Go on, get out—last words are for fools who haven't said enough.
(To his housekeeper, who urged him to tell her his last words so she could write them down for posterity.)
–Karl Marx, German political philosopher, d. March 14, 1883

Is it not meningitis?
–Louisa M. Alcott, American writer, d. March 6, 1888

How were the receipts today at Madison Square Garden?
–P. T. Barnum, American entrepreneur, d. April 7, 1891

Turn up the lights, I don't want to go home in the dark.
–O. Henry (William Sidney Porter), American writer, d. June 4, 1910

Get my swan costume ready.
–Anna Pavlova, Russian ballerina, d. January 23, 1931

Is everybody happy? I want everybody to be happy. I know I'm happy.
–Ethel Barrymore, American actress, d. June 18, 1959

I'm bored with it all.
(Before slipping into a coma. He died 9 days later.)
–Winston Churchill, English statesman, d. January 24, 1965

You be good. You'll be in tomorrow. I love you.
–Alex, highly intelligent African Gray parrot, d. September 6, 2007

REFERENCE